Library of
Davidson College

VOID

*Robert W. McGee*
has extensive experience
in public accounting, industry, and teaching.
He has written
numerous magazine and journal articles
and has three more books in progress.
Dr. McGee is a professor of
accounting, finance, and taxation
at Pace University in New York City

# Accounting for Inflation

## STATING A TRUE FINANCIAL POSITION

*Robert W. McGee*

Prentice-Hall, Inc., Englewood Cliffs, N.J. 07632

*Library of Congress Cataloging in Publication Data*
Main entry under title:

Accounting for inflation.

    (A Spectrum Book)
    Includes bibliographical references.
    1. Accounting–United States–Effect of inflation on
–Addresses, essays, lectures.  2. Financial statement–
United States–Addresses, essays, lectures.  I. McGee,
Robert W.
HF5658.5.A23     657'.48'0973     81-1447
ISBN 0-13-002337-X     AACR2
ISBN 0-13-002329-9 (pbk.)

657.4
A172

This Spectrum Book can be made available to businesses and organizations at a special discount when ordered in large quantities. For more information, contact: Prentice-Hall, Inc., General Book Marketing, Special Sales Division, Englewood Cliffs, New Jersey 07632

Editorial/production supervision and interior design by Carol Smith
Cover design by Linda Rettich
Manufacturing buyer: Barbara A. Frick

© 1981 by Prentice-Hall, Inc., *Englewood Cliffs, New Jersey 07632*

A SPECTRUM BOOK

All rights reserved. No part of ths book may be reproduced
in any form or by any means
without permission in writing from the publisher.

10  9  8  7  6  5  4  3  2  1

Printed in the United States of America

83-9469

PRENTICE-HALL INTERNATIONAL, INC., *London*
PRENTICE-HALL OF AUSTRALIA PTY. LIMITED, *Sydney*
PRENTICE-HALL OF CANADA, LTD., *Toronto*
PRENTICE-HALL OF INDIA PRIVATE LIMITED, *New Delhi*
PRENTICE-HALL OF JAPAN, INC., *Tokyo*
PRENTICE-HALL OF SOUTHEAST ASIA PTE. LTD., *Singapore*
WHITEHALL BOOKS LIMITED, *Wellington, New Zealand*

# CONTENTS

PREFACE, vii

INTRODUCTION, 1

# 1

## Inflation Accounting in the United States

THE HISTORY OF
INFLATION ACCOUNTING
IN THE UNITED STATES
*by William D. Milligan, Jr., MBA, CPA,* 9

THE ARB'S AND ARS NO. 6
*by William D. Milligan, Jr., MBA, CPA,* 12

APB STATEMENT NO. 3
*by William D. Milligan, Jr., MBA, CPA,* 17

FASB EXPOSURE DRAFT:
DECEMBER 31, 1974
*by William D. Milligan, Jr., MBA, CPA,* 20

ASR 190
*by William D. Milligan, Jr., MBA, CPA,* 27

FASB EXPOSURE DRAFT:
DECEMBER 28, 1978
*by William D. Milligan, Jr., MBA, CPA,* 34

STATEMENT OF FINANCIAL
ACCOUNTING STANDARDS NO. 33
*by William D. Milligan, Jr., MBA, CPA,* 42

CONCLUSION
*by William D. Milligan, Jr., MBA, CPA,* 47

INFLATION ACCOUNTING:
PURSUING THE ELUSIVE
*by Philip L. Defliese,* 53

ARE YOU ACCOUNTING
FOR INFLATION IN YOUR
CAPITAL BUDGETING PROCESS?
*by D.D. Raiborn and Thomas A. Ratcliffe,* 63

PROPOSING A MORE APPROPRIATE
DIVIDEND POLICY
*by Eugene L. Zieha and Thomas T. Cheng,* 68

# 2

## General Price-Level Accounting

CONSTANT DOLLAR ACCOUNTING
*by Robert D. Baumann, MBA,* 77

EXAMPLES OF
PRICE-LEVEL ADJUSTMENT
COMPUTATIONS, 82

THE TWO-DIMENSIONAL
TIME FRAME
OF COMMON DOLLAR STATEMENTS
*by Andrew D. Bailey Jr. and Daniel L. Jensen,* 90

PURCHASING POWER
GAINS AND LOSSES
*by Robert D. Baumann, MBA,* 94

# 3

## Current Value Accounting

CURRENT COST ACCOUNTING
*by Robert D. Baumann, MBA,* 101

WHAT *IS* CURRENT VALUE?
*by Laurence A. Friedman, CPA, Ph.D.,* 106

REPLACEMENT COST ACCOUNTING:
HOW WE DID IT
*by W. Howard Wells, Jr.,* 112

REPLACEMENT COST ACCOUNTING:
PROGRESS OR REGRESSION?
*by Michaela M. Marcil,* 115

CURRENT VALUE ACCOUNTING—
COCOA OR REPCO?
*by R.J. Chambers, MEA,* 118

PROBLEMS WITH
CURRENT VALUE ACCOUNTING, 129

HOLDING GAINS AND LOSSES
*by Robert D. Baumann, MBA,* 136

# 4

**Inflation Accounting
in Other Countries**

EXTRAORDINARY INFLATION:
THE ARGENTINE EXPERIENCE
*by Ke-young Chu, MEA,
and Andrew Feltenstein,* 143

ACCOUNTING FOR INFLATION: BRAZIL
*by Manoel Riberio da Cruz Filho
and Amandio da Silva Machado,* 148

HOW BRASILIA DOES IT
*by Peter Myers,* 151

REPORTING THE IMPACT
OF CHANGING PRICES
IN GREAT BRITAIN
*by M. Zafar Iqbal,* 153

ACCOUNTANTS AND ACCOUNTANCY:
IS IT ONLY ACCOUNTANTS
WHO CANNOT RECOGNIZE
THE EFFECT THAT INFLATION
HAS HAD ON ACCOUNTANCY?
*by R.F.J. Dewhurst, MA, FCA, MEA,* 163

ACCOUNTANTS AND ACCOUNTANCY:
SOME FURTHER COMMENTS
ON "INFLATION ACCOUNTING"
*by John M.J. Boersema,* 166

C.C.A.:
A COMPARISON
OF THE AUSTRALIAN
AND U.K. PROPOSALS
*by Russell G. Marriott,* 170

REPORTING THE IMPACT
OF CHANGING PRICES
IN NEW ZEALAND
*by M. Zafar Iqbal,* 174

COMPARISON OF
CERTAIN CURRENT COST
ACCOUNTING PROPOSALS, 180

KEEPING UP WITH INFLATION
THE CANADIAN WAY
*by Peter Myers,* 182

CURRRENT VALUE
ACCOUNTING PREFERENCES:
THE CASE FOR CANADA
*by Haim Falk,* 188

**Appendixes**

APPENDIX A: FASB-33
FINANCIAL REPORTING
AND CHANGING PRICES,
SEPTEMBER 1979, 203

APPENDIX B:
SAMPLE
FINANCIAL STATEMENTS, 213

# PREFACE

This book is intended to provide the reader with a basic understanding of inflation accounting as practiced both here in the United States and abroad. Starting from a historical perspective, the two acceptable methods—general price level and current cost—are explored in some depth. Applications of each approach are discussed, as are criticisms. Practices in a few representative countries are also analyzed.

This book may be used both as an introduction to the subject of inflation accounting and as a ready reference for the practitioner. The "how to" approach is combined with the underlying theory to present a more complete and comprehensive treatment than could be had by confining the analysis to either practice or theory alone.

Few books have been written on the topic of inflation accounting that cover the American system. Until recently, there was little need for such a book because the rate of inflation was moderate, and no generally accepted accounting principles existed. With the issuance of FASB-33 in September, 1979 this has all changed. Practitioners and theoreticians are now studying the various approaches to inflation accounting with ever-increasing zeal.

This volume presents a more detailed historical analysis of inflation accounting than has ever been previously attempted. Recent developments both here and abroad are also discussed in some depth. The appendix provides illustrations of a few representative reporting formats as well as the reproduction of the original (FASB-33) pronouncement itself, complete with dissents. This book should prove to be a useful addition to your accounting library.

# INTRODUCTION

Ever since Friar Luca Pacioli formulated the first balance sheet nearly five hundred years ago, accountants have been recording transactions based on their historical cost. Historical cost has become a broad or pervasive accounting principle. In fact, financial statements must be presented in an historical cost format, although certain items, such as inventory, may reflect market value under the lower of cost or market method.

Among the strengths of the historical cost method is the fact that it has stood the test of time. The method has evolved over the span of several hundred years and has been continuously refined in the process. No other accounting method has enjoyed such wide application and acceptance over such an extended period of time.

Another principal strength of historical cost statements is their objectivity. There is only one way to reflect financial statement items, and that is original cost. While some subjectivity is involved in determining certain items, such as estimating depreciable lives or the allowance for doubtful accounts, the historical cost method is more objective than any proposed or existing accounting method.

The historical cost method does have some shortcomings, however. This method assumes that the basic monetary unit is stable, which has not been true in recent years. Land acquired in 1953 for $10,000 is reflected on the balance sheet at $10,000, even though its fair market value at the balance sheet date might be $40,000. The purchasing power of the dollar has declined almost every year since 1953. Excluding any change in market value, a $10,000 purchase made in 1953 would require more than $25,000 today.

The objective of publishing financial statements is to render a fair presentation of a company's activities and current position. Therefore, it can reasonably be argued that the historical cost method does not achieve this objective in times of changing price levels. While most accountants would readily agree with this statement, many problems arise as soon as possible alternatives are discussed. Should the 1953 land purchase be reflected on the balance sheet at $40,000, $25,000, or some other figure?

The two major alternative methods that have been discussed most frequently are indexing and current value accounting. There are several available sub-options within each of these alternatives, some of which will be explored later.

**Accounting Research Study No. 6**

Accounting Research Studies (ARS) were designed to define an accounting issue and give practitioners and other interested parties the opportunity to respond with comments before the Accounting Principles Board issued a final pronouncement (called an APB Opinion).

In 1963 the AICPA's Research Division issued Accounting Research Study No. 6 entitled "Reporting the Financial Effects of Price-Level Changes." ARS No. 6 outlined the basic problem and evaluated several alternatives. The study was more than 250 pages in length and took two years to complete. In arriving at their final recommendations the Research Division evaluated many sources, both foreign and domestic, as far back as 1920. While many areas were touched upon, the study concentrated on (1) a clarification of the meaning of "price level adjustments" of accounting data by the use of an index of the general price level; (2) a study of the indexes currently available; and (3) an exploration of the forms that disclosure of price-level changes has taken or could take.

The basic problem stems from the fact that the dollar is an elastic measuring device; it is not stable, as is assumed in historical financial statements. The 1940 dollar could purchase different quantities of goods and services than can today's dollar. If assets purchased with 1940 dollars are combined (on the historical financial statements) with assets purchased in the current year, the resulting total is meaningless, in the same manner that adding Swiss francs to U.S. dollars would produce a meaningless total. Yet this is precisely the result when historical financial statements are prepared.

The study made a distinction between monetary and nonmonetary items, and suggested that an arbitrary cut-off date of 1945 be used for indexing pre-1946 prices since many of the goods and services currently available resulted from technology developed during and after World War II. In other words, pre-1946 purchases would be assigned a 1945 index.

The idea of indexing has been around for a long time. Irving Fisher's book entitled *The Money Illusion,* cited in the study, mentions a Massachusetts law, passed in 1780, that pegs the payment of certain state issued notes to an amount of money equal to the value of a group of commodities. Modern indexes are based on the same concept. Price indexes are computed and published for particular industries, segments of the economy, and the economy as a whole. Among the indexes considered in the study were the Gross National Product Implicit Price Deflator, the Composite Construction Cost Index, the Consumer Price Index for All Urban Consumers (CPI-U) and the Wholesale Price Index.

The Gross National Product Implicit Price Deflator includes the goods and services produced by all segments of the economy, weighted according to relative dollar value. This is the most comprehensive index, and is often advocated for that very reason. One drawback to this index is that it is only published quarterly. Another drawback is the fact that this index combines all goods and services into one total, obliterating the individual components. It is an economic fact that the price of all goods and services does not increase or decrease at the same rate. The dollar value of electronic calculators could decrease by 20 percent while the dollar value of petroleum products could increase by 60 percent, yet an oil company and an electronics company would both adjust their financial statements using identical indexes.

To avoid the problem, some accountants have suggested that specific indexes be used for specific industries. This method would enable companies to more fairly reflect their activities and current position. However, problems arise when a company's activities do not fit precisely within one category. Even small companies may have activities in several distinctly different areas, and conglomerates may be in more than one hundred such areas. While using several indexes would more accurately reflect a company's activities and current position, the computations involved would be excessively burdensome in many instances.

The Composite Construction Cost Index is comprehensive, but deals only with the construction segment of the economy, and this is its major weakness.

The Consumer Price Index measures changes in a consumer "basket" of goods and services such as food, clothing, transportation, entertainment, etc. It is not nearly as comprehensive as the GNP Deflator, and this is its major weakness, although it changes at the same rate and moves in the same direction as the GNP Deflator. One advantage of this index is that it is published monthly.

The Wholesale Price Index includes items from the agricultural, mining and manufacturing segments of the economy. Since it is based on a relatively small sample of possible commodities, it is not as comprehensive as the GNP Deflator Index.

ARS No. 6 preferred the GNP Deflator Index because of its comprehensiveness.

The third area of concentration of the study was how the price-level change information should be presented. The possibilities fell into four main categories: (1) the basic financial statements could be adjusted for the effects of changes in the price level; (2) unadjusted statements could be supplemented by price-level information; (3) an adjustment to depreciation charges resulting from recorded revaluations of fixed assets could be made; or (4) an adjustment could be made for depreciation only.

It was finally decided that supplementary statements, completely adjusted, should be prepared, with the historical statements left intact. Adjustments (on the supplementary statements) would be recorded as of the end of the accounting period, and would be expressed in terms of end of period dollars. Only non-monetary items would be affected. Gains or losses in purchasing power would be reported as a separate item.

At the time the study was released in 1963, the annual inflation rate was approximately 1 percent, which is probably why no action was taken at that time.

## APB Statement No. 3

In 1969 the Accounting Principles Board issued Statement No. 3 (not promulgated GAAP) entitled "Financial Statements Restated for General Price-Level Changes." This Statement was based on the recommendations made by the AICPA's Accounting Research Division Staff in ARS No. 6. The Statement confined its application to the general price level. No measurement was to be made of the changes in the relationships between specific prices of individual goods and services.

A major reason given for the need for supplementary statements is that inflation has a cumulative effect on the financial statements over time. Although annual inflation might be less than 2 percent, fixed assets purchased in 1950 would experience a cumulative inflation effect of 54 percent (using the GNP Deflator Index) by the time the financial statements for 1968 are prepared.

The Board determined that it would not be necessary to present general price-level financial statements in order to have a fair presentation of financial position. However, if a company elects to present general price-level statements they should be presented as supplementary information and should not replace historical statements.

Many suggestions were given to companies that wanted to present supplementary price-level information. The index used should be an index that measures general rather than specific prices. The Consumer Price Index may be used, unless it deviates substantially from the GNP Implicit Price Deflator Index, in which case the latter index should be used. Monetary items should be distinguished from nonmonetary items when preparing the statements. Items having both monetary and nonmonetary characteristics should be classified according to the purpose for which they are being held. Nonmonetary items and income statement items should be restated to dollars of current general purchasing power at the end of the period. Monetary items should not be restated.

General price-level gains and losses should be included in current net income as a separate item.

## FASB Exposure Drafts

The Financial Accounting Standards Board has issued several Exposure Drafts in the area of inflation accounting. The first Exposure Draft, issued on December 31, 1974, was entitled *Financial Reporting in Units of General Purchasing Power.* This draft borrowed heavily from APB Statement No. 3, and gave updated and very detailed illustrations demonstrating how general price-level information should be presented. The Exposure Draft called for comprehensive restatement in units of general purchasing power. Reporting for interim periods was not required. Only the Gross National Product Implicit Price Deflator could be used to convert nonmonetary items. A detailed list classifying items as either monetary or nonmonetary was also presented.

The minimum information that must be disclosed on all income statements presented in units of general purchasing power included: (1) total revenue; (2) depreciation of property, plant and equipment; (3) net general purchasing power gain or loss from holding monetary assets and liabilities; (4) income from continuing operations; (5) net income; (6) net income per common share; and (7) cash dividends per common share.

An Exposure Draft entitled *Financial Reporting and Changing Prices* was issued December 28, 1978. This Draft expanded the reporting possibilities by including current value accounting as an alternative to general price-level changes. If a current value method is used rather than the historical cost/constant dollar (general purchasing power) method, items may be reflected either at current cost, net realizable value or value in use. This is different from the SEC's Accounting Series Release No. 190, which restricts the available methods to one—replacement cost.

This Exposure Draft also called for

separate disclosure of foreign exchange gain or loss on net monetary items. A five year summary of certain financial data would also be required. The requirements of the Exposure Draft, when adopted, would be effective for fiscal years ending on or after December 25, 1979.

An Exposure Draft entitled *Constant Dollar Accounting* was issued on March 2, 1979 as a supplement to the Exposure Draft that was issued in 1974. Six changes to that exposure draft were proposed. They were:

1. *The Consumer Price Index for All Urban Consumers (CPI-U), rather than the GNP Implicit Price Deflator Index, is to be used for constant dollar accounting;*
2. *Certain foreign currency items, previously classified as nonmonetary items, were to be classified as monetary;*
3. *Deferred income tax items were to be reclassified as monetary items;*
4. *The five year summary may be stated either in base year dollars or end of current year dollars;*
5. *Comprehensive restatement of the basic financial statements would no longer be required; and*
6. *Fewer enterprises would be required to present supplementary constant dollar information.*

**CURRENT VALUE ACCOUNTING**

The alternative to constant dollar accounting is current value accounting. Current value accounting restates items to estimated current value. There are three principal methods by which this may be accomplished: the entry value system, the exit value system, and the value-in-use system.

*The entry value system,* also referred to as the current cost system or the replacement or reproduction method, is based on cost of replacement or reproduction.

Replacement cost is the estimated cost of acquiring new and equivalent property at current prices after adjusting for depreciation. Reproduction cost is the estimated cost of producing new and equivalent property at current prices after adjusting for depreciation.

The three common methods of estimating such costs are direct pricing, unit pricing, and indexing. Direct pricing may be used to determine replacement costs of inventory and other assets that have readily ascertainable market prices by using invoice prices, vendor's firm price lists, or catalog prices. For other assets such as buildings and machinery, more complicated procedures are required.

Price lists are generally not available for buildings since every building is somewhat unique. An appraiser can be hired to estimate the fair market value of all buildings owned by the company. However, this may be costly, especially if the company owns many buildings.

There are several methods of computing an asset's fair market value using unit pricing. For buildings, an estimate could be made based on construction costs per square foot, multiplied by the number of square feet for each building. One major drawback to this method is that the building's location does not enter into its value. Another criticism is the fact that fair market value may be different than cost to construct, and in fact usually is different. Furthermore, unless an allowance for depreciation is made, a forty-year-old building having 50,000 square feet would be valued at the same figure as a ten-year-old building having comparable square footage.

For machinery, fair value may be estimated on a cost per unit basis. This may be particularly useful if the productive life in terms of units can be accurately estimated and if cost per unit figures are available. One drawback to this approach lies in the fact that plant size and location are not considered. Larger or more modern plants may operate at a lower cost per unit, which makes computations involving different size locations inaccurate.

A third entry value method is indexing. Specific price indexes are available for many types of assets, especially plant assets. One advantage of using specific price indexes is that appraisers need not be hired. This method is also much faster and easier to use. A possible deficiency would be that assets are not treated individually. For example, a company could own two 1957 Chevy automobiles, one of which is driven by a car buff who has the car washed and waxed every week; the other is driven by a slob who never washes the car and who uses the upholstery to extinguish his cigars. The cars would be valued equally, since the 1957 index would be used for both.

The second major current value method is *the exit value system*, which is based on net realizable value in the ordinary course of business. Net realizable value is the estimated selling price of the asset less any costs to complete or dispose. Using this method violates the basic accounting principle of going concern, which states that an enterprise is treated as a continuing entity. Some advocates would limit its use to assets that are about to be sold. One major limitation is that the exit value is based on an estimate. For assets having a readily ascertainable market value an accurate estimate may be made; for unique assets, or for assets whose market value cannot easily or accurately be determined, this is not the case.

The third major current value method is *the value-in-use method*, which measures current value using the present value of future net cash flows. Discounted future cash flow is the present value of estimated cash inflows, or cost savings, discounted at an appropriate rate of interest. This method, unlike the exit value or net realizable value system, recognizes the time value of money. This approach would most probably be used to value fixed assets and inventory items that are not expected to be sold in the immediate future. The major problem inherent in this approach is the high degree of subjective judgment involved. Forecasting future cash flow projections is highly subjective. Choosing the appropriate interest rate is another problem. Assets would most probably be valued by groups rather than individually, since inflows (revenues) and outflows (expenses) are associated with groups of assets (plants, divisions, cost centers, etc).

## FASB No. 33–Financial Reporting and Changing Prices

This Statement was issued in September, 1979 and applies to public enterprises having either (1) inventories and property, plant, and equipment (before deducting accumulated depreciation) amounting to more than $125 million, or (2) total assets amounting to more than $1 billion (after deducting accumulated depreciation).

No changes are to be made in the primary financial statements; the information required by the Statement is to be presented as supplementary information in published annual reports.

For fiscal years ended on or after December 25, 1979, enterprises are required to report:

a. *Income from continuing operations adjusted for the effects of general inflation;*
b. *The purchasing power gain or loss on net monetary items.*

For fiscal years ended on or after December 25, 1979, enterprises are also required to report:

a. *Income from continuing operations on a current cost basis;*
b. *The current cost amounts of inventory and property, plant, and equipment at the end of the fiscal year;*
c. *Increases or decreases in current cost amounts of inventory and property, plant, and equipment, net of inflation.*

However, information on a current cost basis for fiscal years ended before December 25, 1980 may be presented in the first annual report for a fiscal year ended on or after December 25, 1980.

Enterprises are required to present a five-year summary of selected financial data, including information on income, sales, and other operating revenues, net assets, dividends per common share, and market price per share. In the computation of net assets, only inventory and property, plant and equipment need be adjusted for the effects of changing prices.

This book is organized into four distinct parts. Part 1 gives a broad overview of inflation accounting in the United States. Parts 2 and 3 deal with general price level accounting and current value accounting, the two accepted methods used to reflect the effect of changing prices. Part 4 examines the approaches to inflation accounting in a few other, representative countries.

Mandatory reporting for the effects of changing prices is of recent origin, and the parameters of this sphere of knowledge are virtually undefined. As time passes and concepts become refined, the approach to reporting for changing prices will become more structured and, hopefully, more meaningful. Until then, the key words, at least in the United States, are flexibility and experimentation.

# Inflation Accounting in the United States

# THE HISTORY OF INFLATION ACCOUNTING IN THE UNITED STATES

*by William D. Milligan, Jr., MBA, CPA*

## INTRODUCTION

Inflation, defined by Accounting Principles Board Statement No. 3 as a decline in the general purchasing power of money as the general level of prices of goods and services rises,[1] and by *Webster's Dictionary* as a disproportionate and relatively sharp and sudden increase in the quantity of money or credit, or both, relative to the amount of exchange business (which always results in a decline in the general purchasing power),[2] has become a matter of fact situation for the past forty years. In essence, it has become a quantitative question of, what rate of inflation will the economy have to endure?, rather than the qualitative question of, will the prevailing economic conditions which confront the economy result in inflation?

This situation, coupled with the compound effect of inflation over many years (for example, a constant 2% rate of inflation results in 49% cumulative general price-level change in twenty years), has brought to the forefront many serious questions concerning the accuracy, comparability, and, ultimately, the credibility of financial statements as they are currently being prepared. The focal point of these questions does not necessarily criticize Generally Accepted Accounting Principles or Generally Accepted Auditing Standards, the cornerstones of the foundation from which financial statement opinions are based, but encompasses the ability of financial statements to prove useful to investors, creditors, management, employees, government officials, and others who are concerned with the economic affairs of business enterprises.[3]

### Statement of the Problem

As early as 1922 Professor William Paton noted, "The value of the dollar—its general purchasing power—is subject to serious change over a period of years ... accountants ... deal with an unstable, variable unit; and comparisons of unadjusted accounting statements prepared at intervals are accordingly always more or less unsatisfactory and are often positively misleading."[4] In 1978 the contested ability of financial statements to perform adequately prompted the Financial Accounting Standards Board, in Concepts Statement No. 1, "Objectives of Financial Reporting by Business Enterprises," to conclude "that financial reporting should provide information to help investors, creditors, and others assess the amounts, timing and uncertainty of prospective net cash inflows to the enterprise (paragraph 37)." It also calls for "the provision of information about the economic resources of an enterprise in a manner that provides direct and indirect evidence of cash flow potential (paragraphs 40 and 41)" and it concludes that "management is accountable to the owners for 'protecting them to the extent possible from unfavorable economic impacts of factors in the economy such as inflation or deflation' (paragraph 50)."[5]

### Chronological Overview of the Problem

The Concepts Statement, however, was by no means the first indication by a formal accounting rule-making body that there was a need for some form of recognition of the effects of

---

William D. Milligan, Jr., "A Chronological Analysis of Previous Pronouncements on Recording the Effects of Inflation in Financial Statements with FASB No. 33" (Master's thesis, Pace University, May 1980). Used by permission of William D. Milligan, Jr.

[1] "Accounting Principles Board Statement No. 3" American Institute of Certified Public Accountants, paragraph 7 (1969).

[2] *Webster's New International Dictionary* (2nd ed., World Publishing Company, 1971), p. 1275.

[3] "Accounting Principles Board Statement No. 3," paragraph 7.

[4] "FASB Statement of Financial Accounting Standards No. 33," paragraph 71.

[5] Ibid., paragraph 2.

price-level changes in financial statements. The Committee on Accounting Procedure, the predecessor of the Accounting Principles Board, issued Accounting Research Bulletins in 1947, 1948, and 1953 on the subject of general price-level changes. These Bulletins were short and precise. They dealt with the possibility of changing acceptable methods of depreciation so that an additional write-down of assets could be made against current income; the purpose of which would be to cover changes in replacement costs.

In 1963, through the Accounting Research Division, the AICPA issued Accounting Research Study No. 6, "Reporting the Financial Effects of Price-Level Changes," which, when issued, was designed to stimulate discussion on the topic of general price-level financial statements. This study did not require mandatory participation by enterprises, but its extensive analysis of the issue provided the groundwork for Accounting Principles Board Statement No. 3, "General Price-Level Financial Statements," in 1969. However, like its initiating document, APB Statement No. 3 was a pronouncement which did not make the presentation of general price-level information mandatory. As a result, little or no application of the APB's recommendations was evident.

The decade of the seventies brought about a resurgence in the movement against the distorted results obtained from historical cost financial statements. This was a direct result of double digit inflation, which had resulted in the effects of inflation being observed almost immediately rather than five or ten years hence, as was the case when low annual inflation rates were the norm and it took time for the compounding effect to surface.

In December 1974, the Financial Accounting Standards Board issued an Exposure Draft entitled "Financial Reporting in Units of General Purchasing Power." This draft was issued in conjunction with a FASB Sponsored Field Test of 100 companies, to gather feedback on the receptability and applicability of general price-level Financial Statements. This statement, from a procedural point of view, is basically the same as APB Statement No. 3 and "The Board acknowledges the usefulness of APB Statement No. 3, 'Financial Statements Restated for General Price-Level Changes,' in preparation of this Statement."[6] This exposure draft, however, due to a voluminous number of letters of comment and desire for further analysis of the field test results, was never, in its original or an amended form, issued by the FASB as a statement which required mandatory compliance. Thus, another attempt at the initiation of developing adjusted financial statements, which would give at least some supplemental information to financial statement users concerning the effects of inflation, was allowed to expire. The issue itself, however, did not become complacent and the attack on the comparability and credibility of financial statement reporting continued.

In 1976 the Securities and Exchange Commission issued Accounting Series Release 190. Although announcing at the time of issuance that it was not intended to prejudge or be competitive with the FASB proposal, ASR 190 made replacement cost information about inventories, cost of sales, and production capacity (along with its respective depreciation expense) a requirement for certain publicly held corporations. This requirement, a positive step in presenting a form of adjusted financial statement information, affected the corporation's 10-K report and, to a minimal extent, the corporation's Annual Report to stockholders.

In 1977, a *Morgan Guaranty Survey* stated, "In today's world of persistent—and seemingly endless—inflation, the old rules are found by many to be inadequate and misleading. For instance, under generally accepted accounting principles—which carry productive assets at cost of acquisition—true costs of replacing such equipment in an inflationary environment are not reflected. The result is that costs are understated, that income is overstated, and that, often, earnings are nothing more than phantom profits."[7]

The May 1979 issue of *The Journal of Accountancy* stated, "How best to overcome such

---

[6] "Financial Accounting Standards Board Exposure Draft" (December 31, 1974), p. 1.

[7] "Inflation Accounting," *Morgan Guaranty Survey* (July, 1977).

10

inadequacies without destroying the usefulness, wide acceptance, and understanding of traditional accounting based on established standards and practices—is the core of the debate."[8]

In December 1978, a study based on exhaustive computer analyses of a hypothetical U.S. manufacturing investment at various levels of inflation, prepared jointly by the Sun Company and Coopers and Lybrand (a Big Eight Accounting Firm), stated that taxable manufacturing profits were being artificially overstated because U.S. tax rules on depreciation fail to adjust for inflation. The study also noted that as inflation rises the nominal rate of return rises. However, after adjustments for inflation, the real rate of return drops. This "illusion effect" is attributable primarily to the absence of any upward adjustment in allowable depreciation charges under U.S. tax law. The study also finds that while tax incentives have helped companies cope with these inflation related problems, full scale indexing of depreciable assets may be the only way of providing "automatic and properly measured relief from inflation."[9]

In a similar intonation, Joseph E. Conner, CPA, Chairman of Price Waterhouse & Co., stated, "It is time to recognize that the cost of inflation, that is, the amount necessary to maintain the equivalent purchasing power of business capital, is a necessary charge to earnings."[10]

Mr. Conner stressed that the present accounting model produces "record" earnings due to the failure to record the erosive impact of inflation on the corporate capital base due to taxation. The accounting world, though still unable to develop mandatory requirements to deal with financial statement reporting under inflationary conditions, continued to compile doubters and critics.

In December 1978, the Financial Accounting Standards Board issued an exposure draft of proposed standards, Financial Reporting and Changing Prices, with the expectation of issuing a final standard before the end of the third quarter, 1979. The exposure draft would require certain large publicly held companies to disclose supplementary information about the effect of changing prices.

This information would be presented on an historical cost/constant dollar (General Purchasing Power) basis or on a current cost basis. The term "constant dollar accounting" is used in the statement to describe the methodology referred to as "general price-level accounting" and "accounting in units of general purchasing power" in the FASB Exposure Draft of December 1974, "Financial Reporting in Units of General Purchasing Power," and in APB Statement No. 3, "General Price-Level Financial Statements." The current cost accounting information called for in this statement has some similarities to that used in compliance of ASR 190. (However, the differences between the two sets of data are important and will be discussed later in this paper.)

In March 1979 the FASB issued a supplement to the 1974 proposed statement on general purchasing power adjustments. This exposure draft, however, in a similar pattern of previous pronouncements of the FASB, did not give a new outlook or require mandatory participation by corporations.

The Board, recognizing inherent problems in their approach, organized six special task groups to study measurement problems of price changes in specific industries. Furthermore, the Board sponsored a Conference on Financial Reporting and Changing Prices in New York City on May 31, 1979. Here, more than four hundred financial executives, analysts, accounting professors, and public sector policy-makers heard the comments of fourteen speakers representing all segments of the Board's constituency.[11]

Harold Williams, Chairman of the SEC, described an urgent need to report the effects of inflation on corporate financial statements. He said, "Conflicting reports of record profits, on the one hand, and inadequate earnings to

---

[8] "FASB Sponsors National Conference on Reporting Effects of Inflation," *Journal of Accountancy* (May 1979), p. 16.

[9] "Inflation Cuts Companies' Profitability but Not Income Taxes," *CPA Journal* (April 1979), p. 17.

[10] Joseph E. Conner, "Inflation Taxes Capital," *CPA Journal* (May 1979), p. 6.

[11] "FASB Statement of Financial Accounting Standards No. 33," paragraph 82.

maintain and expand capacity, on the other, serve only to confuse the public and political leaders. Furthermore, they raise questions about the integrity of financial reporting."[12] Donald J. Kirk, chairman of the FASB, said that traditional accounting model results "do not convey the effect of inflation on, or the change in value in, the dollar" and that what is at stake is the "credibility not just of financial statements but of American business profits."[13]

Finally, in September 1979, the Financial Accounting Standards Board issued mandatory requirements for certain public companies with regard to reporting the effects of inflation on financial statements. Entitled "Financial Reporting and Changing Prices," FASB Statement No. 33 required enterprises to report, in supplementary form, Historical Cost/Constant Dollar information and Current Cost Measurements. This Statement, for all practical reasons, is very similar to the Exposure Draft of December 1978. The key difference lies in the fact that both forms of reporting are mandatory, rather than optional as they were first proposed.

Therefore, in dealing with what Michael O. Alexander, the FASB director of research and technical activities, calls "the most important issue that has ever faced those who are involved with financial reporting...,"[14] the Financial Accounting Standards Board required two methods of implementation as "a basis for studying the usefulness of the two types of information."[15]

Therefore, the problem of accounting for the effects of inflation does not rest in a question of necessity. Private enterprises, as well as private and public rule-making bodies, agree that, somehow, somewhere, these effects must be reported. The question presently resides in what approach should be used. However, the methods currently proposed by the Financial Accounting Standards Board, constant dollar and current value, have been the subject of intensive study for many years.[16]

---

[12] "Special Report—FASB Conference on Financial Reporting and Changing Prices," *Journal of Accountancy* (July 1979), p. 7.
[13] Ibid., p. 7.
[14] Ibid., p. 10.
[15] "FASB Statement of Financial Accounting Standards No. 33," p. 6.
[16] Ibid., p. 5.

---

## THE ARB'S AND ARS NO. 6

*by William D. Milligan, Jr., MBA, CPA*

---

### THE ARB'S

**Introduction**

In 1944 a *Journal of Accountancy* article used a unique analogy in describing the problem of inflation (or deflation). Comparing the situation with a pilot bringing a ship into a foreign port, the article said, "It is true that the accountant today is befuddled with countless regulations and complex laws. However, even the best he is doing is not enough. If he expects to act as a pilot bringing the client through a dangerous period it will be necessary for him to continue reading all available information so that he may keep himself posted on social and economic problems as well as accounting."[1]

During 1947 there was widespread support in business circles for the proposition that rising costs of asset replacement justified increased depreciation charges against current

---

William D. Milligan, Jr., "A Chronological Analysis of Previous Pronouncements on Recording the Effects of Inflation in Financial Statements with FASB No. 33" (Master's thesis, Pace University, May 1980). Used by permission of William D. Milligan, Jr.
[1] C. P. Wilcox, "Inflation Problem," *Journal of Accountancy* (March 1944), pp. 236-237.

income. An October 1947 editorial, entitled "Depreciation and Inflation," in the *Journal of Accountancy* reported that management was not willing to accept the answer that this was not in accordance with Generally Accepted Accounting Principles. Furthermore, due to the pressure of wage demands and dividend payments based on reported income, management was not receptive to the suggestion of increased retention of current income for replacement purposes. The accounting profession was in a dilemma. Depreciation is an allocation process, not a process of valuation, and if the profession approved occasional charges to net income without adopting a permanent principle from which departure would be an exception, there would be no consistency in income reporting and net income figures would lose their significance.[2]

## ARB No. 33

In December 1947, the Committee on Accounting Procedure issued Accounting Research Bulletin 33, dealing with the subject of depreciation and high costs. The committee gave extensive consideration to the problem of making adequate provision for replacement of fixed assets with respect to increases in the price-level. The committee acknowledged that there was no doubt that management must take into consideration the probability that assets will be replaced at costs much greater than those of facilities now in use. However, the committee explicitly stated that it did not believe that increasing depreciation charges against current income was a satisfactory solution. The committee was in favor of adherence to Generally Accepted Accounting Principles until the dollar stabilized at some level because such a change would be a radical change in accounting principles and "should not be undertaken, at least until a stable price-level would make it practicable for business as a whole to make the change at the same time."[3]

In October 1948, the committee, in a published letter to the membership, reaffirmed this opinion. The letter stated:

> *1. That no change in accounting treatment of depreciation was practicable or desirable under present conditions. 2. That, after intensive study of the opinions of hundreds of businesses, such a change would confuse financial statement readers and nullify any gain which resulted from the more accurate presentation. 3. Should inflation result in original costs losing their practical significance it might become necessary to restate all assets in terms of depreciated currency.*[4]

The letter also pointed out that the immediate problem should and could be met by financial management and gave full support to the use of supplemental schedules, explanations or footnotes by which management may explain the need for retention of earnings.

Thus, in a span of approximately ten months the Committee on Accounting Procedure warranted two statements necessary with regard to price-level changes and their effect on financial statement reporting. However, their acknowledgment of the problem and support for the use of supplemental schedules, explanations and footnotes was negated by the recommendation that no specific action be taken until price stability was maintained. This was because companies would not incur an expense today which could be put off indefinitely and most companies realized that with maintenance of prices any form of action would be even less likely.

## Comments on ARB No. 33

In a November 1948 issue of *Journal of Accountancy,* Mr. George Baily, while referring to the comments of Mr. Daily, a partner with Touche (a Big Eight accounting firm), pinpointed four aspects which should be considered regarding the effects of inflation. The first dealt with the necessity for public understanding of changing values and financial statements and the need for increased retention of

---

[2] "Depreciation and Inflation," *Journal of Accountancy* (October 1947), p. 265.

[3] "Depreciation and High Costs," ARB No. 43 (June 1953), Chapter 9A.

[4] Ibid.

income. The second aspect was the need of management to evaluate the past effects of inflation as well as to reach a conclusion on future trends. This would enable management to set policy on pricing, dividends, and investment maintenance. The third aspect was the necessity of tax reform which would limit the taxation of reserves established to replace assets. The fourth aspect was that of accounting. Here, Mr. Baily primarily agreed with ARB No. 33 and cited the need for more experience, corporate and individual interpretation of financial statements in light of conditions, and encouragement of acknowledgment in financial reporting by either a schedule or footnote.[5]

A January 1949 article from the *Journal of Accountancy* said, "A great deal of theoretical consideration is being given to the effect of inflation on accounting and the determination of income; most agree that income is overstated today, that capital is being taxed and paid out in dividends."[6] The article pointed to a Yale University Study which examined the financial statements of nine steel companies which, according to the American Iron and Steel Institute, were doing 80 percent of the nation's steel business. The results showed that, in current dollars (1948), income retained to provide additional capital was $543,000,000 but in 1935-1939 dollars, dividends, interest and income taxes paid out of capital was $409,000,000.

## ARB No. 43

In 1953, a revision and restatement of previous Bulletins was issued in the form of ARB No. 43. Chapter 9 of that bulletin recognized the continuing importance of the subject and expressed approval of the basic conclusions asserted in the two previous publications.

These announcements were all similar in nature and, because there was no implementation required (nor was there any threat of mandatory requirements), the response of the business and professional circles was relatively sparse. However, the problem of inflation was still apparent and the subject of price-level adjusted financial statements and "illusionary" profits would not remain dormant long.

## ARS NO. 6

### Introduction

The period of the 1950's, one of relative economic calm and security to the country, was a period of only minor inflation. As a result, the issuance of ARB No. 43 was the only pronouncement of the decade concerning changing prices and financial reporting. However, the 1960's cast a different light on matters, and in 1963 the Accounting Research Division of the AICPA issued Accounting Research Study No. 6, "Reporting the Financial Effects of Price-Level Changes." This study was designed to stimulate discussion on the topic of general price-level financial statements.

### Initiation and Assumption of the Study

This study commenced on April 28, 1961 when the APB Board Minutes read, "... The Board ... agreed that the assumption in accounting that fluctuations in the value of the dollar may be ignored is unrealistic, and that therefore the Director of Accounting Research should be instructed to set up a research project to study the problem and to prepare a report in which recommendations are made for the disclosure of the effect of price-level changes upon the financial statements. In this study, special attention should be paid to the use of supplementary statements as a means of disclosure."[7] Supplementary schedules have marked advantages in a period of education, experimentation, and transition and the study, once underway,

---

[5] George D. Baily, "Relationship of Accounting to Other Factors in Accurate Reporting of Inflationary Income," *Journal of Accountancy* (November 1948), p. 362.

[6] Ralph Coughenour Jones, "Effect of Inflation on Capital and Profits, the Record of Nine Steel Companies," *Journal of Accountancy* (January 1944), p. 9.

[7] Raymond C. Lauver, "Accounting Research Study No. 6, 'Reporting the Financial Effects of Price-Level Changes'—Some Observations and Perspective," *New York Certified Public Accountants* (October 1964), p. 756.

assumed that they would be used to disclose price-level effects.

**Purpose of Price-Level Adjustments**
In this study, the use of the term price-level change is limited to the changes in general purchasing power of the dollar that occurs during the period of inflation (or deflation). Accordingly, the purpose of a price-level adjustment is to express each item in the financial statements in terms of a common dollar, or, in terms of dollars of the same general purchasing power. This is important because the accounts of the income statement and balance sheet will be expressed in dollars of the same size. The inferences drawn from that will effect owners, management, creditors, investors, and the government as a result of reevaluation of business policies, loans and taxes because the figures can logically be compared and more meaningful conclusions can be drawn.

On the subject of comparability George O. May wrote: "It has been said that the proposal put forward contemplates a departure from the accepted manner of using the monetary unit as the unit of accounting. It has even been suggested ... that the proposal involves the adoption of an elastic yardstick. But the yardstick used has always been elastic and its usefulness has been impaired (though not destroyed) by that fact ... the proposal does not contemplate discontinuance of the use of the yardstick. It is intended only to use the yardstick intelligently with frank recognition of its defects, rather than to close one's eyes to its shortcomings."[8]

W. E. Parker, a London partner of Price Waterhouse, wrote, "The problem is whether accounting should take cognizance of changes in purchasing power of money ... and if so how best to reflect in accounts the effects and consequences of such changes."[9] However, as the committee pointed out, the bulk of the study was, in essence, a study of the most sophisticated techniques devised to make logical and meaningful comparisons of financial statements, general price-level accounting.

**Prior Reluctance to Price-Level Adjustments**
Prior to this time accountants had been reluctant to record the effects of inflation in the financial statements. Reporting methods either ignored, declined recognition of, or masked the effects of management's financial policies, as a result of its operating policies, on the net income of the firm.[10] The reasons for this were that accountants: (1) had believed a revision of previously recorded figures would confuse more than enlighten, (2) distrusted proposed techniques for dealing with the problem, (3) felt that inflation is not an accounting problem, and (4) were skeptical that inflation could continue unabated in our country.[11] These reasons may have been valid for a certain period of time. However, after twenty years of not answering the call for disclosure, continued procrastination by the profession would be dangerous. This was obvious from the loss of credibility which resulted from the unrest in the business sector, and the growing feeling that the only way to reform would be to incorporate, in some form, adjustments in the financial statements.[12]

**Study Conclusions**
The study came to the conclusion that price-level changes should come in the form of fully adjusted statements supplemental to the conventional financial statements. The adjusted statements could be presented in multicolumn form, presented separately or adjacent to the primary statements based on historical cost. Furthermore, the study suggests that, as a

---

[8] "Reporting the Effects of Price-Level Changes," ARS No. 6 (1963), p. 15.

[9] W. E. Parker, "Changes in the Purchasing Power of Money," *Price Waterhouse Review* (Spring 1963), p. 7.

[10] Philip M. Piaker, "Comments on AICPA Accounting Research Study No. 6–'Reporting the Financial Effects on Price-Level Changes,'" *New York Certified Public Accountants* (Nov. 1964), p. 818.

[11] Ibid., p. 816.

[12] D. H. Bonham, "Reporting the Financial Effects of Price-Level Changes," *Canadian Chartered Accountant* (May 1964), p. 384.

minimum, the following be presented on an adjusted basis with comparisons for a period of years:

a. *Sales or other major source of revenue*
b. *Net profit*
c. *Common stockholder's equity*
d. *Purchasing power gains and losses on monetary items*
e. *Other information might include a comparison of adjusted and unadjusted depreciation and cost of goods sold.*

Also, if the financial data was presented in terms of the price-level at the balance-sheet date, any prior years' figures included for comparative purposes would also have to be restated in terms of the same price-level.

**Impact on Financial Statements**

These recommendations, however, despite the clear expression of displeasure with current methods of reporting, were not without controversy. The impact on financial statements varied depending on which price index was employed. The study recommended the Gross National Product Implicit Price Deflator but did not rule out alternatives. This index would be applied directly to "non-monetary" items (e.g., assets that are not in the form of money or claims to money) and, as a result, would have a tremendous impact on the comparability, and credibility, of the restated figures.

The reporting of purchasing power gains and losses provides further complications. Monetary items are those the amount of which is defined by statute or contract and is therefore not affected by a change in price-level.[13] The amounts ascribed to the item must be restated in terms of dollars at some other point in time. This would result in a gain or loss as the purchasing power of the dollar increases or decreases. This gain or loss, however, has no counterpart in conventional accounting. Therefore, with regard to these balance sheet accounts, the discussion revolved around the placement of the gain or loss on the income statement.

Ralph C. Jones, in an article for the American Accounting Association in 1956, said, "Since no comparable item is found on conventional income statements and since the separation of current (operating) monetary capital from other monetary accounts is difficult and uncertain, managements generally may prefer to treat purchasing power changes in all monetary accounts as a separate category."[14] This was in agreement with the Study's opinion that the net gain or loss on monetary items would be reported (1) in the statement of changes in owner equity, (2) as a component part of the calculation of Net Income for the period, or (3) in the statement of Net Income. Inflationary gain or loss, because it is a new category in accounting . . . should be distinctly labeled and separately set forth. An alternative to this, however, results from the serious question as to whether a credit difference arising in this manner should be disclosed, as the study indicated, or whether it would be better to show it as a deferred amount.[15]

With regard to the income statement, depreciation is usually the most drastically affected item, since it typically reflects the value of the dollar at different points in time depending on when the various depreciable assets were acquired. Cost of goods sold have a similar effect, only to a lesser degree due to a shorter turnover period. As conventionally shown, the Income Statement may lead to unintended results:

1. *As a basis for Income Taxes*
2. *Thwarting the objective of dividend restrictions—preservation of a buffer for creditors*
3. *In comparability of statements if significant price-level changes have occurred.*[16]

**Results of ARS No. 6**

Although some companies, such as Kodak and Indiana Telephone, adopted price-level adjusted statements for internal use around the time that ARS No. 6 was issued, the effects of the study,

---

[13] "ARS No. 6," p. 138.
[14] "ARS No. 6," p. 149.
[15] Bonham, p. 384.
[16] "ARS No. 6," p. 24.

from an application point of view, were not overwhelming. The study was acclaimed the best of its type up to that time and, despite the general consensus that further study of methodology, as well as education of financial statements' users, was needed before any permanent ruling could be made, the study had accomplished its number one objective of increased discussion on price-level changes. Therefore, even though the same objections to change were heard that were used in the past, the calls for change continued and despite a 1965 re-affirmation of Chapter 9 of ARB No. 43, concerning depreciation and rising prices, in APB Opinion No. 6 ("Status of Accounting Research Bulletins"), the pressure for some form of price-level recognition continued to grow.

# APB STATEMENT NO. 3
## by William D. Milligan, Jr., MBA, CPA

## INTRODUCTION

**The Effects of Inflation**

For nearly forty years there had been at least one occurrence common to almost every country in the world. That event had had dramatically different effects on the economies of the world as well as the industries which comprise those economies. This common element was inflation.

During inflation, the general purchasing power of money declines as the general level of prices of goods and services rises. The effects of inflation on a business enterprise and on its financial statements depend on the change in the general price-level and the composition of the assets and liabilities of the enterprise.[1] The effects of inflation on the financial statements compound over a period of years (for example, a constant 2% rate of inflation results in a 22% cumulative price-level change in ten years)[2] and, as a result, may have a substantial effect on financial statement representation even though the amount of inflation each year had been relatively small.

Under these prevailing circumstances the APB minutes of April 28, 1961 stated: "The assumption in accounting that fluctuation in the value of the dollar may be ignored is unrealistic..."[3] and, as part of a program to determine appropriate accounting under conditions of inflation, the Accounting Research Division of the AICPA issued ARS No. 6 to stimulate discussion on this important accounting matter.

**Accounting Principles Board Comments**

In 1969, the Accounting Principles Board issued APB Statement No. 3, "General Price-Level Financial Statements," using ARS No. 6 as its groundwork. In fact, Statement No. 3 is so parallel in nature to the research study that the opening paragraph of the APB Statement, through a footnote disclosure, refers the reader to ARS No. 6 for a more detailed discussion of general price-level financial statements.

The Board stated that changes in the general purchasing power of money have an impact on almost every aspect of economic affairs, including such matters as investment, wage negotiation, pricing policy, and government fiscal policy. The effects of changes in the

---

William D. Milligan, Jr., "A Chronological Analysis of Previous Pronouncements on Recording the Effects of Inflation in Financial Statements with FASB No. 33" (Master's thesis, Pace University, May 1980). Used by permission of William D. Milligan, Jr.

[1] "Accounting Principles Board Statement No. 3" paragraphs 7 and 13.

[2] Ibid., paragraph 14.

[3] Paul Rosenfeld, "Accounting for Inflation—A Field Test," *Journal of Accountancy* (June 1969), p. 45.

general purchasing power of money on economic data expressed in monetary terms are widely recognized, and economic data for the economy as a whole are commonly restated to eliminate these effects. With this in mind the Board felt that general price-level financial statements, or pertinent information extracted from them, should prove useful to investors, creditors, management, employees, government officials, and others who are concerned with the economic affairs of business enterprises.[4]

## RECOMMENDATIONS OF APB STATEMENT NO. 3

In order to facilitate the usefulness of general price-level financial statements, APB Statement No. 3 recommended:[5]

1. *The same accounting principles used in preparing historical dollar financial statements should be used in preparing general price-level financial statements except that changes in the general purchasing power of the dollar are recognized in general price-level financial statements.*
2. *An index of the general price-level (preferably the GNP Deflator) should be used to prepare general price-level financial statements.*
3. *General price-level financial statements should be presented in terms of general purchasing power of the dollar at the latest balance sheet date. This is because current economic actions must take place in terms of current dollars, and restating items in current dollars expresses them in the context of current action.*
4. *Monetary and non-monetary items should be distinguished for the purpose of preparing general price-level financial statements.*

   *Monetary assets and liabilities are those whose amounts are fixed by contract or otherwise in terms of numbers of dollars regardless of changes in specific prices or general price-level.[6] These items should appear in general price-level financial statements at the same amounts as in the historical dollar balance sheet.*

   *Non-monetary assets and liabilities are described as those other than monetary[7] and should be restated to dollars of current general purchasing power at the end of the period.*

5. *The amounts of income statement items should be restated to dollars of current general purchasing power at the end of the period.*
6. *General price-level gains and losses should be calculated by means of the general price index and included in current net income by being reported as a separate item in general price-level income statements.*

   *General price-level gains and losses on monetary items arise from changes in the general price-level, and are not related to the receipt or payment of money. Therefore, the gains or losses are recognized in the period in which the general price-level changes.*

   *The gain or loss (net) are separately identified on the Income Statement because they are not part of historical dollar financial statements.*

7. *General price-level financial statements of earlier periods should be updated to dollars of the general purchasing power at the end of each subsequent period for which they are presented.*
8. *The Board further recommended that the general price-level be compared with general price-level financial statements and not historical data financial statements because the two are prepared on different bases. To encourage this, the Board suggested that the general price-level information be explained in the*

---

[4] "Accounting Principles Board Statement No. 3," paragraph 6.
[5] Ibid., paragraphs 25-48.
[6] Ibid., paragraph 18.
[7] Ibid., paragraph 19.

*footnotes and other appropriate places, and that the two sets of data be presented in separate schedules rather than in parallel columns.*

## EFFECTS OF THE STATEMENT'S RECOMMENDATIONS

Paul Rosenfeld, in a June 1969 article in the *Journal of Accountancy,* described a study which involved eighteen U.S. companies, of various industries and sizes, and the outcome of applying the Gross National Product Deflator as an index of the general price-level.[8]

With respect to Net Income, various effects were reported as a result of the different nature of the industries participating in the test. These differences stemmed from the upward restatement of the firm's assets, purchased years before the balance sheet date, and subsequent increased depreciation, depletion, and amortization charges which decreased net income. This restatement of depreciable assets caused a particularly large discrepancy between capital intense companies and companies with a more liquid financial structure.[9] This wide variation was also affected by the debt structure of the firm.[10] Holders of monetary assets lose purchasing power whereas holders of monetary liabilities gain general purchasing power during periods of inflation simply as a result of general price-level changes.[11] These two aspects of the APB requirements may detect an overstatement or understatement of historical-cost based net income for the firm as a result of the nature of business activities and management decisions on equity structure, rather than operation.

The study also pointed out that the interest rates paid by the firms could be altered dramatically from the statutory rate, cash dividends distributed were a higher percentage of restated income than historical income, and the rate of return (net income divided by owners equity) was lower for restated numbers for all of the companies available.[12]

### Responses to APB Statement No. 3

The eighteen companies involved in the study, as described by Rosenfeld, agreed that the supplemental financial statements would provide a basis for more intelligent, better informed allocation of resources and that practical problems did not represent a major barrier to preparation of general price-level financial statements.[13]

Similar responses regarding the degree of usefulness of Price-level Adjustment Information were reported in a survey of financial analysts, bank officers and credit people, and financial executives performed by Ralph W. Estes. Mr. Estes reported that 56 percent of the financial executives, 70 percent of the financial analysts, and 80 percent of the bank officers and credit people felt that the information was useful.[14]

However, the idea of general price-level adjusted financial statements did not appeal to everyone. In the *Journal of Accounting Research,* William A. Paton states "The essential function of the financial measurement and information system known as accounting is to foster sound decision-making in resource utilization and in business operation generally, and this function cannot be adequately served by procedures and reports that fail to recognize the effects of a continuing and substantial erosion of the monetary unit of measure..."[15] Mr. Paton agrees that a general index number is sufficient to take cognizance of the gains or losses from holding monetary assets or liabilities but that "current value based" accounting

---

[8] Rosenfeld, "Accounting for Inflation," p. 47.
[9] Ibid.
[10] Ibid., p. 48.
[11] "Accounting Principles Board Statement No. 3," paragraph 18.
[12] Rosenfeld, "Accounting for Inflation," p. 49.
[13] Ibid., p. 50.
[14] Ralph W. Estes, "Assessment of the Usefulness of Current Costs and Price-Level Information by Financial Statement Users," *Journal of Accounting Research* (Autumn 1968), pp. 204-205.
[15] William Paton, "Observations on Inflation from an Accounting Stance," *Journal of Accounting Research* (Spring 1967), p. 114.

is undoubtedly superior to "cost-based" accounting from the standpoint of providing owners and managers with significant data on which to base decisions as to utilization and disposition of resources.[16]

Russell Matthews, in a *Journal of Accounting Research* article, thought that general price-level adjusted financial statements failed to recognize a specific need for specific adjustment and thus provided no indication as to how the analysis of different price changes might be included in this framework. Mr. Matthews added "General price-level adjustments are statistical procedures of relatively minor significance compared with specific price adjustments..."[17]

Other negative opinions expressed with regard to general price-level financial statements were the amount of education necessary to train users of such financial statements,[18] the possibility of issuing a liquidating dividend under restated income even though the dividend was distributed in accordance with a normal percent of historic income, the ability of management to increase restated income through debt financing while at the same time having difficulty meeting current cash flows (and possibly approaching insolvency), and the idea of government tax reform with the effective tax rate based on general price-level adjusted income rather than historical cost based income.

The negative response to the conceptional aspects of APB Statement No. 3 and the additional cost of constructing these financial measurements combined with the non-mandatory nature of the APB Statements resulted in almost no response to the Board's recommendations.

---

[16] Ibid., p. 83.

[17] Russell Matthews, "Price-Level Controversy: A Reply," *Journal of Accounting Research* (Spring 1967), p. 114.

[18] Paul Rosenfeld, "Re: General Price-Level Accounting and Current Accounting," *Journal of Accountancy* (March 1970), p. 30.

---

# FASB EXPOSURE DRAFT: DECEMBER 31, 1974

*by William D. Milligan, Jr., MBA, CPA*

## INTRODUCTION

**Review of Previous Proposals**
Entering 1974 the accounting profession had put forth five pronouncements on the subject of the effects of price-level changes on financial statement reporting. From 1947 through 1953 the Committee on Accounting Procedure issued three pronouncements. These pronouncements recognized the problem and gave full support

---

William D. Milligan, Jr., "A Chronological Analysis of Previous Pronouncements on Recording the Effects of Inflation in Financial Statements with FASB No. 33" (Master's thesis, Pace University, May 1980). Used by permission of William D. Milligan, Jr.

---

to the use of supplemental schedules, explanations, or footnotes by which management could explain the effects of the increasing price-level on their financial statements. However, these acknowledgments were negated by the fact that implementation was not mandatory and the response of business and professional circles was relatively sparse.

In 1963 ARS No. 6, issued by the AICPA to stimulate discussion on the topic of general price-level financial statements, recommended comprehensive disclosure of adjusted financial statements. The study was an in-depth one which explored various alternatives and, in addition to stimulating discussion, may have been responsible for several companies adopting price-level adjusted financial statements for internal use. Unfortunately, ARS No. 6 lacked mandatory participation requirements and, despite bringing the problem to the forefront, did not receive overwhelming acceptance.

In 1969, the Accounting Principals Board issued APB Statement No. 3. Based on ASR No. 6, this statement also recommended comprehensive restatement of general price-level financial statements. However, due to the high cost of implementation and the non-mandatory nature of its recommendations, little or no application resulted.

**The Situation after APB Statement No. 3**

In the years following APB Statement No. 3, the rate of inflation increased markedly. The level of prices increased 20% in the United States between 1970 and 1973[1] and "In light of this continuing and increasing inflation, a number of the members of the Financial Accounting Standards Advisory Council, at their meeting in December 1973, urged the Board to consider the effects of recent general price-level increases on financial reporting."[2] Accordingly, the Board placed the subject on its agenda for 1974. However, as John C. Burton, then Chief Accountant of the SEC pointed out, if the rate of inflation was at a low level (3% per annum) historical cost financial statements would be adequate or if the rate of inflation was at a dramatic level (25% per annum) it would be generally agreed that historical cost financial statements are of little value and actions to supersede them would be necessary. It was the middle range rate of inflation, the rate which the nation had been experiencing, where practical answers were not easy to arrive at.[3] Therefore, the situation was not a simple one and debate, from the outset, appeared inevitable.

In January 1974, a *CPA Journal* article referred to two surveys concerning price-level adjusted financial statements taken around the time of APB Statement No. 3's issuance. The first survey, taken in 1968, asked financial analysts, executives, and bankers to rate price-level adjusted financial statements. The results were that 32% thought they were very useful, 38% thought they were somewhat useful, and 30% thought they were of no use. The second survey, prepared in 1969, asked financial analysts if price-level adjusted financial statements should be prepared. Here, 23% said yes, 20% were undecided, and 57% said no.

However, as the same article pointed out, *Accounting Trends and Techniques* 1970, 1971, and 1972 editions showed little or no presentation of financial statements adjusted to a common dollar basis. This gap between advocacy and practice was a result of confusion as to the meaning of adjusted statements and the continued dependence on historical cost financial statements to furnish desired information. Furthermore, firms intuitively took action to cope with changing prices, and the uncertainty regarding the reliability and accuracy of price indices and their different effects on firms with different asset structures caused hesitance towards acceptance. In the meantime, the subject of specific price changes was also being weighed.[4]

The Financial Accounting Standards Board issued a Discussion Memorandum on February 15, 1974 which referred extensively to APB Statement No. 3. The Board received 139 position papers, letters of comment and outlines of oral presentations in response to the Discussion Memorandum. Of these, approximately 40% were in favor and 60% against. Those responding negatively were, primarily, connected with industry. The Accounting Standards Division of the AICPA, in a statement presented to the FASB, recommended that the effects of general price-level changes "be required as information supplemental to conventional historical-dollar financial state-

---

[1] "Measuring and Reporting the Impact of Inflation through Price-Level Accounting," Arthur Young & Co. (1975), p. 5.

[2] "Financial Accounting Standards Board Exposure Draft" (December 31, 1974), paragraph 61.

[3] J.C. Burton, "Accounting That Allows for Inflation," *Journal of Accountancy* (November 30, 1974), p. 68.

[4] Clyde P. Stickney, "No Price Level Adjusted Statements, Please," *CPA Journal* (January 1974), pp. 25-31.

ments."[5] The public accounting firms, which comprised a large majority of the 40% in favor, took the same position as the Accounting Standards Division.

The Financial Executives Institute, though not entirely opposed, stated grave reservations about the use of general price-level financial statements. The Institute expressed the opinion that further research was needed, along with education, so as to assure consistent application and understanding of the adjusted statements. The Institute also felt that the total disregard for APB Statement No. 3 was a clear indication that the testing and development of general price-level adjusted financial statements could not be accomplished without an FASB-sponsored program.[6]

Another opinion put forth during this period was typified by a Coopers and Lybrand Newsletter. The Newsletter said that the initial collection and summary of historical data into categories appropriate for restatement represented the major obstacle to price-level adjusted financial statements. The Newsletter also pointed out that those who favor price-level adjusted financial statements generally endorsed APB Statement No. 3. Categories specifically noted were the adjustment of non-monetary items on the balance sheet, restatement of income as a result of adjusted depreciation and cost of goods sold, and the inclusion of general purchasing power gains or losses.[7]

Still another opinion was put forth in *Business Week* magazine, in an article entitled "Need for Inflation Accounting." Accountants, by attempting to measure income through GAAP, ignore the fact that, unlike physical standards, no unit of currency does or can maintain a constant measure of value. With the exception of LIFO (last in, first out), the accounting profession continues to uphold the original cost concept and is more concerned with transactions in pieces of inventory of units of property than with real capital. As a result, in times of inflation, conventional accounting condones a dangerous inclusion of excessive profit.[8]

The amount of these profits, according to Treasury Department chief Economist Dr. Herman Lieblig, accounted for "a little over half" of the gain in corporate profits in the first half of 1973.[9] This was a result of the use of the FIFO (first in, first out) method of inventory valuation and low depreciation charges, according to Dr. Lieblig.

The 1973 price-level adjusted financial statements of Shell Oil and Indiana Telephone provided numerical proof of the excessive profit theory. Being capital intense companies adjusted depreciation charges exceeded purchasing power gains on net monetary items and resulted in lower profits and return on capital figures. Profits dropped 10.5% and 35%, return on capital 3% and 4.3%, for Shell and Indiana, respectively.[10] C. Meyrick Payne of the management consultant firm of McKinsey and Co. said, "Corporate management is faced with a serious problem during inflationary periods because stockholder's equity—the nucleus of the company's ability to operate in the future—is in danger of depletion"[11] because taxes and dividends are cash distributions based on conventionally computed earnings.

**Questions Remained**

However, despite the theoretical backing of the AICPA and the public accounting firms, and despite numerical proof as provided by Shell, Indiana Telephone and others, serious questions remained as to the appropriateness

---

[5] "Institute Urges Disclosure of Inflation Impact," *Journal of Accountancy* (May 1974), p. 20.

[6] Ibid., p. 20.

[7] "Effects of Inflation on Financial Statements," *CPA Journal* (October 1974), pp. 81-82.

[8] W. Blackie, "Need for Inflation Accounting," *Business Week* (March 30, 1974), p. 16.

[9] "Numbers Game: The Accountants Grapple with Inflation," *Forbes* (March 1, 1974), p. 49.

[10] "Controversial Method of Allowing for Inflation (Price-Level Accounting)," *Business Week* (September 14, 1974), p. 92.

[11] J. F. Lyons, "Inflation Accounting: The Coming New Groundrules," *Financial World* (May 15, 1974), p. 29.

of price-level adjusted financial statements. Some typical questions included:

1. Would such financial statements benefit or confuse users?
2. Is replacement cost more relevant than a general purchasing power adjustment?
3. Can general price-level financial statements be comparable with the technological changes in today's industry?
4. Would prior years' records be adequate for the development of financial statements with integrity?
5. Would a cost-benefit analysis support general price-level financial statements?[12]

## RECOMMENDATIONS OF THE EXPOSURE DRAFT

Thus, with evidence at hand that some disclosure was necessary, but serious questions and opposition still present, the Financial Accounting Standards Board issued, on December 31, 1974, the Exposure Draft entitled "Financial Reporting in Units of General Purchasing Power." The Exposure Draft recommended that:[13]

1. The same accounting principles used in preparing historical cost financial statements should be used in preparing financial information stated in units of general purchasing power.
2. General purchasing power financial statements should be presented when historical cost financial statements are presented at the end of the fiscal year and these general purchasing power financial statements should be presented in terms of the general purchasing power at the most recent balance sheet date.

---

[12] K.M. Frey, "Survey of Price-Level Accounting in Practice," *CPA Journal* (May 1975), p. 32.
[13] "Financial Accounting Standards Board Exposure Draft," (December 31, 1974), paragraphs 31-54.

3. The Gross National Product Implicit Price Deflator should be the index of the general purchasing power of the dollar used in preparing general purchasing power financial information.
4. Monetary and non-monetary items should be classified as such for the purpose of preparing general price-level financial statements.

   *Monetary items would be classified as follows:*

a. Assets: Cash and Claims to cash that are fixed in terms of dollars regardless of changes in prices.
b. Liabilities: Liabilities for which the amount owed is fixed in terms of number of dollars regardless of changes in prices.
c. Stockholders' equity: Items that are fixed in terms of number of dollars, such as preferred stock that is carried in the balance sheet at an amount equal to its fixed liquidation or redemption price.

   *Monetary items are stated at identical numbers in terms of general purchasing power at the current balance sheet date.*

   *Non-monetary items are those balance sheet items other than those classified as monetary by the conditions set forth above.*

5. Financial information stated in units of general purchasing power shall be prepared by comprehensive restatement of historical cost financial statements. However, the amount of income tax expense shall be based on the amount of income tax included in determining net income on the historical cost basis.
6. The net gain or loss of general purchasing power that results from holding monetary assets and liabilities should be included in determining net income in units of general purchasing power.

   *This purchasing power gain or loss should be presented as a separate item on the general purchasing power income statement. This amount, however, would* not include gains or losses of general purchasing power that result from monetary stockholders' equity items. Those items would be charged or credited directly to common stockholders' equity in the general purchasing power financial statements.

7. If general purchasing power information for earlier periods was presented for purposes of comparison with general purchasing power information, the earlier periods would be "rolled forward" to units of the purchasing power at the end of the current period.

8. Financial Statements of foreign branches, subsidiaries and other investees that are expressed in units of a foreign currency should first be translated into United States dollars and then be restated for changes in the general purchasing power of the United States dollar in accordance with this Statement.

9. The following information, at a minimum, was to be presented in units of general purchasing power:

a. Income Statement

   1. Total Revenue

   2. Depreciation of property, plant and equipment

   3. Net general purchasing power gain or loss

   4. Income from continuing operations

   5. Net Income

   6. Net Income per common share

   7. Cash dividends per common share

b. Balance Sheet

   1. Inventories

   2. Working Capital

   3. Total property, plant and equipment, net of accumulated depreciation

   4. Total Assets

   5. Total common stockholders' equity

These presentation requirements were intended to allow flexibility for enterprises to determine the method and extent of presentation most suitable in their circumstances. This, the opinion states, allows presentation of complete or condensed general purchasing power financial statements.

## RESPONSES TO THE EXPOSURE DRAFT

### Business Community

The general business community had various reactions to the Exposure Draft. Those in favor stated that one objective of external financial reporting was to "provide information useful to investors and creditors for predicting, comparing and evaluating potential cash flows to them in terms of amount, timing and related uncertainty."[14] This, of course, was a reason given in the Exposure Draft, APB Statement No. 3 and ARS No. 6.

Archie Monroe, Controller for Exxon Corporation, said, ". . . The added education effort and compilation time would be more than justified by the more meaningful restatement which results."[15] Mr. Monroe also stated that general price-level statements, while still following historical cost principles (GAAP), isolated inflation and gave a better idea of actual earnings and rates of return.

In the September 14, 1974 issue of *Business Week,* Robert T. Sprouse, a member of the FASB, said "There's a serious question whether you get a meaningful measure of income by deducting 1940 dollars from 1974 dollars" and that financial executives and accountants were finally conceding what Wall Street had figured out—earnings were overstated due to inflation. In the same article, W.W. Brown, assistant comptroller with AT&T, simply stated, "if you're going down the river because of inflation, your financial statements ought to let you, your investors, and your regulators know about it."[16]

---

[14] Lawrence Revsine, "Accounting for Inflation—The Controversy," *Journal of Accountancy* (October 1974), p. 73.

[15] Archie L. Monroe, "Experimenting with Price-Level Reporting," *Financial Executive* (December 1974), p. 38.

[16] "Controversial Method. . .," p. 91.

## The Controversy:
### GPP or Replacement Cost

However, rather than the number of supporters for general price-level financial statements increasing, the number of critics appeared to increase after the Exposure Draft. This situation developed, not so much because of disagreements with the particular Exposure Draft, but as a result of the expanded debate over the use of general price-level financial statements or replacement cost financial statements. Both forms of restated financial statements reported consistently lower results than historical cost financial statements, and the debate centered around which was more accurate and beneficial to investors and other financial statement readers.

The Securities and Exchange Commission, through the issuance of Securities Act Release No. 5608, in August 1975, added to the debate by announcing proposed disclosure requirements of certain replacement cost data in the notes to the financial statements. Although it announced that this proposal was in no way related to, or to be directed at, the FASB Exposure Draft, the connection was immediate. John C. Burton, Chief Accountant for the SEC, stated that the first objective of financial statements (according to the Trueblood Committee) was "to provide users with information for predicting, comparing and evaluating enterprises' earning power."[17] Mr. Burton added that in a period of rapidly changing costs there was a strong argument for current (replacement) costs as a means of properly matching revenues and expenses.

The nature of the debate had changed dramatically. John E. Conner, a Partner with Price Waterhouse & Co., stated it very simply, "Forbearance is now required from the SEC to allow FASB to come to grips with problems..."[18]

---

[17] Burton, "Accounting That Allows for Inflation," p. 69.
[18] Joseph E. Connor, "Putting Accounting Developments in Perspective," *Financial Executive* (May 1974), p. 75.

## The Big Eight Firms

Among the Big Eight accounting firms, the Exposure Draft prompted formal responses or editorials from Ernst & Ernst (now Ernst & Whinney), Arthur Young & Company, Price Waterhouse & Co., and Peat, Marwick, Mitchell & Co.

The PMM & Co. editorial appeared in a June 1975 Executive Newsletter. The Newsletter is published periodically by PMM & Co. as a service to its clients with the objective of alerting top executives to important matters relating to financial reporting, accounting principles, taxation, and business management. The editorial pointed out that the debate over current replacement value accounting and general purchasing power had "baffled" many businessmen because in some cases the two methods may be similar, but the purposes and results were different. The editorial concluded "the debate and confusion surrounding the two methods is not expected to be resolved without considerable additional study and experimentation by accountants and businessmen."[19]

Unlike the PMM & Co. editorial, the other firms listed gave comprehensive analyses of the Exposure Draft proposals. Price Waterhouse & Co., in its opening comments to the FASB, as submitted on September 18, 1975, said "We agree with the concept of measuring and reporting the effects of inflation on the operation of business enterprises and believe that selected general purchasing power information can be useful to informed investors... Unfortunately, it is our judgment that the method of presenting adjusted results of operations is so complex that the information will likely be misunderstood and possibly will be misleading. It seems to us that two conditions should exist before the preparation of purchasing power information is required: (1) better understanding and (2) demonstrated demand."[20] This

---

[19] "Current Replacement Value vs. General Purchasing Power," Executive Newsletter. Peat, Marwick, Mitchell & Co. (June 1975), pp. 1-2.
[20] "Financial Reporting in Units of General Purchasing Power (Exposure Draft: December 31, 1974)," Price Waterhouse & Co. (September 18, 1975), p. i.

commentary also pinpointed several points of question about the Exposure Draft.

The September 1975 comments of Price Waterhouse & Co. were supplemented by a March 2, 1977 position paper entitled "Common-Sense Accounting in an Era of Persistent Inflation."[21] In this position paper Price Waterhouse restated that it believed General Purchasing Power was a valid concept, directly responsive to inflation, and that the main source of resistance to the restatement proposed by the Exposure Draft was the complexity of the restatement. Therefore, Price Waterhouse recommended presentation of simplified general purchasing power data, based on the GNP deflator, to supplement traditional financial statements. This would give important additional information to investors and creditors. The objective of the general purchasing power presentation would be common sense use for practical purposes and could be achieved by:

1. *Streamlining the mechanics of preparation.*
2. *Keeping the presentation simple.*
3. *Highlighting the inflationary impact on reported results.*
4. *Segregating price-level gains on long-term obligations.*

Price Waterhouse concluded "It borders on disgraceful that theoretical debates at high levels of abstraction go on and on, while capital-intensive businesses underreport actual costs and money-intensive businesses fail to report significant economic facts. U.S. investors, creditors, and business management are ill-served by accounting inaction that allows business capital to be bled away invisibly via income taxes based on illusory earnings that fail to tell the inflation story . . . Price Waterhouse supports that solution (supplementary price-level data). We believe that it represents common sense accounting in an era of persistent inflation—practical action, directly responsive to an identified problem, entailing negligible cost and no disruption in a useful, long established framework of financial reporting."[22]

Arthur Young & Co., in a 1975 Management Briefing entitled "Measuring and Reporting the Impact of Inflation Through Price-Level Accounting," pointed out that "the many conflicting views presented by business and financial spokesmen during the early stages of the FASB deliberations demonstrated that there was no consensus as to usefulness at that time. Until the application of price-level accounting becomes widespread, it is doubtful that we will have a meaningful basis for assessing its value."[23] The Briefing stated that the following aspects of the Exposure Draft would be useful:

1. *The proposed requirements provide management with an objectively determined quantification of the impact of inflation on its business operations.*
2. *Increased comparability of financial statements would be maintained because the same objective procedures and the same price index would be used by each enterprise.*
3. *The effect of inflation on key ratios and trends could be shown.*
4. *A new light would be placed on taxes and dividends.*
5. *The need for funds and financing as created by inadequate depreciation and excessive taxes and dividends would be clarified.*[24]

Whether or not price-level accounting becomes a requirement, Arthur Young and Company believes that "discussion and experimentation are desirable . . . The development of meaningful financial information is of sufficient importance to all of us to warrant the commitment of our resources and support."[25]

In an August 1975 edition of its Fi-

---

[21] "Common-Sense Accounting in an Era of Persistent Inflation," Price Waterhouse & Co. (March 2, 1977), pp. 10-11.

[22] Ibid., pp. 11-12.
[23] "Measuring and Reporting . . . ," p. 25.
[24] Ibid., pp. 26-77.
[25] Ibid., p. 31.

nancial Reporting Development, Ernst & Ernst discussed Price-level Accounting. Entitled "Financial Reporting in Units of General Purchasing Power," Ernst & Ernst gave the following reasons for not supporting general purchasing power disclosure as proposed by the FASB:

1. *The proposal introduced numerous non-cash charges and credits into the determination of the general purchasing power net income. (Specifically mentioned were the adjusted depreciation expense and the general purchasing power Gain or Loss on the company's net monetary position.) These, Ernst & Ernst believed to be at variance with basic financial statement objectives of equating net income with past or future cash flow as nearly as possible.*
2. *The two costs involved in presentation of general purchasing power of financial statements (preparation and education) would far outweigh any benefits derived.*
3. *The concept of general purchasing power accounting had been virtually ignored for almost forty years since it had been developed. Ernst & Ernst perceived no change in the general demand or need for general purchasing power financial data which would warrant the imposition of disclosure requirements for all entities.*[26]

The December 31, 1974 Exposure Draft was never issued as an official pronouncement with mandatory participation by enterprises. In fact, the results of the field test, in which one hundred and one business enterprises participated, were not issued until May of 1977. At that point the idea of issuing the Exposure Draft as an Official Pronouncement was not a viable option to the FASB. The FASB was involved in the much greater issue of whether general price-level or replacement cost financial statements would provide greater quality information to financial users.

---

[26] "Price-Level Accounting (Financial Reporting in Units of General Purchasing Power)," Ernst & Ernst (August 1975), p. 1.

---

# ASR 190

*by William D. Milligan, Jr., MBA, CPA*

## INTRODUCTION

The theoretical debate which flourished between the supporters of general price-level and replacement cost financial statements following the December 31, 1974 Exposure Draft of the FASB basically "squared off" the FASB and the Securities and Exchange Commission. However, the apparent catalyst to this debate, Securities Act Release No. 5608 (August, 1975), should not have provided the spark because it was not the first time the SEC had made its views known on the subject of restated financial statements. On October 4, 1973 the SEC, through Securities Act Release No. 5427, proposed amendments to Regulation S-X which would require registrants to indicate "the effect on Net Income, if significant, of using current replacement cost (for valuing inventories) in the computation of cost of sales."[1] The Commission received a large number of comments on the Release concerning the effectiveness of and the problems of implementation which existed

---

William D. Milligan, Jr., "A Chronological Analysis of Previous Pronouncements on Recording the Effects of Inflation in Financial Statements with FASB No. 33" (Master's thesis, Pace University, May 1980). Used by permission of William D. Milligan, Jr.

[1] "Accounting Series Release No. 151," *Federal Securities Law Reporter* (1979), p. 62353.

at that time. The SEC considered these and "concluded that it would not be desirable to adopt final requirements in this area which would be effective for 1973 financial statements,"[2] but repeated that the recognition of the impact of inventory profits was significant, and the failure to make such disclosures would mean that inadequate information as to the source and replicability of earnings would be transmitted to investors.

In January 1974, the SEC, pointing to the generally rapid increase of prices in 1973 (which included a rise in consumer prices of 8%, in wholesale prices of 16%, and in crude industrial materials of 30%), as well as wide fluctuations in prices of different individual items, concluded that "under such conditions the usefulness of the traditional accounting measurement model based upon historical cost is significantly reduced. The process of matching costs against revenues is less likely to produce meaningful economic information . . ."[3] This conclusion, as reached in ASR 151, pointed to the inclusion of inventory profits in historically reported earnings as having the most significant and immediate impact on earnings. The inventory profit was a result of holding the inventory in a period of rising inventory costs and was measured by the difference between the historical cost and its replacement cost at the time of sale. These profits do not reflect an increase in the earning power of a business because they are not normally repeatable in the absence of continued price-level increases. Therefore, if material, the SEC encouraged disclosure of this fact because it would be important to investors in assessing the quality of earnings.[4]

ASR 151 further recognized:[5]

1. *Registrants do not normally compute cost of goods sold on historic and current value basis. Therefore, the computation may require estimation by the registrant.*
2. *Inventory profits may be recognized by different methods and these methods, provided they were properly disclosed, would be encouraged until final requirements were issued.*
3. *Inventory profits are directly affected by the responsiveness of the companies' selling prices to the increase in the price-level and that if the length of the lag is sufficient, it might result in a negative increase in earnings.*
4. *The impact of price-level changes does not fall equally among companies.*

Thus, the SEC had issued a proposal which encouraged disclosure of inventory profits almost one year before the FASB's Exposure Draft. However, the debate was not a major one until after the Exposure Draft issuance because it was not until August 21, 1975 that the SEC, after deciding that it was not satisfied that registrants were making sufficient attempts to quantify and disclose the effects of changing cost on their businesses, issued Securities Act Release No. 5608.

Securities Act Release No. 5608 proposed amendments to Regulation S-X which would require footnote disclosure of certain data regarding current replacement cost. The amendments were designed to enable investors to obtain more relevant information about the current economies of an enterprise. The SEC received more than three hundred and fifty letters of comment and, after consideration, a somewhat revised form of Securities Act Release No. 5608 was issued in the form of ASR 190.

**Requirements and Commission Comments**

Under ASR 190, the required disclosures which are to be presented in a note to the financial statements or in a separate section following the notes are as follows:[6]

---

[2] Ibid.

[3] "Inflation Impairs Value of Traditional Accounting," *Journal of Accountancy* (February 1974), p. 16.

[4] "Accounting Series Release No. 151," p. 62353.

[5] Ibid., p. 62534.

[6] "A New Accounting Model—Where Are We?," Executive Newsletter. Peat, Marwick, Mitchell & Co. (June 1976), p. 4.

1. Current replacement cost of inventory shown in annual balance sheets.

2. Cost of sales for two years approximated on the basis of current replacement cost at the time of sale.

3. Replacement cost (new) of "productive capacity" and depreciated replacement cost of such assets shown in the annual balance sheets.

4. Depreciation, depletion, and amortization for two years based on average replacement cost of productive capacity.

5. A description of the methods used in determining the disclosures required by one through four above.

6. Any additional information which management believed was necessary to prevent the above information from being misleading.

These required replacement cost disclosures are to be presented in a note to the financial statements or in a separate section following the notes. If shown in a separate section, a brief note, possibly in the accounting policies section of the footnotes, to act as a cross-reference, would be appropriate. Furthermore, whichever presentation method is adopted, it should be designated as "unaudited."

These disclosures must be made by all companies filing with the SEC if, at the beginning of the fiscal year, their total of inventories and gross property, plant and equipment (i.e., before deduction of accumulated depreciation, depletion and amortization) was $100 million or more, and that total is 10% or more of total consolidated assets (approximately 1200 companies in 1976). They are required in financial statements for fiscal years ending on or after December 25, 1976 except that the disclosures are not required until fiscal years ending on or after December 25, 1977 for mineral resource assets and assets located outside the North American continent and the countries of the European Economic Community. Comparative data for years ending prior to December 25, 1976 or for interim periods was not required.[7]

The Commission noted that because there were difficult conceptual and empirical judgments which must be made in light of different specific factual circumstances in developing the data, replacement cost cannot be calculated with precision and standardized techniques are not, and may never be, available.[8] The SEC felt that the imprecision, if properly explained, would not be misleading and the disclosure would provide valuable information to management and investors. In fact, in order to assure that alternative approaches would be acceptable, the SEC proposed a "safe harbor" rule. Under this proposal, companies would be insulated from liability under federal securities laws if the replacement cost information was prepared with reasonable care, had reasonable factual basis, represented managements' good faith judgment, and was accompanied by a statement disclosing both the basis on which the information was calculated and its inherent imprecision.[9] Furthermore, the Commission established an advisory committee to assist its staff in providing guidance to registrants and suggested that industry groups and associations consider special problems, possibly develop specific price indices applicable to certain asset groups, and suggest uniform industry-wide reporting approaches.

As a result of the large number of comments received, which urged a delay in mandatory reporting until precision could be achieved, the Commission made the following comments:

1. Under current economic conditions the date concerning the impact in changes of specific goods and services on a business was of great significance to investors in developing an understanding of any firm.

2. Specific costs change more rapidly than the general price-level.

---

[7] "Replacement Cost: Implementation of ASR 190," Peat, Marwick, Mitchell & Co. (1976), pp. 29-30.

[8] "Accounting Series Release No. 190," *Federal Securities Law Reporter* (1979), p. 62505.

[9] "A New Accounting Model . . .," p. 5.

3. *From a practical standpoint, the SEC would never be able to anticipate every possible circumstance and, therefore, experimentation would be acceptable as long as the information was carefully prepared and the methods used adequately disclosed.*
4. *By requiring full disclosure of the methods used and permitting flexibility in presentation the SEC was confident that the message would be adequately communicated to investors.*
5. *While certain standards and guidelines may be developed after experimentation, it was highly unlikely that procedures would be developed to make it a mechanical process.*[10]

The Commission viewed that information disclosed in ASR 190 as limited and ASR 190, itself, as the first step in a process of providing more meaningful disclosure about current costs. Finally, and probably in an attempt to reduce any confrontation with the FASB, ASR 190 included the following:

> *The Commission does not believe its new requirements prejudge any conclusion which may arise from the FASB's study of the conceptual framework of financial statements... It believes that experimentation with replacement cost information of the sort that will result from the implementation of this rule will materially assist the FASB in its study as well as providing meaningful supplemental disclosure to investors in the interim.*[11]

**Effect on Financial Reporting**

Although ASR 190 required disclosure of the balance sheet amounts of inventories and productive capacity at replacement cost, the SEC considered such disclosures secondary to the income statement amounts of depreciation and cost of goods sold being disclosed on a replacement cost basis. The key emphasis on the effects on financial reporting, however, is that a single set of financial statements was retained because the SEC required only specified supplemental disclosures rather than a revised financial accounting model. These disclosures would appear in the financial statements, the 10-K report and the annual report to shareholders. The annual report disclosure was limited to a generalized description of the impact and reference to the 10-K report.

Therefore, the major effect of ASR 190 was not the representation of financial statements, as it was with previous proposals, but the considerations necessary for implementation of replacement costs. One consideration was a detailed analysis of inventory and assets to determine the applicability of replacement cost information (ASR 190 and Staff Accounting Bulletins issued by the SEC staff offered guidance in this area). Another consideration was the determination of the technique to be used to determine the replacement cost. The SEC staff stated four broad types of techniques which were generally applicable:

1. *Indexing—involved estimating replacement cost by applying an index to historical cost amounts.*
2. *Direct Pricing—measured replacement cost by reference to the current price of specific replacement assets.*
3. *Unit Pricing—a structured variation of direct pricing whereby a building, inventory lot, or other type of asset was directly priced upon labor, material, and overhead estimates, and then divided into a unit measure.*
4. *Functional Pricing—measured the cost of productive capacity based on the number of units which could be produced within a particular time period. (Technological change is taken into consideration and this technique could be applied to a heterogeneous group of assets.)*[12]

**Comparison to**
**December 31, 1974 Exposure Draft**

The replacement cost information required by the SEC in ASR 190 differs dramatically from the proposed requirements of any previous pro-

---

[10] "Accounting Series Release No. 190," p. 62505.

[11] Ibid., p. 62507.

[12] "Replacement Cost...," p. 11.

nouncements regarding the recognition of the impact of inflation on financial reporting. A comparison of column C in Chart II and column C in Chart I in the *Conclusion* will indicate specific differences between ASR 190 and the FASB's December 31, 1974 Exposure Draft.

The mandatory requirements of the SEC and the proposed requirements of the FASB are, from both a theoretical and practical viewpoint, almost completely different. Thus, the debate surrounding general price-level and replacement cost, as it was mentioned in the previous chapter, was inevitable because the two predominant rulemaking bodies had selected almost opposite approaches to deal with problems both had recognized to be the same.

## Responses to
## Replacement Cost Requirements

The response to ASR 190 disclosure requirements was varied. In February 1976 the SEC commentary section of the *CPA Journal* stated that investors, management, makers of tax policy, and the FASB would benefit from ASR 190's disclosure requirements. The article cited additional current economic data, increased current internal use by macroeconomic decision makers, the explicit definition of the effects of present taxes on economic capital and the conceptual framework as reasons for each group.[13] The article also saw the retention of a single set of financial statements, obtaining comparable data without the need for repetitive restatement, and the expression of economic measurement through current replacement cost as other attributes of ASR 190.

Paul Gross, Vice President of Professional Services for American Appraisal Co., said that even when inadequate records were maintained, any organized, good-sense approach provided an acceptable method for achieving replacement cost compliance. This, Gross said, was necessary, because, "Simply stated, private industry is unable to fully replace its plant and machinery in the current inflationary economy under the present corporate tax structure. Dollars of annual depreciation claimed as an expense against operations, when calculated on the basis of historical cost and lives assigned, are woefully inadequate to replace productive assets in today's marketplace."[14]

Many comments made about ASR 190 were mixed within themselves. In March 1976, Sydney Davidson, author and professor at the University of Chicago, and his co-author, wrote, "if we had to choose one of the two new disclosures, we would prefer the SEC version. But the two methods are not mutually exclusive and both contain useful information. The ideal financial statement, in our opinion, will combine elements of both."[15] The authors also pointed out that if both the SEC requirements and the FASB proposed requirements were necessary at the same time, that would be at least one too many and referred to the following statement of a major CPA firm: "The SEC and the FASB should carefully consider their respective proposals on inflation accounting. Adopting both would require reporting of financial data using three substantially different bases: historical cost, GPP (price level), and replacement cost. This would be an adverse development not in the best interests of financial statement users."[16]

Albert M. King, in January 1976 had stated that the SEC approach to dealing with the specific impact of inflation on a company was in distinction to, and was consciously chosen as preferable over, any of the following:

1. *General price-level*
2. *Liquidation or exit value*
3. *Discounted cash flow*
4. *Reproduction cost of existing facilities—the cost to replace actual or specific facilities on hand, whether or not economic conditions would call for such action. (This does not take*

---

[13]"SEC Proposes Disclosure of Replacement Cost Data," *CPA Journal* (February 1976), p. 48.

[14]P. H. Gross, "Replacement Cost Accounting, Highlighting the Hidden Cost of Inflation (ASR 190)," *Management Reviews* (December 1976), p. 6.

[15]Sydney Davidson and R. L. Weil, "Inflation Accounting: The SEC Proposal for Replacement Cost Disclosures," *Financial Analysts Journal* (March 1976), p. 57.

[16]Ibid., p. 58.

*technology into effect as replacement cost does.)*[17]

King also said that "Observers may wish that the SEC had gone in a different direction. But if one accepts the thesis that agreement on any specific direction is inherently impossible, then movement per se is probably better than sticking to the status quo."[18] Benefits cited by King were that the replacement cost information obtained could be used for tax assessment, proper placement of insurance, establishing pricing policies to ensure economic recovery of current costs, and for enabling the periodic review of capital investments.

However, King also expressed several negative opinions about the replacement cost disclosures. They included the following:

1. *Quite simply, while replacement cost can always be determined and disclosed, there is no reason to believe that because an asset can be replaced, it will be replaced.*

2. *Isn't it possible that the absence of generalized replacement cost data is not an accident? That managers really don't need it to run the business?*

3. *The SEC forces the assumption that today's capacity would be replaced. It would not—most companies would increase investment in profitable lines.*

4. *Replacement of expired capacity, like for like, has not been a problem, is not now a problem, and given the freedom to make its own capital expenditure decisions, need not be a problem for U.S. business.*[19]

A June 1976 article referred to an August 1975 article in which Paul Rosenfeld said that current replacement value accounting was "only a dead end" on the "road to improvement in accounting."[20] Rosenfeld, the later article said, took this position because current replacement value accounting "relies on an erroneous assumption that keeping physical operating capacity at least level is necessary for survival of an enterprise" and "is based on the fallacy that progress does not start until survival is assured."[21]

Ronald Ma and M. C. Miller, writing in the Autumn of 1976, said, "No single accounting system can be considered ideal with the present abysmal lack of knowledge of users' objectives and their decision models. But it is believed that the cause for reporting current value in the financial statements has been overstated for a variety of reasons . . . Many of the benefits claimed for the periodical mandatory reporting of comprehensive current value data have an "Alice in Wonderland" quality and evaporate on close scrutiny. The most important illusion has been in respect to the relevance of aggregates and allocations of current values for decision making."[22]

**Results of ASR 190**

In the October 1977 issue of the *Journal of Accountancy*, C. W. Bastable, Professor at Columbia University's Graduate School of Business, examined the implementation of ASR 190 from the then-released 1976 annual reports and 10-K forms. After examining fifteen "Forbes Assets 500" companies and five smaller companies, Bastable observed that every corporation in the group commented on replacement cost and that there was considerable variation in the number of words used (the range was under 76 to 825 words). The location of the replacement cost data for nineteen out of the twenty companies was in the last or next to last note to the financial statement. In all but one case the disclosures were identified as "unaudited" and that all expressed qualifica-

---

[17] Alfred M. King, "Current Value Accounting Comes of Age," *Financial Executive* (January 1976), p. 18.
[18] Ibid., p. 19.
[19] Ibid., pp. 20-21.
[20] Tom K. Cowan, "Current Replacement Value Accounting: Not a Dead End," *Journal of Accountancy* (June 1976), p. 83.
[21] Ibid., pp. 83-84.
[22] Ronald Ma and M. C. Miller, "Inflation and the Current Value Illusion," *Accounting and Business Research* (Autumn 1976), p. 250.

tions "to keep the data from being misleading."[23]

Two of the corporations made rather pointed observations about the disclosure requirement itself. One stated, "the value of these data for the purposes set forth has not yet been demonstrated to the satisfaction of the Company." The other wrote, "the mandated disclosures fall far short of meeting the stated purposes of the SEC ... Nevertheless, the data have been assembled solely to comply with the SEC requirements."[24]

Bastable concluded:

1. *That the sole positive fact about ASR 190 was that the SEC faced the fact that an inflationary environment impaired the validity of historical cost data.*
2. *ASR 190 neither provided a discussion of alternatives nor explained why the SEC decided on replacement costs. In most instances, the author pointed out, this information would be useful.*
3. *Much of the after-the-fact criticism of the requirement was made known to the Commission before adoption, yet it hastily and prematurely imposed the costly (estimated at between $10,000 and $800,000 for the companies in question) exercise on American Business.*
4. *Had the FASB issued a similar release, the consequence might have been the demise of that organization.*
5. *On the basis of the evidence at hand, the SEC should go back to square one and do its homework.*[25]

Thus, it appears that the post issuance criticisms of the SEC disclosure requirements were as critical, and in many cases the same, as those prior to issuance. The business community was not pleased with the effectiveness of or the cost of the implemented material. However, the SEC held fast to its requirements, and ASR 190 was not to be amended or cancelled.

The SEC disclosure requirements were the first mandatory requirements imposed by any authoritative force concerning the effects of inflation on financial reporting. This chapter revolves around the replacement cost disclosures, as required by the SEC, and the serious discussion which resulted from these requirements. These discussions, combined with the opinions stated in the previous chapter (concerning general price-level financial statements) left the accounting profession in a precarious position. The SEC and the FASB, the two major rule-making bodies, were at opposite positions.

---

[23] Charles W. Bastable, "Is SEC Replacement Cost Data Worth the Effort?" *Journal of Accountancy* (October 1979), p. 72.
[24] Ibid., p. 71.
[25] Ibid., p. 76.

# FASB EXPOSURE DRAFT: DECEMBER 28, 1978

by William D. Milligan, Jr., MBA, CPA

## INTRODUCTION

**The Debate Continues**

The mandatory participation requirements of the SEC, as shown in the preceding chapter, had the effect of stimulating the discussion on reporting the effects of inflation in financial reporting. The arguments against the SEC requirements did not come to a standstill after the participating companies had complied. Allen H. Seed, in July 1978, said, "Despite dislocations caused by inflation, the historical cost accounting conceptual framework should be retained. The focus of financial reporting, however, needs to be modified in an inflationary environment. The funds statement and income statement need to be improved. Additional supplemental disclosure is also needed, but not the replacement cost data called for by the SEC under ASR 190."[1] Seed continued, "Business managers, lenders, and investors contend that they already recognize the reality of inflation and are currently applying judgment to reflect its impact. Inflation is considered in the context of the economic, competitive, and financial environment as a whole rather than as an isolated force."[2]

In September 1978, William C. Norby complained, "While the SEC continues to require disclosure of replacement costs of inventory and fixed plant in 10-K filings, almost all companies refuse to provide this information in their annual reports. Footnotes to financial statements typically state that the information has been developed and is available, upon request, in the 10-K. However, the 10-Ks usually provide such objective data they are not really very helpful either."[3]

"'What do I think of replacement accounting?' snapped venture capitalist Dan W. Lufkin. 'It is one of the stupidest orders ever put out by the SEC. It causes two forms of instant misrepresentation. It overstates assets... Then it automatically understates earnings by creating phantom extra depreciation and cost of goods sold charges so management looks like it is doing a poor job.'" In agreement with Lufkin in this June 12, 1978 article in *Forbes* was General Motors Corp., which, after it published the required figures, said they were "of no value."[4] "Yet, *Forbes* agrees with the SEC and disagrees with General Motors about the value of the exercise. The numbers, while far from precise, are extremely useful in pinpointing problems that conventional corporate reporting ignores."[5]

The general purchasing power viewpoint of financial reporting could be typified by Harold O. Davidson. Writing in November 1979, Davidson stated that between six and sixteen billion dollars of U.S. corporate resources were confiscated through archaic accounting methods each year, because income tax liabilities were created on what really represented recovery of capital.[6] This, the author pointed out, resulted from conventional reporting ignoring changes in the purchasing power of the dollar. Davidson claimed that the constant dollar (general pur-

---

William D. Milligan, Jr., "A Chronological Analysis of Previous Pronouncements on Recording the Effects of Inflation in Financial Statements with FASB No. 33" (Master's thesis, Pace University, May 1980). Used by permission of William D. Milligan, Jr.

[1] Allen H. Seed, "Inflation: Its Impact on Financial Reporting and Decision Making," *Financial Executive* (July 1978), p. 38.

[2] Ibid., p. 40.

[3] William C. Norby, "Accounting for Inflation," *Financial Analysts Journal* (September 1978), p. 75.

[4] "The Hidden Cost of Replacement," *Forbes* (June 1978), p. 107.

[5] Ibid., p. 108.

[6] Harold O. Davidson, "Conventional Accounting Confiscates Capital," *Harvard Business Review* (November 1979), p. 13.

chasing power) method was the superior solution for two reasons. First, the constant dollar method retained the transactional foundation of historical-cost accounting while eliminating a major flaw of conventional accounting methods; their implementation. Second, the constant dollar method is the logically correct choice for capital recovery, which is the operational function of depreciation accounting.[7]

Many businessmen and accountants, however, still supported historical cost accounting as a fair and adequate basis for reporting corporate performance. Rather than disregard it, they suggested that accountants begin providing reasonable explanations of the material effects of inflation on a case-by-case basis.[8]

**The Conceptual Framework**

Entering 1978, the FASB had been working on a conceptual framework for a number of years. As a result of the continued debate and division among accountants over the propriety of historical cost, general price-level, and replacement cost information, the FASB was pressed for an answer. As one author saw it,

> While trying to maintain at least a semblance of reason within financial reports, the accountant now sees inflation rearing its ugly head and challenging the validity of one of the basic tenets of accounting—the stability of the U.S. dollar as the unit of measure. As a result, the accountant has been forced to return to his work bench to examine his conceptual framework—and to find a way of mending his stool before it collapses.[9]

The FASB's answer to the conceptual framework problem was the FASB Statement of Financial Accounting Concepts No. 1, "Objectives of Financial Reporting by Business Enterprises," dated November 1978. That Statement "concludes that financial reporting should provide information to help investors, creditors, and others assess the amounts, timing, and uncertainty of prospective net cash inflows to the related enterprise (paragraph 37)." It also calls for "the provision of information about the economic resources of an enterprise in a manner that provides direct and indirect evidence of cash flow potential (paragraphs 40 and 41)." It also concludes "that management is accountable to the owners for '... protecting them to the extent possible from unfavorable economic impacts of factors in the economy such as inflation or deflation ...' (paragraph 50)."[10]

The Concepts Statement, however, required no changes in the basic financial statements. It pointed to two important reasons for supporting the dominant focus of present financial statements on historical prices:

> 1. It is fitting that financial statements depend on actual transactions of the enterprise because those transactions determine the results of its operations in the long run. Business enterprises invest cash in assets in order to earn more cash. Historical prices provide the elementary measures of both the amounts invested and the amounts received in return.
> 2. Because historical prices generally are the result of arms-length bargaining, they provide a basis for reliable measures of the results of transactions. Accordingly, financial statements prepared on the basis of historical prices tend to be capable of independent verification and can be prepared and used with confidence that the information presented is what it purports to be: the result of past transactions.[11]

The result of persistent and significant inflation, however, had continuously raised questions about the need for supplementing historical cost financial statements with information about the effects of the variation in pur-

---

[7] Ibid., pp. 14-15.

[8] Elwood C. Miller, "What's Wrong with Price-Level Accounting?" *Harvard Business Review* (November 1978), p. 111.

[9] Ibid., p. 112.

[10] "Financial Accounting Standards Board Exposure Draft" (December 28, 1978), paragraph 5.

[11] Ibid., paragraph 3.

chasing power of the units of money in which prices in past transactions were fixed and the effects of changes in the current cost of goods purchased and produced and plant utilized.[12] Recognizing this, the FASB issued, on December 28, 1978, an Exposure Draft, entitled "Financial Reporting and Changing Prices," which would establish standards for reporting those effects.

**Recommendations of the Exposure Draft**
"Financial Reporting and Changing Prices" was an attempt by the FASB to unite the supporters of the replacement cost and general purchasing power theories of financial reporting, while at the same time maintaining historical cost financial statements for the reasons detailed in the Concepts Statement. The requirements of the Draft would affect publicly held enterprises that had both inventory and plant, property and equipment (gross of depreciation) amounting to more than $125 million dollars, and total assets amounting to more than $1 billion dollars at the beginning of the fiscal years for which financial reports were being prepared.

This Draft used terms which should be clarified. The term "constant dollar accounting" was used to describe the methodology referred to as general price-level accounting and accounting in units of general purchasing power in the December 31, 1974 Exposure and in APB Statement No. 3. The term "current cost accounting" was used to describe a methodology similar to, yet importantly different from, replacement cost accounting as described in ASR 190. The differences between *current cost* and *replacement cost* will be described in the following section of this chapter.

The Exposure Draft recommended the following:[13]

1. There would be no change in the standard of financial accounting and reporting used for the preparation of the basic financial statements of an enterprise.

2. *No comprehensive restatement of financial statements was necessary.*

3. *EITHER (a) Supplementary information on income from continuing operations on a current cost basis and on holding gains or losses net of inflation.*

   *OR (b) Supplementary information on income from continuing operations in a constant dollar basis be presented as part of the minimum supplemental information.*

   *To choose between the alternatives, the following guidelines were given:*

   *(1) All enterprises were encouraged to present the information in terms of current cost disclosures values unless constant dollar information better reflects the effect of changing prices.*

   *(2) Constant dollar information might be sufficient information if cost of goods sold and depreciation are not significant, or if cost of goods sold and depreciation are significant but price changes have been approximately the same as the change in the general price-level.*

4. *A holding gain or loss for any period was defined:*

   *(1) For inventory: The increase or decrease in the current cost of inventory between the start of the period or the date of acquisition, whichever was later, and the date of realization or the end of the period, whichever was earlier.*

   *(2) For plant, property and equipment: The increase or decrease in the current cost of the unexpired service potential of such assets between the start of the period or the date of acquisition, whichever was later, and the date of expiration of the service potential or the end of the period, whichever was earlier.*

   *The holding gain or loss should be adjusted for inflation in accordance with the principles of constant dollar accounting.*

5. *An enterprise should measure assets and expenses, under current cost accounting, as follows:*

---

[12] Ibid., paragraph 4.
[13] "Financial Accounting Standards Board Exposure Draft" (December 28, 1978), paragraphs 16-38.

*(1) Inventories and Cost of Goods Sold:* At current cost or lower appropriate value (appropriate only when net realizable value or value in use, whichever was applicable, was lower than current cost) at the balance sheet date or date of sale. Proper valuation methods included current invoice prices, vendors' firm price lists or other firm quotations or estimates, standard manufacturing costs that reflect current costs and revision of historical acquisition cost.

*(2) Plant, property and equipment and the related depreciation, depletion, and amortization expense* should be determined by direct pricing, unit pricing, or indexation. Enterprises should give consideration to availability, reliability, and cost in choosing a valuation method.

6. The amount of the inflation gain or loss on net monetary items should be presented as part of the minimal supplemental information.

7. The amount of foreign exchange gain or loss calculated in accordance with GAAP, net of any attributable income tax expense as described in APB Opinion No. 11 (paragraph 52), should be presented as part of the minimal supplemental information.

8. The index used to prepare constant dollar information should be the Consumer Price Index for All Urban Consumers (CPI-U).

9. Information for the current year on income from continuing operations on a constant dollar basis should be stated in constant dollars as of the end of that year.

10. Information on income from continuing operations would be presented either in a statement format (disclosing revenues and expenses) or in a reconciliation format (disclosing adjustments to the revenues and expenses that are shown in the historical cost income statement).

11. Each enterprise to which this statement applied should disclose the information shown in the table for each of the five last recent fiscal years:

| | Basis of Presentation | |
|---|---|---|
| Information to Be Presented | Under Current Value Approach | Under HC/Constant Dollar Approach |
| Net sales & other operating revenues | HC* | HC/CD† |
| Income from continuing operations | CC** | HC/CD |
| Holding gain or loss, net of inflation, & income tax effects of realized gains or losses | CC | Not required |
| Inflation gain or loss on net monetary items | HC/CD | HC/CD |
| Foreign exchange gain or loss, net of income tax effects | HC | HC/CD |
| Net assets at fiscal year-end | CC | HC/CD |
| Earnings per common share from continuing operations | CC | HC/CD |
| Cash dividends declared per common share | HC | HC/CD |
| Market price per common share | HC | Restated in CDs |

*Historical cost  †Constant dollar  **Current cost

Specific requirements for constant dollar accounting were not given in the December 28, 1978 Exposure Draft. The Board addressed this point by referring to a document on constant dollar accounting which would be released. Entitled "Constant Dollar Accounting," this document was issued on March 2, 1979 in the form of an Exposure Draft. Unlike normal Exposure Drafts, however, this Draft was issued as a supplement to the December 31, 1974 Exposure Draft. It contained appropriate changes necessary for enterprises preparing constant dollar data to conform with the December 28, 1978 Exposure Draft requirements. These changes, some of which have already been included in the recommendations listed, will be identified in the next section of this chapter.

Furthermore, the Board, observing the fact that a substantial learning process was necessary, encouraged experimentation within the guidelines of the Statement. As a result, the Statement was written to be flexible.

**Comparison to Previous Proposals**

The charts in the *Conclusion* will serve as a guide to the differences between the constant dollar and current cost requirements of the December 28, 1978 Exposure Draft (Chart I, column B) and the December 31, 1974 Exposure Draft (Chart I, column C) and ASR 190 (Chart II, column C). The major differences are indicated by an asterisk (*). However, certain differences, which are indicated but not explained in the chart or are not indicated in the chart, will be explained presently.

Most of the differences concerning constant dollar information are self-explanatory. The CPI-U was designated as the index to be used instead of the GNP Deflator because the CPI-U is calculated monthly (rather than quarterly), is not revised after its initial publication, and because use of the CPI-U would tend to produce results comparable to the GNP Deflator.[14] The option to use base period dollars in the five-year summary represented a change from the 1974 Exposure Draft, which proposed that all prior year disclosures be "rolled forward" to dollars of purchasing power as of the end of the latest year presented. This was a result of the suggestion by the 1975 FASB field test participants that the use of base year dollars would enhance the understandability of comparative constant dollar information. The Board concluded that such experimentation would be permitted.[15]

The differences concerning current cost information and replacement cost information, as shown in the chart, are straightforward. The FASB requires additional information (inflation gain or loss on net monetary items and holding gains or losses) to be presented. However, a major omission in the chart is the theoretical differences between current and replacement cost. The following schedule outlines these theoretical differences between current cost (FASB) and replacement cost (SEC).[16]

| *Current Cost* | *Replacement Cost* |
|---|---|
| 1. Emphasized the measurement of the assets owned by the enterprise. | 1. Focused attention on assets that would replace those owned if replacement were to occur currently. |
| 2. Provided a choice among current cost, net realizable value, or value in use, as the measure of the asset and of its consumption, depending on which was applicable in the circumstances. | 2. Required the use of replacement cost, with separate disclosure of net realizable value whenever it was lower. |
| 3. All plant assets and land were included in the Board's current cost accounting provisions. | 3. Land and productive capacity provided by plant assets that were not to be replaced by the enterprises were excluded from replacement cost disclosures. |
| 4. Required presentation of a computation of income from continuing operations. | 4. Called for information that was not suitable for integration into a computation of income. |

---

[14] "Financial Accounting Standards Board Exposure Draft" (March 2, 1979), paragraph 3.

[15] Ibid., paragraph 7.

[16] "Financial Accounting Standards Board Exposure Draft" (December 28, 1978), pp. iii-iv.

Specifically, the changes noted in the chart are these:

*For Constant Dollar:*

1. The December 28, 1978 Exposure Draft recommends either constant dollar or current cost disclosure rather than just changes in the general purchasing power.
2. The Consumer Price Index replaced the GNP Deflator as the index of the general purchasing power.
3. Financial data presented may be presented in either end-of-current year dollars or in base-year dollars rather than the previously recommended end-of-current year dollars.
4. Classification of some Monetary and Non-Monetary items was clarified.
5. Comprehensive restatement of financial statements was not required.

*For Current Cost:*

1. As opposed to ASR 190, which required replacement cost disclosure, the Exposure Draft recommended either constant dollar or current cost disclosure.
2. Monetary and Non-Monetary assets are considered relevant under the Exposure Draft, and inflation gain or loss on net monetary items should be presented with current cost information.
3. The Exposure Draft required the disclosure of holding gains and losses.

The differences between the 1974 and 1978 Exposure Drafts, although they appeared numerous, did not propose changes of major importance. The change in the classification of certain items from non-monetary to monetary would not have a major effect on inflation gains or losses for most companies, and the use of the CPI-U, as already noted, would produce results similar to the GNP Deflator. The requirement of only selected information, and the basic omission of a restated balance sheet, rather than comprehensive restatement was, also, minor because the key emphasis of restatement was always indirectly on balance sheet accounts, and directly on the income statement. In this proposed Statement the effect on the balance sheet (inventory and plant, property and equipment) would be reported in the presentation of net assets in the five-year summary.

The differences noted between current cost and replacement cost information was basically in the theoretical assumptions explained earlier. However, the FASB had attempted, in this proposal, to deal with the effects of changes in current cost more fully than the SEC by including more information in its disclosures and by including current cost information directly in the computation of income. Therefore, the FASB's current cost represented a more practical, less confusing version of replacement cost.

## RESPONSES TO THE EXPOSURE DRAFT

### FASB Member

In January 1979, immediately following the Exposure Draft's issuance, Robert T. Sprouse, Vice Chairman of the FASB, tried to clarify the reasoning behind the proposed Statement. Stating that the representations that would be required by the Exposure Draft were still in a stage of remarkably dynamic development, Sprouse cited two distinctly different perceptions of the problem. The first was "... that inflation is only a symptom that has served to reveal deep-seated deficiencies in financial statements constructed on the basis of transactions and historical exchange prices: As a symptom, inflation requires no direct treatment, the disease to be eliminated is the reliance on transactions and historical exchange prices." Those holding this first view would support current cost disclosure. The second perception was that inflation itself was the disease. "Those who diagnose the problem in this way consider that the sole accounting impact of inflation is its effect on the unit of measurement ... The concern can be readily alleviated by restating all accounting measurements in terms of units of general purchasing power ... " Those holding this second view would support constant dollar disclosure.[17]

---

[17] Robert T. Sprouse, "Inflation: Symptom or Disease?" *Financial Analysts Journal* (January 1979), p. 11.

Sprouse pointed out that distinguishing between inflation and specific prices was essential because the objective, technique, and results of accounting for each are quite different; no correlation need exist between the general price-level change and the specific price-level change for one particular segment of an industry. Sprouse also said that the use of supplementary disclosures by the FASB would allow management, auditors, and users of financial statements to gain experience with the new concepts and allow for the development of a sound conceptual basis before any changes in the basic financial statements would be made.[18] He thought the use of a combination of both current cost and constant dollar disclosure was the best way to develop such a basis.

## Members of Business and Accounting Firms

However, despite Sprouse's attempt to clarify the FASB's reasoning and the FASB's explanation of its reasoning in the Exposure Draft, opinions about the Exposure Draft were mixed. In September 1979, John McEnroe and Loren Nikolai, in light of the proposal by the FASB, reviewed six applicable research projects involving the possible implementation of general price-level and current replacement cost which took place between 1969 and 1979. "The results of these research efforts for the most part have found virtually no evidence that either general price-level or current cost information is superior to historical cost information for investor decision purposes... Perhaps by requiring general price-level and or current cost information on a supplemental basis, the FASB may be functioning in an educational capacity by exposing users to this information and at the same time providing a framework for further research studies."[19]

William C. Norby, in November 1978, said, "While, during an experimental period, companies will have some freedom to choose between a price-level approach or a combined price-level/current cost approach, the Board seems to give primary emphasis to the general purchase power method, which it has renamed the constant dollar method. It is difficult to understand why this method continues to hold enchantment for the accounting profession, in view of the fact that its utility for investment or management decisions has never been demonstrated."[20] In March of 1979, Norby, continuing the discussion, said, "Grading the value of some experimentation, this latitude may merely confuse users and thus defeat the purpose of experimentation. More comparability between companies will be necessary to stimulate interpretation. The Exposure Draft should reduce flexibility by providing (1) more specific criteria for selecting between the current cost and constant dollar approaches, (2) greater standardization of formats, and (3) fewer options in the five-year summary."[21]

Others also saw the flexibility built into the Exposure Draft as a weakness. Dennis Beresford of Ernst and Whinney reasoned, "It's hard to say that the FASB prohibits a company from using the method it chooses" while accounting analyst Ted O'Glove believed the guidelines were a "glaring loophole, too flexible. Too many companies will opt for constant dollar because it's cheaper to do."[22]

However, not everyone felt the flexibility question was a major one. Terry Aranoff, manager of technical policy of Coopers and Lybrand, said, "People are misreading it. It is just not that flexible, and it will be the job of the auditors to make sure the loophole is closed."[23]

The Financial Executives Institute, writing in July 1979, took an opposite view from Norby's November 1978 opinion. They termed the proposed Statement as "too limited" and criticized the FASB for being "strongly biased"

---

[18] Ibid., pp. 12-13.

[19] John E. McEnroe and Loren Nikolai, "How Useful Is Inflation Accounting?" *CPA Journal* (September 1979), p. 9.

[20] Frank E. Block, "Inflation Accounting," *Financial Analysts Journal* (November 1978), p. 77.

[21] William C. Norby, "FASB Exposure Draft on Inflation Accounting," *Financial Analysts Journal* (March 1979), p. 18.

[22] "Inflation Accounting," *Duns Review* (March 1979), p. 103.

[23] Ibid., p. 103.

in favor of current cost disclosure over constant dollar disclosure.[24]

Positive reaction was received for the Exposure Draft from General Electric's vice president of corporate financial administration, Terence E. McClary. Rating the proposal a "nine" on a scale of ten, McClary said the proposal was a "realistic evaluation of a company's performance for both investors and management," and University of Chicago professor Roman Weil said, "The FASB current cost method is more useful and relevant for decision-making than either historical cost or SEC replacement cost."[25]

Robert C. Thomson, Vice President-Finance of Shell Oil, in December 1978, said that his company "believes that financial statements based on historic cost and expressed in units of money fail to adequately disclose the effects of inflation, and that inflation's effects can be explained best and most completely in supplemental as opposed to primary financial statements. The FASB's proposal on this subject represents the only objective and tested mechanism which deals with the entire impact of inflation."[26]

**Comments to the SEC**

The liaison between the FASB and the SEC staff had been close prior to the issuance of the Exposure Draft. This was a direct attempt by the two rule-making bodies to avoid large theoretical disparities in the proposed Statement between the FASB and SEC. Sidney Davidson, and co-authors, in May 1979, said, "In our opinion, the SEC should allow companies to substitute FASB current cost disclosures for SEC replacement cost disclosures. In that case, current cost disclosure would appear more attractive to firms subject to the FASB disclosure rules because it would satisfy both sets of requirements, killing two birds with one stone. On the other hand, in the unlikely event that the SEC accepts the FASB's constant dollar presentation in place of its own ASR 190 presentation, we can expect widespread use of constant dollar disclosure."[27]

Thus, the Commission was in a dilemma. Having concurred with the FASB on the Exposure Draft, it basically agreed with the FASB proposal requirements. However, the situation Davidson referred to was a serious one and would require careful consideration by the SEC.

---

[24] "Financial Executives Institute Calls FASB Inflation Proposal 'Too Limited,'" *Journal of Accountancy* (July 1979), p. 12.

[25] "Inflation Accounting," p. 103.

[26] Robert C. Thomson, "Accounting for Inflation," *Financial Executive* (December 1978), p. 56.

[27] Sidney Davidson et al., "Financial Reporting and Changing Prices," *Financial Analysts Journal* (May 1979), p. 53.

# STATEMENT OF FINANCIAL ACCOUNTING STANDARDS NO. 33

*by William D. Milligan, Jr., MBA, CPA*

## INTRODUCTION

The FASB's recognition, with reminders from the SEC, of an urgent need to reflect the effects of inflation on corporate financial reports prompted the FASB, after the release of the December 28, 1978 Exposure Draft, to sponsor a conference on financial reporting and changing prices. Here, more than four hundred members of the accounting profession, business executives and bankers discussed the problem.

Harold Williams, chairman of the SEC, indicated the severity of the situation when he said, "Continuing reports of record profits, on one hand, and inadequate earnings to maintain and expand capacity, on the other, serve only to confuse the public and political leaders." Williams maintained that the business community and accounting profession "are running out of time in which to develop meaningful solutions to this problem ... We need to make substantial progress and make it now."[1]

Donald J. Kirk, chairman of the FASB, said that the results produced by the traditional accounting model "do not convey the effect of inflation on, or the change in value in, the dollar" and there was a need for action by the private sector "based on careful study of the alternatives and selection of those that seem most likely to provide investors with information they need."[2]

Paul W. McCracken, former chairman of the President's Council of Economic Advisors, agreed with Williams and Kirk when he told the conference "a fundamental erosion has occurred in the capability of the American economy to sustain gains in productivity on real income."[3]

Not everyone at the conference, however, was as optimistic as Williams, Kirk, and McCracken about the need for inflation accounting. Members of the banking industry cited a lack of enthusiasm about inflation accounting because, in their industry, changes in the information they already received would not significantly reduce loan losses. David M. Roderick, chairman of the United States Steel Corporation, said, "the American economy doesn't need just one more index of inflation, it needs a practical and effective means of reducing inflation." As a result, he also urged against the FASB's proposal.[4]

Thus, the result of the conference was to tell the FASB something it already knew. Accountants, government, and business were still divided on the subject of the need for inflation accounting after the issuance of the 1978 Exposure Draft. Harold Williams said the proposals offered "significant potential for meaningful progress" to what Michael O. Alexander, the FASB director of research and technical activities, called "the most important issue that has ever faced those who are involved with financial reporting ..."

The FASB was clearly in a position where it had to deliver an official pronouncement to preserve its position as public accounting's rule-making body. Delay was no longer an alternative and the SEC, as Chairman Williams declared, "... would not look positively at the loss of another year. We are not closed minded as to the approach, and we recognize that we may need to consider safe harbors to encourage experimentation, but we are not flexible as to the need for progress."[5] Therefore, the FASB, while still able to work in coordination with

---

William D. Milligan, Jr., "A Chronological Analysis of Previous Pronouncements on Recording the Effects of Inflation in Financial Statements with FASB No. 33" (Master's thesis, Pace University, May 1980). Used by permission of William D. Milligan, Jr.

[1] "Special Report—FASB Conference on Financial Reporting and Changing Prices," *Journal of Accountancy* (July 1979), p. 7.
[2] Ibid.
[3] Ibid., pp. 7-8.
[4] Ibid., p. 8.
[5] Ibid., p. 7.

and with the cooperation of the SEC, would issue an official pronouncement in September of 1979.

## RECOMMENDATIONS OF FASB STATEMENT NO. 33

### FASB Comments

In the introduction to Statement of Financial Accounting Standards No. 33 the FASB, as it did in the 1978 Exposure Draft, referred to Concepts Statement No. 1, "Objectives of Financial Reporting by Business Enterprises" and its conclusion that financial reporting should provide information to help investors, creditors, and others to help make decisions on investment, lending and other matters. The Statement is intended to help users in the following specific ways:

1. *Assessment of Future Cash Flows–when prices are changing, measurements that reflect current prices are likely to provide useful information for assessment of future cash flows.*
2. *Assessment of Enterprise Performance– measurements that reflect current prices can provide a basis for assessing the extent to which past decisions on the acquisition of assets have created opportunities for earning future cash flows.*
3. *Assessment of the Erosion of Operating Capability–information on the current prices of resources that are used to generate revenues can help users to assess the extent to which and the manner in which operating capability has been maintained.*
4. *Assessment of the Erosion of General Purchasing Power–investors typically are concerned with assessing whether an enterprise has maintained the purchasing power of its capital.*[6]

The Statement also said there are several reasons for believing that the effects of inflation cannot be understood adequately until they are measured and disclosed in financial reports because:

1. *The effects depend on the transactions and circumstances of an enterprise and users do not have detailed information about those factors.*
2. *Effective financial decisions can take place only in an environment in which there is an understanding by the general public of the problems caused by changing prices; that understanding is unlikely to develop until business performance is discussed in terms of measures that allow for the impact of changing prices.*
3. *Statements by business managers about the problems caused by changing prices will not have credibility until specific quantitative information is published about those problems.*[7]

However, in accordance with the theories set forth in the Concepts Statement, FASB Statement No. 33 does not require any changes to historical cost financial reporting. Therefore, the information required to transmit the above mentioned information to investors and creditors is, as it was in the Exposure Draft, to be presented in supplemental disclosures to the financial statements.

### Recommendations

The requirements which FASB Statement No. 33 mandated for participating companies are the same as the 1978 Exposure Draft with the following departures.[8]

| *Final Statement* | *Exposure Draft* |
|---|---|
| 1. Requires both constant dollar and current cost disclosures. | 1. Required companies to choose between constant dollar disclosure or current cost disclosure. |
| 2. Effective for the 1979 annual report. | 2. Is effective for 1979 annual reports of com- |

---

[6]"FASB Statement of Financial Accounting Standards No. 33" (September 1979), paragraph 3.

[7]"FASB Statement... No. 33" (September 1979), paragraph 5.

[8]Reprinted from "Accounting for Changing Prices: Executive Overview," Coopers & Lybrand (October 1979), pp. 8-9. Used by permission.

| *Final Statement* | *Exposure Draft* |
|---|---|
| However, since it may be impracticable to present the 1979 current cost disclosures in 1979, their presentation may be delayed until the 1980 annual report. | panies with fiscal years ending after December 24, 1979. |
| 3. Exempts natural resource industries (oil and gas, forest products, mining) and real estate from the current cost provisions of the Statement pending additional deliberation by the Board; a separate exposure draft is to be issued. | 3. Did not exempt any industries from required disclosures. |
| 4. Calls for constant dollar disclosure in the average-for-the-year dollar of the latest year. However, if a comprehensive restatement of the financial statements is made, either average-for-the-year or end-of-the-year dollars may be used for the disclosures. | 4. Required constant dollar disclosure in end-of-the-year dollars. |
| 5. Same presentation as Exposure Draft, except that Holding Gains are now called Increases or Decreases in Current Cost Amounts. | 5. Called for Holding Gains to be presented as a separate item on the supplemental income statement. |
| 6. Does not permit tax allocations for Increases or Decreases in Current Cost Amounts. | 6. Required allocation of historical cost income tax expense between (1) Income from Continuing Operations before Holding Gains (Losses) and (2) Realized Holding Gains (Losses) for purposes of preparing current cost information. |
| 7. Expresses no preference for the use of one method over another for determining current cost. | 7. Indicated an order of preference for methods that can be used to develop current cost of inventory and fixed assets. |
| 8. Does not require foreign exchange gains and losses to be separately disclosed from Income from Continuing Operations. | 8. Required foreign exchange gains and losses net of tax effect to be disclosed as a separate item on the face of the supplemental income statement. |

The decision by the FASB to require both constant dollar and current cost disclosure was based on the fact that "the Board believes that both types of information are likely to be useful ... and ... that further experimentation is required on the usefulness of the two types of information and that experimentation is possible only if both are provided by large enterprises."[9] FASB chairman Kirk added that the Board felt each had strong merits. "We felt we needed more weight of evidence before deciding which is preferable and we were willing to let the marketplace be a factor in that decision by gaining more information and experience on both methods."[10] Other changes initiated by the FASB eased the requirements of participating corporations. Certain corporations are exempt, certain disclosures and allocations eliminated, and current cost disclosure is, basically, an option to the participants for 1979 reports. Another simplification is the use of average-for-the-year dollars for constant dollar disclosure unless comprehensive restatement is presented (if comprehensive restatement either average or end-of-the-year dollars may be used). For many account balances this

[9] "FASB Statement of Financial Accounting Standards No. 33" (September 1979), p. iii.
[10] "Inflation Accounting: Nobody Likes the FASB's New Approach—But What Else Is There?" *Business Week,* p. 74. Reprinted from the October 15, 1979 issue of *Business Week* by special permission, © 1980 by McGraw-Hill, Inc. New York, NY 10020. All rights reserved.

means one less computation because they are assumed in average dollars of the year and the once needed conversion to end-of-the-year dollars is eliminated (i.e. sales).

Thus, the FASB had taken the Exposure Draft of December 28, 1978, reduced some of the requirements, while, at the same time, under the emphasis of needed experimentation, avoiding the decision to choose between current cost and constant dollar reporting. At the point of issuance the focal point switched from the FASB to business leaders, accounting firms and the SEC for their reaction.

## RESPONSES TO FASB STATEMENT NO. 33

### Business Leaders

Approximately 1,350 of the largest U.S. corporations would be required to comply with FASB Statement No. 33 disclosures and, hopefully, many more will participate voluntarily. The numbers will be rough, controversial, and perhaps confusing but they will be able to generate information about the future of U.S. industry which, without these requirements, would not be possible. In fact, recent data from the Commerce Department suggests that corporate profits may be overstated by 30%-40%, and for many companies the crunch is far more acute than the broad government measures indicate.[11] For the first time, the new standard will force the accounting profession, outside of the SEC disclosures, to acknowledge that rampant inflation does distort traditional financial reporting.

The FASB's option to require both constant dollar and current cost disclosures left many business leaders confused, and the same arguments heard in the past are being reheard. *Business Week* reported on October 15, 1979 that "forced to choose between the two most commonly proposed inflation accounting methods, most executives would opt for the constant-dollar approach, one based on a single price index, rather than have to wrestle with the more involved current-cost approach. Proponents argue that the former method is far simpler and less costly to apply. The results, they add, are based on objective, verifiable data and thus can be audited and relied on."[12] One such executive is B. E. Landstrom, assistant vice-president of Sunbeam Corporation. He reasoned, "Constant-dollar accounting is more apt to be accepted by tax authorities who probably would never allow a depreciation deduction based on judgment or subjective valuation."[13]

Opponents to constant dollar (proponents of current cost) made some of the following comments: (1) David D. Hale, an Economist at Kemper Financial Services Inc., said Current Cost Data "are potentially very useful for evaluating the economic positions of firms." (2) IBM concluded that general price-level financial statements give "unrealistic results" that simply do not represent economic reality. (3) Roger W. Rasmusen, a Financial Vice-President of Dekalb AgResearch Inc., said that applying the CPI-U as an index is "a pointless exercise" and that "current cost is distinctly preferable." (4) Kidder, Peabody & Co.'s Barre W. Littel and Robert Levine put their disdain of price-level adjustments such as the CPI-U more to the point when they asked, "How many companies do you know that have the 'urban family of four' in their inventories?"[14]

Not all businessmen, however, reverted to the petty arguments and excuses which were heard in the past. Thomas O. Thorsen, vice-president and comptroller of General Electric Co., said that since 1973 GE had used inflation-adjusted data for internal corporate decision

---

[11] "Inflation Accounting...," p. 68. Reprinted from the October 15, 1979 issue of *Business Week* by special permission, © 1980 by McGraw-Hill, Inc., New York, NY 10020. All rights reserved.

[12] "Inflation Accounting...," p. 70. Reprinted from the October 15, 1979 issue of *Business Week* by special permission, © 1980 by McGraw-Hill, Inc., New York, NY 10020. All rights reserved.

[13] "Inflation Accounting...," p. 70. Reprinted from the October 15, 1979 issue of *Business Week* by special permission, © 1980 by McGraw-Hill, Inc., New York, NY 10020. All rights reserved.

[14] Ibid., p. 71.

making and that the benefits have more than justified the costs. He said, "We probably have more benefits ahead of us as we continue to evolve inflation adjusted measurements in reporting...."[15] The *Wall Street Journal* observed, "FASB 33, for all its limitations, will dramatize the problems of taxation and dividend policy, and give those who care about capital formation some carefully determined, and sophisticated ammunition."[16]

**Accounting Firms**

The response to FASB Statement No. 33 from the Big Eight accounting firms came primarily in the form of booklets aimed at answering questions and aiding in the implementation of the Statement. Two firms, Coopers & Lybrand and Arthur Young & Co., published booklets which dealt with management and other executive decisions which would be needed to deal with FASB Statement No. 33 properly.

The firms, however, did not, for the most part, express extensive opinions about the proposal. Peat, Marwick, Mitchell & Co. said, "The guidance and interpretations in this booklet were developed based on an initial review and study of the Statement. Although it is intended to provide guidance, this booklet does not constitute firm policy."[17] Coopers and Lybrand commented, "For many companies, the initial restatement process will undoubtedly be burdensome... The disclosures are by their nature approximations, and thus restatement should not involve excessive effort just for the sake of immaterial precision. The development of shortcut techniques could materially help smooth transition and report preparation time."[18]

Arthur Young and Company said of FASB Statement No. 33, "Although by no means perfect, FASB 33 provides opportunities for constructive accomplishment. By requiring companies to report more meaningful cost information and, hence, more meaningful income measures, FASB 33 can help American business alter public perceptions of the level of business income, reconcile the conflicting signals leading to public confusion, and move a few significant steps toward reversing public policies that have sapped the American economy of much of its former vitality... If erroneous public perceptions and policies can begin to be corrected by the addition of a page or two in an annual report, the return on investment may be considerable."[19] Price Waterhouse & Co., "is disappointed with this Statement which results in three different measurements of income in the same annual report. Nevertheless, the Statement constitutes a focal point for practical experimentation and on-going dialogue..."[20]

Arthur Andersen & Co. simply said, "The purpose of this booklet is to aid companies affected by these new disclosure requirements to better understand the intricacies of the Statement and to provide guidance for individuals responsible for calculating and reporting the information required by the new disclosures. We welcome questions concerning the Statement's requirements."[21] Andersen & Co. did expand on its comments in the October 15, 1979 issue of *Business Week*. There, Andersen charged that many managements are unwilling to acknowledge that a significant portion of the growing profits they report are not real. Management wants to be rewarded for increases in earnings per share, but at the same time, complains to Congress that taxation of these "paper profits" is destroying their ability to retain or raise capital.[22] Hopefully, the requirements of FASB Statement No. 33 will properly indicate those situations, where they exist, and

---

[15] Ibid., p. 74.

[16] "Financial Reporting and Changing Prices," Arthur Young & Co. (November 1979), p. 9.

[17] "Statement of Financial Accounting Standards No. 33: A Review of the Key Provisions of the Statement and Answers to Questions about Them," PMM & Co. (November 1979), p. 2.

[18] "Accounting for Changing Prices," p. 23.

[19] "Financial Reporting and Changing Prices," Arthur Young & Co. (November 1979), p. 13.

[20] "Financial Reporting and Changing Prices," Price Waterhouse & Co. (November 1979), p. 1.

[21] "Financial Reporting and Changing Prices," Arthur Andersen & Co. (1979), p. 1.

[22] "Inflation Accounting...," p. 70.

the appropriate steps will be taken to alleviate the situation.

**SEC Response**

As reported in the *Journal of Accountancy* in December 1979, the SEC, through the issuance of ASR No. 271, eliminated the requirement for disclosure of replacement cost information, as required under ASR 190, once the requirements of FASB Statement No. 33 were fully effective. Technically, this would be December 24, 1980 except for registrants who voluntarily implemented FASB Statement No. 33 for 1979 annual reports. Such companies would have ASR 190 requirements waived immediately.

SEC chairman Harold Williams said that FASB Statement No. 33 "is more comprehensive than the commission's replacement cost rule, in that it requires information on both a constant-dollar and a current-cost basis" and that the SEC will extend its safe harbor rule that now exists for disclosing replacement cost data to disclosures under FASB Statement No. 33.[23]

---

[23] "Replacement Cost Data Waived by SEC," *Journal of Accountancy* (December 1979), p. 32.

# CONCLUSION

*by William D. Milligan, Jr., MBA, CPA*

"The value of the dollar—its general purchasing power—is subject to serious change over a period of years . . . accountants . . . deal with an unstable, variable unit; and comparisons of unadjusted accounting statements prepared at intervals are accordingly always more or less unsatisfactory and are often positively misleading."[1] This statement, by Professor William Paton, was made in the year 1922. Since that time, the debate concerning the effect of a continuously changing price-level on historical cost financial reporting has been a dominating one in the accounting and business communities. Not until September of 1979, however, fifty-seven years after Mr. Paton's statement, did the Financial Accounting Standards Board issue Statement of Financial Accounting Standards No. 33 requiring approximately 1,350 of the largest U.S. corporations to present supplementary information concerning the effects of changing prices on financial reporting.

The process of developing this statement was an evolutionary one which involved five major sources of accounting theory and procedure. They are the Committee on Accounting Procedure, the Accounting Principles Board, the American Institute of Certified Public Accountants, the Securities and Exchange Commission and the Financial Accounting Standards Board. This paper has examined the recommendations of each pronouncement, discussed the theoretical effects of the implementation of the recommendations on Financial Statement reporting, and explored the responses of corporate leaders, major accounting practitioners and journalists in a chronological manner by comparing the most recent pronouncement with immediately preceding pronouncements. As a result of this examination it is quite obvious that the pros and cons of both price-level adjusted and current cost financial statements have not been altered dramatically over time. In fact, the quotes of the businessmen and accountants, as used throughout this paper, are, for the most part, interchangeable.

---

William D. Milligan, Jr. "A Chronological Analysis of Previous Pronouncements on Recording the Effects of Inflation in Financial Statements with FASB No. 33" (Master's thesis, Pace University, May 1980). Used by permission of William D. Milligan, Jr.

[1] "FASB Statement of Financial Accounting Standards No. 33," paragraph 71.

What has been altered, however, is the viewpoint of the rule-making bodies. The Committee on Accounting Procedure said that, although it would support the use of supplemental schedules, explanations or footnotes to explain the effects of inflation on the financial statements, it thought this change would confuse financial statement users and nullify any gain which resulted from the more accurate presentation. On the other hand, the Financial Accounting Standards Board, in Concepts Statement No. 1, explicitly stated the need for information concerning the effects of inflation on financial reporting. The evolutionary change in accounting thought is evidenced through the issuance of numerous pronouncements and FASB Statement No. 33, the most current of the pronouncements, represents only a stage in the evolutionary process and is a combination of the previous pronouncements. The evolution of the pronouncements described in this paper is illustrated in the following two charts. The first represents the change in constant dollar pronouncements and the second represents the change in current cost pronouncements.

The first chart, dealing with pronouncements concerning constant dollar financial statements, clearly shows the constant dollar requirements of FASB Statement No. 33 as a synopsis of previous proposals. The effects of evolution, however, as indicated by an asterisk(*), are summarized as follows:

1. *Accounting theory has moved from general purchasing power disclosures to the requirement of both constant dollar and current cost disclosures.*
2. *Constant dollar information, at first required in purchasing power of the dollar at the latest balance sheet date, evolved to presentation in either average-for-the-year dollars or end-of-the-year dollars, depending on the type of disclosure.*
3. *The index of the general purchasing power changed from the GNP Deflator to the Consumer Price Index for All Urban Consumers.*
4. *Minor changes, mainly for the purpose of clarification, occurred in the breakdown of monetary and nonmonetary items.*
5. *The idea of fully adjusted financial statements evolved to the presentation of selected financial data.*
6. *The format of presentation, although always liberal in nature, evolved to the point where presentation must be disclosed separate from the primary financial statements.*

These changes have been discussed in several chapters of this book and, as indicated in those chapters, do not represent major changes in constant dollar theory. Rather, the changes made from pronouncement to pronouncement were usually designed to either simplify or clarify the theory or application of a previous pronouncement. Therefore, the constant dollar requirements of FASB Statement No. 33 are not original, but, instead, a product of numerous proposals and pronouncements.

The second chart illustrates current cost pronouncements. This chart gives evidence to the fact that the FASB, outside of its clarification of the procedures dealing with foreign owned assets and the omission for most companies of current cost information in 1979, retained the proposed requirements of the December 28, 1978 Exposure Draft. Thus, because the differences between the Exposure Draft and ASR 190 were detailed in a previous chapter, an explanation of the evolution of the current cost disclosures required under FASB Statement No. 33 is not necessary.

Therefore, FASB Statement No. 33 has taken two theories, which at one time were considered mutually exclusive, and required that information obtained under the two assumptions be disclosed in the same annual report. This is just one more step in the evolution of reporting the effects of inflation on financial statement reporting. It is by no means, however, the last step in that evolutionary process. The FASB has already committed itself to review the requirements of FASB Statement No. 33 within five years after its issuance. That review, however, will undoubtedly occur before the end of that five year period due to the severity of the problem, the necessity for a satisfactory solution, and the continuing debate over the appropriateness of the dual requirements of FASB Statement No. 33.

The nature of that review will depend upon the ability, both economically and practically, of corporations to comply with the requirements, the rate of inflation, and the usefulness, as stated by management, investors and creditors, of the information provided under FASB Statement No. 33. In light of current economic conditions the rate of inflation will apparently remain at historically high percentage and, based on the ability of corporations to comply with ASR 190, corporations will be able to meet the requirements of the FASB without much difficulty. Therefore, the major area of the review will be centered around the usefulness of the information provided. In this area the FASB will find itself facing an old nemesis—the debate between constant dollar and current cost which has been exemplified throughout this paper. In this review, however, the answer should not be difficult for the FASB. Having made the disclosure of information under both theories mandatory, the FASB should not alter those requirements. Rather, they should gradually incorporate simplifications in methodology and procedure which will inevitably develop for both theories. Also, the scope of the participants under FASB Statement No. 33 should, upon the development of these simplified techniques, be expanded until almost every company which prepares financial statements will be required to present supplementary information.

Increasing the number of participants under FASB Statement No. 33 should not be the only change. The FASB should also move toward the mandatory disclosure of comprehensive financial statements under both theories in lieu of the limited disclosures under the current statement. This will provide further information to management, investors and creditors and add tremendously to the credibility and comparability of that information.

Therefore, while dealing with a subject which has been in a continuous state of change over the past half century, the FASB should provide continuous guidance to the business and accounting communities. This guidance, along with the proposed expansion of present requirements, will help provide the information necessary to maintain the comparability, and more importantly, the credibility of financial statements in the future.

## CHART I   CONSTANT DOLLAR PRONOUNCEMENTS

| FASB No. 33 Constant Dollar | December 28, 1978 Exposure Draft Constant Dollar | December 31, 1974 Exposure Draft | APB Statement No. 3 | ARS No. 6 |
|---|---|---|---|---|
| 1. The requirements of GAAP should be followed. However, both constant dollar and current cost disclosures are required. | 1. *The requirements of GAAP should be followed. However, either constant dollar or current cost disclosure is required as supplemental information. | 1. Same as ASR-6. | 1. Same as ARS-6. | 1. The requirements of GAAP should be followed except that changes in the general purchasing power of the dollar are recognized. |
| 2. Information for the current year on income from continuing operations on a constant dollar basis should be stated in average-for-the-year dollars. However, if comprehensive restatement is made, average-for-the-year dollars may be presented. | 2. Information for the current year on income from continuing operations on a constant dollar basis should be stated in constant dollars as of the end of that year. | 2. Same as ASR-6. | 2. Same as ARS-6. | 2. General price-level financial statements should be presented in terms of the general purchasing power of the dollar at the latest balance sheet date. |
| 3. Same as 1978 Exposure Draft. | 3. *The Consumer Price Index for All Urban Consumers should be the index of constant dollar information. | 3. The GNP Deflator should be the index of the general purchasing power. | 3. Same as ARS-6. | 3. Suggests the use of the GNP Deflator as the index of the general price-level. |
| 4. The five-year summary of selected financial data may be presented in either average-for-the-year dollars or end-of-the-year dollars; whichever is used for measurement of income from continuing operation in two, above. | 4. **The five-year summary of selected financial data may be presented in either end-of-current year dollars or in base-year dollars (i.e., the base year used by the Bureau of Labor Statistics in calculating the CPI-U). | 4. Prior years' financial statements should be "rolled forward" or restated to the same units of general purchasing power. | 4. Same as ARS-6. | 4. Prior years financial statement should be restated. |
| 5. States that both information concerning specific and general price level changes are of great significance to investors. | 5. States that both information concerning specific and general price-level changes are of great significance to investors. | 5. States restatement in terms of a stable measuring unit would contribute to an understanding of the effects of the changing purchasing power of the dollar or individual enterprises. | 5. Same as ARS-6. | 5. States restatement would be useful to investors, management, creditors and all others concerned with economic affairs of enterprise. |

| FASB No. 33 Constant Dollar | December 28, 1978 Exposure Draft Constant Dollar | December 31, 1974 Exposure Draft | APB Statement No. 3 | ARS No. 6 |
|---|---|---|---|---|
| 6. Monetary and Non-Monetary terms remained the same as the December 30, 1978 Exposure Draft. | 6. *Definitions of Monetary and Non-monetary items are unchanged (according to March 2, 1979 Exposure Draft). However, foreign currency on hand, claims to foreign currency, foreign currency obligations and deferred income tax items should be classified as monetary items. | 6. Defines: Monetary items are classified and defined in terms of assets, liabilities, and stockholders' equity; with the common feature of the amounts being fixed in terms of number of dollars. Non-monetary items are those balance sheet items other than monetary. | 6. Defines: Monetary items are those whose amounts are fixed by contract or otherwise. Non-monetary items are those other than monetary. | 5. Defines: Monetary items are those whose amounts are fixed by contract or otherwise. Non-monetary items not in the form of money or claims to money. |
| 7. Same as 1978 Exposure Draft. | 7. Inflation gain or loss on net monetary items should be presented as a separate item in the five-year summary. | 7. General purchasing power gain or losses should be included in Net Income by being reported as a separate item in general price-level statements. | 7. Same as ARS-6. | 7. General price-level gains and losses included in Net Income by being reported as a separate item in general price-level income statements. |
| 8. Same as 1978 Exposure Draft. | 8. *Comprehensive restatement of financial statements was not required. | 8. Financial information stated in units of general purchasing power should be prepared by comprehensive restatement of historical financial statements. | 8. States that partially restated financial statements, and information based on them, are likely to be misleading and should not be presented. | 8. Concluded that price-level changes should come in the form of fully adjusted statements. |
| 9. Same as 1974 Exposure Draft. | 9. Translation of foreign owned assets was not covered. | 9. Financial statements of foreign branches that are expressed in units of foreign currency should first be translated into United States dollars and then restated for changes in the general purchasing power of the U.S. dollar. | 9. Same as ARS-6. | 9. Financial statements of foreign branches or subsidiaries to be combined with their U.S. parent company should be translated into U.S. dollars and then restated. |
| 10. Same as 1978 Exposure Draft. | 10. Disclosure would appear as supplemental information to financial statements. Flexibility and necessary allowances for experimentation are present. | 10. No specified format was suggested for presentation. | 10. Suggests that this supplementary information be presented in multicolumn or narrative form opposite from historical. | 10. Suggests that this supplementary information be presented in multicolumn form either separate or adjacent to historical. |

## CHART II  CURRENT COST PRONOUNCEMENTS

*December 28, 1978*

| *FASB No. 33* <br> *Current Cost* | *Exposure Draft* <br> *Current Cost* | *ASR 190* |
|---|---|---|
| 1. The requirements of GAAP should be followed. However, both constant dollar and current cost disclosures are required. | 1. *The requirements of GAAP should be followed. However, either constant dollar or current cost disclosure is required as supplemental information. | 1. Historical Cost financial statements should be presented in accordance with GAAP. Supplemental disclosure of replacement cost is mandatory. |
| 2. Except in 1979, where current cost disclosures may be omitted, both current cost and constant dollar information are required. | 2. If current cost information is presented, constant dollar information is optional. | 2. No general purchasing power financial statements are presented. |
| 3. Determination methods of current cost information are flexible. | 3. Determination methods of current cost information are flexible. | 3. Replacement costs are flexible—the calculation may use one or several indices, if and when an index is used. |
| 4. Current cost is the cost of acquiring the same service potential as embodied by the asset owned. The increase or decrease in current cost amounts shall be reported both before and after eliminating the effects of general inflation. | 4. Current cost is the cost of acquiring the same service potential as embodied by the asset owned. The increase or decrease in current cost amounts shall be reported both before and after eliminating the effects of general inflation. | 4. Replacement costs are not altered in subsequent periods. |
| 5. States that both information concerning specific and general price-level changes are of great significance to investors. | 5. States that both information concerning specific and general price-level changes are of great significance to investors. | 5. States that data concerning the impact in changes of specific goods and services on a business is of great significance to investors in developing an understanding of any firm. |
| 6. Monetary and Non-monetary items are relevant. See 7, below. | 6. *Monetary and Non-monetary items are relevant— see (7), below. | 6. Monetary and Non-monetary items are not relevant to replacement cost procedures. |
| 7. Inflation gain or loss on net monetary items should be presented in the current cost five-year summary in terms of constant dollars. | 7. Inflation gain or loss on net monetary items should be presented in the current cost five-year summary in terms of constant dollars. | 7. Does not require specific disclosure of the impact on earnings. |
| 8. Increases or decreases in current cost amounts (formally called holding gains and losses) as well as the disclosure of expenses and | 8. *Called for the disclosure of expenses and assets at current cost as well as holding gains and losses. | 8. Disclosed only the specific cost impact on inventory, productive assets and their related expenses. |

| FASB No. 33<br>Current Cost | December 28, 1978<br>Exposure Draft<br>Current Cost | ASR 190 |
|---|---|---|
| assets at current cost should be presented.<br>9. If measured in a foreign currency, the amount shall be translated into dollars at the current exchange rate (for depreciation and cost of sales) or the rate at the balance sheet date (for inventory and plant, property and equipment). | 9. Translation of foreign owned assets was not covered. | 9. Certain foreign owned assets would be excluded from 1976 disclosures but, in the future, GAAP would be followed for translation or replacement costs. |
| 10. Disclosure would appear as supplemental information to financial statements. Flexibility and necessary allowances for experimentation are present. | 10. Disclosure would appear as supplemental information to financial statements. Flexibility and necessary allowances for experimentation are present. | 10. Disclosure would appear in notes to financial statements or in a separate section following the notes. Similar to the FASB, the SEC has allowed for considerable experimentation in this. |

# INFLATION ACCOUNTING: PURSUING THE ELUSIVE

by Philip L. Defliese

Despite anticipated record-year 1978 earnings of over $12 per share, General Motors last November declared a smaller year-end extra dividend than in 1977 ($6 total for 1978 vs. $6.80 for 1977). The question must be asked: Did GM know what it was doing? GM stock sold off immediately and took the entire market with it for several days, as Wall Street interpreted the action as bellwether GM's concern over a dim outlook for 1979. Yes, GM did know what it was doing, and why, but it failed to communicate adequately its motives. Hence the market reaction. Responsibility for the inadequate communication must, however, be shared by the accounting profession. And soon, if hopes are realized, something will be done about it—the comment period on the Financial Accounting Standards Board's exposure draft, *Financial Reporting and Changing Prices,* has just ended.

Blue-chip companies generally follow the policy of declaring a sustainable percentage of earnings as cash dividends, plowing back the remainder for growth. Inflation has impacted this practice considerably as companies have learned that a greater portion of earnings must be retained to cover the excess of replacement cost over original cost of consumed inventory, plant and machinery (in GM's case, tools, dies, jigs, etc.) to permit them to maintain their existing level of operations without adding heavy debt.

Buried in the GM communiques, inadequately emphasized, was the fact that GM expects to spend $5 billion for capital expenditures in 1979 vs. records of $4.5 bil-

---

Copyright © 1979 by the American Institute of Certified Public Accountants, Inc.

lion and $3.6 billion in 1978 and 1977, respectively. In 1978, depreciation provided only $3.04 billion, a shortfall of $5.11 per share. Unfortunately, we cannot determine what portion of these expenditures relates to replacement and what portion to growth. Nevertheless, GM knows that its historical cost determined earnings are inflated in an economic sense, and that the dividend must be smaller to make up for excess replacement costs—its 1978 payout ratio was the lowest in recent history.[1]

How this message can be conveyed in a more quantified and objective fashion has confounded accounting standard setters around the world for some time.[2] In 1976, the impatient Securities and Exchange Commission created a hornet's nest when it issued Accounting Series Release no. 190 requiring disclosure of replacement cost depreciation and cost of sales. Businessmen generally dislike any disclosure that disparages historical cost generated earnings. Many companies (including GM) understandably buried the data in the Form 10-K report rather than include it in their annual reports to shareholders. Some considered the implications misleading and said so in no uncertain terms. Even finance-trained GM Chief Executive Thomas Murphy has said that few, if any, businessmen viewed ASR no. 190 with any kindness. He accused the SEC of having opened "a Pandora's box providing the unscrupulous with the opportunity to present and manipulate hypothetical data which can only serve to confuse those it should inform." True, ASR no. 190 has its drawbacks. It was hastily rammed through without research and was premised on a hypothetical future replacement rather than on equipment in use. More on that later.

The SEC cautioned that such replacement data should not be used to reconstruct net income. I shall disregard this caveat—with poetic license—only to illustrate that some adjustment of earnings must be made to communicate the need for an additional dividend limitation which, I believe, GM undertook subconsciously, if not overtly. Based on GM's 1978 10-K disclosure of replacement costs, which it said was hypothetical and probably not useful for this purpose, its $12.24 per share earnings would be reduced by between $3.17 and $3.66, depending on which theory (described later) you subscribe to for the effect of net monetary liabilities (see Figure 1).

Now comes the FASB's proposed solution. The exposure draft issued in December (for comments by May 1 with the possibility of public hearings thereafter) fulfills the board's promise to require disclosure of the effect of changing prices as supplementary data, leaving undisturbed the traditional historical cost accounting model as the basic reporting vehicle. Almost all accounting standard-setting bodies throughout the world have now seen the wisdom of this conclusion and are proceeding along these lines. Unless the monetary unit is regularly officially restructured, as in Brazil, a dollar is a dollar is a dollar—historical cost earnings are objectively determined earnings (within present limitations), and the results are in actual dollars. Thus, a company could distribute those dollars if it intended to liquidate and all other things remained equal. The fact that those dollars can no longer buy what they once did is another matter, but more a matter of economics than of accounting. Nevertheless, it is a matter that calls for *interpretation* of the reported historical dollar results by those best qualified to do so. And this is where we now are. It should be noted, of course, that inflation is just one element of the broader concept of "changing prices." The recent severe erosion of purchasing power by inflation has emphasized the need for action but has also served to confuse the issues.

Opinions among accountants and businessmen differ widely on how to interpret reported earnings in an inflationary environment—the FASB itself is undecided and of-

---

[1] In its 1978 report to shareholders, GM for the first time restated operations on a constant dollar basis for the years 1973-1978, using the consumer price index for 1973 as a base.

[2] The confusion over whether the objective is to redetermine past income on some better economic basis or to predict future cash flows to the investor adds to this problem.

**FIGURE 1  ILLUSTRATION OF SUGGESTED FIRST APPROACH TO THE PROBLEM OF CHANGING PRICES**

Supplemental earnings data—1978* (in millions of dollars)

|  |  | Amount | Per common share |
|---|---|---|---|
| Net income per income statement (historical cost) |  | $3,508.0 | $12.24 |
| Earnings reserved to cover estimated excess of current cost over historical cost of |  |  |  |
|     Depreciation and amortization | $  862.1 |  |  |
|     Cost of sales | 180.9 |  |  |
|  | $1,043.0 |  |  |
| Less: Portion attributable to net monetary debt capital (12.4%) | 139.3 |  |  |
| Portion attributable to shareholders' capital |  | 903.7 | 3.17 |
| Earnings available for expansion and distribution |  | $2,604.3 | $ 9.07 |

*Amounts based, for illustration only, on General Motors' 1978 10-K disclosures of replacement cost in compliance with ASR no. 190. Replacement cost is not the exact equivalent of current cost. The adjustment for depreciation and amortization is not precise because ASR no. 190 requires straight-line and GM uses accelerated methods for historical cost. As a matter of interest, it should be noted that the GM 1978 annual report showed $2,390.8 million and $8.34 as the constant (1973) dollar equivalents of net income and earnings per share, respectively. See footnote 1.

---

fers two ways (see Figure 2) of doing it. Not even the much maligned Accounting Principles Board had the temerity to offer a choice on an important issue, except when forced to by the SEC (remember the investment credit debacle[3]). No doubt this is a sop to the opposing current cost and constant dollar (price level) factions, a Solomonic decision that may, or may not, temper the fierce controversy between them.

In fairness, it must be reported that the FASB says it is attempting to encourage experimentation that "would help to develop techniques for accumulating, reporting, and analyzing data on the effects of price changes." Thus, we will now have mandatory experimentation. Previous experimentation was voluntary[4] and was understandably conducted under the cloak of secrecy because companies, on a selective basis, didn't want to publicize any but their official results. Now everybody will have to let it all hang out, one way or the other. The proposed standard will apply only to publicly held companies with over $125 million of inventory and plant, or assets over $1 billion. It is estimated that 1,000 U.S. companies will be affected. If experimentation is needed (and it is), one wonders why companies shouldn't report the data both ways so users may make relevant comparisons. As it is, if GM chooses the constant dollar model (as it did in its 1978 report) and Ford chooses the current cost model, how can comparisons be made? It's not clear whether the choice is that optional, as explained below.

This proposal is another step in the board's quest for a conceptual framework

---

[3] The first APB opinion (no. 2) required one uniform method; when the SEC permitted two methods, the APB amended its opinion (issued as Opinion no. 4) to permit two also.

[4] In 1975 the FASB conducted a voluntary field test of the general purchasing power exposure draft on 101 companies (report issued in 1977). In 1977 the AICPA conducted a test of four types of accounting models designed to reflect changing prices; 23 companies participated voluntarily (report issued 1979). Both tests were on a confidential basis.

**FIGURE 2   ANNUAL SUPPLEMENTAL STATEMENTS: CHOOSE EITHER ONE.**

| (a) Current cost model | | (b) Historical cost/constant dollar model | |
|---|---|---|---|
| Condensed statement of current cost income from continuing operations and other data pertaining to changing prices | | Condensed statement of constant dollar income from continuing operations in December 31, 1978, dollars and other data pertaining to changing prices | |
| For the year ended December 31, 1978 | | For the year ended December 31, 1978 | |
| Net sales and other operating revenues | $50,000 | Net sales and other operating revenues | $*52,000 |
| Cost of goods sold at current cost | 21,900 | Cost of goods sold at restated historical cost | 21,200 |
| Depreciation and amortization expense at current cost | 12,100 | Depreciation and amortization expense at restated historical cost | 11,800 |
| Other operating expenses | 9,000 | Other operating expenses | 9,360 |
| Interest expense | 1,000 | Interest expense | 1,040 |
| Provision for income taxes | 3,000 | Provision for income taxes | 5,200 |
| Current cost income from continuing operations | $ 3,000 | Constant dollar income from continuing operations | $* 3,400 |
| Net holding loss on inventories and property, plant and equipment resulting from a holding gain ($4,500) less inflation component ($4,000) and less income tax ($2,000) on amounts realized | $(1,500) | Inflation gain on net monetary items | $*  600 |
| | | Foreign exchange loss net of tax† | $*  500 |
| Inflation gain on net monetary items | $  575 | $*December 31, 1978, dollars. | |
| Foreign exchange loss net of tax | $ (500) | †It is assumed that the foreign exchange loss is stated at the same amount as in the basic income statement. | |

These illustrations of alternative presentations of supplemental data are from the FASB Exposure Draft, *Financial Reporting and Changing Prices.*

for financial reporting, following its issuance, also last December, of its long-awaited Statement on Financial Accounting Concepts no. 1, *Objectives of Financial Reporting.* That statement, in line with previous proposals, affirmed the objective of providing users with information "on the relative standing and performance of a business enterprise . . . *on which to base estimates required for investment and lending decisions."* [Emphasis supplied.] Most preparers, and perhaps many users, will be happy to see that the board acceded to the almost universal clamor to avoid injecting price-change concepts into the basic model, i.e., it did not tinker with historical cost. On the other hand, it's never been made clear just what analysts want or need as supplemental information in this area. We can only surmise, but the emphasis given to "future cash flows of the enterprise" in the objectives statement leads directly to one conclusion—an investor needs to know what to expect in terms of cash dividends and stock price appreciation. The relationship to the need for a better interpretation of reported earnings is obvious.

The present low price-earnings ratios tell us that the efficient market has discounted most reported historical cost earnings as inflated. The constant lowering of the percentages of earnings distributed during the current decade (despite the absolute increases in earnings) tells us that managements have also seen the need to retard distributions to cover excess replacement costs. Presumably, what users need is some better indication of earnings available for distribution and growth, after allowing for excess replacement cost. On the other hand, as a consumer, the shareholder has his problems with the declining purchasing power of the dollar he receives as dividends and his share price on resale; perhaps he also needs something to put his cash flow in perspective. The FASB proposal for a five-year summary provides data that go a long way in this direction.

The proposal appears to provide something for everybody—shareholders, analysts, theoreticians (all camps) and management. It would require a plethora of data from every affected company from which presumably the most useful data (to whom?) will ultimately be chosen or plucked. Presumably, the marketplace will choose, but will Gresham's law operate? Will the useless data drive out the useful? The proposal also has the capability of creating considerable confusion, because only the most sophisticated will understand the implications of each disclosure, especially since the disclosures are discrete, ostensibly incapable of being consolidated into a useful new indicator of earnings available for distribution and growth.

Somehow the FASB cannot resist mixing apples and oranges. Yes, every choice but one provides, more or less, a mixture of current or historical cost with constant dollar (price level) concepts (see Figure 2). The one exception is the brief statement of asset values at year-end (see Figure 3), which compares historical cost amounts of inventory and plant with their related current cost (not necessarily current value). This statement is required only for those choosing the current cost format. Presumably it is needed to provide some idea of the asset values used to derive current cost income. It is hoped that the Internal Revenue Service will give Lifo (last in, first out) companies permission to make this disclosure, as it did for the ASR no. 190 disclosures. Also, we can only hope that users will not add the differences to equity to reconstruct the debt—equity ratio; on this point, however, views will differ.

Now, let us look at the choices, their premises, their advantages and their drawbacks. While the draft seems to permit a free choice between the two different bases, it provides guidelines that "shall be considered" in making the choice. These specify that the current cost format should be used "unless ...constant dollar...better reflects the effects of changing prices...," i.e., the constant dollar basis "may be sufficient...if cost of sales and depreciation are not significant" (paragraph 25) or when specific price changes follow the general price level. (Then why not use specific prices?) Does this mean that those choosing the constant dollar model must defend their choice? This vague permissiveness in the guidelines must be clarified. Financial institutions will need to use the constant dollar basis. With the dollar as its commodity, does a bank worry about the dollar's purchasing power? It simply adjusts the interest rate, and its investors look for a different rate of return.

### FIGURE 3 CURRENT COST MODEL

Statement of asset values at December 31, 1978

| | Net historical cost per balance sheet | Net current cost |
|---|---|---|
| Inventory | $ 5,435 | $ 6,920 |
| Property, plant and equipment | 40,000 | 50,000 |
| | $45,435 | $56,920 |

These illustrations of alternative presentations of supplemental data are from the FASB Exposure Draft, *Financial Reporting and Changing Prices.*

## CURRENT COST MODEL

This model (see Figure 2[a]) attempts to determine income from continuing operations using current costs for cost of sales and depreciation.[5] Current cost is defined as the "current cost of acquiring the same service potential (that is, the same operating costs and output capacity) as embodied by the asset owned." This assumption may be made when the asset can be replaced in its present mode (used condition). Much latitude is allowed, including the use of indexes, in setting current cost values. The methodology differs considerably from that of the SEC's release on replacement cost, especially since the FASB model would permit operating cost differentials to be considered when the only available measure embodies replacement with new technology.

Income from continuing operations—the draft's new concept of recurring net income—excludes holding gains and losses, both realized and unrealized (adjusted for inflation), and foreign exchange loss (net of tax) computed in the same manner as in the historical cost income statement. Considering the flak the FASB has been getting on Statement no. 8, *Accounting for the Translation of Foreign Currency Transactions and Foreign Currency Financial Statements,* it is understandable that it would want to segregate these translation effects.[6]

It is unfortunate that the term "holding gain" has entered our literature in this area, since in many instances there is no "gain" at all in an economic sense. Price changes of inventories and plant assets reflect the combination of a change in the purchasing power of the dollar and in the intrinsic value of the item itself. Often there is only a new monetary denomination without an intrinsic gain, as most homeowners today realize. This model attempts to squeeze out the inflation factor to determine the true holding gains (or losses—especially since the related actual income tax is deducted from those realized). Much debate will center on whether this item should include unrealized gains or losses. (The consumer price index is used to measure inflation, as discussed later.)

The most controversial item in this model will be "inflation gain on net monetary items." This is the same item that created so much controversy in previously proposed constant dollar (price level) models—both the APB's and the FASB's. Many companies operate with a net monetary liability, because heavy long- and short-term debt usually outweigh inventory. (Even the colossus GM had a net monetary liability of about $2.5 billion in 1978.) There is a presumption that, because of this phenomenon, each year's inflation results in a gain from the fact that cheaper dollars will ultimately be used to repay the debt. This can cause a sizable gain for a highly leveraged company.

In the past, the prime controversy was whether this gain (if it exists) should be included in income immediately, as it was in the original price level model, or spread over the periods during which the offset—higher annual replacement cost depreciation of the assets financed—takes place. The FASB model begs the question by presenting the amount as a discrete item for the reader to interpret as he wishes. A few theorists believe no real gain takes place—they say the gain resides in the assets purchased by the debt.[7] One can also take the position that backlog depreciation (inflation's effect on prior years' original cost depreciation) more than offsets any such gains on net monetary liabilities.

A simple example will illustrate: Assume a plant with a 30-year life built 10 years ago for $10 million and financed entirely with 30-year debt has a current replacement cost of $20 million. The current year's inflation rate is 10 percent, resulting in an assumed net monetary gain on the debt of $1 million.

---

[5] An alternative presentation (also illustrated in the FASB draft) reconciles current cost income with historical cost income. A similar option is given for the constant dollar model.

[6] The FASB has announced that it intends to modify Statement no. 8.

[7] Jack C. Robertson, *Business Income Determination Through Use of Current Cost Accounting* (New York: Coopers & Lybrand, 1977), p. 7.

The excess of current cost depreciation over historical cost depreciation for the year is only $666,667 ($20,000,000 ÷ 20 − $10,000,000 ÷ 30).

The British have proposed, in their Hyde guidelines,[8] that only those excess current cost adjustments financed by shareholders' equity should be taken into account; those financed by debt are omitted. This is accomplished by applying a net monetary debt-to-total-capital ratio to the adjustment. Thus, if the plant in the above example was financed 50 percent from debt and 50 percent from equity (an oversimplification), the current cost adjustment would be $333,333, with no reference made to a net monetary gain. The theory behind this is that only the shareholders' portion of employed capital needs inflation protection (creditors must rely on their interest rates) and that bondholders will later refinance their portion of the higher replacement cost.

Of course, the British are interested in arriving at a surrogate net income figure, based on current costs, that represents an amount available for distribution and growth, after allowance for the added replacement cost applicable to the shareholders' portion of the investment. The FASB's model does not do this; the reader is given various data (some of which are interrelated, as described earlier), and he must reach his own conclusions. Certainly, the items in the current cost model should not be added together, although—unlike the SEC in ASR no. 190—the FASB does not caution against this.

## CONSTANT DOLLAR MODEL

This is our old friend, price level accounting or historical cost restated in current dollars —current purchasing power, with some var-

---

[8]Interim Recommendation of the Inflation Accounting Steering Group, U.K. Accounting Standards Committee, November 1977, following rejection of ED 18, the so-called Morpeth response to the Sandilands report (1975).

[9]A supplement to the exposure draft entitled *Constant Dollar Accounting,* was issued for comment in March 1978. In addition to the

iations.[9] Removed from current income are the controversial "inflation gain on net monetary items," discussed above, and "foreign exchange loss net of tax" (on a historical cost basis), resulting in "constant dollar income from continuing operations." Only realized holding gains (adjusted for inflation) flow through into continuing income; the old price level model included all these items in net inome. Here they are pulled apart and separately disclosed for obvious, or perhaps not so obvious, reasons. Unrealized holding gains are ignored; the old model carried them directly to equity.

Another new twist is the index used. Instead of the gross national product implicit price deflator, the consumer price index for all urban consumers is used on the assumption that shareholders can relate to this index: their dividends and share prices are affected in relation to the consumer dollar. But it is also assumed that shareholders must be concerned about preserving the purchasing power of their corporate assets—a negation of the entity theory. No doubt this will stir some controversy. Those who oppose price level accounting conceptually will point out that the CPI—heavily influenced by the market basket of the consumer (food, health care, rent)—has absolutely no relevance to a company in the copper fabricating business, for example. In their view, it was bad enough to use the GNP deflator rather than specific indexes. Even some price level believers will have trouble with CPI. Of course, the availability and reliability of CPI over other indexes is an advantage.

## FIVE-YEAR COMPARISON DATA

This summary is by far the most impressive new creation. At first blush, considering the illustrations presented (see Figure 4a and 4b),

---

differences referred to above, the draft differs principally from the old price level model in the following ways: (1) foreign currency on hand and foreign currency claims and obligations are classified as monetary items, and (2) deferred income tax items are classified as monetary items.

**FIGURE 4    FIVE-YEAR SUMMARIES: CHOOSE ONE OF THREE**

*(a) Current cost model*

Five-year comparison of selected financial data

| | Years ended December 31 | | | | |
|---|---|---|---|---|---|
| | 1974 | 1975 | 1976 | 1977 | 1978 |
| Consumer price index average for year | XX | XX | XX | XX | XX |
| Net sales and other operating revenues | $XX | $XX | $XX | $XX | $XX |
| Current cost income from continuing operations | XX | XX | XX | XX | XX |
| Holding gain (loss) on inventories and plant assets net of inflation and tax | XX | XX | XX | XX | XX |
| Inflation gain (loss) on net monetary items | XX | XX | XX | XX | XX |
| Foreign exchange gain (loss) net of tax | XX | XX | XX | XX | XX |
| Net assets at year-end | XX | XX | XX | XX | XX |
| Current cost income from continuing operations per common share | XX | XX | XX | XX | XX |
| Cash dividends declared per common share | XX | XX | XX | XX | XX |
| Market price per common share at year-end | XX | XX | XX | XX | XX |

*(b) Historical cost/constant dollar model*

Five-year comparison of selected financial data in December 31, 1978, dollars

| | Years ended December 31 | | | | |
|---|---|---|---|---|---|
| | 1974 | 1975 | 1976 | 1977 | 1978 |
| Net sales and other operating revenues | $* XX | $* XX | $* XX | $* XX | $*XX |
| Constant dollar income from continuing operations | XX | XX | XX | XX | XX |
| Inflation gain (loss) on net monetary items | XX | XX | XX | XX | XX |
| Foreign exchange gain (loss) net of tax | XX | XX | XX | XX | XX |
| Net assets at year-end | XX | XX | XX | XX | XX |
| Constant dollar income from continuing operations per common share | XX | XX | XX | XX | XX |
| Cash dividends declared per common share | XX | XX | XX | XX | XX |
| Market price per common share at year-end | XX | XX | XX | XX | XX |

$*December 31, 1978, dollars.

*(c) Current cost/constant dollar model* (not illustrated in the draft)

These illustrations of alternative presentations of supplemental data are from the FASB exposure draft, *Financial Reporting and Changing Prices*.

it appears that the choice between the current cost and constant dollar frameworks must follow the choice made for the supplemental income determinations. Actually, a third choice is available—those choosing current cost may present the five-year summary on a current cost/constant dollar basis (not illustrated in the draft). One's views concerning current cost vs. constant dollar concepts must necessarily carry over into this summary.

**Current cost model.** In this model the CPI is presented first for each of the five years. The CPI is relevant here because actual cash dividends per share and market prices per share are shown for the five-year period (users must make their own conversions), and we can presume that shareholders (including millions of pensioners) can relate those cash flows, when adjusted, to their needs.

Actual net sales for the five years are given in this model; presumably one should interpret them in the light of the changes shown in the CPI. However, an index tuned to the product being sold would provide a better indicator of volume trends. The other items—notably income from continuing operations—are the adjusted figures from the current cost supplemental income statement. As indicated previously, the CPI index may instead be applied to all the current cost data to produce the current cost/constant dollar format (the unillustrated third choice).

***Constant dollar model.*** This summary requires all items to be presented in either current dollars or dollars of a base period, such as 1967 = 100. The latter choice—proposed officially for the first time—is designed to avoid the confusion of constantly restating prior years' figures. This model facilitates trend analysis because all years presented are on the same selected wavelength. Shareholders will be interested, and perhaps astonished, to see past dividends, earnings per share and market prices restated in current dollars. Managements will understandably be concerned about such disclosures and may opt for the current cost model instead.

## BASES FOR CONCLUSIONS

The draft includes a 43-paragraph appendix stating the board's bases for the conclusions reached. Here emphatic support is given to its two-pronged approach, intended to provide flexibility during an experimental period. There is a reassessment and restatement of all the classic arguments for and against each methodology. Several themes come through that are worthy of mention.

Preservation of the investor's purchasing power is the overriding rationale for the need for supplemental information and for the relevance of the CPI whenever an index is used; the shareholder presumably can personally relate to that index when evaluating his investment. The company's cash flows are presumed to be the same as the shareholders'. One cannot deny that dividend and appreciation expectations are dependent on a company's cash flows, but neither can one deny the irrelevance of the CPI to those flows. Shareholders own an enterprise, but not its assets. On this issue, I suppose, disputants will always agree to disagree.

One also senses a mild preference for the current cost/constant dollar option. This is evidenced by the board's permitting the use of the current cost/constant dollar presentation in the five-year summary even though the current cost method is used in the annual supplemental report, as previously discussed.

The major flaw in this section may be found in paragraphs 59 and 60, entitled "Adherence to the Financial Concept of Capital." Repeating in condensed form the arguments for the financial concept and against the physical capital maintenance concept[10] contained in its conceptual framework discussion memorandum, the changing prices draft concludes in no uncertain terms that the financial concept should prevail. This certainly supports the board's conclusion that the historical cost framework should continue to be used for the basic financial statements. The separate disclosure of holding gains in the current cost model also conforms to this concept. But if the term "current cost income from continuing operations" is to have meaning for the current cost model, the financial capital concept certainly appears incompatible. The board finesses this inconsistency by characterizing current cost as "value to the business" or "current cost of acquiring the same service potential," which on careful analysis boils down to current replacement cost for many of the items—undeniably a physical capital maintenance concept. This will need some sorting out.

## AUDITOR'S INVOLVEMENT

The proposal specifies that the required information "is to be presented in supplementary statements, schedules, or notes in financial reports." Interim reporting is not required.

---

[10] The draft defines the two concepts as: "a. The financial concept of capital: Capital is maintained when the money value of net assets (measured either in nominal dollars or in units of purchasing power) remains constant. b. The physical productive capacity concept of capital: Capital is maintained when the net assets remain sufficient to produce a fixed quantity of goods and services."

The natural question is: Must the data be audited and covered by the auditor's opinion? There is no answer and since the location of the data in the report often has a bearing, the auditing standards board of the American Institute of CPAs will have to grapple with the issue. My guess is that the same approach taken with ASR no. 190 will be followed. Thus, initially the information will be labeled "unaudited" and auditors will "review" the material but not opine thereon. In the long run, once the experimentation period is over and methodologies are shaken down, I believe the material will be required to be audited.

**OVERVIEW**

The pressures placed on the FASB to get something out on inflation accounting are understandable. SEC Chairman Harold M. Williams has been harping on the need, and the board wants to show progress. Thus, the current draft shows the effect of hasty action. Nevertheless, it is the culmination of the board's long consideration of the issues, and only because views on the subject are so diverse does the outcome seem flawed and loaded with options. A good consensus in this area is almost impossible because the introduction of elusive economic theory and subjective measurements into an accounting model does not please objective accountants.

The draft will be criticized—justifiably—for being too complicated, understandable by only the most sophisticated accountants and analysts. But so is the subject. Attempts at simplification, such as mine, below, will be criticized for not recognizing all facets of the problem.

As one who has gone up the hill and down again in attempting to devise a framework for accounting that will more closely approximate economic income (whatever that is) and reflect changing prices and values caused by inflation or otherwise, I know that this is a never-ending quest for the impossible dream. Once we leave the solid mooring of objective historical (actual) cost accounting and introduce macroeconomic measurements, such as consumer price indexes and hypothetical replacement cost measurements into the complexities of accounting, we enter a never-never land reminiscent of medieval doctoral dissertations. Financial analysts are expected to make subjective judgments, and differences of opinion among them are commonplace; accountants, accustomed to the tenets of their discipline, will disagree sharply when asked to enter this realm. And the public won't tolerate such disagreements for the same reason—it expects preciseness and objectivity from accountants. Can we safely overcome these hurdles? Perhaps, but only if we walk before we run.

Nevertheless, users today—shareholders and their analysts—need better indications of future cash flows from an investment. If nothing else, the FASB draft will help everyone zero in on that need and the ways of satisfying it. I am sure that something useful will come out of this effort when the FASB carefully analyzes the comments it will stimulate, polishes up the draft and monitors the results of the experimentation.

The board has done a noble deed in sticking to basics—historical cost—for the official reporting model; fears of its being tinkered with are allayed, and so the reaction to the draft will be less heated. But an experiment of such consequences cannot offer so many choices, it cannot be so complicated, nor can its objectives or uses be so elusive.

Let me suggest—as a first step—a simple approach to the determination of what I believe shareholders are looking for: a rough estimation of the portion of reported historical cost earnings that needs to be reserved as some approximation of the current cost of replacing assets in use, before dividends and growth can be accommodated. My suggestion for this reserve is: the excess of current cost depreciation and cost of sales over related historical cost applicable to the shareholders' portion of the capital invested in related assets (vs. creditors' portion), a la the Hyde guidelines previously discussed. This offers what appears to be a simple solution to a complex problem; this approach is illustrated in Figure 1. In my view it will provide more relevant and understandable data for the user. But it's not as simple as it looks; refining its elements could provide the basis for considerable future experimentation and research to search out the answers to the inflation question. Obviously, a lot more thought will have to be applied before the inflation puzzle can be solved. Is it within our grasp? The FASB exposure draft seems to suggest that it is if we recognize how far we have to go.

# ARE YOU ACCOUNTING FOR INFLATION IN YOUR CAPITAL BUDGETING PROCESS?

*by D.D. Raiborn and Thomas A. Ratcliffe*

Capital budgeting involves the evaluation of capital investment proposals in terms of amount, timing, and uncertainty of cash inflows and outflows and the selection between project alternatives based upon certain investment criteria. An often overlooked aspect of capital budgeting relates to the impact of inflation on capital budgeting techniques, particularly that of incorporating price level changes into the net present value model.

## EFFECT OF INFLATION ON THE CAPITAL BUDGETING PROCESS

In a taxless world, inflation would affect cash flows and the applicable discount rate in a comparable manner, therefore, the effect on present value calculations would be irrelevant. In the traditional model,

$$NPV = C_0 + \sum_{t=1}^{x} \frac{\overline{C}_t}{(1 + K)^t},$$

inflation is contained implicitly in the overall discount rate (K) and remains constant throughout the life of the project. The implicit assumption of a constant price level is erroneous because the general price level in fact changes over the life of the project.

Given the unrealistic assumption that the price level remains unchanged throughout the life of the project, estimation of future cash flows is usually based on existing prices. The acceptance criterion, the rate of return demanded by investors, is based on current capital costs which embody a premium for anticipated inflation. If the acceptance criterion embodies an element of anticipated inflation, the cash flows of the project must be stated on an equivalent basis with the acceptance criterion.

An increase in the general price level index would then increase future revenues, wages, and material costs of the project. The effect of anticipated inflation on the outflows and inflows of the project may not always be in the same direction; therefore, the assumptions used in the analysis must be carefully stated. Various price level change assumptions should be analyzed to test the sensitivity of the project's acceptance to the different general price level changes. Probability analysis also can be incorporated into the model by assuming various price level changes and estimating the probability of their occurrence.

The traditional capital budgeting process involves the following steps:

1. *Determine the initial net capital investment and the estimated useful life of the project;*
2. *Determine incremental cash flows involving:*
   a. *Estimation of future revenues, and*
   b. *Estimation of future expenses by estimating:*
      *(1) Incremental materials and labor,*
      *(2) Incremental depreciation, and*

---

Reprinted from *Management Accounting*, September 1979, Copyright © 1979, National Association of Accountants, New York, N.Y. All rights reserved.

**TABLE 1 THE EFFECTS OF INFLATION ON CAPITAL BUDGETING PROCEDURES**

| Capital Budgeting Procedures | Effect of Inflation |
|---|---|
| 1. Determination of initial net capital investment and life of project | No effect (The asset is purchased currently.) |
| 2. Estimation of incremental future revenues | Effected (Future revenues increase or decrease with general price level effects on sale of goods and services.) |
| 3. Estimation of incremental future expense | Effected (Future expenses increase or decrease with general price level effect on materials and labor.) |
| 4. Determination of incremental depreciation | No effect (The depreciation charge is fixed at the time of asset acquisition.) |
| 5. Determination of incremental taxes | Effected (Incremental taxes are affected by the increase or decrease in sales and expenses and the tax consequences of depreciation charges based on historical cost.) |
| 6. Determination of incremental cash flows | Effected (Depreciation is based on historical cost; therefore, depreciation is constant as revenues and expenses increase or decrease with the price level.) |
| 7. Discount cash flows to present value | Effected (The discounting term should be multiplicative not additive in nature.) |

  (3) *Incremental taxes;*
 c. *Compute incremental cash flows.*

3. *Discount net cash flows at the required rate of return.*

The steps in the capital budgeting process that are affected by inflation are shown in Table 1 and are discussed in depth below.

## MODIFICATIONS TO THE NET PRESENT VALUE MODEL

Budgeting in inflationary periods involves the following modifications to the traditional process.

 *1. Cash flow estimates*

Cash flows are affected by anticipated inflation in several ways:

a. *Cash inflows arising from the sale of a service or product are affected by future prices;*

b. *Cash outflows affect future wages and material costs;*

c. *Depreciation charges are not affected because once the asset is acquired the charges are known with certainty.*

*2. The discount rate*

The cost of capital to a corporation involves three components; the pure interest rate (i), an inflation adjustment (n), and the premium associated with the degree of risks (p).

Their relationship is traditionally expressed in the denominator of the present value equation as: $(1 + K)^t$. The traditional relationship can be further defined as $(1 + n + p + i)^t$, where n is the inflation adjustment factor, p is the premium associated with risk, and i is the pure interest rate.

The additive relationship of the discount rate components ignores the fact that discount rates are stated as of the end of each period, but the discounting process occurs on a continuing basis; therefore, the cost of capital will be understated and the real net present value overstated if the additive denominator is used and the compounding effect is ignored. The relationship may be properly stated in the multiplicative form as $(1 + n)^t (1 + i + p)^t$. Only if the product of the inflation rate (n) and the real discount rate (i + p) is sufficiently small can the relationship be shown as additive: $(1 + i + p + n)^t$. Table 2 illustrates the conversion of the traditional model to a model that incorporates general price level changes. From the illustration, it should be evident why net cash flows cannot be adjusted as a single amount for price level changes, but the revenues

---

**TABLE 2  CONVERSION OF THE TRADITIONAL NET PRESENT VALUE MODEL**

The net present value model is adjusted to incorporate general price level changes as follows:

Traditional net present value model   $\quad NPV = C_o + \sum_{t=1}^{x} \dfrac{\overline{C_t}}{(1+K)^t}$

Changes to the model

*Description*  *Mathematically*

We may expand the numerator, $\overline{C_t}$, to:   $\overline{C_t} = [(I_t - O_t)(1 - T)] + D_t T$

*Where*
$\overline{C_t}$ = estimated net cash flows for period t
$I_t$ = estimated net cash inflows for period t
$O_t$ = estimated net cash outflows for period t
T = corporate tax rate
D = fixed noncash charges (i.e. depreciation)

$\sum_{n=1}^{m} n[(I_t - O_t)(1 - T)] + D_t T$

To allow for inflation the numerator may be changed to:
*Where*
n = inflation adjustment (GPL Index)   $\quad (1 + i + n + p)^t$

The denominator may be expanded to:
*Where*
i = pure interest rate
n = inflation adjustment
p = premium associated with risk

To incorporate the compounding effect, the expanded   $(1 + n)^t (1 + i + p)^t$
arithmetic denominator should be changed to the multiplicative
form which incorporates the compounding effects:

Substituting the conversion of the numerator
and denominator, the revised NPV model is:   $\quad NPV = -C_o + \sum_{t=1}^{x} \sum_{n=1}^{m} \dfrac{n[(I_t - O_t)(1 - T)] + D_t T}{(1+n)^t (1+i+p)^t}$

and expenses (excluding depreciation) must be adjusted. To allow for inflation, the first part of the numerator is multiplied by the inflation adjustment factor. The second part of the numerator, the tax savings from depreciation, is not multiplied by the inflation index. The expansion of the denominator to allow for inflation is also illustrated.

## HOW INFLATION AFFECTS CAPITAL BUDGETING DECISIONS

The following case illustrates the hazards of capital investment selection when inflation is ignored. CRR Company is reviewing a project that involves a net cash outflow of $100,000 for a new machine which is determined to have a useful life of four years. The company depreciates equipment on a straight-line basis. The controller says the company's *real* cost of capital unadjusted for inflation is 12%. The cost rate was computed by using a historical, pure interest rate of 4% plus an average premium demanded by the investors of 8%. He also determined from his economic advisors that the general price level index should rise by 10% a year for the next four years. The company anticipates the following revenues and expenses:

| Year | 1 | 2 | 3 | 4 |
|---|---|---|---|---|
| Revenue: | $60,000 | $75,000 | $75,000 | $45,000 |
| Expenses: | | | | |
| Labor | $10,000 | $10,000 | $10,000 | $ 8,000 |
| Materials | 8,000 | 12,000 | 12,000 | 8,000 |

**TABLE 3   NET PRESENT VALUE COMPUTATION**

*Project A*
*Assumption: No change in general price level*

|  | Year 1 | Year 2 | Year 3 | Year 4 |
|---|---|---|---|---|
| Revenues: | $60,000 | $75,000 | $75,000 | $45,000 |
| Expenses: | | | | |
| Labor | 10,000 | 10,000 | 10,000 | 8,000 |
| Materials | 8,000 | 12,000 | 12,000 | 8,000 |
| Depreciation | 25,000 | 25,000 | 25,000 | 25,000 |
| Total expenses | (43,000) | (47,000) | (47,000) | (41,000) |
| Before-tax profit | 17,000 | 28,000 | 28,000 | 4,000 |
| Taxes (50%) | (8,500) | (14,000) | (14,000) | (2,000) |
| After-tax profit | 8,500 | 14,000 | 14,000 | 2,000 |
| Add back: | | | | |
| Depreciation | 25,000 | 25,000 | 25,000 | 25,000 |
| After-tax cash flows | $33,500 | $39,000 | $39,000 | $27,000 |

*Conversion to present value of cash flows*

| After-tax cash flows | Discount factor (12%) | Present value of cash flows |
|---|---|---|
| $33,500 | .89286 | $ 29,910.81 |
| 39,000 | .79719 | 31,090.41 |
| 39,000 | .71178 | 27,759.42 |
| 27,000 | .63552 | 17,159.04 |
| | | 105,919.68 |
| Less cost of project | | (100,000.00) |
| Net present value | | $   5,919.68 |

66

After-tax cash flows, assuming no adjustment for price level changes, are computed in Table 3. And Table 4 illustrates the real cash flows of the machine purchase, assuming a price-level increase in each of the next four years of 10%.

The project which at first appears acceptable now appears unacceptable.

Without incorporating inflation adjustments into the process, the net present value computation is overstated. The net present

**TABLE 4   NET PRESENT VALUE COMPUTATION**

*Project A*
*Assumption: General price level increase of 10% each of the next four years.*

|  | Year 1 | Year 2 | Year 3 | Year 4 |
|---|---|---|---|---|
| GPL index | 1.10 | 1.21 | 1.331 | 1.464 |
| Revenues: | $66,000* | $90,750 | $99,825 | $65,880 |
| Expenses: |  |  |  |  |
| Labor | 11,000 | 12,100 | 13,310 | 11,712 |
| Materials | 8,800 | 14,520 | 15,972 | 11,712 |
| Depreciation | 25,000 | 25,000 | 25,000 | 25,000 |
| Total expenses | (44,800) | (51,620) | (54,282) | (48,424) |
| Before-tax profit | 21,200 | 39,130 | 45,543 | 17,456 |
| Taxes | (10,600) | (19,565) | (22,771) | (8,728) |
| After-tax profit | 10,600 | 19,565 | 22,772 | 8,728 |
| Add back: |  |  |  |  |
| Depreciation | 25,000 | 25,000 | 25,000 | 25,000 |
| Nominal after-tax cash flows | $35,600 | $44,565 | $47,772 | $33,728 |

*Conversion of nominal cash flows to real cash flows*

| Nominal after-tax cash flows | General Price Level Index | Real after-tax cash flows |
|---|---|---|
| 35,600 | 1.10 | 35,600/1.10 = 32,363.64 |
| 44,565 | 1.21 | 44,565/1.21 = 36,830.58 |
| 47,772 | 1.331 | 47,772/1.331 = 35,891.81 |
| 33,728 | 1.464 | 33,728/1.464 = 23,038.25 |

*Conversion to present value of real cash flows*

| Real after-tax cash flows | Discount factor (12%) | Present value of cash flows |
|---|---|---|
| 32,363.64 | .89286 | 28,896.20 |
| 36,830.58 | .79719 | 29,360.97 |
| 35,891.81 | .71178 | 25,547.07 |
| 23,038.25 | .63552 | 14,641.26 |
|  |  | 98,445.50 |
| Less cost of project |  | (100,000.00) |
| Net present value |  | ( 1,554.50) |

*Revenue and cash expenses were converted to purchasing power equivalents of each year, i.e., Year 1 revenues of $60,000 × 1.1 = $66,000.

value in Table 3 is $5,919.68. Cash flows are computed for four years and then discounted by 12%, the pure interest rate (4%) plus the risk premium (8%). The 12% discount factor contains no provision for inflation.

Table 4 multiplies the revenues, materials, and labor estimates by general price level index. An annual 10% inflation rate compounds to yield the following indexes:

| Year 1 | 1.0   | × 1.1 = 1.1   |
| Year 2 | 1.1   | × 1.1 = 1.21  |
| Year 3 | 1.21  | × 1.1 = 1.331 |
| Year 4 | 1.331 | × 1.1 = 1.464 |

The indexes are used first to inflate the revenues and appropriate expenses to approximate cash flows expected each year and used to deflate the resulting nominal cash flows. Nominal cash flows are converted to real cash flows (constant dollars) by dividing the nominal flows by the index applicable to each year. The real cash flows are then discounted by the 12% factor to yield a net present value of $1,554.50.

## CAPITAL BUDGETING WITH PRICE LEVEL ADJUSTMENTS

Incorporating general price level adjustments into the present value model will not always reverse the decision as to whether a particular project alternative should be accepted, but the adjustment will always yield a different net present value result. The adjustments should be considered to improve decision-making analysis. The following factors should be considered in the capital budgeting process when price level adjustments are used.

1. *Even though sales dollars, profits, and cash flows may increase with a rise in the general price level, the real rate of return (IRR) will decrease with inflation.*
2. *During a period of inflation the real cost of an asset is not totally reflected in the depreciation charges; therefore, taxable income is overstated.*
3. *The real income tax rate increases with the rate of inflation and the age of the asset (Step 2 of Table 2 illustrates this phenomenon.)*
4. *The effect of inflation is usually more significant for individual projects than for portfolios, depending on the size of the general price level adjustment, the pattern of cash flows between given projects, and the diversity of the portfolio.*
5. *General price level changes can affect the evaluation of mutually exclusive projects.*

To prevent the erroneous acceptance of capital investment projects and provide optimum resource allocation, the proposed technique should be incorporated into the capital budgeting process during times of changing prices.

# PROPOSING A MORE APPROPRIATE DIVIDEND POLICY
### by Eugene L. Zieha and Thomas T. Cheng

Currently accepted accounting principles and practices result in the recording of transactions in dollars at the time they occur. This historical

Reprinted from *Management Accounting*, September 1979, copyright © 1979, National Association of Accountants, New York, N.Y. All rights reserved.

cost approach has been criticized on the grounds that the purchasing power of the dollar changes and, therefore, accounting reports aggregate dollar balances that have different economic meanings than they had at the time the original transactions occurred. Particular concern has been expressed about using historical dollar-based accounting data for computing income tax. The ultimate criticism is that the mode of accounting measurement results in a taxing away of economic capital. We will make no attempt to solve the underlying problems of inflation and taxation. Rather, we will seek an accounting measurement on which management can base a dividend policy that will enable them to operate efficiently within the existing system.

## WHAT PROFITS SHOULD BE MAINTAINED?

Corporate managers find themselves in an ambiguous position over the possible deterioration of economic resources. There are legal restrictions on dividend payments that require dollar capital to be maintained intact. But stockholders have the practical expectation that their economic position will be continued, and this carries an implication of an obligation to maintain economic capital. This article will go beyond the minimum legalistic requirement and assume that management and stockholder alike desire the maintenance of economic capital.

In order for the corporation to maintain the economic resources committed to it by the stockholders under present conditions, it must retain some reported earnings. What we need, then, is a measurement of the amount of reported earnings that must be retained—that must be considered not available for dividends—so as to offset the impact of inflation upon the economic resources that represent the stockholders' interest. The question is: what amount of accounting measured profits must be retained so that the economic resources of the stockholders at the beginning of the period are still present at the end of that period?

## THE DIVIDEND POLICY

Our proposal is that dividend policy or, more specifically, its obverse—earnings retention—be used to maintain the economic capital represented by the stockholder equity. It is more commonplace to equate dividend policy and corporate growth. The usual idea is that the declaration of dividends in an amount less than reported profits results in corporate growth when corporate size is measured on a dollar basis. But given inflation, does the corporation grow, remain constant, or contract under such a dividend policy if corporate size is measured in real economic terms?

Let us, therefore, seek a dividend policy that is appropriate under conditions of inflation. What amount of reported earnings should be retained in order to maintain the economic resources of the company? The guideline we propose is dependent on the validity of the hypothesis that retaining an amount of reported earnings equal to the product of the residual stockholder equity multiplied by the inflation rate for the period will protect both the residual owners and the corporation from the economic impact of inflation.

In order to get a clearer image of the hypothesis, we will make several simplifying assumptions. Then we can turn to a more complicated case after the simplified case is understood.

*Assumption One*—The corporation is financed entirely by stockholder contributions except for the routine short-term credit items that are a part of the working capital computation.

*Assumption Two*—The reported after-tax profits are sufficient, or more than sufficient, to offset any erosion of capital that is occurring because of monetary inflation. The possibility of retaining enough reported earnings to offset inflation must exist if dividend policy is to provide a practical solution to the problem.

*Assumption Three*—The company desires to be in a maintenance of capital mode, not in a contraction mode or in a growth mode. Therefore, all reported earnings beyond those needed to maintain stockholder economic capital will be distributed to the stockholders as dividends.

Note that reported profits are those computed by using currently accepted accounting methods. What we will call for is a retention of some of such reported profits in order to maintain economic capital. This may imply to some that reported profits retained to maintain capital are not really profits. In order not to digress, let us emphasize that the question of what is profit and what is not profit is not the subject of this article.

## TESTING THE POLICY

Our proposed policy is relatively easy to state and apply. Each year a part of the reported income is retained to provide for the maintenance of economic capital. The amount retained is calculated by multiplying the common stockholders' equity as of the start of the year by the rate of inflation during that year.

This equity is usually the sum of common stock, the premium on common stock, and retained earnings. Consideration should also be given to any other accounts that are a part of the residual equity. Several acceptable inflation indices are readily available from public sources. For example, the period's beginning and ending GNP deflators (1972 = 100) may be used to arrive at the rate to be used. The technical aspects of what is the amount of common stockholders' equity and which is the appropriate price index to use are not relevant here. The important question is whether the proposed policy will protect both the stockholders and the company against the expropriation of capital by inflation. More specifically, will the policy protect them against capital impairment caused by dividend payments based on reported profits calculated from historical cost figures in times of price-level increases?

The hypothesis was tested by use of the "Accountancy Model for Analysis of Business Policy."[1] The accountancy model is based on a series of computer programs that accept various relationships and factors and provide a "what if" series of balance sheets and income statements. Proper handling of changes in the value of the monetary unit require that both real and monetary units be used in the projections. Productive capacity and sales are stated in terms of units of goods and then translated to dollar amounts dependent on the price factors of the respective years.

The model is constructed so that the sales potential is held steady in terms of units for the multiple year "what if" projection. The model starts in a steady-state position with 10% of the productive capacity necessary to produce the goods to be sold having been obtained in each of the prior ten years. Physical assets are given a ten-year life for both depreciation and useful life purposes with no salvage value. Additional computer logic instructs the model to replace expired assets in order to maintain the productive capacity necessary to produce the number of units the market will take. The full productive capacity will not, however, be replaced if the financial resources are not available.

This model experimentation features a series of steps by which the inflation rate is applied to the beginning stockholder equity so as to calculate the amount of reported profits to be retained. All profits above this amount are distributed as dividends. This means that the funds available to replace fully-depreciated and expired fixed assets are equal to the sum of current period depreciation and the retained earnings computed therein.

Given other conditions compatible with the investigation, the test is whether or not the company can replace productive capacity as time progresses. Capital impairment would be indicated if the fixed assets could not be replaced. In this case, the dividend policy (reported profit retention policy) would be deemed unsatisfactory. The policy could also be questioned if there were an accumulation of funds over the amount needed to provide fixed asset replacements.

Successive runs of the model, each a 20-year projection, were undertaken. We used inflation rates of 0%, 3%, 6%, 9%, and 12%.

---

[1] The "Accountancy Model for Analysis for Business Policy" is a series of computer programs developed by E.L. Zieha for accountancy and business research and for instructional purposes. A discussion of the steady-state starting point as regards fixed assets appears in E.L. Zieha, "Gross Fixed Asset Analysis." *Budgeting* (now *Managerial Planning*), November/December 1967.

The steady-state starting position included the application of these sets of successively higher costs to each 10% of productive capacity block of assets obtained in the ten preliminary years. Additional experimentation included a one-time change to a higher price level, a move from one price plateau to another.

The application of the dividend policy (profit retention policy) resulted in the maintenance of real capital in each of the runs and did not result in an accumulation of excess funds. These experiments in which we used simplifying assumptions uphold the validity of the policy in maintaining the economic capital of common stockholders and company alike.

## AN ILLUSTRATION

The twenty-year "what if" computer simulation we used to test the proposed policy produces results too voluminous to present here. We will, however, provide an abridged example to illustrate the basic idea in the analytical approach.

Let's assume an ongoing business whose only assets are depreciable fixed assets. A portion, one-fifth on a physical measurement, have been acquired on the first day of each of five consecutive years. The present time is immediately before closing on the last day of the fifth year. Straight-line depreciation is used and both economic life and physical life are five years. Prices are increasing at the rate of 6% each year.

The five blocks of assets, each with a productive capacity of 10,000 units, cost successively larger amounts as shown in column A of Table 1. Column B shows the accumulated depreciation and Column C shows the asset book values as they were carried during the fifth year. Any current assets that exist are assumed to be exactly offset by current liabilities. Therefore, the common stockholders' equity during the year, prior to computation of fifth year results, is equal to the fixed asset book value at that time of $35,135.

The fifth year is profitable. The company follows the policy of paying out as dividends all reported earnings above an amount computed by multiplying the common stock equity by the inflation rate for the year ($35,135 x .06 = $2,108). Therefore, the common stock equity going into the sixth year will be $37,243.

The important question is whether or not the company is able to replace its assets as they depreciate. The case in point is the block of assets acquired in the first year that has a productive capacity of 10,000 units and costs $10,000. This block of assets is fully depreciated and goes out of service at the end of the fifth

TABLE 1 FIXED ASSET DATA AND EQUITY; FIFTH YEAR PRIOR TO CLOSING; INFLATION RATE 6% PER YEAR

| Year Asset Acquired | A<br>Asset Cost | B<br>Accumulated Depreciation | C<br>Book Value | D<br>Current Depreciation |
|---|---|---|---|---|
| 1 | $10,000 | $8,000 | $ 2,000 | $ 2,000 |
| 2 | 10,600 | 6,360 | 4,240 | 2,120 |
| 3 | 11,236 | 4,494 | 6,742 | 2,247 |
| 4 | 11,910 | 2,382 | 9,528 | 2,382 |
| 5 | 12,625 | —0— | 12,625 | 2,525 |
| Total (equity = book value) | | | 35,135 | 11,274 |
| 6% Capital maintenance | | | 2,108 | 2,108 |
| Equity for year six | | | $37,243 | |
| Resources available* | | | | $13,382 |

*Cost of replacement assets is $12,625 x 1.06 = $13,382.

year. As there was a 6% per year increase in the price level, the cost of a block of assets with a productive capacity of 10,000 units is 6% higher than the cost of similar assets in the fifth year. This sixth year cost ($12,625 × 1.06 = $13,382) is also $10,000 times $(1.06)^5$, which is $13,382. Therefore, it will take that amount of funds to replace the assets that cost $10,000 five years ago with assets of an equal productive capacity.

Depreciation charges for the fifth year are shown in column D. In this example, they indicate an equal amount of funds flow of $11,274. The dividend policy, as noted previously, left $2,108 of the reported profits for the fifth year in the retained earnings account as an addition to common stockholders' equity. This also would be offset by an equal amount of funds. Therefore, the funds available to replace the fully depreciated assets ($11,274 + $2,108 = $13,382) represent exactly the cost of a block of assets with a productive capacity of 10,000 units at the start of year six.

Table 2 shows the asset cost, accumulated depreciation, and book value on the books at the start of, and during, the sixth year after acquiring the new block of assets. This better illustrates how the model moves forward through time.

So far, what we have presented illustrates analytical support of the proposed policy under the simple assumed conditions. We obtained similar supportive results with assets of other years of life and with other depreciation methods. Such tests included the use of sum-of-the-years-digits and declining balance depreciation.

## COMPLICATING CONDITIONS

The test of the proposed dividend policy (reported profit retention policy) under simplified conditions gave us encouraging results. The simplified conditions include a constant rate of inflation; equal physical blocks of fixed assets being acquired each year; and 100% common stock financing. Now let's continue the experimentation by relaxing each of the simplified conditions.

Is the proposed policy valid in a case in which the rate of inflation is not constant over the life of the string of assets? Preliminary evidence indicates a validity that may be difficult to trace or illustrate with multiple changes in the rate of inflation. Therefore, the proposed policy is first tested with a projection in which only one price change occurred during the term of years. No inflation or deflation is assumed except in one year in which a 6% inflation is assumed. Another case included a constant 6% per year inflation except for a single year in which the rate was only 3% and

### TABLE 2 FIXED ASSET DATA AND EQUITY; SIXTH YEAR PRIOR TO CLOSING; INFLATION RATE 6% PER YEAR

| Year Asset Acquired | A<br>Asset Cost | B<br>Accumulated Depreciation | C<br>Book Value | D<br>Current Depreciation |
|---|---|---|---|---|
| 2 | $10,600 | $8,480 | $ 2,120 | $ 2,120 |
| 3 | 11,236 | 6,741 | 4,495 | 2,247 |
| 4 | 11,910 | 4,764 | 7,146 | 2,382 |
| 5 | 12,625 | 2,525 | 10,100 | 2,525 |
| 6 | 13,382 | —0— | 13,382 | 2,676 |
| Total (equity = book value) | | | 37,243 | 11,950 |
| 6% Capital maintenance | | | 2,235 | 2,235 |
| Equity for year seven | | | $39,478 | |
| Resources available* | | | | $14,185 |

*Cost of replacement assets is $13,382 × 1.06 = $14,185.

yet another assumed a constant 6% inflation rate except for one year in which the price change was 9%. The results supported the proposed policy in each of these cases even though the results were not evident in a single year. They could only be reconciled with the policy by considering all the years in which the assets obtained at a higher or lower price were in use.

The case in which higher prices occurred in only one year resulted in resources being increased in that year beyond the amount required to replace the assets going out of service. The inflation factor was applied to a common stockholders' equity which was equal to the sum of the book value of five blocks of fixed assets. But only one block of fixed assets had to be replaced in that year. The current inflation adjustment in each of the next four years was in itself insufficient to provide the additional funds needed to replace the assets going out of service. However, a drawing upon the excess funds provided in the year of price level increase made possible the replacement of the physical assets in each of the four succeeding years. The excess provision in the one year was exactly equal to the sum of the deficiencies in the next four years. Similar, but opposite, results were obtained in the case in which the rate of inflation was lower in one year than in the others.

This timing difference between provision of funds and replacement of assets may cause some confusion. The danger exists that management may view a temporary excess of funds as funds either available for growth or free to be used for some other purpose. But those assets that offset the portion of reported profits retained for capital maintenance are needed for the replacement of fixed assets, either currently or eventually. Temporary use of such funds elsewhere is reasonable if management recognizes the timing problem. Additional provisions of funds are required if true corporate growth is to be achieved.

A similar experiment tested the case in which the physical amount of assets acquired was not equal in each year. Fixed assets with a productive capacity of 10,000 units had been acquired each year at increasingly higher prices in the basic model. This simplifying assumption was relaxed by a case in which physical assets with a productive capacity of 14,000 units were acquired at the end of the sixth year. Additional common stockholder investment was required to provide for the purchase of assets with the 4,000 units of increased capacity. In the years seven through ten, the funds available (equal to current depreciation plus capital maintenance adjustment) exceeded the amount needed to replace the 10,000 units of productive capacity that went out of service in each of these years. Depreciation on the extra 4,000 unit capacity was being recognized in these years. The funds provided currently in year eleven under the proposed policy would not be sufficient to replace assets with a productive capacity of 14,000 units. However, the insufficiency in year eleven would be exactly offset by the excesses from years seven through ten. This experiment yielded additional evidence to support the validity of the proposed capital maintenance policy.

## DEBT FINANCING

The debt financing of fixed assets must be given consideration in the test of the proposed policy. This proposal differs from various suggestions for price level adjusted accounting in that the proposed adjustment is based on the common stockholders' equity rather than on the company assets. To the extent fixed assets are financed by debt, no specific provision is made for their replacement at a higher cost. The additional funds needed will have to be obtained by borrowing a larger number of dollars.

Such additional borrowing does not increase the debt position of the company in real terms. This is because the borrowing is in terms of physical assets rather than dollars. Assume that 30% of the dollar cost of an asset was financed by debt several years ago. Now the asset is to be replaced and the dollar cost has risen because of monetary inflation. The financing of 30% of a replacement asset of the same productive capacity, therefore, does not represent a new level of economic debt even though the dollar amount has increased.

The basic model can also be used to test

the validity of this debt approach. Assume a situation in which 30% of all fixed assets are financed by long-term debt. Assume further that regular debt payments are made equal to 30% of current depreciation. Debt will be equal to 30% of asset book value and, therefore, also equal to 30% of total corporate equity.

Now refer back to Table 1. Under the assumed debt policy, the equity of $35,135 shown in column C would be represented by $24,594 (70%) common stockholders' equity and $10,541 (30%) long-term debt. The new block of assets to be purchased at the start of year six has a dollar cost of $13,382.

Three sources of funds are used to provide for the purchase of the replacement assets. Assuming the business is profitable, the depreciation of $11,274 is offset by an equivalent amount of funds. Payment of debt uses $3,382 (30%) of this amount and the balance of $7,892 (70%) is available for asset replacement. In addition, a capital maintenance adjustment of $1,476 represents 6% of the $24,594 common stockholders' equity. Furthermore, debt financing of $4,015, which is 30% of the $13,382 new asset cost, is the third source of funds. The amounts available summarized:

| | |
|---|---:|
| Depreciation equivalency | $ 7,892 |
| Capital maintenance adjustment | 1,476 |
| Debt financing | 4,015 |
| Total available | $13,383 |

A further reconciliation of these figures over time can contribute to the understanding of this test of the proposed policy. Assets will be as shown in Table 2 at the completion of the indicated acquisition. The total equity will be $37,243, of which $26,070 (70%) represents stockholders' equity, and $11,173 (30%) represents debt. The stockholder figure can be reconciled by taking the $24,594 shown above and adding the $1,476 capital maintenance provision to obtain $26,070. The debt figure can be reconciled by starting with the $10,541 shown above, deducting the $3,382 payoff, and adding the new debt of $4,015 to obtain $11,174. This example of debt financing provides additional evidence to support the validity of the proposed policy.

**COMPOSITE OF SIMPLE CASES**

Separate favorable examples have dealt with a change in the rate of inflation, a change in the quantity of physical assets, and debt financing. Actual business situations usually include multiple changes in inflation rates and asset quantities during the life of the chain of assets. Debt financing is the general expectation. A computer model run or worksheet analysis that would consider all these conditions simultaneously would be very complicated to present and reconcile. The complicated real situation, however, can be viewed as a composite of many simple cases, some of which we have just covered. We hold that the individual underlying forces are there even though they are shielded from view.

# General Price-Level Accounting

# 2

# CONSTANT DOLLAR ACCOUNTING

*by Robert D. Baumann, MBA*

Constant dollar disclosures are conventional historical cost disclosures adjusted for changes in the general purchasing power of the dollar. As a result, constant dollar disclosures do not change the accounting principles used to develop financial information and are analogous to restating financial statements from one currency to another, much like what is required by FASB #8, Accounting for the Translation of Foreign Currency Transactions and Foreign Currency Financial Statements. Conventional historical cost disclosures are based on dollars with varying amounts of purchasing power; constant dollar disclosures merely adjust these dollars of varying purchasing power to dollars with equivalent purchasing power. Constant dollar disclosures change the measuring unit used in the disclosures from the historical dollar to the general purchasing power dollar.

## USEFULNESS OF AND NEED FOR CONSTANT DOLLAR ACCOUNTING

We are living in a period characterized by a high rate of inflation. In 1979, the general rate of inflation rose by 13.3%, one of the highest levels ever to be achieved in the United States. The problem which this spiraling inflation brings about for accountants is that in the present-day financial statements where measurements are made in nominal dollars, there is no allowance explicitly made for changes in the purchasing power of the dollar. In order to measure the impact of inflation on accounting, we must address the changes in the general purchasing power of the monetary unit used in accounting measures.[1] Therefore, many people feel that information is needed based on measurements that are indeed made in units having the same general purchasing power, rather than arbitrarily, and wrongly, assuming that the units of measure in the financial statements are stable, as the present-day historical cost statements do. The method which attempts to do this very thing is known as "constant dollar accounting."[2]

At stake here is more than just the possibility, or better yet the probability, that users of these historical cost financial statements will make an uneducated or wrong decision, but the theoretical framework itself of these historical cost/nominal dollar statements which rely on the assumption of a monetary system where the unit of measure is stable. It is the belief of some that in order to uphold the confidence now placed in financial reporting, one must recognize that earnings do not represent the recovery of the real cost of investment, but that as mentioned earlier, there can be no earnings unless the purchasing power of capital is maintained.[3]

In trying to determine just why it is that people invest, one finds that one of the main purposes is that they expect or would like to earn a return on their investment which will sooner or later be available in the form of cash to meet any expenditures which might arise. Some people, especially those not investing in growth but high yield stocks, are looking for a cash flow pattern which is rela-

---

Robert D. Baumann, "Critical Analysis of FASB No. 33" (Master's thesis, Pace University, May 1980). Used by permission of Robert D. Baumann.

[1] Robert T. Sprouse, "Inflation: Symptom or Disease?" *Financial Analysts Journal* (January/February, 1979), p. 75.

[2] Financial Accounting Standards Board, *Statement of Financial Accounting Standards No. 33* (Stamford, Conn.: Financial Accounting Foundation, 1979), p. 4.

[3] Ibid., p. 27.

tively constant, enabling them to meet any fixed expenditures that they may have. One also finds that investors are also very much concerned not only with the absolute amount of cash which they receive, but also with its purchasing power. Receiving a fixed amount of money each year does no one any good if the purchasing power of these fixed dollars is declining. The investors' need for this type of information can be met by the use of a constant dollar measuring unit.[4]

## REQUIRED DISCLOSURE

As mandated by FASB #33, there are certain disclosure requirements associated with the constant dollar approach to financial reporting. Information derived by using constant dollar methods is required on income from continuing operations for the current fiscal year for which the statements are issued. As a minimum, an enterprise must also restate individually its inventory, property, plant and equipment, cost of goods sold, and depreciation, depletion and amortization expense on a constant dollar basis. Also, it must restate to a "recoverable amount" any inventory or property, plant and equipment if these recoverable amounts are less than the traditional historical cost amounts. The term "recoverable amount," as defined in the statement, means the "current worth of the net amount of cash expected to be recoverable from the use or sale of an asset."[5] This measure need only be used if for a group of assets their value measured in recoverable amount is materially and permanently lower than their value based on an historical cost/constant dollar calculation. The above amounts, with the exception of the recoverable amounts, will be converted by using the average level over the fiscal year of the Consumer Price Index for All Urban Consumers. As was stated, these are the minimum requirements. An enterprise is free to, and even encouraged to, make a comprehensive restatement of the financial statements on a historical cost/constant dollar basis. If this be the case, the enterprise has its choice of using either the average or year-end Consumer Price Index for that fiscal year. The accounting principles used in computing both the historical cost/constant dollar and historical cost/nominal dollar income should be the same. The only item which is changed for the purposes of this measurement is the measuring unit itself. Also required to be included in the supplementary information is the purchasing power gain or loss on net monetary items in the current fiscal year.[6]

## METHODS OF CALCULATION

### Calculation of Lower Recoverable Amounts

There are only two acceptable ways of measuring the recoverable amounts of assets mentioned in FASB #33; either the *net realizable values* or the *value in use* of the assets concerned may be used. Most accountants are familiar with the term "net realizable value." This amount is used in determining market for the lower of cost or market valuation for some assets. Net realizable values are quite simply the amounts of money one would expect to receive upon the sale of an asset less the costs which would be incurred in order to sell the asset. The alternative method, which most people would agree would be the theoretically correct method of valuing all assets on the balance sheet, but which is quite literally impossible to do objectively, is called "value in use." An asset's value in use is represented by the net present value of all future cash flows expected to be received from the use of the asset by the firm. The key question here is: at what rate should these flows be discounted? It is doubtful that any firm will attempt to use this method of valuation in deriving an asset's recoverable amount.[7]

### The CPI as a Measuring Unit

The only other types of measurements involved with the constant dollar approach are those using the CPI. While the calculations involving the CPI are fairly easy, the real problem here,

---

[4] Ibid., p. 68.
[5] Ibid., p. 21.
[6] Ibid., pp. 11-21.
[7] Ibid., pp. 21-22.

and indeed with all of constant dollar accounting, is the theoretical justification for using the CPI. In trying to determine just what base should be used for the measuring unit, the FASB considered three alternatives. The first alternative was to use dollars whose purchasing power was equal to those of dollars used in the base year used by the Bureau of Labor Statistics in constructing the CPI. At present, this base period is 1967. The CPI is stated in terms of whether or not the purchasing power of the dollar has increased or decreased since 1967. Quite obviously, it has decreased significantly. The second alternative was to use dollars whose purchasing power was equivalent to that of a dollar represented by the average level of the CPI for the fiscal year under consideration. The third alternative was to use dollars whose purchasing power was equivalent not to that of a dollar represented by the average level of the CPI for the year under consideration, but equivalent to a dollar represented by the year-end level of the CPI for the fiscal year under consideration. The Board opted for the second alternative.[8]

The Board felt that using a unit based on the average purchasing power for the year dollar had a number of advantages over the other alternative. One computational advantage is that any revenue and expenses which are spread out evenly throughout the year can be assumed to already be expressed in historical cost/constant dollar amounts. Also, the cost of goods sold and depreciation expense measurement on a current cost basis tend to be very close to their measures in the average for the year constant dollar measurement. Therefore, comparing the current cost and historical cost/constant dollar amounts with those in the primary financial statements will cause less confusion if some of the new amounts are measured similarly.[9]

## CONSUMER PRICE INDEX

The CPI is by far the most widely used index to measure the effects of inflation. It is felt that this index is the most valid because it is relevant to more people than any other index. Implicit in the CPI index are several basic assumptions which go into its makeup. Whether these assumptions are valid or not is the key to the use of the CPI in constant dollar accounting.

The CPI assumes that everyone spends the same percentages of their income in each of seven major categories. These categories are food, housing, transportation, medical, apparel, entertainment, and other. For each of these categories, further subdivisions irrelevant to this discussion are made. The CPI weights these various spending components arbitrarily and ignores completely important items such as income and social security taxes in its calculations.[10] The weights assigned by the CPI to these various categories were determined by a study of consumer purchases back in 1972 and 1973. An immediate problem which comes to mind is the possible irrelevancy of these weights. Everyone knows that the same mix and/or products are not, in all probability, being bought today. A prize example of this would be energy, and more specifically, oil. Today, the American people are cutting back drastically on their use of oil, whereas in 1972 and 1973, people were almost wasting it. Also, the proportion of people's income which goes to energy today is easily double that of the proportion which went to it in 1972 and 1973.[11]

Another controversial point is that included in the CPI category of housing is the fact that these housing costs are developed based on the assumption that each home is being rebought and refinanced every month. In the CPI for October of 1979, housing costs alone raised the index by 1.5%; this accounts for almost 12% of the total rise. It is significant to note that most consumers never feel this bite. Along these lines is the fact that the CPI fails to take into account that almost all real estate is increasing in value, partially offsetting these higher costs. It would appear then, that the major problem presen-

---

[8] Ibid., p. 91.
[9] Ibid., p. 92.

[10] Mark F. Polanis, "Will Accountants Go Off the Dollar Standard?" *Magazine of Bank Administration* (November, 1978), pp. 43-44.
[11] *New York Times*, October 22, 1979, Sec. IV, p. 2, Cols. 1-2.

ted by the CPI is that it may very well overstate the effects of inflation for the man on the street. It may overstate it due to the three factors just mentioned: the choice of the base period, the weight assigned to each category, and the effects of the assumptions concerning housing costs.[12]

## GROSS NATIONAL PRODUCT DEFLATOR

The other widely used inflation indicator is the GNP implicit price deflator. The GNP deflator measures the increase in cost only of goods actually produced. For the week ending October 19, 1979, the GNP deflator for the third quarter had an annualized rate of 8.4%. The CPI, on the other hand, had increased at an annualized rate of 12.7%. The CPI is just over half again as big, or fifty percent more than the GNP deflator. In general, the GNP deflator has shown much smaller increases than the CPI for many reasons, only the major two of which will be mentioned here. Since relatively few homes are produced in any given period, while the GNP deflator takes this into account, the CPI does not. The amount of housing costs alone raised the CPI by 1.5%; in the last period this figure represents almost 20% of the GNP deflator for the same period. You can see the effect that such an assumption has on the perceived effect of inflation on the economy. The second major reason for the disparity between the two measures is the way in which energy is handled. The GNP deflator takes into account the decreased use by Americans today of energy, while as mentioned previously, the CPI assumes that they are as lax in their use of energy today as they were in 1972 and 1973. This clearly is not the case.[13]

Turning to the other side of the coin, one invalid assumption which is partly responsible for the GNP deflator constantly being smaller than the CPI is the fact that the GNP deflator only measures domestic economic activity, so that an item such as increased prices for imported oil never enters into its calculation. For all the reasons stated above, it is felt by most experts that the true rate of inflation lies somewhere in between the two indices.[14]

## ADVANTAGES OF CONSTANT DOLLAR ACCOUNTING

Just discussed were some of the major assumptions which go into the makeup of the two most widely quoted indices for measuring inflation. Since FASB #33 mandates the use of the CPI, the discussion here will center around that index. Also, in discussing the validity of constant dollar accounting, one must necessarily devote much of the discussion to its main feature, the CPI. That is exactly what will be done here in presenting the advantages and disadvantages of constant dollar accounting.

One of the main benefits that constant dollar accounting has going for it is the simple fact that it is now, today, ready for implementation. It is the most readily available method for coping with the impact of inflation on accounting. It is not even experimental; the only thing experimental about constant dollar accounting concerns what the results will tell about a given enterprise. Some people even go so far as to say that the CPI, when used as a basis for constant dollar accounting, gives the maximum achievement of the quality of relevance of any method presently under consideration.[15] Another great advantage of constant dollar accounting is that the CPI is reliable. By this is meant that the CPI is objective as compared to using any of a wide array of current cost valuations. Many people also argue that the CPI is a relevant measure when dividends per share and market price per share are shown, because stockholders can relate these cash flows to their own cash flow needs. The CPI is the index which makes the most sense for the shareholder. The shareholder can relate better to this index in view of the fact that the dividends and market

---

[12] Ibid.

[13] Ibid.

[14] Ibid.

[15] Robert T. Sprouse, "Inflation: Symptom or Disease?" *Financial Analysts Journal* (January/February, 1979), p. 14.

prices for his or her shares are directly affected by the purchasing power of the consumer's dollar. This relates back to a consumer's initial reason for investing, to get back a dependable pattern of cash flows in order to meet expenses. Lastly, when a base period is used, such as 1967 in the CPI, trend analysis is facilitated. Trend analysis, it should be mentioned, is one of the more important areas into which financial analysts look when evaluating an enterprise.[16]

## DISADVANTAGES OF CONSTANT DOLLAR ACCOUNTING

The CPI, of course, is not without its disadvantages as a measure of inflation. First of all, the CPI, as are all indexes of this type, is merely an average. As most people will agree, in reality, this so-called average probably does not apply to anyone. The average consumer just does not exist, nor does the average enterprise. What this says is that while the CPI will give an approximation of the effect of inflation on the consumer or firm, it will be specific for no one person or no one firm. A sharp critic of constant dollar accounting is Harold M. Williams, the chairman of the SEC, who states that he cannot see how any company which has a major investment in its inventory and property, plant and equipment can use constant dollar accounting and have it convey any meaningful or relevent data for any given period of time.[17]

Getting back to the idea of the average firm, the CPI has absolutely no relevance to many companies such as the steel and oil companies. Using this index, little will be known about the preservation of the purchasing power of the corporate assets.[18]

Another argument against the constant dollar method is that it does not really reflect changing prices. It implicitly assumes that the assets of major corporations are affected by inflation like all other sectors of the economy. This is just not so. As was stated earlier, the CPI is "worked up" based on a history of consumer purchases. How relevant can a figure derived in this manner be to capital intensive industries such as steel and public utilities, even though it might serve a useful purpose for some manufacturing and consumer goods firms. Lastly, one of the most basic problems is that the meaning or results of constant dollar accounting are not easily understood. Specifically, the meaning of general price level adjusted cost is ". . . neither what it would cost to buy the item nor what the item could be sold for. It is the cost of the item when originally purchased expressed in current sized dollars."[19] Since this price probably does not exist or appear in the real world, an interpretation of this figure will be and is most difficult at best. Knowing the textbook definition of constant dollar accounting and interpreting the results are two extremely different matters.

---

[16] Philip L. Defliese, "Inflation Accounting: Pursuing the Elusive," *Journal of Accountancy* (May, 1979), p. 61.

[17] "Inflation Accounting," *Business Week* (October 15, 1979), p. 72.

[18] Philip L. Defliese, "Inflation Accounting: Pursuing the Elusive," *Journal of Accountancy* (May, 1979), p. 60.

[19] Laurence A. Friedman, "What Is Current Value?" *Motor Freight Controller* (February, 1979), p. 7.

# EXAMPLES OF PRICE-LEVEL ADJUSTMENT COMPUTATIONS

The purpose of the following demonstration is to provide a simplified illustration of the essential features of price-level adjustments of financial statements, and to contribute to an understanding of the effect of price-level changes. It is not intended to provide a detailed technical guide for the use of an accountant in preparing a set of adjusted financial statements for an actual case.[1] It will be followed by comments on certain variations and special problems not covered in the basic demonstration.

The illustration will include a two-year period, beginning with the opening of business. Adjusted income statements will be prepared for each of the two years, and adjusted balance sheets for the opening of business, the close of the first year, and the close of the second year.

The following price-level index numbers are assumed for use in the demonstration:

| | | | |
|---|---|---|---|
| Opening of business | 150 | Second year—average | 190 |
| First year—average | 160 | Second year—end | 200 |
| First year—end | 175 | | |

The financial statements will be restated in terms of the *dollar at the end of the second year*, that is, in terms of the *"current dollar"* when the index is at 200.

Other assumptions are:

1. The inventory is priced on a first-in, first-out (Fifo) basis.
2. All revenue and expenses, except for depreciation and that portion of the cost of goods sold represented by the *beginning inventory, are earned or incurred evenly throughout each year, i.e., in effect, the transactions occur at the average price level of the year.*
3. *Dividends are declared and paid at the end of each year.*
4. *At the beginning of the second year, $50,000 of the long-term liabilities are paid in cash, and $300,000 are converted to capital stock.*
5. *Acquisitions of plant and equipment take place at the opening of business and at the close of the first year. The land on which the plant is located is held under a lease, so all items of plant and equipment are subject to depreciation. The average depreciation rate is 10 per cent a year on the straight-line basis.*

## ADJUSTMENT OF INCOME AND RETAINED EARNINGS STATEMENTS

### Sales

Sales took place evenly throughout the year, so, in effect, they took place at the average dollar of the year, i.e., when the price index was at the average for the year. The adjustment of the sales amounts to the end-of-second-year dollar, or the current dollar, would be:

First year:   $ 800,000 × 200/160 = $1,000,000
Second year: $1,000,000 × 200/190 = $1,052,632

### Cost of Goods Sold

Under the first-in, first-out (Fifo) method of inventory pricing, the cost of goods sold is

---

From *Accounting Research Study No. 6,* "Reporting the Financial Effects of Price-Level Changes." Copyright 1963 by the American Institute of Certified Public Accountants, Inc.
[1]Technical aspects of price-level adjustments are discussed in the following publications, among others: Ralph C. Jones, *Price Level Changes and Financial Statements—Case Studies of Four Companies.* American Accounting Association, 1955. Ralph C. Jones, *Effects of Price Level Changes on Business Income, Capital, and Taxes.* American Accounting Association, 1956. Ralph D. Kennedy and Stewart Y. McMullen, *Financial Statements—Form, Analysis, and Interpretation,* 3rd ed., Chaps. 17-21. Richard D. Irwin, Inc., 1957. Perry Mason, *Price-Level Changes and Financial Statements—Basic Concepts and Methods.* American Accounting Association, 1956.

### 1: COMPARATIVE INCOME STATEMENT (HISTORICAL BASIS)

|  | First Year | Second Year |
|---|---|---|
| Sales | $800,000 | $1,000,000 |
| Operating Expenses: | | |
|   Cost of goods sold | $470,000 | $ 600,000 |
|   Depreciation | 30,000 | 40,000 |
|   Other expenses (including income tax) | 280,000 | 300,000 |
| Total Operating Expenses | $780,000 | $ 940,000 |
| Net Profit from Operations | $ 20,000 | $ 60,000 |

### 2: COMPARATIVE STATEMENT OF RETAINED EARNINGS (HISTORICAL BASIS)

|  | | |
|---|---|---|
| Retained Earnings, Beginning of Year | $ — | $15,000 |
| Net Profit from Operations | 20,000 | 60,000 |
| Total | $20,000 | $75,000 |
| Dividends to Stockholders | 5,000 | 10,000 |
| Retained Earnings, End of Year | $15,000 | $65,000 |

### 3: COMPARATIVE BALANCE SHEET (HISTORICAL BASIS)

|  | Opening of Business | End of First Year | End of Second Year |
|---|---|---|---|
| **Assets** | | | |
| Cash, Receivables and Other Monetary Items | $200,000 | $195,000 | $235,000 |
| Inventories | 250,000 | 300,000 | 200,000 |
| Plant and Equipment | 300,000 | 400,000 | 400,000 |
| Less: Accumulated depreciation | — | (30,000) | (70,000) |
| Total Assets | $750,000 | $865,000 | $765,000 |
| **Liabilities** | | | |
| Current Liabilities | $100,000 | $200,000 | $100,000 |
| Long-term Liabilities | 350,000 | 350,000 | — |
| Total Liabilities | $450,000 | $550,000 | $100,000 |
| **Stockholders' Equity** | | | |
| Capital Stock | $300,000 | $300,000 | $600,000 |
| Retained Earnings | — | 15,000 | 65,000 |
| Total Stockholders' Equity | $300,000 | $315,000 | $665,000 |
| Total Liabilities and Stockholders' Equity | $750,000 | $865,000 | $765,000 |

measured by the beginning inventory plus a portion of the merchandise purchased during the period.

*First year.* The beginning inventory was acquired at the opening of business when the index number was 150. The merchandise purchases were made at the average price level of the year, or when the index number was 160. The adjustments to express the cost of goods sold in terms of the current dollar would be:

| | | |
|---|---|---|
| Beginning inventory | $250,000 × 200/150 = | $333,333 |
| Portion of merchandise purchases | 220,000 × 200/160 = | 275,000 |
| Cost of goods sold | $470,000 | $608,333 |

The traditional calculation of cost of goods sold could have been used. (The merchandise purchases of $520,000 is derived from the other related figures.)

| | | |
|---|---|---|
| Beginning inventory | $250,000 × 200/150 = | $333,333 |
| Merchandise purchases | 520,000 × 200/160 = | 650,000 |
| | $770,000 | $983,333 |
| Ending inventory | 300,000 × 200/160 = | 375,000 |
| Cost of goods sold | $470,000 | $608,333 |

*Second year.* The beginning inventory of $300,000 at historical cost, or $375,000 as adjusted to the current dollar, is carried forward from the close of the first year. An additional $300,000 (historical cost) is a part of the merchandise purchased during the second year when the price index was at 190. The adjustments are:

| | | |
|---|---|---|
| Beginning inventory | $300,000 × 200/160 = | $375,000 |
| Portion of merchandise purchases | 300,000 × 200/190 = | 315,789 |
| Cost of goods sold | $600,000 | $690,789 |

## Depreciation

The most time-consuming step in the adjustment process is the "aging" of the depreciable property and the corresponding adjustment of the periodic depreciation. Strictly speaking, the date of acquisition of each item of property must be determined as well as its cost, and the corresponding depreciation must be adjusted to the current-dollar basis. Once the "aging" process has been carried out, however, it can be kept up to date with a relatively small amount of time and effort. Various simplifications can be introduced. All items acquired at approximately the same time, such as a month or a quarter, can be grouped together and treated as a single item, unless the depreciation charge to operations must be broken down for more detailed accounting purposes. An arbitrary cut-off point can sometimes be used for the older items of property, which are often a small proportion of the total, and all items acquired prior to a certain point of time can be treated as though they were all acquired at the cut-off point. Where a very large number of similar units of equipment are in use, statistical methods are available for the aging calculation. Survivorship tables, similar to the mortality tables used by insurance companies, may be employed to determine under rules of statistical probability how many items are in use, classified by date of acquisition.

Ordinarily the simplest way to revise the depreciation charges is to apply the normal depreciation rates to the adjusted cost amounts. In the demonstration, the $300,000 of plant and equipment used during the first year was acquired at the beginning of that year, and the addition of $100,000 was acquired at the close of the first year. The calculations are:

| | |
|---|---|
| Plant and equipment, acquired at beginning of first year, $300,000 × 200/150 | $400,000 |
| Plant and equipment, acquired at end of first year, $100,000 × 200/175 | 114,286 |
| Total adjusted cost of plant and equipment, beginning and end of second year | $514,286 |
| Depreciation, first year — 10% of $400,000 | $ 40,000 |
| Depreciation, second year — 10% of $514,286 | 51,429 |

## Other Expenses

The other expenses, which include income tax expense, were incurred evenly throughout each year or at the average dollar of the year. The adjustments are:

First year,   $280,000 × 200/160 = $350,000
Second year, $300,000 × 200/190 = $315,789

## Dividends

Dividends to stockholders were declared and paid at the end of each year. The adjustments are:

First year,   $ 5,000 × 200/175 = $5,714
Second year, $10,000 × 200/200 = $10,000

## Gain or Loss on Monetary Items

A loss in purchasing power of monetary items arises from holding monetary assets during a period of rising prices or from maintaining liabilities during a period of falling prices. A gain is the reverse; it arises from holding monetary assets during a period of falling prices or from maintaining liabilities during a period of rising prices.

The purchasing-power gain or loss on monetary assets and liabilities appears only on adjusted financial statements. Differences of opinion exist as to the method of reporting these gains and losses,[2] but for purposes of this demonstration, they will be treated in a statement of income and inflation gain or loss as separately disclosed elements immediately following the determination of net profit.

The amount of the accumulated net gain or loss on monetary items can be calculated by

---

[2] Various methods of presentation in financial statements are illustrated and discussed in Appendix C, page 137, of ARS 6.

---

### 4: NET CURRENT MONETARY ITEMS

|  | Opening of Business | End of First Year | End of Second Year |
|---|---|---|---|
| Cash, receivables, and other monetary items | $200,000 | $195,000 | $235,000 |
| Current liabilities | 100,000 | 200,000 | 100,000 |
| Net monetary assets (liabilities) | $100,000 | ($5,000) | $135,000 |

| First Year | Unadjusted Amount | Multiplier | Adjusted Amount |
|---|---|---|---|
| Net monetary assets—beginning | $100,000 | 175/150 | $116,667 |
| add — | | | |
| Sales | 800,000 | 175/160 | 875,000 |
| | $900,000 | | $991,667 |
| deduct — | | | |
| Purchases of merchandise | $520,000 | 175/160 | $568,750 |
| Other expenses | 280,000 | 175/160 | 306,250 |
| Dividends paid at end of year | 5,000 | 175/175 | 5,000 |
| Plant and equipment purchased at end of year | 100,000 | 175/175 | 100,000 |
| | $905,000 | | $980,000 |
| Net monetary assets—end | ($5,000) | | $ 11,667 |
| | | | (5,000) |
| Purchasing-power loss | | | $16,667 |

85

determining the amount needed to balance the financial statements after making all adjustments of the nonmonetary accounts. A more detailed analysis, however, is desirable as a verification of the net gain or loss and to analyze it as to types of monetary items. The calculation in the demonstration will be made in two parts: (1) the gain or loss on the net current monetary items, and (2) the gain or loss on the long-term liabilities.

There are several ways of computing the gain or loss from holding monetary items. The computations which follow are in more detail than would ordinarily be needed because in an actual case calculation could be facilitated by grouping together items to be adjusted by the same multiplier. Regardless of the method chosen, however, care must be used to insure consistency. That is, both sides of a transaction must be adjusted by the same index number. In our illustration, for example, the choice of the index number at the end of the first year to adjust the acquisition of plant and equipment dictates that the outlay of monetary assets for plant and equipment in that year be adjusted by the index at the same date.

$16,667 x 200/175 = $19,047 (Loss)

| Second Year: | Unadjusted Amount | Multiplier | Adjusted Amount |
|---|---|---|---|
| Net monetary assets – beginning | $(5,000) | 200/175 | $(5,714) |
| add – | | | |
| Sales | 1,000,000 | 200/190 | 1,052,632 |
| | $ 995,000 | | $1,046,918 |
| deduct– | | | |
| Retirement of debt at beginning of year | $50,000 | 200/175 | $57,144 |
| Purchases of merchandise | 500,000 | 200/190 | 526,316 |
| Other expenses | 300,000 | 200/190 | 315,789 |
| Dividends paid at end of year | 10,000 | 200/200 | 10,000 |
| | $ 860,000 | | $ 909,249 |
| Net monetary assets – end | $ 135,000 | | $ 137,669 |
| | | | 135,000 |
| Purchasing-power loss | | | $ 2,669 |

### 5: LONG-TERM LIABILITIES

| | First Year | Second Year |
|---|---|---|
| Balance at beginning of year | $350,000 | $350,000 |
| Balance at end of year | 350,000 | – |
| Decrease during year | None | $350,000 |

Since this loss is stated in terms of the dollar at the end of the first year, it must be converted into terms of the dollar at the end of the second year for inclusion in the adjusted statements [shown in the table above].

*First year.* The $350,000 of long-term liabilities remained constant throughout the year. The calculation of the purchasing-power gain for the year, converted into terms of the dollar at the end of the second year is:

$350,000 × 175/150 = $408,333;
$408,333 − $350,000 = $ 58,333;
$ 58,333 × 200/175 = $ 66,667 (gain).

*Second year.* There is no gain or loss of purchasing power because the decrease took place at the beginning of the year [see Table 6.]

The adjusted comparative income statement can now be prepared in terms of "end-of-second-year" dollars and appears as follows. [See Tables 7 and 8.]

### 6: SUMMARY

|  | First Year | Second Year |
|---|---|---|
| Loss on net current monetary assets | $19,047 | $2,669 |
| Gain on long-term liabilities | 66,667 | — |
| Net gain or loss | $47,620 (Gain) | $2,669 (Loss) |

### 7: ADJUSTED COMPARATIVE STATEMENT OF INCOME AND INFLATION GAIN (LOSS)

|  | First Year | Second Year |
|---|---|---|
| Sales | $1,000,000 | $1,052,632 |
| Operating Expenses: |  |  |
|     Cost of goods sold | $ 608,333 | $ 690,789 |
|     Depreciation | 40,000 | 51,429 |
|     Other expenses (including income tax) | 350,000 | 315,789 |
| Total Operating Expenses | $ 998,333 | $1,058,007 |
| Net Profit (Loss) From Operations | $ 1,667 | $ (5,375) |
| Inflation Gains or Losses |  |  |
|     Gain (loss) on short-term monetary items | $ (19,047) | $ (2,669) |
|     Gain (loss) on long-term debt | 66,667 | — |
| Net Inflation Gain (Loss) | $ 47,620 | $ (2,669) |
| Net Profit and Net Inflation Gain (Loss) | $ 49,287 | $ (8,044) |

### 8: ADJUSTED COMPARATIVE STATEMENT OF RETAINED EARNINGS

|  | First Year | Second Year |
|---|---|---|
| Retained Earnings, Beginning of Year | $ — | $43,573 |
| Net Profit and Net Inflation Gain (Loss) | 49,287 | (8,044) |
| Total | $49,287 | $35,529 |
| Dividends to Stockholders | 5,714 | 10,000 |
| Retained Earnings, End of Year | $43,573 | $25,529 |

## ADJUSTMENT OF THE BALANCE SHEET

### Monetary Items

The amounts of the monetary items at the end of the second year require no adjustment since they are, as legal tender, or by agreement with the debtors and creditors, receivable or payable in current dollars. The amounts at the opening of business and at the end of the first year, however, must be restated in order to express them in terms of the purchasing power of the dollar at the end of the second year.

Cash, Receivables, and Other Monetary Items:
Opening of business, $200,000 × 200/150 = $266,667
End of first year, $195,000 × 200/175 = $222,857
End of second year, $235,000 × 200/200 = $235,000

Current Liabilities:
Opening of business, $100,000 × 200/150 = $133,333
End of first year, $200,000 × 200/175 = $228,570
End of second year, $100,000 × 200/200 = $100,000

Long-term Liabilities:
Opening of business, $350,000 × 200/150 = $466,667
End of first year, $350,000 × 200/175 = $400,000
End of second year, None

### Inventories

The merchandise inventory at the opening of business was acquired at the price level of that date. The inventories at the end of the first and second years were, under the Fifo pricing method, assumed to have been acquired at the average price level of each of the respective years. The adjustments to the current-dollar basis, therefore, are:

Opening of business, $250,000 × 200/150 = $333,333
End of first year, $300,000 × 200/160 = $375,000
End of second year, $200,000 × 200/190 = $210,526

### Plant and Equipment

The adjustment of the plant and equipment was demonstrated in the previous section, "Adjustment of the Income Statement." The adjusted amounts for the plant and equipment were:

Opening of business, $400,000
End of first year, $514,286
End of second year, $514,286

The adjusted amount of accumulated depreciation can be derived from the adjusted annual depreciation, as follows:

End of first year, 10% of $400,000        $40,000
Depreciation during second year,
  10% of $514,286                          51,429
Accumulated depreciation, end
  of second year                          $91,429

### Capital Stock

The first $300,000 was issued at the opening of business. The next $300,000 was issued by conversion of long-term liabilities at the beginning of the second year. Expressed in terms of the current dollar, the adjusted capital stock appears as follows:

Issued at opening of
  business,            $300,000 × 200/150 = $400,000
Issued at beginning
  of second year,      $300,000 × 200/175 =  342,854
Total, end of
  second year                                $742,854

### Retained Earnings

The adjusted retained earnings are derived from the series of adjusted income statements. As a matter of informative disclosure for purposes of this demonstration, the retained earnings from ordinary operations will be shown separately from the accumulated gain or loss on monetary items. [See Tables 9 and 10.]

Accumulated gain or loss on net monetary items:

Gain on net monetary items, first year    $47,620
Loss on net monetary items, second year     2,669
Accumulated gain on net monetary items   $44,951

#### 9: RETAINED EARNINGS FROM OPERATIONS:

|  | First Year | Second Year |
|---|---|---|
| Carried over from previous year | $ — | ($4,047) |
| Net profit or (loss) from operations | 1,667 | (5,375) |
|  | $1,667 | ($9,422) |
| Adjusted dividends | 5,714 | 10,000 |
| Retained earnings from operations | ($4,047) | ($19,422) |

## 10: ADJUSTED COMPARACTIVE BALANCE SHEET

|  | Opening of Business | End of First year | End of Second year |
|---|---|---|---|
| **Assets** | | | |
| Cash, Receivables, and Other Monetary Items | $ 266,667 | $ 222,857 | $235,000 |
| Inventories | 333,333 | 375,000 | 210,526 |
| Plant and Equipment | 400,000 | 514,286 | 514,286 |
| Less Accumulated Depreciation | – | (40,000) | (91,429) |
| Total Assets | $1,000,000 | $1,072,143 | $868,383 |
| **Liabilities** | | | |
| Current Liabilities | $ 133,333 | $ 228,570 | $100,000 |
| Long-term Liabilities | 466,667 | 400,000 | – |
|  | $ 600,000 | $628,570 | $100,000 |
| **Stockholders' Equity** | | | |
| Capital Stock | $ 400,000 | $ 400,000 | $742,854 |
| Retained Earnings: | | | |
| From Operations (after dividends) | – | (4,047) | (19,422) |
| Accumulated Gain or (Loss) on Net Monetary Items | – | 47,620 | 44,951 |
| Total Stockholders' Equity | $ 400,000 | $ 443,573 | $768,383 |
| Total Liabilities and Stockholders' Equity | $1,000,000 | $1,072,143 | $868,383 |

## ADDITIONAL COMMENTS

The demonstration assumed that no adjustment of the financial statements had been made prior to the end of the second year. This required the restatement of the historical income statement for the first year and of the historical balance sheets at the beginning and end of the first year in terms of the current dollar in order to make them comparable with the adjusted financial statements for the second year. If adjustments had been made at the end of the first year, the results at the end of the second year would have been the same, but the procedure would have been somewhat different. Each amount in the adjusted statements prepared at the close of the first year would have been multiplied by the fraction 200/175 in order to restate them for use in the comparative financial statements prepared at the close of the second year. Other calculations involving items carried over from the first to the second year would correspondingly be modified.

It was assumed in the demonstration that the inventory was priced on a first-in, first-out (Fifo) basis. Other pricing methods would require variations in the computations. For example, if the last-in, first-out (Lifo) method had been used, the inventory at the end of the first year would have consisted of $250,000 acquired at the opening of business when the price-level index was 150, and $50,000 acquired during the first year when the average price-level index was 160. The calculation for the adjustment to the current dollar would have been:

$250,000 × 200/150 = $333,333
  50,000 × 200/160 =   62,500
$300,000             $395,833

The corresponding amount of goods sold would have been acquired entirely from the first year's purchases of merchandise and the adjustment calculation of the cost of goods sold for the first year would have been

$470,000 × 200/160 = $587,500

For the purposes of the demonstration, price-level index numbers were available only for the beginning, the end, and the average of each year. Index number series are usually available at monthly or quarterly intervals and should be used if greater refinement of the restated amounts is considered desirable. On the other hand, a still greater simplification than the one used in the demonstration could be employed when the movement of the price level is relatively slow by assuming that the index number at the beginning of each year applied to all transactions during the year. The results might be sufficiently accurate for most purposes.

In the demonstration, the accumulated gain or loss on monetary items and the accumulated undistributed earnings from ordinary operations were shown as separate portions of the retained earnings. This was possible because the illustration started with the opening of business and the accumulations could readily be computed over the two-year period. Where the price-level adjustment technique is put into effect for a company which has been in existence for a great many years, the accumulated adjusted retained earnings are obtained as a balancing figure in the first set of financial statements. To isolate the accumulated gain or loss on monetary items would not be feasible since it would require calculating the purchasing-power gain or loss on monetary items back to the date of origin of the company. Either the accumulated amount must be left as an undivided and unidentified portion of the retained earnings, or a practical compromise must be adopted such as starting the accumulation at a practicable date and disclosing this limitation of the accumulated amount by means of a footnote.

# THE TWO-DIMENSIONAL TIME FRAME OF COMMON DOLLAR STATEMENTS

*by Andrew D. Bailey, Jr. and Daniel L. Jensen*

Common dollar financial statements add a second time dimension to financial reporting that beginning students of accounting may find difficult to grasp. The second time dimension may be called *money time* to distinguish it from *statement time*. Statement time is simply the day or period a statement reflects; money time is the date of the dollar unit represented by the reported magnitude. It is particularly difficult for students to understand the roll-forward adjustment and the distinction between monetary and nonmonetary items in relation to a set of comparative financial statements.

The authors find that students' difficulty is alleviated when common dollar statements are introduced with a two-dimensional display. The display, which is based on a simple numerical example, is shown in Table 1.

Reprinted by permission of *The Accounting Review*, January 1977.

The columns of the table represent different statement times, and the rows represent different money times. In this way the full history of common dollar financial statements can be displayed in a single exhibit.

**ILLUSTRATION**

The numerical example describes a company with two assets acquired for $2,000 cash at time zero: (1) a ten-period bond purchased at par for $1,000 and paying 6 percent per period paid at the end of each period; and (2) a machine depreciated on a straight-line basis with a cost of $1,000, an estimated life of ten periods and no salvage value. The company leases the machine to an outside agency for a fee of $200 per period—payable in cash at the end of each period. The only expense incurred is depreciation, and the company holds all cash collected in a checking account. The

## TABLE 1  COMMON DOLLAR FINANCIAL STATEMENTS

| Money Time | Time Zero (Position Statements) | | Period One (Income Statements) | | Time One (Position Statements) | | Period Two (Income Statements) | | Time Two (Position Statements) | |
|---|---|---|---|---|---|---|---|---|---|---|
| Money Time Zero (Index 100) | Assets | | | | | | | | | |
| | Cash | $ 0 | | | | | | | | |
| | Bond | 1,000 | | | | | | | | |
| | Mach. | 1,000 | | | | | | | | |
| | | $2,000 | | | | | | | | |
| | Equity | $2,000 | | | | | | | | |
| Money Time One (Index 110) | Assets | | Revenue | | Assets | | | | | |
| | Cash | $ 0 | Rent | $200 | Cash | $ 260 | | | | |
| | Bond | 1,100 | Int. | 60 | Bond | 1,000 | | | | |
| | Mach. | 1,100 | | $260 | Mach. | 1,100 | | | | |
| | AcDp. | (0) | Expense | | AcDp. | (110) | | | | |
| | | $2,200 | Depr. | $110 | | $2,250 | | | | |
| | | | PP Loss: | | | | | | | |
| | | | Cash | 0 | | | | | | |
| | | | Bond | 100 | | | | | | |
| | | | | $210 | | | | | | |
| | Equity | $2,200 | Income | $ 50 | Equity | $2,250 | | | | |
| Money Time Two (Index 120) | Assets | | Revenue | | Assets | | Revenue | | Assets | |
| | Cash | $ 0 | Rent | $218 | Cash | $ 284 | Rent | $200 | Cash | $ 520 |
| | Bond | 1,200 | Int. | 66 | Bond | 1,091 | Int. | 60 | Bond | 1,000 |
| | Mach. | 1,200 | | $284 | Mach. | 1,200 | | $260 | Mach. | $1,200 |
| | AcDp. | (0) | Expense | | AcDp. | $ (120) | Expense | | AcDp. | (240) |
| | | $2,400 | Depr. | $120 | | $2,455 | Depr. | | | $2,480 |
| | | | PP Loss: | | | | PP Loss: | | | |
| | | | Cash | 0 | | | Cash | 24 | | |
| | | | Bond | 109 | | | Bond | 91 | | |
| | | | | $229 | | | | $235 | | |
| | Equity | $2,400 | Income | $ 55 | Equity | $2,455 | Income | $ 25 | Equity | $2,480 |

index of the general price level stands at 100 when the assets are purchased at time zero. The index stands at 110 throughout period one and at 120 throughout period two.

## THE ROLL-FORWARD ADJUSTMENT

As statements are reissued for purposes of comparison with current statements, statement time and money time diverge, i.e., money time advances while statement time remains fixed. The progression of time-zero position statements is shown in the far left-hand column of the table. Statement time remains at zero, as indicated in the column heading, and money time advances from zero to one, etc., with each reissuance of the first position statement. The statement is said to be "rolled forward" from one money time to the next. In general, the roll-forward adjustment is characterized by movement from one row of Table 1 to the next and is accomplished by multiplying the dollar amount of each statement item on the earlier statement by the ratio of the current to the earlier index. *The roll forward permits interstatement comparisons in dollars of the same money time, i.e., dollars of the same purchasing power.*

## RELATIONSHIP AMONG COMPARATIVE STATEMENTS

The sequence of comparative statements within any row reveals the response of common dollar statements to advances in statement time while money time remains fixed. Consider the progression of statements from left to right within any row of the table. Successive position statements separated by income statements are related in the usual way, except that all account balances and implied transactions are given effect in terms of dollars of the same purchasing power regardless of statement time.

The cash account rises by 260 actual dollars each period—$200 from the rentor and $60 from the bond. After two years, the account contains $520 ($520 = $260 · 2) as is shown on the time-two position statement given in time-two dollars. One year earlier, the position statement (again, in time-two dollars) shows cash of $284, which is the $260 time-one cash balance in time-one dollars restated in time-two dollars. The activity and related balances of the cash account all stated in time-two dollars can be summarized as follows:

| CASH ACCOUNT IN TIME-TWO DOLLARS | |
|---|---:|
| Time-Zero Cash Balance | $—0— |
| Add: Period One Cash Receipts | |
| ($260 · 120/110) | $284 |
| Time One Cash Balance | $284 |
| Add: Period-Two Cash Receipts | 260 |
| Subtotal | $544 |
| Deduct: *Purchasing Power Loss* | (24) |
| Time-Two Cash Balance | $520 |

Notice that adding the $260 collected in the second period to the cash balance at the beginning of the second period (stated in time-two dollars) yields $544 which exceeds the $520 ending cash balance. The time-two cash balance in time-two dollars is $520, the cash on hand. The $24 difference between $520 and $544 is a loss of purchasing power, the result of holding cash through the second period.

The activity in the bond account also can be reconstructed in common dollars by a similar procedure as is shown below:

| BOND ACCOUNT IN TIME-TWO DOLLARS | |
|---|---:|
| *Time-Zero Bond Balance* | |
| ($1,000 · 120/100) | $1,200 |
| Add: Interest Income | |
| ($60 · 120/110) | 66 |
| Deduct: Coupon Payment | |
| ($60 · 120/110) | (66) |
| Subtotal | $1,200 |
| Deduct: *Purchasing Power Loss* | (109) |
| *Time-One Bond Balance* | |
| ($1,000 · 120/110) | $1,091 |
| Add: Interest Income | 60 |
| Deduct: Coupon Payment | (60) |
| Subtotal | $1,091 |
| Deduct: *Purchasing Power Loss* | (91) |
| *Time-Two Bond Balance* | $1,000 |

Notice that the two purchasing power losses during the second period—$91 due to holding the bond and $24 due to holding cash—are reported in total ($115) in the period two income statement.

An important distinction is drawn among monetary items (e.g., cash—long-term investments in bonds and long-term or short-term payables) and nonmonetary items (e.g., land, machinery, inventories and retained earnings). Monetary items are assets and equities for which a current cash equivalent is fixed by contract, the market or some other means. Since customary accounting procedures assign such items their current cash equivalents, they are reported at the same amount on the current position statement whether or not statements are adjusted for general price-level changes. As a consequence, *the holding of monetary items gives rise to gains and/or losses in purchasing power reflected as they occur in common dollar income statements.*

**MACHINE-RELATED ACCOUNTS IN TIME-TWO DOLLARS**

|  | Original Cost | Accumulated Depreciation | Net Book Value |
|---|---|---|---|
| Time-Zero Balance (1000 · 120/100) | $1,200 | $—0— | $1,200 |
| Period-One Depreciation (1200/10) |  | 120 | (120) |
| Time-One Balance | $1,200 | $120 | $1,080 |
| Period-Two Depreciation (1200/10) |  | 120 | (120) |
| Time-Two Balance | $1,200 | $240 | $ 960 |

In contrast, *purchasing power gains and losses on nonmonetary items are not recognized until their ultimate sale or other disposition.* The machinery cost and accumulated depreciation accounts of the example demonstrate the point. Consider the statements issued in dollars of time two as represented in the third row of Table 1. The original cost of the machine is $1,200 in time-two dollars ($1,200 = $1,000 · 120/100 = $1,100 · 120/110). Since there is no activity in the account containing the original cost, the balance is $1,200 on all three position statements in time-two dollars; thus, the roll forward is a capital adjustment rather than a purchasing power gain or loss for current income statement purposes. The accumulated depreciation account, however, rises by one period's depreciation, or $120 ($120 = $1,200/10) in each period. Notice that the periodic common dollar depreciation is a constant one-tenth of the original cost in time-two dollars, regardless of statement time, which accords with the straight-line method. The activity and balances of the machine-related accounts can be summarized in time-two dollars as [shown above].

As the summary of the accounts indicates, no gain or loss in purchasing power is recognized. If the machine were sold for $1,050 cash just before the end of the second period, then customary accounting practice would recognize a gain of $250 ($1050 − $1000 · 8/10). A common-dollar income statement for the second period would report a gain on the sale of only $90 ($1050 − $960)—the other $160 of the gain ($250−$90) being viewed as fictional or eroded by the rise in the price level. In this way, the gain on disposition of nonmonetary items measures the deviation of proceeds from the net book value of assets adjusted for changes in the general price level.

# PURCHASING POWER GAINS AND LOSSES

*by Robert D. Baumann, MBA*

## MONETARY AND NONMONETARY ITEMS

Before defining what the gain or loss on net monetary items is, the monetary and nonmonetary items themselves must be defined. A *monetary asset* is either money or a claim held by an enterprise for the future receipt of money whose amount is either fixed or is determinable without reference to the future price of a specific good or service. A *monetary liability* is just the converse. It is an obligation to pay an amount of money whose amount is either fixed or is determinable without reference to the future price of a specific good or service. *Nonmonetary assets* and liabilities are defined as any asset or liability which is not monetary.[1] Now the purchasing power gain or loss on net monetary items can be defined.

## PURCHASING POWER GAIN OR LOSS DEFINED

During times of inflation, holders of monetary assets such as cash and receivables lose purchasing power because monetary assets buy fewer goods and services as the general level of prices rises. Conversely, those holders of monetary liabilities recognize a "gain" because these liabilities will be paid by dollars having less purchasing power than the dollars received when the liabilities were incurred. The net gain or loss in purchasing power, therefore, is part of the overall impact of inflation on the company's operations. This net gain or loss is determined by restating in terms of average dollars for the year the "opening and closing balances of, and transactions in, monetary assets and liabilities."[2]

Concerning gains and losses on specific items, merely holding cash does not by itself result in a gain or loss, but during inflationary times, it will result in a loss of purchasing power. If one has $10 at the beginning of the year and the rate of inflation is 10 percent that year, there is a loss in purchasing power on the $10 held of $1. At the end of the year, one would need $11 to purchase the same goods the original $10 could have purchased at the beginning of the year. In order to recognize a gain on holding cash, just the opposite circumstances would have to hold true. Also, if holding cash is a losing proposition, so is holding a claim to cash, such as receivables; the same logic applies. Conversely, being the holder of a payable in inflationary periods would result in a gain of purchasing power. One would compute the gain from payables (monetary liabilities) and the loss from receivables (monetary assets) the same way a loss on holding cash is computed.[3]

Many firms, it turns out, will have a net monetary liability position, due largely to the fact that long- and short-term debt comprise a major part of many firms' balance sheets, often surpassing their cash and receivables position. In 1978, General Motors had a net monetary liability of $2.5 billion.[4] Highly leveraged companies such as General Motors can and will experience a large gain from this because it is presumed that each year's inflation will result in a gain due to the fact that cheaper dollars will be used in the future to pay off the debt.

---

Robert D. Baumann, "Critical Analysis of FASB No. 33" (Master's thesis, Pace University, May 1980). Used by permission of Robert D. Baumann.

[1] Financial Accounting Standards Board, *Statement of Financial Accounting Standards No. 33* (Stamford, Conn.: Financial Accounting Foundation, 1979), p. 16.

[2] Ibid.

[3] Ibid., pp. 73-74.

[4] Mark E. Steakley, "Inflation Accounting Techniques: How They Compare," *Management Accounting* (September, 1979), p. 59.

## EXAMPLE OF A PURCHASING POWER GAIN

In order to clarify the concept of what a purchasing power gain is, we will look at an example of one, which has been adopted from FASB #33.

Assume that Enterprise X has $1,000 of invested capital and that Enterprise Y has borrowed $1,000 at an annual interest rate of 15 percent. Also assume that both firms buy inventory at a cost of $1,000 and sell it one year later for $1,500; the general rate of inflation is 10 percent per year. Working through an historical cost/constant dollar income statement we find that both firms have gross margins of $400 ($1,500 sales less $1,000 cost of goods sold; [$1,000 × 110/100] ). Subtracting out interest expense of $150 ($1,000 × 15%) for Enterprise Y, one finds Enterprise X with net income of $400 while Enterprise Y has net income of $250. One also sees that while firm X has no purchasing power gain or loss, firm Y has a purchasing power gain of $100, resulting in a real cash surplus for X of $350. This is so because while Enterprise Y has received $1,500 in revenue, it needs to repay only $1,150 ($1,000 × 115%), representing the principle and interest. In light of this, it would appear that Enterprise X's net income would understate the true increase in the purchasing power which was earned for its equity investors.[5]

## ADVANTAGES OF RECOGNIZING THE GAIN OR LOSS

Now that monetary items have been defined, along with the purchasing power gain or loss, and an example of such a gain has been presented, the advantages and disadvantages of recognizing these gains or losses will be looked at.

To begin with, some people believe that this gain may serve as an indication of how well a company is managing its monetary resources during times of inflation, the presumption being that having net monetary liabilities is the goal, because this results in a gain. Others feel that to the extent that purchasing power is lost as the business cycle progresses, this loss would indicate that the company's ability to purchase inventory or other nonmonetary assets is diminishing. On the other hand, as long as a firm's resources are invested in its inventory, it is protected to some degree from inflation.[6]

In disclosing a separate figure for the monetary gain or loss, investors and analysts may well be able to improve their assessments of the firm's future cash flows. Disclosing this figure gives investors a broader base on which to base their decision concerning the future prospects of a firm. Since the holding of monetary assets and liabilities is to a large degree up to the firm's own discretion, the net gain or loss on such items provides an indication of management's efficiency with regard to such items and is considered part of management's stewardship responsibility. It is the sign of a successful management when a purchasing power gain results from an amount of debt, the funds from which have been wisely invested in assets whose purchasing power has either been maintained, or at least has been decreasing less rapidly than monetary items.[7] Explicitly recognizing these gains and losses will provide investors with an increased understanding during inflationary periods of the implications and ramifications of the monetary components of working capital and the amount of debt which is included in the capital structure of an enterprise.

Lastly, some people feel that this information can be useful if the purchasing power gain on debt is looked at in the light of it being a reduction in the interest expense of a firm. Others, though, argue that if this be the case, why isn't the gain included in income from con-

---

[5] FASB, *Statement of Financial Accounting Standards No. 33*, pp. 75-76.

[6] Robert Kaplan, "Purchasing Power Gains on Debt: The Effect of Expected and Unexpected Inflation," *Accounting Review* (April, 1977), pp. 370-371.

[7] Ernst and Whinney, *Financial Reporting Developments: Inflation Accounting* (New York, N. Y.: Ernst and Whinney, 1979), p. 66.

tinuing operations? This will be discussed further momentarily.[8]

## DISADVANTAGES OF RECOGNIZING THE GAIN OR LOSS

For every advantage inherent in recognizing the gain or loss, there appears to be a corresponding disadvantage. These disadvantages will be discussed presently.

To begin with, in spite of the advantages mentioned above, many people believe that it is not easy to find a use for this purchasing power gain or loss. They draw an analogy to FASB #8 and the foreign exchange gain or loss item on the balance sheet. Both gains and losses are arrived at similarly, except here the CPI is used versus the foreign exchange rates in FASB #8. They go on to state that few analysts have found a use for the foreign exchange gain or loss, and that they feel the same will be the fate of the purchasing power gain or loss.[9] Others feel that holding either a net monetary asset or liability position is normal and necessary for the continuation of business activities. Therefore, the effects of holding one position or the other is a "joint effect" with income from continuing operations; this being the case, separation of the two figures is not valid. The two figures should be shown as one; the gain or loss should be included in the net income from continuing operations figure.[10]

Others who oppose explicitly recognizing this gain or loss state that one is implying in this recognition that an enterprise can be better off by borrowing than if it had not borrowed. They point out that these gains are only paper gains, that they have not been earned, and that this new figure makes it look good for a company to have a high debt to equity ratio which normally is considered unwise. Recognition of this new figure, in effect, makes debt a profit center. This statement makes highly leveraged firms recognize large monetary gains and therefore look "better" than would a firm which has not used such large amounts of financing. Clearly, they say, this should not be the case. Opponents feel that this figure may easily be misinterpreted and serve to confuse the readers and users of financial statements. They believe that when current cost depreciation is measured, any gain on net monetary liabilities is more than offset and therefore should not be shown. They mention the fact that while FASB #33 defines and computes the gain or loss on net monetary items, nowhere does it indicate specifically how it can be used in an investment or credit decision.[11]

Another major drawback to the use of this figure is that it cannot be used anywhere for reconciliation purposes. Normally, the change in retained earnings from the beginning of the period to the end of the period should be able to be reconciled by using the net income or loss figure. This is not the case for the purchasing power gain or loss on net monetary items. Take for instance the current cost income statement. This new figure cannot be part of the reconciliation because, in effect, it is continuously reflected in the balance sheet figures. This is so because, by definition, the figures used for net monetary assets are always stated at current value. Therefore, this gain or loss figure can be computed, but it cannot actually appear anywhere or be reflected in the financial statements. Also brought out is the fact that purchasing power gains do not represent cash available for distribution to shareholders.[12]

Lastly, an oft presented argument is that since interest expense is intended, at least in part, to compensate lenders for lost purchasing power during inflationary periods, and there-

---

[8] Kaplan, "Purchasing Power Gains on Debt," pp. 370-371.

[9] Bear, Stearns and Company, "Understanding the FASB's Inflation Accounting Proposal," *Accounting Issues* (March 21, 1979), p. 22.

[10] FASB, *Statement of Financial Accounting Standards No. 33*, p. 58.

[11] "Inflation Accounting," *Business Week* (October 15, 1979), p. 74.

[12] Bear, Stearns and Company, "Understanding the FASB's Inflation Accounting Proposal," *Accounting Issues* (March 21, 1979), p. 23.

fore is computed in the contractual rate of interest on the debt, the gain should be regarded as a reduction in interest expense and included in income from continuing operations. Not to do so, many people believe, is to mislead financial statement readers as to the true meaning of a purchasing power gain on net monetary items.[13]

---

[13] Arthur Young, *Financial Reporting and Changing Prices* (New York, N. Y.: Arthur Young, 1979), p. 17.

# Current Value Accounting

**3**

# CURRENT COST ACCOUNTING

*by Robert D. Baumann, MBA*

Current cost accounting is a method of measuring and reporting assets and expenses associated with the use or sale of assets at their current cost or lower recoverable amount at the balance sheet date or at the date of use or sale. Current cost is defined as the "cost of acquiring the same service potential as embodied by the assets owned."[1] Therefore, it emphasizes measurement of the current costs of assets actually owned by the enterprise rather than some hypothetical replacement. These costs are based on estimates of the costs to acquire or produce today assets which have the ability to produce the same goods or services at the same operating costs as the assets presently owned. Unlike the previously discussed historical cost/constant dollar information, current costs are not derived from historical cost financial statements, and therefore, they are a departure from historical cost. Instead of restating historical costs, current cost accounting replaces these figures with current cost. Current costs are not necessarily the same as costs that would actually be incurred if existing assets were in fact to be replaced currently. In many situations, the existing assets would be replaced with technologically superior assets, and therefore, adjustments would have to be made to determine the costs that would be associated with the same service potential and operating costs as the old assets. In other situations, the assets would not or could not be replaced at all. Current costs are not equivalent to costs in the usual sense of the word. They do not represent money spent or obligations incurred by a firm, but rather they represent hypothetical transactions based on estimates of what the company would have to spend currently.

Concerning current cost valuations, FASB #33 gives an indication of how to define current costs for certain specific types of assets. For inventory, current cost is defined as the price a firm would have to pay today to acquire goods identical to those in inventory, or the price the firm would have to pay today to produce these same goods, whichever method would be appropriate for the firm under consideration. The current cost of property, plant and equipment is the cost of acquiring the same service potential presently derived from the asset. This same service potential is measured by both the operating cost associated with the asset and its physical output capacity. The firm, in measuring these current costs, should use methods which reflect whatever way the firm would normally go about acquiring an asset given the firm's specific circumstances.

The term "lower recoverable amount" was mentioned previously. For all intents and purposes, this is equivalent to the net realizable value of the asset, which is the current amount of cash which could be expected to be received from the sale of an asset, less the costs incurred to sell the asset. If for a group of assets taken as a whole, their recoverable amount is materially and permanently lower than the historical cost restated in constant dollars or the current cost of the asset, then this recoverable amount figure should be used to measure both the asset and the expenses associated with the use or sale of the asset.[2]

---

Robert D. Baumann, "Critical Analysis of FASB No. 33" (Master's thesis, Pace University, May 1980). Used by permission of Robert D. Baumann.

[1] Philip L. Defliese, "Inflation Accounting: Pursuing the Elusive," *Journal of Accountancy* (May, 1979), p. 59.

[2] Financial Accounting Standards Board, *Statement of Financial Accounting Standards No. 33* (Stamford, Conn.: Financial Accounting Foundation, 1979), pp. 19-21.

## NEED FOR CURRENT COST INFORMATION

Now that current costs have been defined, a look will be taken at the perceived need for such information. Whereas constant dollar restated financial statements were based on the premise that prices *in general* are rising, current costs are based on the fact that the prices for specific goods are changing also, independent of the rise in the general price level. The prices of specific goods fluctuate due to changes in supply and demand factors and due to technological innovations in the specific product area. Since these changes are an integral feature of all capitalistic economies, many people feel that when financial statements fail to take these changes into account that these statements are failing to provide information which is necessary to make informed financial decisions. The historical cost financial statements in use today fail to take into account these changes in specific goods and services.[3]

The need for such disclosure has been perceived by educators, financial analysts, and especially the SEC, as can be seen by ASR-190, which deals with the disclosure of replacement costs. It should also be noted, though, that at present, based on the current literature, it does not appear that issuers of financial reports and auditors in particular perceive as strong a need for current costs as do the parties previously mentioned. The issuers do not perceive as strong a need for one of three reasons. Either they just do not believe in general that there is a need or that this information would be helpful, or they believe the costs are greater than the benefits, or they believe that the current cost model needs more development before it is ready for implementation. Let it be made clear, though, that these parties do not feel that the present day statements are adequate.[4]

Another reason current costs are necessary is that the values of many assets on the balance sheet are understated. The prices of assets are rising, but no recognition of this fact is reflected in the financial statements. While it would not be proper to reflect these changes on the books of a firm due to the cost principle, there is no reason why these increased values cannot be supplementarily disclosed in the financial statements. The historical cost financial statements just do not assess the true present worth of a firm, an assessment which is important to all the parties associated with a particular firm or its financial statements.

Advocates of current cost do not view the decline of the purchasing power of the monetary unit as the primary problem. Instead, they feel that the real problem has to do with deficiencies in the historical exchange price model in use today. Using current costs, they feel that the values of assets are automatically stated in the same current unit of measurement, so that the effects of inflation on the general purchasing power of the dollar is already accounted for.[5]

## REQUIRED CURRENT COST DISCLOSURE

Just what types of disclosure dealing with current costs are required by FASB #33? The pronouncement states that income from continuing operations derived using current costs is required to be disclosed, along with the current costs of a firm's property, plant and equipment, as of the end of the fiscal year for which the financial statements are presented. Also shown will be the changes in the current cost figure for property, plant and equipment and inventory, net of the effects of inflation, for the current fiscal year. These changes are determined by measuring the difference in the current costs of the assets at the beginning of the year or date the asset was acquired, whichever is appropriate, and the current costs of the assets at the end of the year or the date of use or sale, again whichever

---

[3] L. S. Rosen, *Current Value Accounting and Price-Level Restatements* (Toronto: The Canadian Institute of Chartered Accountants, 1972), p. 72.

[4] FASB, *Statement of Financial Accounting Standards No. 33,* p. 28.

[5] Robert T. Sprouse, "Inflation: Symptom or Disease," *Financial Analysts Journal* (January/February, 1979), p. 12.

is appropriate to the firm's specific situation. These changes should be reported both before and after the effects of the general rate of inflation have been eliminated.

When the amount of income from continuing operations on a current cost basis is not materially different from the same figure derived on an historical cost/constant dollar basis, then the information described above need not be presented, but a note to the financial statements must disclose the reason for the absence of such information.[6]

## METHODS USED
## TO MEASURE CURRENT COSTS

One of the most debated issues concerning current costs is that of its measurement. FASB #33 leaves the door open for an abundance of methods, most of which will be discussed presently.

Based on a number of financial statements recently published which this writer has read, it appears that the majority of firms will be using internally generated indexes to measure an asset's current cost. This method was sanctioned by the pronouncement, along with indexes which are generated externally, to the extent they can be found. Direct pricing is also a means by which current costs can be measured. Direct pricing can be derived by means of current invoice prices, vendors' price lists, or manufacturers' standard costs which presumably reflect current costs. The current cost information may be applied to individual items or to broad categories, whichever a firm sees fit to do depending on the circumstances involved.

It is assumed by the pronouncement that the accounting principles and policies used for current cost calculations will be the same as ones used for both historical cost/nominal dollar and historical cost/constant dollar calculations. Here the statement is specifically referring to depreciation expense and its related estimates. Also, income tax expense for current cost calculations should be the same as the expense used in the primary financial statements. It should be noted that the Board expressed no preferences as to the use of either direct pricing or indexes in deriving the current cost measurements.[7]

## PREVIOUS USE OF
## CURRENT COST FIGURES

Current cost measurements are by no means new to accountants and preparers of financial reports. One example of a current cost measurement in use today is the inventory pricing method known as last-in, first-out (LIFO). This method of pricing inventory usually results in a cost of goods sold figure which approximates the results one would expect to find if current cost valuations were used instead. Another example is when the SEC came out with ASR-190, in which certain large corporations had been requested to disclose in their financial statements replacement cost data, figures which are an approximation of current cost. A third example is the fact that some of the larger corporations in a number of foreign countries have already experimented with supplementary current cost disclosure in their financial statements. It should be apparent, therefore, that current cost disclosures are nothing new. Since replacement cost was required by the SEC in ASR-190 and firms have been complying with it for four years now, this paper will look to an evaluation of ASR-190 to see how effective it has been, and to see what light it can shed on the requirements for current cost disclosure in FASB #33.[8]

## EVALUATION OF ASR-190

In 1976, the SEC issued ASR-190 which required that certain large public corporations disclose on their 10-K's replacement cost data

---

[6]FASB, *Statement of Financial Accounting Standards No. 33*, pp. 11-12.

[7]Ibid., pp. 20-21.

[8]Elmwood L. Miller, "What's Wrong with Price-Level Accounting," *The Certified Accountant* (February, 1979), p. 13.

for cost of goods sold, inventories, depreciation and productive capacity. While these figures were required on annual reports filed with the Commission, few companies included their replacement cost disclosures in their annual reports to shareholders. Due to the filing requirements, ASR-190 included about 20 percent fewer firms than does FASB #33. ASR-190 was hastily promulgated without adequate research.[9]

ASR-190 does not require a new figure to be shown representing income from continuing operations as does FASB #33. It merely requires the replacement costs to be disclosed for certain items which when used alone cannot be used to arrive at a new figure for income from continuing operations.[10] The key conceptual difference between replacement cost and current cost is that the replacement cost theory focuses on the cost of replacing physical productive capacity with current state of the art technology, while the current cost theory focuses on the cost of replacing the assets owned unless they are functionally obsolescent. ASR-190 is based on a hypothetical future replacement rather than on equipment in use.[11] FASB #33 has an alternative figure in recoverable amount when this amount is lower than an asset's current cost, whereas ASR-190 has only one measure, with a separate disclosure of net realizable value if it is lower than replacement cost. ASR-190 made no mention of disclosing the effects of changes in the general price level, unlike FASB #33. The new statement also allows for differences in operating costs to be considered when the only available measure used to compute an asset's current cost contemplates replacing the asset with one embodying new and advanced technology. FASB #33 also requires disclosure of changes in the current costs of assets, as well as the current cost of the land, both of which are not required by ASR-190.[12]

Many firms stated that they disliked ASR-190 due to the fact that it is based on an unrealistic premise, that of replacing one's total productive capacity all at once. They feel that replacement cost does not represent current value.[13] It should be mentioned though, that other firms believe that if applied logically, current cost and replacement cost give approximately the same results. Another problem with ASR-190 is that firms disclosing the figures are allowed to place a disclaimer with the information. It appears that these firms have "attacked" their own disclosures so much that people have been placing little, if any, worth on the disclosed information.[14] Other complaints have been that the replacement cost data is misleading in that it provides the basis for presenting and manipulating hypothetical data which could possibly serve to confuse those it is supposed to inform.

In closing this discussion of ASR-190 and replacement cost, it should be noted that the SEC has ordered ASR-190 to be phased out in response to FASB #33. The SEC's rule terminates when a company reports current cost figures, which will be mandatory for fiscal years ending on December 25, 1980 and thereafter, as required by FASB #33.[15]

## ADVANTAGES OF CURRENT COST MEASUREMENTS

Now that current costs have been defined, the need for them explained, and the methods of calculating them discussed, a summary of both

---

[9] Louis Bisgay, "Inflation Accounting Is Here," *Management Accounting* (December, 1979), p. 6.

[10] FASB, *Statement of Financial Accounting Standards No. 33*, p. 6.

[11] "Inflation Accounting," *Business Week* (October 15, 1979), p. 74.

[12] FASB, *Statement of Financial Accounting Standards No. 33*, p. 7.

[13] R. F. J. Dewhurst, "Accountants and Accountancy," *The Accountant* (October 12, 1978), p. 471.

[14] Bear, Stearns and Company, "Understanding the FASB's Inflation Accounting Proposal," *Accounting Issues* (March 21, 1979), p. 18.

[15] Louis Bisgay, "Inflation Accounting Is Here," *Management Accounting* (December, 1979), p. 6.

the advantages and disadvantages of current costs will be presented.

The main reason that many investors and analysts argue in favor of an accounting framework which uses current cost, as compared to historical cost/constant dollar, is that the general price level tells no one anything about the impact of changing prices on the specific assets of a specific firm. In theory, the average has no relation to any given part of the sample used to devise the average. It is ofttimes a meaningless concept when applied to many situations.[16] If one student receives a fifty on a test, and another student receives a hundred, the average score is seventy-five, which tells one absolutely nothing about their respective scores. As far as investors are concerned, when the current cost of a firm's assets are rising, this rise is synonymous to an increase in the firm's investment in its assets. Hopefully, a firm will and should expect to earn a rate of return on this increased investment, so therefore the current cost information gives investors a basis for assessing their return on investment. Along this same line, of concern to investors is the question of whether or not a firm's operating capability has been maintained. In general, when a figure for current cost income is disclosed, if dividends are less than this figure, the indication is that operating capability has been increased; if dividends are greater than current cost income, it indicates that the operating capability of the firm has decreased.

In determining a firm's future potential, some analysts are concerned with more than just the net income figure; they would like to see a more detailed and comprehensive assessment of a firm's future prospects. They want presented intermediate measures of such items as current cost depreciation, cost of goods sold, and property, plant and equipment in order to judge the firm's profitability. These figures on a current cost basis provide more relevant and up-to-date information about the true costs of these resources to the enterprise as compared to the related historical cost amounts.[17]

Lastly, and in connection with a statement made earlier in this section, the model of current cost accounting may prove to be especially helpful in highlighting an urgent situation in this country's economic policy. Current cost accounting is based on the premise of maintaining operating capability and the amount of income which can be distributed and still leave the firm as well off as it began. These two factors focus attention on that specific point where a firm's reduction in capacity sets in. Indeed, "the whole system pivots on the point where capital investment begins to rise or fall."[18] This information would be most valuable to the legislature in determining an economic policy for the United States.

## DISADVANTAGES OF CURRENT COST MEASUREMENTS

The disadvantages and impracticalities of current cost measurements are numerous. As was mentioned earlier, most firms using current cost measurements at present are deriving their figures using indexes. This could present some practical difficulties in that an appropriate index must be "chosen" and that this index will have to allow for an ever changing technology and asset mix of the enterprise under consideration. If, on the other hand, the direct pricing method is used, great care will have to be taken to ensure that prices which are truly relevant to the situation that the firm is in at the present time are used. Inherent in these two objections to current cost accounting is the fact that these measurements are subjective and may well be open to manipulation, especially of the income figure.

Another problem caused when current cost accounting is used is that one of the most basic tenets of accounting tends to be lost in

---

[16]"Inflation Accounting," *Business Week* (October 15, 1979), p. 70.

[17]FASB, *Statement of Financial Accounting Standards No. 33*, p. 59.

[18]Ibid., p. 26.

the shuffle, the realization principle of income determination. This principle in essence states that income is recognized objectively based on an arm's-length transaction. If some alternative concept of value such as current cost is used, this principle would be undermined through the determination of income by recognition of subjectively arrived at value changes without regard to realization.[19] In other words, when current costs are used to restate balance sheet items, a radical change in the definition of earnings takes place. Earnings currently equal revenues less expenses; this equation emphasized current operating performance. Under the new supplementary approach of current cost, earnings will be equal to the changes in assets and liabilities in a current value accounting scheme. The income statement would no longer be primarily concerned with income from current operations. The market value fluctuations of the firm's resources and long-term debt would be the crucial factors, and they may even overshadow the revenue less expense figure.[20]

---

[19] John M. Boersema, "Accountants and Accountancy—Some Further Comments on Inflation Accounting," *The Accountant* (January 11, 1979), p. 34-36.

[20] Mark F. Polanis, "Will Accountants Go off the Dollar Standard?," *Magazine of Bank Administration* (November, 1978), p. 43.

---

## WHAT *IS* CURRENT VALUE?

by Laurence A. Friedman, CPA, Ph.D.

---

The initial reaction to the SEC's requirement that large firms disclose supplemental replacement cost information has, for the most part, been negative. The requirements that firms disclose the replacement costs of inventory, property, plant and equipment as well as the replacement cost depreciation expense and replacement cost of goods sold is criticized as being costly with no appreciable benefits. For example, General Motors Company characterized the requirements as ". . . of no value because of the subjectivity necessarily involved in making these estimates and because the concept is based on an unrealistic premise, i.e., the total replacement of all productive capacity at one time."[1]

On the other hand, most accountants agree that some measures should be taken to inform users of the effect on financial statements of the inflationary tendency of the economy. Many critics of ASR 190 seem to agree that some measure of the effect of changing prices should be disclosed but that the SEC's version of replacement cost accounting is not appropriate.[2]

Among other things, they criticize the use of replacement costs as defined by the SEC as not representing current values. Approximately 50 percent of the 10-K reports the author examined contained criticisms, such as:

> . . . *replacement cost data . . . are not representative of the current value of existing inventory and productive capacity.*[3]
>
> . . . *it cannot be assumed that the reported replacement cost bears any relationship to the actual current value of*

---

This article reprinted with permission from *The CPA Journal,* published by the New York Society of Certified Public Accountants.

[1] The General Motors Company, annual report, 1976.

[2] C. W. Bastable, "Is SEC Replacement Cost Data Worth the Effort," *Journal of Accountancy,* October 1977, pp. 74-76.

[3] The Dow Chemical Company, 10-K report, 1976.

*existing property, plant and equipment...*[4]

*...replacement cost should not be interpreted as the current value of existing productive capacity.*[5]

Most of the reports give no explanation of what is meant by "current value." But if progress is to be made toward reaching a consensus regarding reporting in periods of changing prices, interested parties must be specific in their suggested solution. Users, preparers and auditors must all make known their needs for current value information and the practical difficulties of meeting those needs. The purpose of this article is to summarize various valuation approaches that could all be called "current value." Perhaps this will enable accountants to understand some of the different methods of current value accounting and will encourage them to come forward with specific suggestions, which they feel can be implemented at reasonable cost for improving reporting in periods of changing prices.

## THE CURRENT PRICE DEBATE

Sterling set up a framework to describe the various valuation approaches. Basically, he suggests that two types of prices exist: input and output. Also, one can examine three different states of time: the past, present and future. Each intersection of time and price provides a possible method of valuation. "Thus, there are four major valuation methods that have been proposed:

1. *Historical cost (HC);*
2. *Replacement cost (RC);*
3. *Exit value (EV); and*
4. *Discounted cash flows (DCF)."*[6]

His classification is reproduced in Table 1.[7]

| | TABLE 1 | | |
|---|---|---|---|
| Price | Past | Present | Future |
| Input | HC | RC | DCF |
| Output | Irrelevant | EV | DCF |

He does not include general price level adjustments because they could be added to any of the above, resulting in four more alternatives. He suggests that one should adjust for changes in the general price level but that selection of the valuation method is a separate problem which must be solved first. The author agrees with this suggestion, but a discussion of general price level adjusted historical costs is appropriate since that is the subject of APB Statement No. 3 and a withdrawn FASB exposure draft.[8]

Before reviewing the various valuation alternatives, however, an attempt is made to discover which of the various valuation alternatives seem to be implied by the use of the term "current value." One report states "Replacement costs . . . should not be interpreted to be current value or the price for which the assets could be sold."[9] Unfortunately, that statement could mean either that current values are current selling prices or that current values are something different from current selling prices. Another report includes that statement that "... replacement cost amounts should not be interpreted to represent amounts at which the assets could be sold or any other measure of current value."[10] This implies that current selling prices are a measure of "current value," but that others exist also.

---

[4] Wheeling-Pittsburgh Steel Corporation, 10-K report, 1976.

[5] Handy and Harman, 10-K report, 1976.

[6] Robert R. Sterling, "Decision Oriented Financial Accounting," *Accounting and Business Research,* Summer 1972, p. 202.

[7] Ibid.

[8] Accounting Principles Board, *Statement No. 3, Financial Statements Restated for General Price-Level Changes,* AICPA, June 1969; and Financial Accounting Standards Board, *Exposure Draft: Financial Reporting in Units of General Purchasing Power,* 12-31-74.

[9] International Business Machines Corporation, 10-K report, 1976.

[10] Kraft, Inc., 10-K report, 1976.

Thus, while the term "current value" may mean selling prices, it may not; it may refer to a variety of valuation approaches. Even if we could define "current value" it is not clear from the statements quoted above (or from any other remarks in the replacement cost footnotes of the companies already cited) that use of some form of "current value" is in fact an appropriate method of accounting in periods of changing prices. Therefore rather than continue to try to determine what is meant by current value, I will briefly summarize the major valuation alternatives which have been suggested, all of which could be considered methods of current valuation.

**REPLACEMENT COST**

A reasonable starting point for this discussion is with replacement cost accounting since this is the current value method mandated by the SEC. The replacement cost of an asset must be considered to be a current value since it is a measure of what current buyers would have to pay for a similar asset.

The SEC is in the process of developing detailed rules and regulations specifying how replacement costs are to be determined. This process is likely to take years. In the meantime, the basic guideline provided requires the preparer of supplemental replacement cost information to determine how much it would cost to replace existing productive facilities and inventories *in the manner in which they would actually be replaced.*

This guideline reflects the SEC's definition of replacement cost and is one of the most serious flaws in the disclosure requirement. The flaw results from the fact that, as most companies replace their productive facilities, they become either increasingly capital intensive or technologically sophisticated. Much of the reason for incurring higher capital outlays is to reduce labor costs and to create tax shelters. But the SEC will not allow a company to reduce the depreciation expense which is based on the replacement cost of the capital intensive productive capacity by an amount equal to the anticipated labor and tax savings. Thus, the information could be misinterpreted.

As an example, consider the United States steel industry. As the industry currently exists, much of its productive capacity is still from an era of reasonably inexpensive labor and is highly labor intensive. As labor costs have increased, the new steel plants which have been built have been more automated, more expensive and less dependent on labor. Evidence exists to indicate that this trend will not change. Therefore, if steel companies calculate replacement costs based on the newer technologically advanced productive capacity, the price will be much higher than the older labor intensive plants. But these additional expenditures probably are economically sound given the size of the anticipated labor savings. The SEC version of replacement cost accounting recognizes the escalating capital costs, but does not require the quantification of the labor savings. Thus, the charges that the SEC's replacement cost numbers are misleading.

The flaw in the SEC's approach is one of implementation, rather than of conceptual weakness. It could be remedied in several ways. One of the most obvious, but least satisfactory from the companies' viewpoint, would be to encourage disclosure of anticipated savings due to replacement of existing productive equipment with technologically superior equipment. But many companies may balk at this type of disclosure because it may be considered proprietary. Also, disclosure of anticipated labor savings would be an extension into forecasting, whereas conceptually replacement cost accounting is concerned with reporting past and present phenomena.

Perhaps a different definition of replacement cost is more appropriate. The SEC's definition of replacement cost is their own and it does not correspond to that in any of the major works dealing with replacement cost accounting. Another definition of replacement cost is the current cost to acquire productive capacity *which would provide the current level of economic services.* In other words instead of using replacement costs for the existing facilities, the measure would be the cost of providing similar economic services.

Continuing the steel industry example, the replacement cost under the alternative definition of replacement cost would be the cost to build a new plant which utilizes approximately the same technology then in existence. This definition is advantageous because the calculation is based on what the company actually has rather than on some nonexistent future plant which the company may or may not build. Thus, the replacement cost figures would be more relevant to the then present activities of the company.

Another advantage of the alternative definition is that the replacement cost figures are based on a plant of the size of that being used. The SEC's definition of replacement cost may result in numbers which reflect much higher levels of productive capacity because newer technology may only be economically feasible at higher output levels.

To summarize, use of replacement cost data might be much less subject to criticism and more valuable as a source of information if a more reasonable definition were adopted. Thus, a more viable method of accounting in periods of changing prices would retain the use of replacement costs, but modify the operational definition so that more reasonable, reliable and meaningful information would be obtained.

## EXIT VALUES

Another measure which may be used to represent "current value" is exit value. Exit value is the amount which may be obtained in the current market by selling an asset. From a theoretical point of view, use of exit values is significantly different from use of replacement costs. From a practical viewpoint, however, most differences may be so small that they are immaterial.[11]

Exit values may be easier to determine because one does not have to be concerned with valuing assets which are no longer produced. We are no longer concerned with buying replacements, but rather with selling those assets we have. Thus, a manager does not have to try to determine what it would cost to buy an asset which cannot be bought. Use of exit values would have several other advantages. One of the major advantages is that it would avoid cost allocation. Depreciation expense is simply the decline in selling price of an asset during a period. Thus, no life estimates are necessary.

Another advantage of an exit value approach is that it is probably the most easily understood of the current value alternatives. The exit value is simply what a company could expect to receive for its assets if it were to sell them in small groups rather than use them or sell the firm as a whole. This is a concept which laymen should be able to easily comprehend. But, valuation problems will still exist for unique assets which are infrequently traded. Estimates will still be necessary to determine what assets could be sold for. A more serious problem relates to defining the hypothetical sale. Would one assume that assets have to be sold immediately (a distress sale) or could the company assume some reasonable time period in order to dispose of its assets in favorable markets? In addition, would the hypothetical costs of selling the assets be deducted from the selling prices?

Exit values have several other disadvantages. One is that an exit value system does not lend itself to traditional income statement presentation. Income, in an exit value system, is simply the difference between the valuation of the net assets at the end of the period, after adjustment for any capital transactions. Thus, revenues and expenses are not an integral part of the system. Furthermore, income, as measured in an exit value system, is time related rather than based on events. Thus, measurements of revenues and expenses are not facilitated by the system. While income

---

[11] Assets which are traded in good markets, such as commodities, are likely to have buying and selling prices which move together. Because of this the income measures based on these prices should also be very similar. Assets which are not actively traded, such as specialized ones, are likely to have a more significant difference in price. Thus, the income measurement for these items will be more divergent. An interesting project would be to try to determine the relative percentage of the assets of a company which are actively traded.

statements have been designed, no general agreement has been reached as to which is most appropriate. Of course, given that the SEC has required disclosure of only supplemental information, this may not be a serious problem.

Another disadvantage of exit value measurements is conceptual: assets are held to be used rather than resold. Thus, the prices reported in an exit value system are based on assumptions which may be contrary to intent. As is the case with replacement cost, exit values may be considered hypothetical. Nevertheless, the exit value approach may be a useful method of accounting in periods of changing prices.

## DISCOUNTED CASH FLOWS

Discounted cash flow valuation is widely discussed by economists and accounting theorists as the theoretically correct way to value assets and measure income. Accountants, however, usually ignore discounted cash flow valuation because of the practical difficulties inherent in implementing such a system. Projecting future cash flows and determining the appropriate discount rate is considered by many to be a completely subjective exercise, not sufficiently objective to be useful for external reporting purposes.

Staubus has suggested that discounted cash flows is the most relevant valuation method. He also recognizes the difficulty of determining discounted cash flows and indicates that they can be approximated by using current market prices.[12] He suggests that net realizable values (current selling prices less costs of selling) be used in valuing inventory, because inventory is held for sale and net realizable value should be a good surrogate for present value of the future proceeds.

On the other hand, Staubus suggests replacement costs be used for assets held for use. He argues that if the company did not have these assets they would have to buy them in the future. These future purchases would require outflows which can be approximated by current replacement costs. The replacement cost provides an indication of what it will cost to use these assets in the future.

Staubus' suggestion makes use of both current market values. Therefore, while the system may be conceptually different from either of the valuation approaches discussed earlier, the practical advantages and disadvantages are the same as for the others.

## GENERAL PRICE LEVEL ADJUSTED HISTORICAL COSTS

As mentioned earlier in this paper, the author concurs with Sterling's and others' suggestion that general price level adjustments be added to any valuation system which is used. Some accountants have suggested that adding general price level adjustments to historical cost amounts would provide sufficient information about changing prices and alleviate any need for current values.

Such an approach has the advantages of being easier to implement than the others and of being objective in the sense that the necessary data are readily available. Implementation is easier because little is added to the historical cost records which are already kept. The historical cost records are adjusted by means of a general price level index. The only extra information needed is the index and the acquisition date of the assets. Since general price level indexes are government developed, they are objective and readily available. The adjustments are relatively simple and could even be programmed on a computer. Thus, the prime advantages of this system are ease of implementation and no loss of objectivity.

Among the disadvantages of the system is that it does not really report the effect of changing prices. Implicit in the system is the assumption that all company assets are affected by inflation in the same manner as are average goods and services in the economy. In other words, each asset's value is determined by adjusting its cost for the price change of the goods and services used in the index con-

---

[12] George Staubus, "The Relevance of Discounted Cash Flow Valuation," *Asset Valuation*, Robert R. Sterling, editor, University of Kansas Press, 1971, pp. 42-69.

struction. Yet it is well known that an index is nothing more than a composite average. It is unlikely that the price of any one asset will change exactly by the same amount as the average of the general index for goods and services. In a period of rising prices in general, some asset prices may fall, some may rise more slowly than average, some faster than average, but few will be exactly average. Therefore, while general price level adjustments may be useful as a general indicator of the effects of inflation, they cannot provide information about the effects on any specific company.

Another disadvantage of general price level adjustments relates to the determination of monetary gains and losses. One of the criticisms leveled at the FASB's general price level exposure draft was that highly leveraged companies would recognize large monetary gains and would look better than companies that do not use such large amounts of debt financing. Furthermore, Kaplan has demonstrated that it is conceptually incorrect to determine monetary gains by applying general price level adjustments to historical amounts of debt. He shows that the correct gain is determined only when current prices are used to value debt.[13] Using historical amounts borrowed to calculate monetary gains is the reason that highly leveraged companies seem to benefit so substantially from general price level adjustments. If current market prices for the debt instrument were used, the magnitude of purchasing power gains from holding debt would probably be much smaller.

The last disadvantage to be discussed is that general price level adjustments are not likely to be easily understood. It is easy to say that these are nothing more than scale adjustments similar to changing feet to yards. But most scale adjustments take place at an instant in time, whereas general price level adjustments are intertemporal. For example, if we measure a board to be six feet long we also know it is two yards long. But if we measured a board as six feet last year, we cannot say it is two yards now unless we know that nothing has happened in the meantime. Yet with general price level adjustments we try to make scale conversions across time while knowing things have changed.

Therefore, if one were to ask the meaning of a general price level adjusted cost the answer would be difficult to understand. It is neither what it would cost to buy the item nor what the item could be sold for. It is the cost of the item when originally purchased expressed in current sized dollars. Since this adjusted price may not actually exist in the world, interpretation is likely to be difficult.

## SUMMARY

In this paper we indicated some of the major valuation techniques which could be considered to provide measures of current value. These techniques include replacement cost accounting, exit value accounting, discounted cash flow accounting and general price level adjusted historical cost. Each of the alternatives uses a price in the valuation process. The difference hinges on the market and time from which the price is taken. One common feature is that all of the methods could be general price level adjusted.

The author hopes that his discussion will enable accountants to be more specific in their thinking on how to account in periods of changing prices. Perhaps one of the systems discussed, or some combination of them is the answer. It is likely that, if the issues are more completely understood and if suggestions become more concrete accountants will find an acceptable method of accounting in periods of changing prices.

---

[13] Robert Kaplan, "Purchasing Power Gains on Debt: The Effect of Expected and Unexpected Inflation," *Accounting Review*, April 1977.

# REPLACEMENT COST ACCOUNTING: HOW WE DID IT

*by W. Howard Wells, Jr.*

In the early part of September 1976, The American Textile Manufacturer's Institute (ATMI), of which the Bibb Company is a member, issued its *Voluntary ASR 190 Implementation Guidelines.* Those Guidelines were our starting point for dealing with replacement cost accounting. Fortunately, we already had a reasonably accurate itemized listing of our productive facilities and it was computerized. Our data base included historical costs and related reserves, methods of depreciation, acquisition dates, original estimated lives, and a reasonably descriptive identification of each productive asset, by location. Without this information we would have found it almost impossible to comply with the regulation. Additionally, several of our key personnel, who would be directly involved with compliance of this regulation, attended several seminars which added to the general guidelines and suggested methods for computing the required data. As a result, we met the challenge, complied with the regulation, and we are better off for our time and trouble.

Our initial goal was to include only such information as relates to calculating the replacement costs and related reserves of our fixed assets, the resultant cost savings and/or increases resulting from technological improvements, and the methods utilized in the formation of this data.

We began by meeting with our independent auditors to discuss the overall problem. During this meeting they suggested that we consider the analysis on an operation by operation basis. We decided that we would write a complete program which would include all of our detailed procedures, assumptions and subsequent revisions.

Reprinted from *Management Accounting*, October 1977, Copyright © 1977, National Association of Accountants, New York, N.Y. All rights reserved.

## PLANNING

The most important factor was that our top management people decided that they would be directly involved with the shaping of our policies. They organized a group to act as a Replacement Cost Accounting Committee, to which they appointed the following individuals:

*The president*

*A manufacturing area executive from Division A*

*A manufacturing area executive from Division B*

*The controller*

*The director of industrial engineering*

*The director of purchasing*

*An assistant controller from operational accounting*

*An assistant controller from financial accounting*

*The tax manager (author)*

Our Committee held its first meeting in late October, 1976, to discuss the requirements of ASR 190 and the voluntary guidelines which had been issued by the ATMI. At that meeting, the following disclosure requirements were discussed: (1) the current cost of replacing our productive capacity and its current depreciated replacement cost, (2) the amount of depreciation that would have been recorded for the year, (3) a complete description of the methods utilized in determining the above information, and (4) any additional information which would be necessary to prevent the above information from being misleading. Our major problems were: (1) developing replacement cost data based upon our fixed asset historical records, (2) determining our out-of-pocket savings based on replacement cost assumptions, and (3) related accounting problems. We also agreed at that meeting that our manufacturing area executives and our director of industrial engineering would decide, on an operation by operation basis, which machines would be replaced and with what types. In addition, we agreed that certain operations should be combined (if they were compatible), that all multi-story buildings should be replaced with single-story structures, and that underlying financial leases should be revalued, based upon the underlying asset. Finally, we agreed to hold a weekly meeting of the full committee to discuss the progress of the overall project, to change assumptions, and to make recommendations with regard to specific operations which would better reflect the best judgment of management.

A working committee was then formed to prepare and summarize the various inputs, and as each operation was completed, it was to report to the full committee. The members of this committee included the tax manager, a senior staff industrial engineer, and a mechanical engineer.

Before any work was begun by the subcommittee, the following questions were asked about each operation:

1. Should this operation be combined with any of our other operations? If so, which one(s)?
2. How many separate and distinct operations are conducted at this location?
3. Based upon new technology, can any of these operations be combined or eliminated?
4. What specific assets are we presently employing in each operation and what types of assets should we replace them with?
5. Based upon the replacement machine size, how many square feet of manufacturing floor space would be required? and
6. Based upon these new square footage requirements, governmental regulations (including OSHA and EPA requirements) and transportation efficiencies, how much would it cost us to replace each building, on a usage basis?

After each of these questions was satisfactorily answered, detailed machinery lists were prepared for each operation. These lists analyzed precisely how many, and, what type of machines should be utilized to replicate present productive capacity.

## REPLACEMENT COST BASIS

There are four generally accepted methods of determining replacement cost. We used all four:

1. *Indexing*
2. *Direct pricing*
3. *Unit pricing*
4. *Functional pricing*

It was determined that each of these methods had certain advantages and disadvantages and that each was more suited to a particular type of fixed asset. Accordingly we used each of these methods where best suited.

### Indexing

If we had purchased a modern and technologically efficient asset, within the past two to three years, and the "state of the art" had not changed, we felt that an indexing method would be appropriate. We also used this method for classes of assets which when compared to the total assets of the company were not of significant value. These classes of assets would include furniture and fixtures, material handling equipment, and miscellaneous machinery and equipment. The indexes used were the "Wholesale Prices and Price Indexes Data for May 1976" from the U.S. Department of Labor, Bureau of Labor Statistics. An illustration of how these indexes were used for furniture and fixtures follows:

| | |
|---|---|
| Cost | $100,000 |
| Annual depreciation | $ 5,000 |
| Accumulated depreciation | $ 70,000 |
| Net book value | $ 30,000 |

*Step 1*
$70,000 ÷ $100,000 = .70
*Step 2*
.70 × 15 years (average life of assets) = 10½ years
*Step 3*
The Wholesale Price Index for 10½ years ago was 93.7 and the current factor is 169.8—a difference of 76.1
*Step 4*
$100,000 × 1.761 = $176,100

The $176,100 was then considered to be the replacement cost for $100,000 of furniture and fixtures purchased (on an average) 10½ years ago.

**Direct Pricing**
The direct pricing method was used in all cases where major units of machinery or readily identifiable machines were to be replaced. In this case, the area executive and the director of industrial engineering decided: (1) what type of replacement machinery would be purchased, (2) whether new or used machinery should be considered, and (3) whether the president's approval for their selections would be required. They then requested that the director of purchasing provide them with the costs of the replacement machines. Used machines would be used to replace current machines only if they were currently available and would continue to be available in the used equipment market, and if in management's judgment they provided a viable alternative to new machinery.

**Unit Pricing**
The only assets which were costed using the unit pricing method were our buildings, all of which would be replaced with single-story structures. As with any specialized industry, certain types of structures could be replaced at different unit costs based upon the functional application of the building. Therefore, a number of square-foot prices were obtained for application to each function, such as manufacturing areas, warehouses, or office buildings.

**Functional Pricing**
There are certain specialized operations for which there are no "direct prices" and indexing would be inappropriate. Therefore, engineering and purchasing applied functional pricing based upon their best estimates of how much it would cost us to replicate certain operations.

## COST SAVINGS OR INCREASES

Since we did not replace each asset with an identical asset and since there had been many technological improvements, resulting in increased efficiencies, there were many direct and indirect savings.

1. *Labor savings—These savings were analyzed, in detail, by department and summarized by operation.*
2. *Fringe benefits—Whenever we incurred direct or indirect labor savings we also computed a fringe benefit savings based on a predetermined percentage of these labor dollars.*
3. *Other labor savings—Whenever the actual number of direct and/or indirect labor employees would be reduced we calculated an additional savings to include such items as training and overtime.*
4. *Utilities—Our mechanical engineer calculated the actual power consumption for the new equipment, and compared these new costs with our historical power consumptions. Any resulting increases or savings were incorporated into our data.*
5. *Property taxes & insurance—Based upon the percentage increase in the net book value of the replacement assets over the net book value of our actual fixed assets, the historical data for these costs were increased with the resultant increases being incorporated into our data.*
6. *Depreciation—Based upon our historical data, we compared the actual depreciation that we would have incurred had we used replacement cost accounting. The replacement cost depreciation was calculated by using the same percentage relationship that historical depreciation bore to historical cost. All depreciation*

*was calculated using the straight line method.*

## OTHER CONSIDERATIONS

Environmental protection devices which are not currently embodied in our existing assets were included in our replacement assets, if these devices were available. In some cases there aren't any machines currently available which *will* meet certain governmental standards. In those cases we used our best judgment as to which machine would be best of those that are currently available. However, asset lives were not adjusted for any technological improvements, and the many small subsidiary assets which were not capitalized on the financial records were ignored. Also, interest carrying costs were not considered due to the fact that there is no way to determine how much of this additional capital would be financed through equity fundings versus additional borrowings. And, the tax effects of the net savings (increases) including substantial investment tax credits were not taken into account.

## COST OF COMPLIANCE

The total costs which have been incurred to date, include 1,500 manhours, and miscellaneous expenses, representing many thousands of dollars. Additional costs have also been incurred for the inventory and cost of sales calculations and the audit fee applicable to this review.

## CONCLUSION

A final report was submitted by the working committee to the full Replacement Cost Committee which summarized our results for the entire company on an operation by operation basis. It led our president to ask: "Now that we have this data, what does it tell us, and what can we do with it to make us a stronger company?" The unanimous consensus was, "It really didn't tell us anything that we didn't already know, but it did highlight a number of areas, which we should analyze more thoroughly, make some minor and some major changes, and become a stronger and hopefully, more profitable company."

# REPLACEMENT COST ACCOUNTING: PROGRESS OR REGRESSION?

*by Michaela M. Marcil*

The professional strength of historical costs has been its claim to objectivity. By using costs which were established in an arm's length transaction, the resulting statements are believed to be more verifiable and subject to audit scrutiny. Opponents of replacement cost statements have long proclaimed that these costs are too "soft" and subject to gross errors of estimation.[1] Replacement cost data must be constructed on the basis of numerous assumptions that are continuously changing and will vary from firm to firm.[2] However, such objec-

Reprinted from *Management Accounting,* February 1979, Copyright © 1979, National Association of Accountants, New York, N.Y. All rights reserved.

[1] Edward J. Bailey, "The SEC and Replacement Cost: An Urgent Need to Find a Better Answer," *Management Accounting,* December 1977, p. 20.

[2] L. Todd Johnson and Philip W. Bell, "Current Replacement Costs: A Qualified Opinion," *Journal of Accountancy,* November 1976, p. 68.

tions fail to consider the broad variety of accounting methods allowed under current generally accepted accounting principles. In fact, "under traditional accounting, variations in classification and allocation procedures can have a significant impact on interperiod and intercompany comparisons."[3] With choices among a number of depreciation methods, estimates regarding useful lives and salvage value, and decisions concerning inventory valuations, one can see how a great deal of subjectivity is unavoidable under the historical cost process.[4]

What current replacement cost figures may give up in "objectivity," however, they may make up in relevance to the user.[5] Indeed, providing relevant data is also among the primary goals of financial accounting. But many corporate executives and accounting practitioners are reluctant to abandon completely the historical cost system because of the great differences that can arise using various replacement cost estimates. More support exists for a supplemental disclosure of these current prices to be issued along with traditional historical cost statements. Unfortunately, there is not a wealth of actual practice in implementing replacement cost systems. Many of the methods necessary, however, to compute replacement cost data are already being used. The lower-of-cost-or-market rule for valuing inventories has necessitated that some firms become cognizant of the procedures for estimating the replacement cost of inventories and investments.[6] Similarly, the purchase method of accounting for business combinations has provided more opportunities for working with current replacement data since assets acquired must be recorded at their fair values.[7] Thus, "many auditing firms are now knowledgeable in the state of the art."[8] In addition, the international scene can provide some further experience. Some variety of current value reporting and/or replacement cost accounting has been used and experimented with in numerous foreign countries.

## SHORTCOMINGS OF ASR 190

Although replacement cost information has been reported for two years now, many executives still complain about the usefulness of the data and its lack of objectivity and comparability. Shortcomings of the SEC ruling include the lack of total conceptual framework—such as regards capital maintenance—from which to calculate the estimates. Also, of concern to many is the incomplete nature of the information required. For example, many firms did not include the estimated cost savings that would result from using new, more efficient plants. Such savings, though admittedly difficult to quantify, can significantly change the replacement cost outcome.[9]

*Liability.* Of paramount interest to those who prepare financial statements containing replacement cost data is the extent of their legal liability in case estimates go awry. Presently, the disclosures required by ASR 190 are covered by the "safe harbor" amendment. In this way, registrants are protected from liability if the data is prepared reasonably and in good faith. Cause for concern may arise in cases where current values are not disclosed inasmuch as the SEC "has supported imposition of liability in cases in which 'special circumstances' would render the balance sheet misleading if textual disclosure of current values is not also made."[10]

---

[3] Morton Backer, *Current Value Accounting* (New York: Financial Executives Research Foundation, 1973), p. 3.

[4] Johnson and Bell, p. 70.

[5] Richard C. Adkerson, "Replacement Cost Accounting: A Time to Move Forward," *Management Accounting,* December 1977, p. 17.

[6] Wayne G. Bremser, "Reporting on Current Replacement Costs," *Management Accounting,* July 1977, p. 34.

[7] Ibid.

[8] Ibid.

[9] Robert W. Berliner, "Replacement Cost Accounting: A CPA's View," *Management Accounting,* December 1977, p. 24.

[10] Backer, p. 9.

*Usefulness.* Replacement cost information is primarily seen as being valuable to current and potential investors and creditors, as well as to management, as a decision-making tool. Knowing the current costs and current expenses enables them to be better able to assess whether one alternative is superior to another in a business decision.[11]

Security analysts are using the new data to provide more information on a company's ability to grow and pay dividends and earn a return on new capital investment.[12] Some firms have found that the current prices increase their borrowing ability as creditors get a better understanding of the current position of the company.[13]

Management already uses a great deal of replacement cost data. These costs can be used in pricing, product planning, and capital planning to great advantage.[14]

The SEC cautions, however, that replacement cost data is not to be used simplistically. The main benefits will be derived by the sophisticated user of this information.

## COSTS OVERESTIMATED

The initial costs of providing the data for the SEC replacement cost disclosures have varied significantly. Texas Instruments of Dallas claimed that it spent $400,000 while Koppers Company, a construction and manufacturing firm in Pittsburgh, paid $100,000.[15]

But many companies overestimated their costs. Because these firms already had much of the data in their own engineering, purchasing, and insurance departments, costs were about one-tenth to one-third what they were first estimated to be.[16] Many of these costs should be a one-time affair.[17]

The position of the SEC is that it believes the benefits to investors outweigh the costs of preparation. Management should also reap additional benefits in more informed decision-making. But aside from these broad generalizations, it is difficult to quantify the benefits to be drawn from preparing replacement cost data.

Replacement cost accounting is not a perfect answer to the problem of how to report useful information on the effects of inflation on the firm. But it does appear to be a step in the right direction, and at least a supplemental disclosure of replacement cost figures appears to be warranted. Increased research and experimentation is still necessary in order to develop a more refined replacement cost system.

---

[11] Johnson and Bell, p. 70.

[12] "Inflation Accounting Is Here to Stay," *Business Week,* December 26, 1977, p. 109.

[13] "How Current Value Data Affect the Balance Sheet," *Business Week,* June 27, 1977, p. 48.

[14] Bremser, p. 34.

[15] Vasil Pappas, "Inflation Accounting in SEC-Order Test Irks Many Companies," *Wall Street Journal,* May 23, 1977, p. 24.

[16] Donald A. Corbin, "SEC Replacement Costs: Suggestions for Full Disclosure," *Management Accounting,* August 1977, p. 13.

[17] Ibid.

# CURRENT VALUE ACCOUNTING—COCOA OR REPCO?

*by R.J. Chambers, MEA*

1. Historical cost accounting has virtually been rejected—at least in most English-speaking countries. It is still practised, and there are still reactionary pockets of people who see nothing wrong with it. But sentiment and argument are strongly against it. Until quite recently the principal alternative contender for "general acceptance" seemed to be current purchasing power (CPP) accounting. The major moves for professional endorsement of CPP, made in the early seventies in the U.K., culminated in the issue in May 1974 of "Statement of Standard Accounting Practice No. 7" (SSAP7). About that time the Australian profession seemed about to follow the same line; and the Canadian and U.S. professions seemed also to be favourably disposed towards it, under the description "general purchasing power" (GPP) accounting. But since then a strong tide of antipathy towards it has set in. Interest has switched to some forms of "current value accounting." Attention is given in this paper to two types of current value accounting, COCOA and REPCO. They will be described, their main features will be analysed and a conclusion on their relative merits will be presented.

2. REPCO is a group of proposals, different in some particulars but relying heavily on the use of replacement costs for asset valuations. Its main idea has a fairly long history. The most elaborate theoretical exposition of it, until the sixties, was in the literature of the Netherlands; and the best known example of it is the accounting of the Philips group, based in the Netherlands. It was given a boost in the sixties on the publication of a book, The Theory and Measurement of Business Income by two American economists, Edwards and Bell. The proposal of the Sandilands Committee[1] and other proposals of the REPCO variety have been heavily influenced by that work.

3. COCOA is a proposal for the use of current money equivalents or resale prices for asset valuations. Its full description is continuously contemporary accounting (hence the abbreviation COCOA). Its systematic exposition is my own work. It took shape in 1962-1964, was published in its original form (Accounting, Evaluation and Economic Behavior) in 1966 and since has been improved and extended. There are traces of some if its main ideas in the "handbook" literature of accounting as far back as 200 years ago; and there are traces of those ideas in accounting practice and in the companies legislation of the last hundred years. A great deal of material illustrative of the widespread significance of information based on the current money equivalents of assets was presented in Securities and Obscurities, published in 1973.

4. There are a number of characteristic features which any system of accounting should be expected to embrace. The analysis will turn on a selection of those features. Reasonably complete and concise descriptions of the systems are given in recent publications of mine—REPCO, in Accounting for Inflation—Methods and Problems; and COCOA in Accounting for Inflation—An Exposure Draft.[2]

---

Reprinted from *Singapore Accountant*, Volume 12, 1977, with the permission of Singapore Society of Accountants and R. J. Chambers.

---

[1] *Inflation Accounting: Report of the Inflation Accounting Committee* (the "Sandilands Report"), Cmnd 6225, H.M.S.O. London, 1975. An extended critical examination of the Report is given in R. J. Chambers, *Current Cost Accounting—A Critique of the Sandilands Report*, ICRA Occasional Paper No. 11, International Centre for Research in Accounting, University of Lancaster, 1976.

[2] These two pamphlets, and *Securities and Obscurities* (mentioned in para. 3), are available from Department of Accounting (H04), University of Sydney, Australia, 2006.

It will be useful for present purposes to give a thumbnail sketch of the method of each of the systems. As there have been many proposals of the REPCO variety, the sketch relating to REPCO will indicate some of the variants only. The variants are drawn principally from the Sandilands Committee's proposal, and from an Australian exposure draft "A Method of Current Value Accounting" (June 1975) and the Australian Provisional Accounting Standard "Current Cost Accounting" (October 1976). The appraisal of the relative merits of REPCO and COCOA is largely independent of the variants of REPCO.

5. REPCO. Under REPCO—

a. *Monetary assets (mainly money and receivables) are stated at their nominal amounts in balance sheets. Non-monetary assets are stated at their estimated replacement costs at balance sheet dates, less amounts, charged against revenues, based on replacement costs. Non-monetary assets which are not essential to the continuation of a firm's operations, or which are not intended to be replaced, are stated at net realisable values. Liabilities are shown at their nominal amounts.*

b. *All transactions are accounted for in the amounts in which they occurred.*

c. *When assets are revalued at current replacement cost, the amount of the revaluation is debited to the asset account and credited to a current cost adjustment account or to an asset revaluation reserve the amount of which is not ordinarily available for distribution as a dividend.*

d. *In calculating net profit for each year, the cost of goods sold is to be determined by reference to the current costs at the time of sale, or at average replacement costs of the year, either by reference to actual replacement costs or by reference to an index of prices representative of the inventories.*

e. *In calculating net profit for each year, the depreciation charge is to be based on the average of opening and closing replacement costs of depreciating assets, or on the average current costs during the period of those assets, or on the closing replacement prices.*

f. *The cumulative provision for depreciation for any asset is to be the "expired" proportion of closing replacement prices. Where, due to subsequent rises in replacement costs, the cumulative depreciation provision is not equal to the expired proportion, the "depreciation gap" or "backlog" is to be made good by a charge against previously reported retained profits, or against the current cost adjustment account, or against the asset revaluation reserve.*

g. *Where there is no year-end equivalent of an asset then in possession, replacement cost is estimated by reference to the current cost of equivalent capacity or equivalent service potential, or by applying an appropriate price index to the original cost of the asset.*

h. *Net income is gross revenues less cost of goods sold and depreciation charges as in (d) and (e), less other expenses at their nominal amounts (as indicated by (b) above).*

6. COCOA. Under COCOA—

a. *All assets are stated at the best approximations to their money equivalents, in their then state and condition, at balance dates.*

b. *All transactions are accounted for in the amounts in which they occurred.*

c. *All variations from the costs or book values of assets, which have not already been brought into account by the sale of assets in the period, are brought into the income account as price variation adjustments. Depreciation charges are one such adjustment.*

d. *There is charged against the total revenues, in calculating income, a capital maintenance adjustment which is obtained by applying to the opening amount of net assets the proportionate change in an index of the general level of prices.*

   e. *Net income is the algebraic sum of the outcomes of transactions, the price variation adjustment and the capital maintenance adjustment.*

7. These descriptions are sufficient to draw a number of conclusions about the merits of the systems. Though we are primarily concerned with those systems, we shall at the same time be able to draw conclusions on the merits of other systems. Most of the characteristics which we will consider have to do with the usefulness of the products of accounting to managers and to outside parties such as investors and creditors. We consider that there is no distinction between the kinds of information required by insiders and outsiders, since both use the information in negotiations, and only one kind of information can be equally fair to both parties to any such negotiations.

**CONTEMPORARY DATA**

8. Both REPCO and COCOA use current prices in deriving asset values. Any financial statements which are to represent the consequences of transactions and events up to a stated date, and which may be used then and thereafter as premises or decisions, should be based on contemporary price data. If any financial statement figures are not based on contemporary prices and money amounts they are false to the stated dates or periods which are part of their descriptions—and misleading to users. Any system such as historical cost accounting and C.P.P. accounting, the price bases of which are in the past, and any system which makes use of future prices, such as discounted cash flow valuations, fails on this point.

**RELEVANCE TO ACTION**

9. A dated balance sheet may properly be expected to represent a firm's financial capacity for action at the date it bears. The kinds of action firms take in the ordinary course of business are buying inventories and services, paying debts and raising loans, paying dividends and taxes, buying and selling plant and other property, issuing shares, and so on. All involve movements in money holdings. Whether or not any conceivable action is possible or feasible depends on knowledge of money holdings, the money equivalents of other asset holdings and the amounts and composition of liabilities. The money equivalent of any non-monetary asset in possession is its market (resale) price, whether or not the firm sells it. Information on resale prices in respect of the assets of firms serves exactly the same function as checking on the selling price of shares one holds. It indicates the firm's present wealth as embodied in its assets. COCOA uses the money equivalents of assets as asset values.

10. REPCO on the other hand uses current purchase prices. These prices do not in principle represent the capacity to do any of the things mentioned in the previous paragraph. A purchase price is what one would have to pay if one did not have the asset in question. It is perhaps indicative of what one would have to pay if one were obliged soon to buy another similar asset. But it does not indicate whether the firm is able to buy the good at the stated purchase price. If a firm were confronted with the question of buying any good, it would deduct the purchasing price from the amount of money (and sometimes the money equivalents of other assets) available or accessible to it. It is not sensible to add an amount of money now held to the purchase price of a good (which one may or may not be able to buy) to find out one's financial position.

**RELEVANCE TO GOING CONCERNS**

11. The typical going concern is continually changing its modus operandi as purchase prices and selling prices of inventories and other assets change, as supplies of goods and services change and as technical devices of production and marketing change. Its behaviour is adaptive. Firms which do not respond to these things sooner or later cease "to go." The information indicative of the capacity to make

any such changes is information on the money and money's worth of assets and on the amount of liabilities from time to time, for money can be spent in any available direction one chooses. A COCOA balance sheet is of this kind (9 above).

12. A REPCO balance sheet, by contrast, is based on the current purchase prices of the specific collection of nonmonetary assets which a firm possesses at balance date. REPCO presumes, in other words, that the firm will continue after any balance date as it did before. The presumption is fallacious; since what is discovered, when financial statements become available, may make it desirable or necessary to do something quite different. A balance sheet based on a specific assumed pattern of future action is clearly irrelevant to the choice between a variety of possible future actions, and irrelevant to any judgment about the general capacity of the firm to continue in business.

## HISTORICITY

13. An account of the past up to some dated present is necessary for all on-going ventures—going on a journey, playing a game, running a business. It is an indication of progress made, and a necessary basis for judgments of that progress and of the advisability of proceeding as before. An account of the past can properly deal only with past actions and events. A statement of the consequences of past actions and events is improper if it omits the consequences of any such action or event, or includes the expected consequences of any future action or event, or includes the hypothetical consequences of any hypothetical action or event, past or future. A statement of any present position is at the same time a statement of the consequences of past actions and events. If the account of the past (say, an income account) cumulated upon a past financial position is not equal to a present financial position, then the account of the past is incomplete and must be adjusted. No better indication can be obtained of a present position than by present discovery or verification of it. In taking observations of the resale prices of assets at balance date, COCOA is strictly historical, completely historical, and non-hypothetical.

14. REPCO fails historicity in several directions. The use of replacement cost entails some notion of future replacement. This is denied by many supporters of REPCO. But a replacement or purchase price is not used or useful in any other context than replacement (except perhaps in indemnity insurance, which is a contract, not an element of financial position). The calculation of net profit by recourse to average replacement prices of inventories or depreciating assets, and the use of indexes for these purposes (see rules 5 (d), 5 (e) above) introduces hypothetical figures into the accounts. The calculation of depreciation charges by reference to expected future lives and expected future resale prices, introduces both future and hypothetical elements into the accounts (as, of course, does the traditional historical cost process). In effect what such a calculation entails is this: Given that the cost of an asset is $1000, if its life turns out actually to be five years, and if its disposal value turns out to be $200, it will have been correct to charge $160 per year on the average. The futuristic and hypothetical nature of the figure should be apparent. COCOA makes no such guesses. Depreciation is simply the ascertained decline (and appreciation is the ascertained rise) in the market resale prices of assets from year to year. In this, as in other respects, COCOA applies strictly and impartially the well-established accrual principle, accruing actually experienced effects, regardless of what may happen in the future. REPCO, by contrast, accrues changes in prices which a firm has not yet experienced and may not experience; for a rise in replacement cost may cause a firm to switch to some other asset rather than replace an existing asset.

15. Under REPCO, if replacement costs rise, past depreciation provisions will have been inadequate to make the accumulated depreciation provision equal to the "expired" proportion of the total amount to be written off. The deficiency is described as "depreciation gap" or "backlog." If the deficiency is charged against the past balance of undistributed profits, no one can ever be sure that an undistributed profits balance is really distribu-

table! The accounts of the past are never complete and reliable! If the amount of the backlog is charged against the amount carried to the revaluation reserve or the current cost adjustment account, the deficiency and the remedy cut across the year-by-year reporting of results and progress. COCOA has no such gaps or backlogs.

16. REPCO introduces other hypothetical elements where replacement costs are not available because equivalent goods are not currently sold. One solution is to find the price of the "nearest equivalent good" and, from that, to calculate a notional replacement cost on the basis of physical capacities. The result is inevitably questionable, since prices have no linear relation to physical capacities (a 10-ton truck is not twice the price of a 5-ton truck). The Sandilands proposal uses specific class price indexes. But the result in this case is also unreliable. The prices of few particular goods are likely to move at the same rate as the price index of the class of goods in which they fall. COCOA does not prevaricate. It seeks a price of the present asset in its then state and condition. It accepts approximations to such prices, based on independent evidence, where there is a going market. But it treats as a sunk cost any outlay for which there is no asset having a current market price.

## CHANGES IN THE GENERAL PURCHASING POWER OF MONEY

17. Particular prices change relatively to one another during inflation; but they do also in the absence of inflation. A rise in the general level of prices is the characteristic feature of inflation. The general purchasing power of money varies inversely with the general level of prices. A fall in the general purchasing power of money means a fall in the general purchasing power of every dollar held, owed, received or paid through the interval of a given quantitative fall. Every firm is thus differentially affected by inflation, and the accounting for every firm must be such that it captures the differential effects. Concurrent changes in particular prices will also have differential effects on particular firms. These also must be captured.

But the important thing about inflationary periods is that the money unit, the dollar, is not the "same" dollar from time to time. All dollars are the same dollars, in name and general purchasing power, at a given date, but not at successive dates. This too must be captured in the accounts.

18. REPCO takes account of changes in particular prices, but not of changes in the general purchasing power of the dollar. The particular processes of REPCO are, in fact, so complex that it is difficult to see what meaning could be attached to the resulting figures if they were adjusted to take account of the depreciation of the dollar. For example, as a replacement cost (or depreciated replacement cost) does not represent purchasing power (see 10 above), it is pointless to make an allowance for the effect on the firm of the decline in purchasing power of its net investment, by use of an index calculation. For a further example, the correction for "backlog" depreciation would be exceedingly difficult to adjust (and if adjusted, impossible to interpret) for changes in the significance of the dollar.

19. COCOA takes account of specific changes in the (selling) prices of nonmonetary assets simply by finding those prices at balance dates and taking up price variation adjustments for assets still in possession. Under COCOA, the total of the money equivalents of assets does represent general purchasing power at the disposal of a firm. The total liabilities represents amounts owing to others, who bear the effect of the fall in the general purchasing power of money. The firm "hedges" against that effect to the extent of its debt. The amount of net assets at the beginning of a period is thus the amount of general purchasing power at risk of depreciation. One simple calculation yields the amount of the fall in general purchasing power during a year of the opening net assets. Let p be the proportionate change in an index of changes in the general level of prices. Then, in terms of general purchasing power, $\$_1 (1) = \$_2 (1 + p)$. If $\$_1 N_1$ and $\$_2 N_2$ represent the net assets at $t_1$ and $t_2$, the change in the firm's command of general purchasing power during the period is $(\$_2 N_2 - \$_1 N_1)$. Substituting $\$_2 (1 + p)$ for $\$_1$, the change is $\$_2 (N_2 - N_1 - pN_1)$. The term $(-\$_2 p N_1)$

is called a capital maintenance adjustment. It is the amount which must be deducted from the total dollar increment in net assets to provide for the maintenance of the general purchasing power of the opening net assets. The calculation is simple; the result is readily interpretable.

**INCOME**

20. The income of a person or firm may reasonably be understood as the extent to which he or it became better off during a year than at the beginning (disregarding consumption for the person and dividends of the firm). "Better off" does not simply mean having more money or money's worth. We do not want money for its own sake. "Better off" means having more general purchasing power. Most claims for higher wages, higher prices, higher dividends, and so on, arise from arguments based on this idea. If the general purchasing power of the opening amount of net assets is the "capital" at risk, net income should be calculated by reference to the maintenance of that capital. That is the function of the capital maintenance adjustment made under COCOA, as described in para. 19 above. The amount of the adjustment is debited in the income account and credited proportionately to undistributed profits and other owners' equity accounts. The net income of the firm is then the net revenues plus or minus net price variation adjustments minus the capital maintenance adjustment. The inclusion of the price variation adjustment is consistent with the generally held view that the gain from a security investment in a period is the dividend received plus the change in the market value of the investment. Net income under COCOA is thus a genuine money surplus, since it is derived by reference only to money and money equivalents.

21. Net income under REPCO is said to be the surplus after providing for the replacement cost of assets used in earning gross revenues. Some expositions speak of this as income after providing for the maintenance of "operating capability" or service potential. In essence this means maintaining a physical capacity. But as we have pointed out (11, above) maintaining a physical capacity has nothing necessarily to do with survival and growth. The Sandilands Report refers to its proposal as calculating income in such a way that if the firm continued as in the past, the same profit would be earned in the future. But this is hypothetical in the extreme. Every firm is subject to the shifts in tactics and expectations of other firms, customers, suppliers, financiers, workers and so on. It is certain that it will not continue as in the past, and a profit calculated on such a basis is therefore irrelevant.

22. The notion of maintaining a physical capacity or operating capability cannot be applied consistently from the formation of a firm, in any case. Its initial "endowment" is a sum of money. What then is to be "maintained" in calculating income in its first year? It can only be some kind of money sum, a financial capacity—not a physical capacity or operating capacity. And if, following some proposals, the depreciation gap must be filled by charges against undistributed profit, the net profits of all or some of the prior years must have been overstated. In any event, as REPCO makes no adjustment for the change in the general purchasing power of money, it ignores one of the factors which influence the "well-offness" of a firm.

**CONSISTENCY**

23. It is a long-standing principle that accounting rules should be applied consistently. It is a principle "more honoured in the breach than the observance." It is usually understood as relating to consistency from year to year. REPCO clearly provides possibilities of inconsistency from year to year. An asset may be "thought to be essential" or "intended to be replaced" in one year, but not in the next. Different valuation rules will be used in the two years (see rule 5(a) above). The Sandilands proposal allows the valuation of inventories at the lower of replacement cost and net realisable value. Thus, again, the same asset may be valued under a different rule in successive years. For both reasons (and there are others) income will not be calculated consistently from year to year. COCOA is consistent from

year to year. The same rule—use of dated money equivalents for all assets—is applied every year.

24. Consistency may also be related to the contents of the accounts of any singular year. Any rule for deriving money amounts of assets or liabilities should be applied consistently. As we have just pointed out, under COCOA one rule is used consistently throughout for the valuation of assets. And liabilities are also expressed in dated money amounts. It follows that the amount of owners' equity is also a dated money amount. And as the amount of income is a dated money amount (see 20 above), the whole of the accounts are consistent within themselves.

25. REPCO has no such consistent rule. The asset total is a mixture of money equivalents (cash, receivables, net realisable values for some non-monetary assets) and depreciated replacement costs. The aggregate of such a mixture has no determinate commercial meaning. As liabilities are shown at dated money amounts, the amount of owners' equity (like the total amount of assets) can have no determinate meaning. The Sandilands variety of REPCO in fact tolerates at least five distinctively different kinds of asset valuation—money equivalents, depreciated replacement costs, lower of replacement costs and net realisable values, discounted present values and historical costs—in any one balance sheet. Such inconsistency cannot yield significant representations of financial positions and results.

## MATHEMATICAL LEGITIMACY

26. Accounting is basically arithmetical. Addition, subtraction and relation are its commonest features. Prices and amounts of money are aggregated throughout any period. Balance sheets and income accounts are aggregations. Financial features of firms are specified in terms of relations between aggregates; the most obvious is the relation of equality between the amounts of assets and equities. It should be expected that all this arithmetical work would be done in a technically correct way, that the rules of arithmetic would not be violated. The principal rule is that only like things may be added or related. Two buying prices may be added; two selling prices may be added; but a buying price may not be added to a selling price. This is not simply a consequence of a logical rule; it is also supported by experience. No meaning can possibly be given to the sum of a buying price and a selling price. Even a pure REPCO system (which excludes the use of net realisable values) fails this rule. For one cannot add a buying price (replacement cost) to an amount of cash and obtain an aggregate having any meaning. The variety of possibilities REPCO provides (see 25 above) is clear violation of the rule for addition. Certainly the numbers, as numbers, can be added; but they make no more sense than adding one's height and one's girth. COCOA, on the other hand, yields balance sheet figures which can properly be aggregated. Its magnitudes relate to one characteristic only of assets—their money equivalents; and their aggregate has the same significance.

27. The previous paragraph related to like properties or things. But the rules of aggregation require also that the magnitudes of like properties be expressed in like units. Money equivalents expressed in U.S. dollars, Hong Kong dollars and Australian dollars cannot be added dollar for dollar. Similarly Australian dollars spent five years ago, last year and last month cannot properly be added, since they are not the same dollars; their general purchasing powers are different. This difficulty can be overcome, however, if we make an appropriate correction for the shift in the general purchasing power of the dollar. We never make such corrections day by day in our ordinary affairs. We only find it useful when looking back over some extended period. And that of course is what periodical accounts are for. The money amounts laid out and received by a firm are bits of history, but they do have a resultant, the amount of money it now has, and the money equivalents of the other things it now has. The only significant question is: is the company better off than it was before? Under COCOA, the function of the capital maintenance adjustment is to enable this question to be answered. Any COCOA balance sheet contains items that can properly be

added—because they are all amounts of "dated dollars"; and the net income is also an amount in the same "dated dollars." Dated financial statements under COCOA are thus contemporary and mathematically legitimate. For a number of reasons already given, the financial statements of REPCO (and any other system) cannot be.

## RELEVANCE TO PAST ANALYSIS OR DIAGNOSIS

28. Business managers and outsiders are the better informed for future action if they know the effects of past actions. The effects are represented by historical accounts, up-to-date and fully inclusive of the financial effects of all past actions and events. Interest centers, however, on the relationships between particular aggregates and sub-aggregates. Thus the ratio of current assets to current liabilities, the ratio of debt to equity (or debt to total assets) and the rate of return, and perhaps other such ratios, are widely used. These ratio calculations are pointless unless the numerators and denominators have significant connections. The current ratio, for example, is taken as a guide to a firm's capacity to meet its debts. As debts must be met in money, the amount of current assets must be an available or accessible money amount. Only under COCOA is this the case. A replacement cost of inventories, or a valuation at the lower of replacement cost and net realisable value, is not a money amount or a money equivalent. It will not yield a proper indication of short term liquidity. A rate of return which relates net profit to a net assets figure based on current replacement costs is not a genuine rate of return on a sum of money actually invested through a period. A rate of return based on net assets at their money equivalents, as under COCOA, is a genuine rate of return on the sum invested at the beginning of a period. It can be compared with rates of return on money contracts such as the bond rate and bank interest rates.

29. Further, no such ratio is legitimate unless the amounts of money in which its numerator and denominator are expressed are in dollars of the same kind. Since COCOA financial statements are expressed exclusively in dated dollars, all ratio calculations are legitimate. No system (REPCO or any other) which does not take steps to express all balance sheet figures and the net profit figure in homogeneous money units as at balance date, can yield mathematically proper and practically useful ratios.

## INTERTEMPORAL COMPARABILITY

30. One aspect of the judgment of past performance is the comparison of the positions and results of two or more successive years. As the dollars of successive years are not the same dollars, the direct comparison of money amounts and aggregates, however they are derived, is not permissible. But properly calculated ratios are comparable. A ratio is a pure number or percentage; it has no "dollar dimension." Since the ratios derived from COCOA financial statements are mathematically legitimate, they are comparable over successive years.

31. Ratios derived from REPCO financial statements are not comparable over successive years both because of the inconsistencies of valuation from year to year (23 above) and because the ratios of any one year are not themselves mathematically valid ratios (28, 29 above).

## INTERTEMPORAL CONNECTEDNESS

32. A set of financial statements of successive years should represent the financial history of a firm. This is possible only if the amounts in the accounts of successive years are progressive. They must be linked year by year to one another by obvious and connected accounting processes which take account of the effects of transactions and events on their magnitudes. The method of COCOA has this characteristic. Money paid and received, increases and decreases in the money's worth of non-monetary assets (price variations), and changes in the general purchasing power of money, are all represented by explicit entries—without omissions, backlogs, hypothetical anticipations,

or switches in the valuations of particular assets.

33. Because REPCO requires that judgments be made about the future (in particular, the "presumed" replacement of assets or operating capability, the "essentiality" or "non-essentiality" of assets—see rule 5 (a) above), each year's accounts will be made up on potentially different presumptions. The accounts will represent the outcomes of the different "outlooks" of a firm's management up on the future of the firm. Differences in outlook from year to year are inevitable. But the history of managerial "outlooks" is not the financial history of a firm. Every change in outlook, if it influences the accounting, constitutes a distinct break in the continuity of progression. The very things which COCOA lacks (see end of 32 above), make REPCO accounts deficient as a complete and progressive account of the financial history of a firm.

**INTERFIRM COMPARABILITY**

34. There being no quantifiable standard by reference to which the solvency, gearing and rate of return of a firm may be judged, comparisons of changes in the position and results of firms (through common periods and therefore similar general conditions) are often made to serve. As between firms of different sizes (in any sense), the only proper comparisons are of ratios or percentages. The accounting of all firms, under COCOA, will be substantially the same, since all must use the same valuation and adjustment rules. Similar assets will be valued similarly—if not at exactly the same amounts, at amounts that are not materially different. The value of p for the capital maintenance adjustment (see 19 above) will be the same for all firms over any given period. For these and other reasons the ratios of firms will be strictly comparable.

35. The ratios of firms under REPCO and other systems will not be comparable. The options available, the exercise of judgments in respect of the valuation rules applied, the omission of the effect of changes in the general purchasing power of the dollars—all of these will make the financial statements of different firms different to unknown degrees. Quite apart therefore from the basic impropriety of the ratios of any particular firm under REPCO, the ratios will not be comparable as between firms.

**OBJECTIVITY**

36. The reliability of any kind of information depends on the way in which it is derived. If it is derived by the application of an accepted non-personal rule applied to the objects in question, and if, therefore, any skilled person independently applying the same rule would derive approximately the same information, the information is said to be objective. Objective information is necessary for all circumstances in which the magnitudes of some objects or the rates of growth of some changing objects are of importance. It is, in fact, one of the functions of auditing to ensure that financial information is reliable; that is why so much is made of independent verification.

37. The method and results of COCOA are objective. There are two basic rules—observation of the magnitudes of the money's worth of assets from time to time, as these are established in the market; and the application of processing rules which conform with the rules for addition and relation. Because the money equivalents of assets are derived by observation of market prices, any qualified observer (in particular, an auditor) can independently check the reliability of figures appearing in the accounts.

38. The method and results of REPCO are not objective. Judgments of the technical similarity of assets, and the choice of other available goods (where goods identical with present assets are no longer procurable) for the purpose of estimating replacement costs, are personal, subjective. Whether an asset should or should not be classed as "intended to be replaced" is a personal judgment. The calculations made of depreciation charges depend on judgments of asset lives and ultimate resale prices. In respect of all these, an auditor cannot check, independently of the persons whose judgments were involved, the propriety of any of the amounts indicated. He can only check

the arithmetic. That is not independent authentication of the amounts shown in financial statements.

## INTELLIGIBILITY

39. The meaning of the singular and aggregate figures in financial statements can only be understood if a reader knows what characteristic is represented by the figures, and that that characteristic is faithfully represented by the figures. It is universally expected that financial statements represent financial positions and results; and as "finance" means "money," the money statements in accounts can only be expected to represent money—in respect of assets, money amounts pertinent to the payment of liabilities, current purchases, wages, taxes, dividends, and so on. This is so elementary and important and understandable a notion that everyone is entitled to expect accounts to represent it, whatever else accounts might show. For the same reasons, users of accounts expect them to represent genuine shifts from time to time in the money amount of the wealth of firms. Further, almost everyone knows the meaning of an annual rate of inflation; that money is not the "same" from year to year is so common a matter of press discussion, governmental concern, wages and price negotiations and so on, that the meaning of a rate of inflation must be considered to be very common knowledge.

    40. COCOA sticks throughout to the money amounts of transactions, the ascertained shifts in money equivalents of goods unsold, and the publicly stated rate of change in the general level of prices. All such amounts are readily intelligible, to lay persons and to "experts."

    41. REPCO, on the other hand, is full of processes which cannot be briefly explained to users of accounts, and figures derived by processes which even an expert could not reconstruct even if they were briefly explained. An outsider, for example, cannot know the line of reasoning or the choices made in deriving a replacement cost estimate; or the estimates of life and scrap value used in calculating annual and backlog depreciation; or the indexes used and methods of finding average replacement costs of inventories. A classical piece of obfuscation occurs in the Sandilands Report. It proposes the use of a value for assets called "value to the business." This is the "written down current replacement cost (current purchase price), except in situations where the written down current replacement cost is higher than both the 'economic value' and the net realisable value in which case the value of the asset to the company is the 'economic value' or the net realisable value, whichever is the higher." What the result of this means, and what the sum of such different values can mean (since any balance sheet could include them all), is unimaginable. Most expositions of REPCO provide for the separate reporting of "operating gains" and "holding gains," following Edwards and Bell. But when some assets must be held for the purpose of operating, it is impossible to grasp the merit of the distinction; as it cannot but be arbitrary, the reported amounts of the two types of gain cannot be intelligible. (Amounts described under COCOA as "price variation adjustments" are much more readily describable and understandable.) Only some of the peculiarities of REPCO have been mentioned here; but enough to indicate that it ranks very low on "intelligibility rating."

## TRUTH AND FAIRNESS

42. A statement of financial position and results cannot be said to give a "true and fair" view if its components are derived by processes specifically chosen by those who report; for by the exercise of particular choices, they can make the report "favourable" to themselves or "satisfying" to others on whose support they rely. Not only must a report be claimed to be fair; it must be seen to be fair. Further, a report cannot be said to give a true and fair view, if it leaves out of account any significant effect—such as the effect of changes in the general purchasing power of money. Indeed, no report can be said to be true and fair which fails such tests as consistency, historicity, relevance to action, mathematical legitimacy, intertemporal comparability, inter-

firm comparability, objectivity and intelligibility. On the grounds previously laid, COCOA does, and REPCO cannot, give a true and fair view of dated positions and results.

## STEWARDSHIP-ACCOUNTING UTILITY

43. That nothing should be overlooked, we turn finally to stewardship, in the judgment of which historical cost accounts have long been said to be preeminently serviceable. If stewardship is judged in any sense at all, it is judged periodically and progressively. Whether such judgment is concerned with the proper use of the resources available to the management of a firm, or the increment obtained from using those resources, it is necessary to know year by year what those resources are at the beginning of each year. This is not possible under "historical cost" accounting, since many resources are represented at their carried-forward book values which have no relationship to contemporary assessments of "resources available." It is possible under COCOA, since the extent of resources available is ascertained afresh year by year, by recourse to the money equivalents of all assets. On similar reasoning, it is not possible under REPCO.

## OTHER ARGUMENTS AND EXTENSIONS

44. It should be clear that COCOA would dispose of many of the "problems" which still plague accounting. A single rule of asset valuation is the greatest possible step towards uniformity (or "the reduction of diversity") in accounting. Countless utterances of committees and individual persons have hailed the desirability of reduced diversity. But some varieties of REPCO have introduced greater potential for diversity than ever before (see 25, 41 above). A new rule of the United States S.E.C. introduced in 1976 requires that replacement cost information on inventories and plant be given in supplementary notes.[3] But the rule leaves the mode of calculation substantially at the discretion of registrant companies. It is possible, therefore, that every registrant will have its own combination of chosen rules. The probability of making valid comparisons between firms on the basis of the resulting figures would shrink to the infinitesimal if this occurred.

45. COCOA does not confuse the valuation of the assets of a business with the valuation of a business as a whole. It excludes all so-called assets which have no significance to going concerns but which might enter into the bargaining base in negotiations for the sale of a going concern; such things as purchased goodwill, development costs, specialised nonvendible assets are written out altogether, or removed to a ruled-off section of the balance sheet, separate from the statement of financial position.

46. Such contingent matters as future tax effects (as in tax effect accounting) and proportionate interests in the earnings of associated companies (as in equity accounting) are treated under COCOA (if treated at all) as contingencies, and appear below the balance sheet, not in it. The whole of the debate about these things is removed by recourse to a long established and technically quite proper device.

47. The affairs of companies having foreign branches and subsidiaries are treated under COCOA in a manner which removes the varied conversion rules now in use or proposed. As all assets are valued at current money equivalents, current rates of exchange can readily be applied to them or their aggregates or differences. The results of such conversions may properly be added to any domestic aggregates—another example of the improvement in mathematical legitimacy. Further, COCOA enables account to be taken of the specific changes in prices and the specific changes in the general level of prices in each different country, improving the capacity for judgment, on the part of a central management, of the relative effects of trading, price movements and inflation.

48. COCOA would also remove the possibility of "puffing" the values of securities or other assets by intercompany sales at notional prices. The necessity of going back

---

[3] United States Securities and Exchange Commission, Accounting Series Release No. 190, Rule 3-17; March 1976.

to market resale prices at the end of each year would "squeeze the water" out of an inflated transfer price. Where there is no market in securities held, the proportionate interest in the net assets of the investee would be an appropriate valuation of the securities. This would squeeze the water out of inflated valuations of securities. It would cut back the opportunity availed of, under present practices, by manipulators who resort to intercompany dealings which have no real substance.

49. COCOA also suggests a rationalisation of "consolidation" accounting. As all companies would value assets according to the same rule, it is perfectly proper to aggregate figures from the balance sheets of companies in groups. It is, of course, quite improper to aggregate figures derived by different companies in different ways, as is possible if not inevitable under REPCO and other systems. Further, as market values are used throughout, there would be no such questionable balance as "goodwill on consolidation."

## CONCLUSION

50. On none of the points discussed has REPCO the advantage of COCOA. Anyone is at liberty to reject some of the points. But reasons for rejection should be expected. I can imagine none. Anyone is at liberty to add additional points. But coverage has been sufficient to indicate that additional points would yield the same evaluation. What form of current value accounting, then, should be adopted? Certainly COCOA rather than any form of REPCO.

# PROBLEMS WITH CURRENT VALUE ACCOUNTING

Two general types of current value proposals have been made: (1) internally consistent theoretical models which give little attention to the problems of application in a wide variety of companies and situations, and (2) somewhat more realistic models directed almost completely to the details of implementation with little concern for theoretical consistency as long as the specific valuation techniques employed fit within the general category of current value.

Although we expect that the more realistic models will be proposed for actual implementation purposes, we feel obligated to consider the theoretical models also because our criticisms run to the basic concepts as well as to the very serious problems of implementation.

This material originally appeared in *Accounting Under Inflationary Conditions,* copyright 1976, Ernst & Whinney, and is reproduced with their permission.

## CONCEPTUAL DIFFICULTIES WITH CURRENT VALUE ACCOUNTING

Theoretical models fall into three types on the basis of the way they value a company's assets: (1) the present value of discounted future cash flows, (2) current realizable value, and (3) replacement cost.

*Change in Present Value of Future Cash Flow.* Most current value proposals are urged as a reasonable approximation of an economic income concept based on the present value of future cash flows which is often cited as the basic economic concept of value. The theory is that if the amount and timing of the future cash flows from a given asset, whether that asset be a security, a machine, or a company, were known, these could be discounted to the present at an appropriate rate of interest and the result would be the value of that asset in the most realistic economic terms.

There is an interesting result in this approach. If a company could be recorded at the present value of its future receipts, the company's net income in any period would then become nothing more than a rate of interest applied to its value. The most revealing information about the differences among companies would be found, not in such a statement of income for each company, but in the calculation of the future cash flows necessary to determine present values. All the differences between companies would be worked out in determining the future cash flows from their anticipated activities. Once the future cash flows were determined and a rate of interest selected, income determination would consist of applying the interest rate to accumulate the present values back up to the amounts of the cash flows.

This approach works ideally with a federal government bond which comes as close to certainty of cash flow as we have in our uncertain world. It would also work for some rental properties under lease for the duration of their lives. But it is quite another matter to apply it to a variety of assets, such as the components of a production line, which must be associated with one another in order to produce an income stream. And, of course, a company is far more difficult to value based on the present value of future cash flows because it includes a variety of assets, not all of which are a matter of record.

For example, how does one determine anticipated cash flows from such intangibles as created goodwill, from a successful marketing program, from a research and development department? Included in the idea of income as the change in the present value of future cash flows is the frequently overlooked idea that if we can approximate the present value of each of a company's individual assets, these can be added to reveal the current value of the company. We have difficulty in accepting the idea, even on a conceptual basis, that all the assets which contribute to a company's cash flows can be identified and valued on any basis that provides dependable information.

Most people concede that, with rare exceptions, the implementation difficulties in applying discounted cash flow concepts of value and net income to the operating assets of many companies on a realistic basis are overwhelming. For the assets of most companies, future productivity is so uncertain that we just do not know and cannot estimate with any degree of objectivity what future cash flows will be. Neither can we find sufficiently reliable evidence of the appropriate interest rate at which they should be discounted. Hence, change in the present value of future cash flows is held by some to constitute an ideal which cannot be attained in practice but should at least be sought.

We do not argue with the idea of present value of future cash flows as a useful economic concept of value. We do disagree strongly with the contention that such a concept has any valid application to the financial statements of a modern corporation. An income concept that presumes (a) to identify as assets all the factors that contribute to a company's future cash flows, (b) to measure the specific cash flows resulting from such factors, (c) to effectively equalize such flows with a discount rate, and (d) then to total the results to obtain the value of the company and to determine its income is so far removed from real world uses and problems of corporate income data as to have little, if any, perceivable relevance to corporate financial reporting.

*Current Realizable Value.* Another group of theorists argues that the major economic decision facing management is whether to continue in its present line of activity or to convert the capital under its control to some other course of action. For example, if the rate of return on government bonds is greater than the return from making steel, the company's assets used for making steel should be disposed of and the amount realized should be invested in government bonds or whatever other available activity promises the highest rate of return commensurate with the risk the company is willing to accept.

But to make such a decision, the argument runs, management must know what the current realizable value of its assets actually is. It does no good to sell the steel mill and find the amount realized is so small that less will be earned on the government bonds than would have been earned if the company still made steel. Therefore, at the end of each period, the current realizable value of the company's assets should be determined. Under this theory, the change in the current realizable value of the company's assets from the beginning of the period to its end, taking into account additional investments and withdrawals, represents its income.

The implementation problems in ascertaining current realizable values are similar to those faced in attempting to discover future cash flows. As a matter of fact, in concept they are much the same. If markets were "perfect," every asset could always be priced at the present value of its future cash flows. In this uncertain world with limited and imperfect markets, a variety of questions arise. What is the current realizable value for a steel mill? Do we plan on selling the assets on a piece by piece basis or seek bids on the plant as a whole? Does one assume forced sale liquidation or disposition on a going concern basis? What value is to be used if no sales of plants of this kind or size have taken place recently?

We have great difficulty in finding any usefulness in such information even if it could be obtained. Certainly management must be alert to the possibility that other opportunities exist for employment of its capital. But going out of business is not a decision that needs to be made at every balance sheet date, nor should possible liquidation dominate financial reporting when the normal expectation is that the company will continue.

*Replacement Cost.* Replacement cost, a term that seems to mean many things to many people, is often advocated as the closest practical approximation of discounted future cash flows. Conceptually, except for market imperfections, replacement cost, current realizable values, and the present values of future cash flows should be the same. The assumption is that the market is willing to pay for any asset no more than the present value of what that asset will produce in the future in the way of cash flows. Thus, the present replacement cost of any asset is the market's estimate of the future cash flows of such an asset discounted at what the market considers to be a reasonable rate of interest.

We have already noted what we consider to be the fundamental flaw in that approach to asset valuation and income determination. Equally serious implementation issues require resolution.

The difficulty with replacement cost arises when we consider the nature and circumstances of the asset to be replaced. A simple staple like a ten-pound bag of sugar will likely be replaced by a ten-pound bag of sugar so similar that telling them apart might be nearly impossible. But replacing a complex piece of production machinery presents another problem entirely. If it were to be replaced at all, it might be by a greatly improved machine designed to perform the same function, or by a substantially different machine designed to use new technology for attaining the same results, or by equipment that produces a different product to perform the same function as the old product. A conceptual question concerns the extent to which replacement cost of property and equipment should recognize technological change.

In general, the following versions of replacement cost are all possibilities:

> *Reproduction Cost of Existing Assets. The cost to replace existing assets without considering technological improvement. Reproduction cost is frequently approximated through price-level adjustment of historical cost amounts using specific price indexes.*
>
> *Replacement Cost of Existing Assets. The cost to replace a single asset or groupings of congruous assets with other assets of equivalent productive capability. Replacement cost is equivalent to reproduction cost only in those relatively rare instances when there has been no technological change.*
>
> *Replacement Cost of Existing Capacity. The cost to replace productive capacity without regard to existing assets or their physical distribution. This approach repre-*

sents a forecast of how the company might proceed if it were to establish a competing business with identical productive capacity. For this purpose, technological change, economies of scale, and other anticipated savings are all considered. Variations in the way these influence replacement cost seem unavoidable.

In addition to the possibility of confusing these, some pose significant implementation shortcomings. The lack of an adequate and accepted technology to develop replacement cost data, absence of a reasonably identifiable set of standards to reduce subjectivity to a satisfactory minimum, and a widespread failure to understand either the purpose or limitations of replacement cost data represent important deficiencies. We believe that adoption of replacement cost for financial statement purposes would introduce problems of measurement and interpretation that would far exceed those now faced in conventional financial reporting.

The SEC has introduced yet another application of replacement cost, one that tends to emphasize implementation over theory.

***SEC Requirement for Supplementary Replacement Cost Data.*** A modification of replacement cost accounting was adopted by the Securities and Exchange Commission on March 23, 1976, in its Accounting Series Release No. 190.[1] The new SEC rule calls for the disclosure on a supplementary basis, by certain large companies, of the following items of information:

*The current replacement cost of inventories at each fiscal year end for which a balance sheet is required.*

*For the two most recent fiscal years, the approximate amount which cost of sales would have been if it had been calculated by estimating the current replacement cost of goods and services sold at the times when the sales were made.*

*The estimated current cost of replacing (new) the productive capacity together with the current depreciated replacement cost of the productive capacity on hand at the end of each fiscal year for which a balance sheet is required.*

*For the two most recent fiscal years, the approximate amount of depreciation, depletion, and amortization which would have been recorded if it were estimated on the basis of average current replacement cost of productive capacity.*

The requirement differs from the typical proposal for replacement cost accounting in both purpose and detail. It does not call for determination of a net income amount based on replacement cost, although an invitation to make such a calculation seems implicit in provision of the replacement cost data. The SEC Release states that the information is offered as supplementary data intended to provide information to investors which will assist them in obtaining an understanding of the current costs of operating the business which cannot be obtained from historical financial statements taken alone. A secondary purpose is stated to be to provide information which will enable investors to determine the current cost of inventories and productive capacity as a measure of the current economic investment in these assets existing at the balance sheet date.

A distinguishing feature of the SEC's replacement cost rule appears in its definition of replacement cost as the current cost to obtain an asset of equivalent productive capability in accordance with management's normal or most likely replacement policy. Thus if a given item of equipment which cost $1,000 and is still profitable could be replaced either by a similar piece of equipment at a current cost of $1,200 or by a technologically improved machine at $1,500, the replacement cost to be used would depend on management's policy.

---

[1] Ernst & Ernst Financial Reporting Developments, *SEC Requires Replacement Cost Disclosures for Large Companies,* April 1976, Retrieval No. 38450.

If it is assumed that management's policy would be to acquire the technologically improved machine at time of replacement, the replacement cost of the machine would be reported at $1,500 under the SEC rule.

In this illustration, SEC replacement cost results in an asset valuation greater than that which could result under other definitions of replacement cost. The difference exists because the SEC calls for replacement cost to be determined using management's normal approach to replacement.

SEC replacement cost and "ordinary" replacement cost will approximate one another when any technological advance is reflected in the asset cost. If that technological advance appears instead in the use of less material because spoilage is reduced, or in lower labor costs, or in energy consumption, replacement cost under the two approaches may be significantly different.

Companies are currently seeking to apply the SEC replacement cost concepts. We expect that most companies will be able to do so, although at some cost and management effort. But to what end? Will the resulting information have any practical use? Nothing in the SEC Release answers the kinds of conceptual and implementation objections we have to replacement cost accounting but we strive to keep an open mind until the considerable experience to be acquired during the next year or two will provide a better basis for evaluating the usefulness of the required information and the implementability of the rule as it stands.

## IMPLEMENTATION PROBLEMS IN CURRENT VALUE ACCOUNTING

As mentioned previously, models advanced by practitioners tend to adopt current value as a general goal of financial reporting, a goal to be reached in specific circumstances by whatever valuation technique seems both available and appropriate. For example, current market quotations would be used for marketable securities; inventories would be valued at the lesser of current replacement cost or current realizable value; income producing property at exit or discounted value; plant and equipment at replacement cost or exit value with replacement cost selected from (1) reproduction cost, (2) the replacement cost of existing assets, (3) the lower of replacement cost or reproduction cost, or (4) the lower of replacement or reproduction cost provided the resulting amount does not exceed the present value of future cash flows.

Although general agreement might be reached among current value advocates on the appropriate valuation procedure for many assets and liabilities, a number of items present special problems. Included among these are intangible assets such as goodwill, patents, and copyrights; land in use under productive facilities; natural resources such as oil reserves; and even long-term receivables and payables when interest rates are changing.

Consider the determination of financial statement amounts for long-term receivables and payables. Some current value proponents would have companies revalue all such long-term items at every balance sheet date. Fluctuations in interest rates would then influence reported income. To the extent that a company has entered into a long-term financing transaction at a current market rate, we feel that rate should govern the accounting for the receivable or payable until settled or until another transaction is consummated.

Neither the lender nor the borrower can control prevailing interest rates, and it is economically impracticable to refinance obligations or dispose of assets at every rate change. Of course interest rates influence the profits of companies engaged in financial activities but we believe financial statement readers are interested in the results of actual transactions, not in every change that would have influenced other transactions if they had been entered into.

*Net Income in Current Value Models.* In reporting net income, current value models exhibit differences similar to those found in their valuation methods. Most models try to subdivide the present net income figure into a variety of components including, for example, operating income, realized value changes, and unrealized value changes. Some would include a provision for capital maintenance based on the decline in the general purchasing power of the dollar. Others would adjust reported income for general purchasing power gains or losses on net monetary items.

Segregation of holding gains (generally defined as the increase in value of an asset during the time it is held by a company) is a relatively common characteristic of current value reporting proposals. This is apparently done on the theory that such gains are so different from operating income that they should not be combined with it. In some cases, the contention seems to be that they are not actually enterprise income at all. The purpose in separating them from other income items is so that financial statement readers will identify holding gains as something they cannot count on to be repeated in future years.

As a practical matter, holding and operations are often inseparable. Manufacturing and sales operations cannot be conducted without holding inventories and other assets for a period of time, and to report these activities as if they were separable can be misleading. In other cases, holding gains are the result of wise management planning and purchasing and are as much a result of management action as are operating gains. We concur that extraordinary market changes may result in holding gains that are not indicative of a company's ability to sustain reported earning power but we feel that such changes can be disclosed without major modificatons to the conventional income concept.

Because we believe the present concept of corporate net income has demonstrated great usefulness, we are opposed to the idea that what is now reported as net income should be subdivided into a number of separate elements with new designations and descriptions. The present concept of net income is so much a part of the way investors, management, credit grantors, labor, regulatory authorities, and others think about business success and failure that proposals to change it in major ways impress us as unreasonable. Such a proposal would place a significant burden on financial statement readers who would then be left to their own devices to formulate and apply some concept of enterprise net income. The failure to identify and determine net income is not likely to be received by financial statement users as progress.

*Loss of Discipline Under Current Value Proposals.* It seems curious that some of those who now complain that present financial reporting already includes far too wide a range of acceptable practices should advocate abandonment of historical cost. One can only conjecture about the total range of asset valuation practices that would be proposed as acceptable if current value amounts were injected into financial statements. Certainly the discipline now incorporated in conventional accounting, the hard-earned results of decades of work by many individuals and organizations, is likely to be sacrificed if a new basis of accounting is adopted, and the long, tedious, and painful process of developing authoritative standards will have to commence anew.

*Financial Statements Adjusted for Changes in General Purchasing Power.* An entirely different method of adjusting accounting data for the impact of inflation was proposed by the Financial Accounting Standards Board in an exposure draft entitled "Financial Reporting in Units of General Purchasing Power." Ernst & Ernst opposed the issuance of that proposal as a financial accounting standard.[2]

Our primary opposition focused on the recommendation that the purchasing power gain or loss from holding net monetary items be included in net income although it is an item that will never constitute realized net income in the sense that most readers of financial statements understand that term. It represents a "gain" that will never be received by the reporting company in cash and as such cannot be reinvested or distributed to shareholders. We commented further:

> *On this point, GPP net income for conservatively capitalized companies will compare unfavorably to that of highly*

---

[2] Ernst & Ernst Financial Reporting Developments, *Price Level Accounting,* Aug. 1975, Retrieval No. 38350.

*leveraged companies, because the latter will include larger purchasing power gains as part of their net income. Users may not understand that income in leveraged companies is influenced by the amount of debt and could erroneously conclude that prospects for leveraged companies are unrealistically better than future cash flows will ever justify. The opposite conclusion may be reached for conservatively capitalized companies. Should this occur, reported net income would be misleading as a measure of past success and future prospects.*

We also objected to the proposal on the grounds of its general lack of understandability, the questionable usefulness of price level adjustments for economic predictive purposes involving specific companies based on a single general index, the cost of not only implementing the proposal but of educating financial statement users to an understanding of its meanings and limitations, and the widespread lack of enthusiasm for a procedure which has been available for years.

We did take that occasion to advocate the reporting on a supplementary basis of depreciation expense adjusted for price level changes, a position included in the recommendations of this present paper.

In June, 1976, the FASB announced that it had decided to defer further consideration of a statement on Financial Reporting in Units of General Purchasing Power.

## CONCLUSIONS ABOUT CURRENT VALUE ACCOUNTING

Our approach to resolving accounting issues is essentially an application of a cost/benefit test. What are the net advantages or disadvantages of historical cost? What are the net advantages or disadvantages of current value? How do they compare? Such an evaluation, of course, should be made keeping in mind the varying interests in and uses of accounting data. We recognize that others may place different evaluations on some of these factors but, given our experience and practical orientation, we find the decision an easy one.

In favor of historical cost we find its demonstrated usefulness over time and under a variety of circumstances. It has wide acceptance and understanding, and is supported by a body of well established standards and practices. Literally innumerable decisions are made every day on the basis of conventional accounting data and those who make them are not the ones calling for a change to current value. On the negative side we recognize its limitations during times of inflation or deflation and the desirability of supplementing it with specific value information under some conditions. Both of these deficiencies can be remedied, the first by the proposals in this paper, the other by supplementary disclosures.

We also support continuing efforts to narrow the range of acceptable practices insofar as this is possible without unduly restricting application of the judgment necessary to recognize the influence of circumstances and conditions on transactions.

Current value advocates claim great usefulness for financial statements prepared on that basis but such claims are as yet completely unsupported by any significant amount of experience. They also claim conceptual conformity with economic concepts, but this claim is subject to challenge. On the negative side are anticipated but as yet unknown problems of implementation. We consider these of great importance. There is also an absence of experience, of acceptance, and of discipline in the form of established standards or accepted practices. An additional negative is the cost of change if current value is substituted for historical cost, a change that can result in great confusion and distress to those who fail to understand the results.

Given such a summary, we can come to no other conclusion than that the clear balance of usefulness at this time remains with the modest departure from historical cost we have recommended. If we put ourselves in the position of corporate managers, investors, analysts, regulators, taxing authorities, creditors, or whatever interest you choose, and consider whether we would prefer to have traditional financial statements, modified as proposed in this paper, or some version of current value with all the disadvantages we envisage in the implementation of that method of accounting, we find historical cost to be the better choice by far. On any cost/benefit test we can apply, society would be ill served by the adoption of current value accounting as the basis for corporate financial reporting.

# HOLDING GAINS AND LOSSES
### by Robert D. Baumann, MBA

## DEFINITION

This discussion of holding gains and losses comes about because in FASB #33, one of the supplementary requirements is to show income on a current cost basis. In general, those who back a current cost accounting scheme believe that income on a current cost basis "represents earnings or losses resulting from the efforts of the enterprise after removing the effects of gains or losses resulting from possessing (holding) assets during a period of changing prices."[1] Therefore, it becomes necessary to break-out and separately disclose from current cost income that part attributable to the holding of assets in times of changing prices.

Holding gains and losses, as discussed here, are referred to in FASB #33 as increases or decreases in current cost, even though in the exposure draft they were indeed termed holding gains and losses. The reason for this difference in terminology is that in response to the exposure draft, many comment letters received by the Board stated that the terms "gains" and "losses" should not be used in connection with these items, mainly because these gains or losses do not constitute income which is available to be distributed without impairing the operating capability of the enterprise.[2] This point will be discussed in further detail in a later section of this chapter. This item will be referred to as a *holding gain or loss* for the purposes of this paper. Regardless of how the item is referred to, this item is calculated by computing the differences in current costs of assets at their entry and exit dates for the fiscal year being reported on. Entry date means either the beginning of the year or the date of purchase, whichever is more recent, and exit date means the end of the year or date of use or sale, again whichever is more recent. Part of the difference in the two measurements is attributable to inflation in general, and part of it is due to economic factors such as supply and demand and new technology which affects the individual prices of the particular assets owned.[3] "This disclosure is designed to show how the increases in the current costs of a firm's resources have fared in comparison with general inflation."[4] It is important to remember that this inflation component does not represent the effect of inflation on the historical costs of assets, but on the current cost measurements. Therefore, this figure should not be interpreted as a compari-

---

Robert D. Baumann, "Critical Analysis of FASB No. 33" (Master's thesis, Pace University, May 1980). Used by permission of Robert D. Baumann.

[1] Peat, Marwick, Mitchell & Co., *Statement of Financial Accounting Standards No. 33* (New York, N.Y.: Peat, Marwick, Mitchell & Co., 1979) p. 16.

[2] Financial Accounting Standards Board, *Statement of Financial Accounting Standards No. 33* (Stamford, Conn.: Financial Accounting Foundation, 1979), p. 66.

[3] Arthur Young, *Financial Reporting and Changing Prices* (New York, N.Y.: Arthur Young, 1979), p. 17.

[4] Ernst and Whinney, *Financial Reporting Developments: Inflation Accounting* (New York, N.Y.: Ernst and Whinney, 1979), p. 77.

son between the current cost and historical cost/constant dollar measurements.

## REQUIRED DISCLOSURES

As far as the disclosures required by FASB #33 are concerned, all the statement asks is that the increases or decreases themselves in the current costs of inventory and property, plant and equipment be disclosed. These figures should be disclosed both before and after the effects of general inflation have been eliminated. If current cost increases at a slower rate than general inflation, the result will be a net change in current cost which is negative. It goes on to state that these amounts should not be included in the figure for income from continuing operations on a current cost basis. Normally, these increases or decreases attributable to the effects of general inflation should be measured in average-for-the-year constant dollars, unless comprehensive supplementary statements are presented. In that case, end-of-year constant dollars could be used as well. Applying constant dollar methods to current cost figures can be looked at "as an adjustment for changes in the general purchasing power represented by the worth of the enterprise insofar as that worth is recognized under current cost accounting."[5] Even though a significant increase or decrease in the specific prices of assets may have a significant effect on net assets on a current cost basis, if the effect on cost of sales and depreciation is immaterial, this current cost information would not be required, but the reasons for its omission must be stated. Just the discussion alone of events such as this in explanatory comments will help to inform readers of some of the effects of changing prices on the specific firm.[6]

---

[5] FASB, *Statement of Financial Accounting Standards No. 33*, p. 19.

[6] Peat, Marwick, Mitchell, *Statement of Financial Accounting Standards No. 33*, p. 23.

## FREQUENCY OF HOLDING GAINS AND LOSSES

Unlike the gains and losses on net monetary items, where the recent published financial statements showed most firms having a gain, these same financial statements have not shown either holding gains or holding losses to be favored. The main criteria or pattern, as far as this writer has been able to discern, revolved around the type of industry the specific firm is in. Firms that design calculators or stereo equipment have seen new technology being rapidly developed in recent years, and therefore the cost of any given item which was on the market yesterday is cheaper to produce today. Firms such as these would experience "losses" due to holding these items in inventory. Other firms such as utilities or steel manufacturers, industries which are capital intensive, are recognizing holding losses for one of two reasons. Since demand is a factor in determining the current cost of assets and there is little demand for the types of assets the aforementioned firms use, their current prices will tend to remain more or less constant based solely on the demand factor. This gives the general rate of inflation a chance to increase at a faster rate, thereby causing a holding loss to appear on the firm's financial statements. The second reason is that the recoverable cost of the assets of these firms is very low (since there is not a big aftermarket for smelters), and that if this amount is less than current cost, it must be used in the calculation, thereby intensifying the holding loss.

In other industries where technology plays no significant role in the cost of the product and the demand is high, such as the food industry and all that it encompasses, these firms will likely show a holding gain, due to the fact that the prices of their goods are rising faster than the general rate of inflation.

## IS A HOLDING GAIN INCOME?

As was mentioned earlier, there had been much debate over whether to call the item under consideration a holding gain or loss or an increase or decrease in current cost. This question, in turn, hinged on whether this item represented income or something else. Let it be made clear at the start that the Board, in FASB #33, has not clearly answered this question.[7] Opponents of the term holding gain or loss state that no real gain takes place or is recognized, and that terming this item a gain would be to disregard the realization principle of income. They argue that the "income" from this gain could not be distributed without impairing the operating capability of the enterprise. This is where the crux of the issue lies, in the capital maintenance theory one subscribes to. Under consideration are both the financial and physical concepts.

If one subscribes to the financial capital concept, then the holding gain would be looked at as income, since income is determined by the difference in dollars invested as compared to the dollars received from that investment. If, on the other hand, one subscribes to the physical capital concept, where income is not considered earned until a firm provides for the maintenance of its productive capacity, then a part, if not all, of the holding gain would not be considered gain at all, but would be considered a capital maintenance adjustment needed to reflect the increasing costs of assets at the end of the period versus the beginning. This figure would be shown as a direct adjustment to equity.

In the exposure draft, the Board stated that they had chosen the financial capital maintenance concept, and accordingly, that holding gains were to be viewed as income. Based on letters in response to the exposure draft though, the Board has changed its position and has decided to remain neutral on the capital maintenance concept. In view of this, they decided that it was preferable to describe this item as an increase or decrease in current cost amounts. The debate still goes on as to whether or not this item represents a gain or income, but the Board has left that up to each individual to decide.[8]

---

[7] FASB, *Statement of Financial Accounting Standards No. 33*, pp. 66-67.

[8] Ernst and Whinney, *Financial Reporting Developments*, pp. 75-76.

## EXAMPLE OF A HOLDING GAIN

To further enhance the reader's understanding of a holding gain, let us look at an example of one.

Assume a firm purchases an unfinished item and exerts effort to finish it and make it available to consumers. Further assume that between the time of purchase and sale, the cost of acquiring the original unfinished item has increased. Since current cost income has previously been defined as the earnings or losses resulting from the efforts of the enterprise after removing the effects of gains or losses resulting from possessing (holding) assets during a period of changing prices, the efforts of the firm are properly computed by measuring the difference between the sale price and the current price of the unfinished item, and not the difference between the sale price and the original cost of the unfinished item. Assume the original cost of the item is $10, the rate of inflation is 10 percent per year, the cost at year-end for the item is $13, and the item is sold for $15. The current cost income would be $2 ($15 original cost less $13 year-end cost). The gross effect of changing prices on the item during the period held is $3 ($13 year-end cost less $10 original cost). Of this $3, $1 is attributable to the effects of general inflation ($10 × 10 percent), and $2 are attributable to the effects of changes in the price of the specific item ($13 year-end cost less [$10 original cost plus $1 effect of inflation]).[9]

## ADVANTAGES OF RECOGNIZING THE GAIN OR LOSS

Now that holding gains and losses have been defined, the disclosure requirements of FASB #33 discussed, the theoretical implications of calling this item a gain looked at, and an example of a gain presented, the advantages and disadvantages of recognizing this item will be brought out.

To begin with, the management of many

---

[9] Peat, Marwick, Mitchell, *Statement of Financial Accounting Standards No. 33*, pp. 16-17.

firms try to call attention to the fact that once a firm is operating at a constant level of output, a holding period between buying and selling must necessarily take place. They go on to state that since this holding period is not absolutely fixed, if as a result of holding inventories, there is a significant rise in the current cost of these inventories due to favorable buying decisions, then it would be and is proper to recognize a gain, especially if these opportunities may not recur.[10]

Next, it is believed by many that separating the income from continuing operations from the holding gains and losses will provide an improved basis for assessing future cash flows, which to many investors is the key factor in an investment decision. The results of each of these two activities will be affected by different economic factors and therefore the two measures may be useful in different ways to assess these future cash flows. It is much easier to follow and account for the numerous factors which affect the patterns of a firm's operating income and changes in the current cost amounts if these two items are presented separately, especially since these two measures have different patterns over time. Also, they can always be added together to give an overall view of a firm's operations if so desired by an investor, but if presented together, most investors could not break down the combined figure into its two component parts.[11]

Lastly, and in spite of the arguments presented above, as we mentioned before, from a purely theoretical aspect, the determining factor as to whether or not the gain should be computed and shown depends on one's concept of capital maintenance. Quite simply put, if one favors the financial capital concept, the gain should be recognized; if one favors the physical capital concept, then the gain should not be shown as such, but rather be labeled as a capital maintenance adjustment.

## DISADVANTAGES OF RECOGNIZING THE GAIN OR LOSS

There are probably more reasons not to recognize the gain than there are in favor of recognition. The most important ones will be looked at now.

To begin with, to the degree which the increase in the current cost of an asset has been realized by a sale of that asset during the year, that increase has already been included in the figure for income from continuing operations on a current cost basis. The same would hold true for fixed assets, only here the doubling up comes from the recognition of current cost depreciation expense. So while the holding gains include both realized and unrealized amounts, nowhere is a firm required to separately disclose these two components. Also, the unrealized portion does not, of course, represent the receipt of cash, so this figure should not be considered as a source for providing funds for reinvestment or for dividend distribution. It is felt that because of this, readers of financial statements may be confused as to what the figure really represents as far as they are concerned.[12]

In view of the fact that the holding activities of a firm are necessary to the continued operations of that firm, many people have severely criticized the ascribing of income to such necessary holding activities. They feel that the figure should not be recognized separately but should properly be included in income from continuing operations on a current cost basis. Opponents of this figure also state that the true significance of it cannot be determined merely by considering its size and whether or not it is positive or negative. They feel that an important consideration for the firm is whether or not the selling prices of their goods are responsive to changes in current cost, without giving consideration to the general rate of inflation.

Lastly, there are those who feel that disclosing only the total increases or decreases in the current cost of assets may not be going far

---

[10] Ernst and Whinney, *Financial Reporting Developments,* p. 25.

[11] FASB, *Statement of Financial Accounting Standards No. 33,* p. 58.

[12] Young, *Financial Reporting and Changing Prices,* p. 17.

enough, that it will not really be of any significance to financial statement users in and of itself. They feel that this figure should be broken down between inventories and property, plant and equipment, since some users may attach greater emphasis to the current cost increases for inventories as compared to property, plant and equipment, because where property, plant and equipment is concerned, "the cash flow consequences are often less direct and more future-oriented."[13]

---

[13] Ernst and Whinney, *Financial Reporting Developments,* p. 25.

# Inflation Accounting in Other Countries

# EXTRAORDINARY INFLATION: THE ARGENTINE EXPERIENCE

*by Ke-young Chu, MEA, and Andrew Feltenstein*

Modern countries have all, almost without exception, suffered periods of inflation. In general these inflations have been controllable, both in their severity and in their duration, but there have been certain instances in which the acceleration in the rate of increase in prices has been seemingly unmanageable. Perhaps the most famous such case, and one of the few instances of true hyperinflation, was the German inflation of 1923, during which the rate of increase in prices rose to a peak of more than 30,000 per cent a month and the economy was reduced to functioning virtually as a barter economy.

In the past 20 years there have been no examples of such violent inflation, but there have been a few countries where for a significant period of time the rate of price increase seemed to be genuinely out of control. Three of the most recent examples were Chile in 1973, when inflation reached an annual rate of more than 650 per cent; Indonesia in 1966-67, with rates of increase in prices of over 170 per cent annually; and Argentina in 1973-76, when the rate of inflation had risen to 50 per cent a month by the spring of 1976 and to almost 350 per cent during the course of that year. The case of Argentina is particularly interesting because a number of the country's economic policies had a significantly adverse impact upon inflation although, paradoxically, they were often designed precisely to reduce the rate of increase in prices. This article summarizes the results of an analysis of the relationship between inflation, price controls, the money supply, and real wages in Argentina for the period 1963-1976.

Price controls were a major characteristic of Argentine economic programs implemented between 1963 and 1976—aimed at both controlling inflation and real wages. In 1963 the economy was operating without any significant

Reprinted from *Finance & Development,* June 1979, Volume 16, Number 2.

controls at a rate of inflation that was approximately the postwar average of about 24 per cent a year; between 1964 and 1966, however, the Government, dissatisfied with this rate of price increase, initiated a system of selective direct controls on the prices of the public sector and of certain private industries, such as agriculture. This program did keep prices down initially, but the rate of inflation eventually rose again, and the system was abandoned at the end of 1966. A new Government introduced an anti-inflation program that simultaneously applied restraints to both wages and prices. In support of these measures, the Central Government significantly reduced its deficit, which had been a major source of monetary expansion and hence of inflationary pressures. During 1967 and 1968 certain selective price controls, which attempted to stem the rate of increase in costs, continued to be used. Between 1968 and 1969 Argentina experienced the lowest rates of inflation in recent history while continuing to reduce its reliance on price controls (see Chart 1).

In 1971 this period of relatively low inflation came to an end. Fiscal policy became expansionary and wage programs were relaxed; in addition, in an unsuccessful attempt to slow the rise in prices, firms were not allowed to pass on increases in wage costs to their output prices. In 1973, the Peron Government returned to power in Argentina, bringing with it the Social Contract, a program whose primary goal was to raise the general level of real wages and to redistribute income. Price controls were a key component of this program: in June 1973, prices for a large number of consumer goods were lowered by 7 to 20 per cent, and, at the same time, nominal wages were raised by an average of 20 per cent. As a result, business profits were severely squeezed, shortages and black markets developed, and by April 1974 there was sufficient pressure to compel the Government to relax its controls. Since wages continued to rise, an inflationary spiral began.

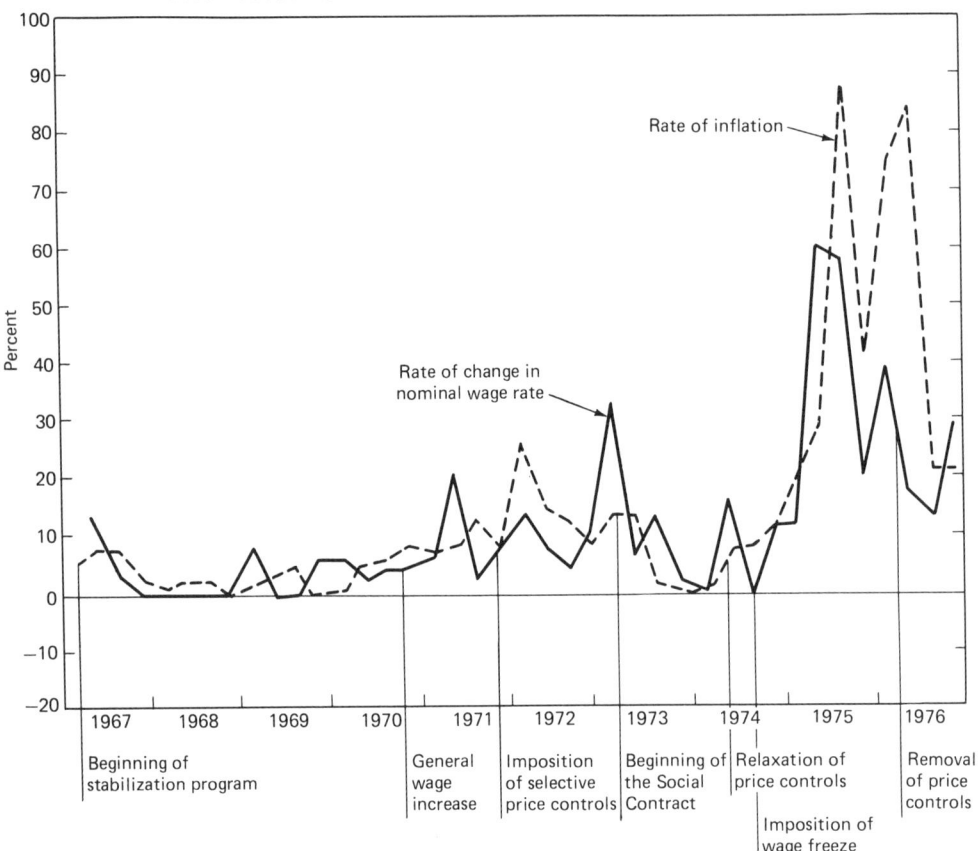

**CHART 1 QUARTERLY RATE OF INFLATION AND RATE OF CHANGE IN AVERAGE NOMINAL WAGE RATE IN INDUSTRIAL SECTOR**

This weakened the Government's fiscal position, as tax receipts failed to keep up with inflation, and there were price distortions in those sectors that were still subject to controls. By March 1976 the rate of inflation had reached 50 per cent a month. After a new Government removed all price controls, however, inflation decelerated sharply and prices rose by only 63 per cent in the second half of the year, compared to a rise of 175 per cent in the first half. At the same time, however, real wages declined sharply.

## CAUSES OF INFLATION

Two studies were made of inflation in Argentina for the period between 1963 and 1976 to test a series of hypothetical links between price controls, government deficits, inflation, and real wages. (The models upon which the analysis is based are described [at the end of this chapter.]) This analysis shows that there were essentially two main causes of the inflation—both of which had an inflationary impact because domestic credit, and hence the money supply, were automatically linked to demand. The first cause was the budget deficit of the Central Government. The size of the deficit was usually set in real terms, as a percentage of gross domestic product (GDP) for example. As the general price level in the country increased, the nominal level of the deficit had to be raised, and this led to an inflated deficit that was generally financed on the basis of a passive expansion in Central Bank credit. At the same time, taxpayers were often allowed to delay paying fixed amount tax obligations, and, again because of inflation, these delays significantly reduced government revenues in real terms, leading ultimately to a further increase in the deficit.

The second, and less apparent, cause of inflation during this period was the very instrument that the Government often used to attempt to check the rise in prices: namely, price controls. The Government frequently turned to selective price controls not only to keep down the prices of key commodities but also in an attempt to control inflation and maintain high real wages. At the same time, the Government subsidized those public and private firms that had made losses because of price controls, either by direct transfer payments or by low interest rate loans made through the banking system. As a result, distortions in sectoral prices and wage-price relationships in key industries gave rise to an excessive creation of credit by the banking system. This ultimately led to a situation in which it was extremely difficult for the Government to defend its original price targets for any length of time.

The analysis estimated the distortions in the price structure of the major sectors in the Argentine economy between 1963 and 1976. It was found that, with a few notable exceptions, these sectors had had their output prices held down considerably below the levels at which they could show a profit during 1973-75, which was the period of the Social Contract. Agriculture, for example, experienced considerable losses during those years, because controls kept the selling prices of agricultural goods below production costs. By the end of 1976, however, when price controls had been removed, the average price level of the sector had risen sufficiently to allow costs to be covered. On the other hand, in a typical public enterprise, such as the electrical industry, price controls were still, to a certain extent, in effect in 1976 and, as a result, the industry was still operating at prices that forced it to make a loss, although the loss was considerably less than those made during the previous three years. In a few select industries, such as construction and leather, where there were relatively high degrees of competition and where controls were never strictly applied, there were no significant differences between zero profit and actual price levels until 1976, when the industries may have taken advantage of the general relaxation of controls to raise prices considerably above their zero-profit levels. Similar distortions in relative prices were found in most other sectors of the economy. The losses due to price controls peaked in 1974 and 1975 and were thought to have almost disappeared by the end of 1976.

In the analysis, the major sources of monetary expansion during 1963-76 were the government deficit, which included the government subsidies to public enterprises, and the estimated losses of private industries induced by price control. A time lag of approximately four quarters was found between the occurrence of losses and the subsequent creation of money. Additional sources of monetary expansion were changes in foreign reserves; the inflationary anticipations of the public were incorporated in a real balance equation. The magnitude of the estimated parameters indicated that, other things being equal, a one-point increase in the real government deficit as a percentage of the stock of real money balances caused, on the average, a 1.28 per cent point increase in the rate of growth in the monetary aggregate, an increase that may be interpreted as an estimate of the money multiplier. On the other hand, the estimation suggests that a one-point increase in the aggregate real loss of the private sector as a percentage of the stock of real money balances caused a 0.19 per cent point increase in the rate of growth in the money supply four quarters later. These percentages were significantly higher during the periods of higher rates of inflation.

Would inflation have increased at the same rate without such a large budget deficit and without price controls? The model was used to simulate three paths of inflation between 1967 and 1976 on the basis of three differing assumptions about the two policy variables: the government deficit and the losses in the public and private sectors induced by price control. This led to the following conclusions. The assumption of a balanced budget throughout the simulation period produced a simulated path of inflation that was significantly lower than the one generated by the assumption of the historical series of the two

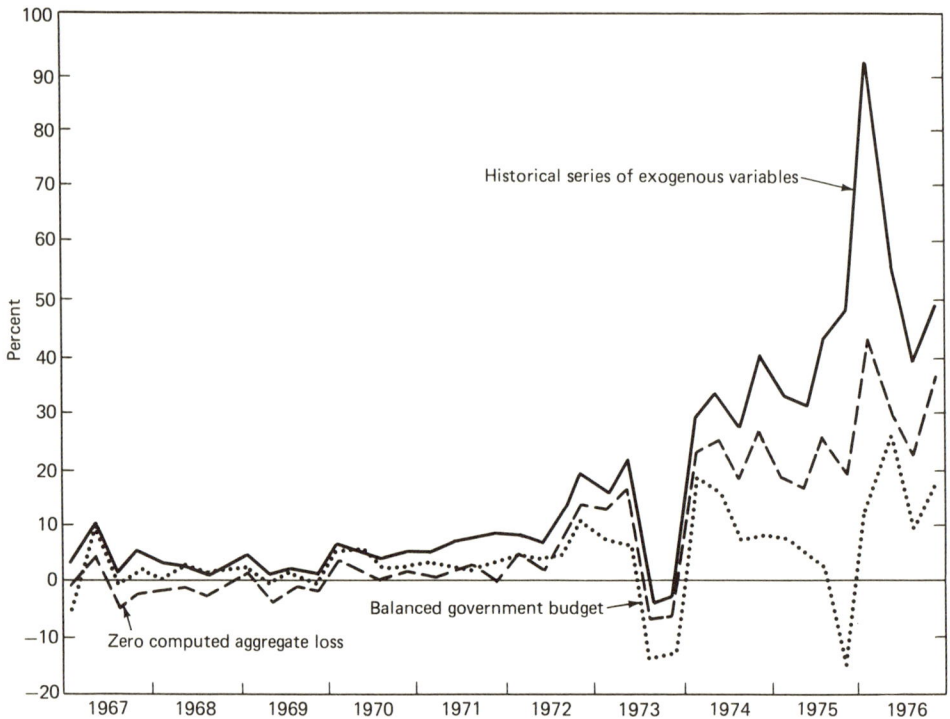

**CHART 2   SIMULATED QUARTERLY RATES OF INFLATION BASED ON DIFFERENT ASSUMPTIONS ON POLICY**

policy variables (see Chart 2). The average simulated quarterly rates of inflation declined from 5.30 to 2.23 per cent for the period 1967-72, from 34.77 to 5.86 per cent for 1973-76, and from 17.09 to 3.68 per cent for 1967-76. The assumption of no price distortions, and hence zero losses induced by controls for the public and private enterprises, also gave a simulated path of inflation markedly lower than the one generated by the assumption of the historical series of the policy variables, with average simulated quarterly rates of inflation being 1.13, 19.66, and 8.54 per cent for 1967-72, 1973-76, and 1967-76, respectively. According to this model, therefore, either a removal of price controls or a balancing of the government budget would have led to significant reductions in, although not a complete elimination of, the high rate of inflation that occurred in Argentina between 1967 and 1976.

## INFLATION AND REAL WAGES

It seems, then, that price controls probably did aggravate inflation in Argentina during the period of the study. Equally paradoxically, they also seemed to have helped to defeat another important objective that they aimed at—the maintenance of high real wages.

Real wages declined during the period of high inflation, probably because nominal wages adjusted to inflationary anticipation rather than actual inflation, and because the public's ability to forecast inflation accurately declined as inflation accelerated. The analysis also showed that an assumption of either a balanced government budget or zero losses from price controls in the public and private sectors would have raised the level of real wages significantly during the period. Thus, the policy of attempting to raise real wages by distorting the wage-price structure may have had significant counterproductive effects.

It is always tempting to overgeneralize the applicability of the results of a study such as this. Although price controls did seem to lead to inflation and an eventual lowering of real wages in Argentina between 1963 and 1976, it does not follow that such a sequence would necessarily occur elsewhere or even in Argentina at other times. The Argentine inflation contained critical and unique institutional elements, particularly the passivity of Central Bank credit. However, for Argentina, two important conclusions emerge from the study. First, and perhaps most important, price controls probably had an adverse impact upon the rate of inflation and the level of real wages, the two variables they were intended to improve. Second, the Central Government deficit was probably the major cause of high rates of inflation during the period in question.

***Models on Creation of Credit, Inflation, and Real Wages in Argentina—A Technical Note.*** The two studies were designed to test a series of hypotheses on sources of money creation. They were also used to simulate the rates of inflation and of changes in real wages that would have occurred under alternative assumptions about government policies, about deficit financing, and about the creation of credit to subsidize industries subject to price control. One study was based on a simple econometric model made up of (1) two stochastic functional relationships (that is, relationships containing elements of uncertainty), which explained the rate of change in the money supply and demand for real balances; (2) several definitional identities for connecting the nominal and real variables; and (3) an input-output system that generated an estimate of the losses in 17 of the 23 industries included in the Argentine input-output table for each quarter from 1963 to 1976.

The model, which was designed to capture the essence of the money creation-inflation spiral process described in the article, has the following features. The rate of increase in the monetary aggregate during the current quarter is largely determined by four variables: the current government deficit, the estimated aggregate loss of private industries during past quarters, current changes in external reserves (all in real terms), and the current and past rates of inflation. The rates of inflation, as determinants of the rate of monetary expansion, capture the degree of passivity of the changes in the money supply to the various pressures discussed earlier, while the use of estimated losses from previous quarters induced by price control is dictated by the institutional setting that allowed a time lag between the occurrence of losses and the actual creation of money.

Our method of estimating the business losses caused by price controls is relatively technical. Argentina has constructed input-output matrices representing the country's production technology for the years 1963 and 1970. Input-output matrices for each of the years 1963-76 were constructed on the basis of these two matrices. The total values added, for our purposes given by the sectoral wage bills, were used to derive the Leontief, or zero-profit, prices for each sector in the input-output matrix for each of the 14 years in our study. These prices may be thought of as being those at which an average firm in each sector of the economy would have made exactly zero profit in the year in question. In a particular year, the difference between the computed price and the actual price is the distortion in the unit price of the sector in question. (In 1975-76 it is sometimes claimed that official and actual price indices differed, but in order to maintain consistency, we have chosen to use official price indices throughout the sample period.) If the actual price is lower than the computed zero-profit price, the distortion is positive, representing a loss to the sector. By multiplying this positive distortion by the total output of the sector, an estimate was obtained of the sector's total loss caused by price controls. Totaling all sectors then gave an estimate of the aggregate loss due to price distortions for the entire economy. By subtracting transfer payments to public enterprises an estimate was made of the aggregate loss due to price controls that needed to be financed by domestic credit expansion.

There is not, however, a one-to-one correspondence between these losses and net domestic credit, since not all enterprise losses actually received financing.

The second study examined the impact of inflation on real wage rates of several sectors of the industrial part of the Argentine economy. The design of the study was simple: a stochastic functional relationship was estimated to explain how the rate of change in nominal wage rates in each sector adjusted to the inflationary anticipation of the public and to simulate alternative paths of real wage rates on the basis of differing assumptions on government policies. One of the additional assumptions maintained throughout the study was that the public anticipated inflation only on the basis of its past experiences with inflation. This adaptive anticipation formula provides one possible reason why the real wage rate could fall even when the nominal wage rate fully adjusts to the anticipated rate of inflation. The estimated equations suggest, among other things, that the inflationary anticipation of the public was a dominant determinant of the changes in nominal wage rates in Argentina during 1963-76.

## ACCOUNTING FOR INFLATION: BRAZIL
*by Manoel Riberio da Cruz Filho and Amandio da Silva Machado*

The new Brazilian corporation law (Law No. 6404, December 15, 1976), its provision to be effective for financial years beginning after January 1, 1978, sets out accounting and financial reporting standards in a manner different than they have been used in Brazil, although the basic and generally accepted accounting principles were maintained. The old legislation's requirements for financial statement were inadequate for evaluating managerial performance and assessing the liquidity of the company, except for publicly held (open capital) companies for which the information needs were more in line with the most developed practices. The new law clearly establishes the form of presentation, account-groupings, and evaluation criteria concerned with the maintenance of purchasing power invested in the company (liquidity approach). It also reduces any influence of other legislation, commercial or fiscal, which used to interfere in financial statements. The principles and requirements of this law were later extended to other legal types of entities like limited partnership companies.

This new law rules that company bookkeeping shall be done without changing accounting methods and statements regulated by it and, in a separate book, a company shall comply with taxation regulations and any other special laws on company activities which may stipulate different accounting methods or criteria, or even require the preparation of other financial statements.

The following financial statements are compulsory:

*Balance sheet*
*Profit and Loss Account or Income Statement*
*Retained earnings*
*Source and application of funds*

The statements above shall be supplemented with explanatory notes indicating: (a) the principal criteria for evaluating assets and liabilities, especially inventories, an estimation of depreciation, amortization and depletion, and a provision for loss and bad debts; (b) investments in other corporations, if they are relevant; (c) increases in an asset value resulting from appraisal; (d) contingencies which result in material losses or liabilities; (e) composition of share capital; (f) interest rates, maturity dates, and guarantees on long-term financing; and (g) previous year's adjust-

---

Reprinted with permission from *Financial Executive,* December 1978.

ments and subsequent events, which have or may have a relevant effect on the financial situation of the company.

## ASSETS AND LIABILITIES

For the balance sheet, the accounting principles and presentation requirements are not that different from other countries' methods. The classification for the balance sheet is:

*Assets*—current, long-term, and permanent (investments, fixed assets and deferred assets).

*Liabilities*—current, long-term, deferred income, and net equity (share capital, capital reserves, assets appraisal reserve, profit reserves, and retained earnings).

The objective of grouping accounts which represent the fixed part of the capital structure (the Net Equity), the application of funds in fixed assets (productive capacity), permanent investments, and deferred assets under the heading Permanent Assets was based on two needs: (1) assessing the stable financial structure of the reporting entity, and (2) enabling the introduction of a new indexation system whereby all accounts stated within these two groups are to be indexed periodically.

The assets' accounts shall be grouped in decreasing order of liquidity. This approach is the basis for two concepts: (a) all balances with associated and controlled companies, directors and stockholders must be classified as long-term receivables, and (b) permanent investments are only those of a long-term character; therefore, the fundamental basis for classification is the economic nature of the acquisition not the legal involvement inherent to any equity investment. Thus, permanent investments are those intended for investment income (dividends) or to guarantee continuous supply of raw materials or other operational support to the investor. Any other type of investment should then be classified as current or long-term asset.

Deferred Assets are those funds application which will contribute to the performance of the company in more than one fiscal period as research and development expenditures, preoperational expenses, interest during construction, etc. They shall be amortized within 10 years.

Either Capital Reserves or Capital Surplus groups funds which exceeds the amount intended to form corporate capital as premium received on stock or debentures issues, proceeds from sale of subscription rights, etc., and the indexation amount of the paid-up share capital which has to be capitalized next year. All other funds mentioned may be used for capitalization or absorption of losses in excess of retained earnings and profit reserves.

Either Assets Appraisal Reserve or Revaluation Surplus is the increase in value of a fixed asset by virtue of a new spontaneous evaluation based on appraisal approved by a stockholders' meeting. This write-up is not tied up with an indexation system. By the time the revalued asset is depreciated or sold such reserve is transferred to retained earnings and it may be distributed.

The law maintains the concept of the lower of cost or market price as the basis for inventory valuation, except for agricultural and mineral products and inventories of livestock which may be valued at market as normal practice. Provisions for estimated inventory depreciation or price oscillation are not allowed. The market value concept is also applicable to other assets in the form of loans or interest bearing securities and foreign exchange variation or indexation of the principal, whose balance is limited to the market value. Similarly, the liabilities subject to foreign exchange or indexation shall be adjusted upward. Both assets and liabilities write-ups are included as income or expenses respectively. In the Brazilian financial market, all medium and long-term local bank loans are indexed by either a prefixed index or the official index (the same applies to the government treasury bonds) adopted for inflation accounting purposes.

The law provides for the indexation of all permanent assets (including accumulated depreciation, amortization and depletion) and net equity accounts. The index applied to each account's balance gives the indexation amount which shall be recorded in the account for the period, except for the indexation of share capital, which shall be recorded in a specific account under the heading of Capital Reserves. The net result is recorded as a gain or loss item in the income statement. If the indexation for the year is a loss, this will be deductible for tax purposes. If the result is a gain, this will be taxable although the company may opt for deferment of tax on that part of the gain deemed to be "inflationary profit" until it is considered to be realized.

## MEASURING THE EFFECTS OF INFLATION

*Inflationary profit* is defined as the net indexation gain recorded as income, less the net foreign exchange and indexation variation incurred during the year on accounts in foreign currency or in local currency subject to indexation on liquidation. For this purpose, the net exchange and indexation variation includes both realized and unrealized gains or losses. If the net variation is a gain, then inflationary profit is limited to the indexation gain on permanent assets and net equity (an indexation gain occurs when permanent assets are bigger than net equity).

The indexation is applied on a monthly or quarterly basis. Quarterly basis is permissible because the averaging of the monthly index variation is not expected to deviate too far from the result on a monthly basis.

The indexation is continuously applied to the past (month or quarter) account's balance. Therefore, at the end of the year the accounts are adjusted to the compound index variation in the same year.

Accrual basis is the mandatory principle to determine the net income for the year. The valuation difference resulting from application of indexation is added to the pertinent account of permanent assets and net equity, and the same procedure is adopted to adjust those assets and liabilities subject to indexation (prefixed or not) or foreign exchange variation. Therefore, both assets and liabilities items more exposed to inflationary erosion are adjusted by two methods: (1) the stable financial structure (permanent assets and net equity) by indexation based on an official index, and (2) the other items by legal or contractual imposition (as foreign exchange fluctuation and prefixed or current indexation on loans, and fixed time deposits). The inflationary effects of these two methods are shown in a different manner in the income statement: the indexation effect of the stable financial structure is shown as the last item before the net profit before tax, and the financial income and expenses in the form of time deposit or loan interest and foreign or local currency variation are recorded as part of the operating profit or loss.

However, the Brazilian system does not reflect inflation's impact on inventories (presently at average cost or FIFO basis) except for real estates on sale. Indeed, the law has oriented the balance sheet to present more the liquidity situation; thus, the reported profit being only adjusted to store the inflation adjustments resulting from the two methods just mentioned. As a consequence there will still be a hidden profit in the inventories which may be compensated by a monetary loss (higher unadjusted monetary assets than monetary liabilities) or, inversely, be added by a monetary gain. This leads management toward working with less monetary assets than monetary liabilities within the limits of risk and financing ability.

## ACCOUNTING FOR INVESTMENTS

Investments in associated or controlled companies, when they each represent more than 10 percent, or, in total, more than 15 percent of the investor's net equity, must be accounted for on the basis of the investor's proportion of their underlying equity at closing dates. The acquisition price shall be broken down between the equity value at the date of acquisition and the difference between price and equity value, representing the premium or discount on acquisition. Such premium or discount must be recorded separately as a permanent asset or net equity respectively, with an indication of the difference between the book and market value of the assets of the investee, its projected profitability in future years, and the value of its intangible assets whatever be the case. The recorded value (cost plus past indexation) of the investment, net of dividends received during the year, is subject to indexation for the year and then adjusted to its underlying equity value based on accounts of the investor closed within the previous two months, including any adjustments necessary to ensure that its accounts have been prepared on a uniform basis with those of the investor. Any reduction in the equity is tax deductible only to the extent that it exceeds the provision for loss, which may have been set up, and the discount on acquisition. The premium or discount on acquisition of an equity investment shall be disclosed in the balance sheet as addition or reduction of the related investment. Any premium or discount attributable to the difference of book and market value of the underlying assets will be amortized in accordance with the realization of the related assets through depreciation, amortization, depletion, or disposal.

Other equity investments bearing a permanent character and not required to be accounted for on an equity basis will continue to be recorded at cost subject also to indexation. Stock dividends (bonus shares) received are not attributed a value for accounting purposes from 1979 on.

Capital gain or loss on sales of fixed assets and investments shall be determined against the adjusted cost by indexation. Where investments are accounted for at the underlying equity value, the capital gain or loss on liquidation will be computed on the net book value adjusted by indexation, including any adjusted balance of premium or discount unamortized, and net of provision for loss.

## CONCLUSION

The Brazilian accounting standards are a combination of historical and inflation accounting. In the past, the Brazilian legislation has been quite fair on accounting regulations concerned with inflation. The new law will be in force for a long time because it really represents a big step from the previous system. Regarding tax legislation, there may be further developments on fiscal incentives and the deductibility of minority shareholders' dividends.

---

# HOW BRASILIA DOES IT

### by Peter Myers

---

Although Brazil has traveled further along the indexation route than any other country, its system does not serve as a particularly practical illustration of how indexation could be applied in the United States. Americans face a similar problem to the one that led Canadians to adopt a partial indexation system—the shifting of wealth among individuals and between the private and public sectors, a result, solely, of inflation. With inflation in the double-digit range, these dislocations may be sufficiently serious to warrant adoption of partial indexation as a means of limiting the most undesirable consequences.

---

Reproduced from *Across the Board*, March 1980.

On the other hand, Brazil turned to indexation in response to a far more critical, and specific, set of circumstances. Its first steps were taken in the early Sixties, when the Brazilian government was virtually bankrupt. Inflation was running at an annual rate of around 100 percent, a circumstance caused in part by the strains of the construction of the country's new capital, Brasilia. At the same time two of the government's most important revenue sources had dried up: nobody would invest in government bonds because their yields were hopelessly inadequate; and few Brazilians bothered to pay their taxes—by the time the government caught up to them, it was far cheaper to pay the bill in devalued cruzeiros, even if the bill included a fine.

So Brazil at first adopted indexation to cope with these two revenue problems. It added automatic escalator clauses to both bond values and unpaid taxes. The idea caught on, and indexation gradually spread throughout the entire Brazilian economy. Today almost every financial measure—including wages, mortgage balances, and other debts—is subject to periodic revision in accordance with a variety of formulas that compensate for the cruzeiro's shrinking value. A parallel system of monetary correction provides for exchange-rate adjustments, and the cruzeiro is formally devalued every couple of months.

One basic problem with this comprehensive approach to indexation is that inflation in Brazil became largely "institutionalized"—there was less incentive to combat inflation directly, and prices have continued to rise at rates that are frightening, even in comparison with current North American inflation levels. Because many economic measures, such as wages, are adjusted on a quarterly basis, Brazilians ride a high-speed roller coaster in dealing with normal living expenses. Their real incomes take a sharp jump after each quarterly adjustment, then wither away over the next three months.

While such difficulties probably are trivial in relation to the situation faced by Brazilians before indexation was adopted, they would seem rather undesirable in the North American context. Economic theorists may argue that full indexation does nothing more than maintain the status quo; in practice, no system can easily cope with the daily adjustments that would be needed to avoid the Brazilian roller coaster.

A further problem with full indexation stems from the need for greater precision in the various adjustment factors that are needed to index different items, and even to index the same items in different regions. Brazilian wage indexation, for example, is based on actual living costs. Not only are there different factors in different cities, such as São Paulo and Rio de Janeiro, reflecting local price levels, but there also are significant variations within each city. To determine such a wide range of index factors, an army of part-time government workers is needed to undertake endless price surveys. Because the system is so complex, many Brazilians suspect that the government fiddles with the many adjustment factors before they are announced. While officials protest that this is not so, clearly there is considerable potential for abuse.

In a less extensive indexation system it is less risky to adopt cruder measures of the inflation rate—such as the national Consumer Price Index used in Canada. Yet heavy reliance on any single indicator can create its own problems. As any CPI is based on a typical "basket" of consumer goods, the selected basket may be totally unrepresentative in many areas of a country. It also may bear little relationship to the actual spending habits of those in relatively high—or relatively low—income categories. The poor, for example, spend high proportions of their incomes on basic necessities such as food and accommodation: the affluent are more affected by the cost of automobiles and vacation travel. So when food and housing prices are rising faster than luxury items, the wealthy may get an unfair "bonus" from indexation.

But probably the most unappealing aspect of indexation to North Americans is that it could further undermine the already shaky public confidence in their dollars. Quite apart from basic economic considerations, both Canadians and Americans have been brought up believing that a buck is a buck—or at least that it ought to be. Any form of indexation constitutes unavoidable evidence that a buck no longer is expected to be worth a buck.

# REPORTING THE IMPACT OF CHANGING PRICES IN GREAT BRITAIN
## by M. Zafar Iqbal

Six accountancy bodies play an important role in accounting standard-setting in the UK:

1. The Institute of Chartered Accountants in England and Wales;
2. The Institute of Chartered Accountants of Scotland;
3. The Institute of Chartered Accountants of Ireland;
4. The Association of Certified Accountants;
5. The Institute of Cost and Management Accountants; and
6. The Chartered Institute of Public Finance and Accountancy.

These independent organizations cooperate with each other in standard-setting and other matters through joint committees. The Consultative Committee of Accountancy Bodies (CCAB) consists of the senior executives of the six bodies. The CCAB presents a unified view of the accountancy profession on important issues including inflation accounting. Another committee called Accounting Standards Committee (ASC), formerly known as Accounting Standards Steering Committee (ASSC), has a more direct role in accounting standard-setting, as explained later. The ASC's operations are financially supported by the six accountancy bodies, the share of contribution by each being determined by the CCAB. Although it is a committee of The Institute of Chartered Accountants in England and Wales, the other five organizations are also included in its membership and constitute minority representation. Members of the ASC contribute their time voluntarily and are supported by a small research staff employed by the English Institute.

The Accounting Standards Committee is a technical working committee. After deliberations and research, it has the authority to issue exposure drafts of proposed Statements of Standard Accounting Practice. Comments received on the exposure drafts are considered and, if agreed upon, are reflected in a revised version of the proposed accounting standard. Approval of a draft by the ASC has the status of a proposal to the council of each of the six accountancy bodies. Each council must formally approve the proposal, the last council to vote being of the English Institute, before the approved draft becomes a Statement of Standard Accounting Practice (SSAP). This is the mechanism normally used in standard-setting process in the UK. Numerous departures from these procedures were made in the case of inflation accounting which, according to some knowledgeable observers, has "travelled a rocky road" in the UK.[1]

In January 1973, Exposure Draft No. 8, "Accounting for Changes in the Purchasing Power of Money" was issued by the ASC. It proposed adoption of current purchasing power (general price level) accounting for supplementary financial statements. These statements were to be subject to audit. General response to ED 8 was positive. A committee organized by the Conference of British Industry issued two reports endorsing the Accounting Standards Committee's proposals contained in ED 8.[2]

---

Excerpted from "SEC Replacement Cost Accounting: Broader Implications" by permission of M. Zafar Iqbal, MBA, Ph.D., CPA, CMA, Professor of Accounting at the California Polytechnic State University, San Luis Obispo. Mr. Iqbal is a member of the American Accounting Association, National Association of Accountants, Beta Alpha Psi, Beta Gamma Sigma, and Sigma Iota Epsilon. He has previously published in numerous professional and business journals.

---

[1] Charles W. Gill and S. Thomas Moser, "Inflation Accounting at the Crossroads," *Journal of Accountancy* (January 1979), p. 76.

[2] Edward Stamp, "Toward Current Value Accounting in the United Kingdom," *Collection of Papers of the American Accounting Association's Annual Meeting, 1977* (Sarasota, Fla.: 1978), p. 20.

On January 21, 1974, only a few days before the ASC was scheduled to vote on the decision to approve ED 8, the government announced the appointment of the Inflation Accounting Committee under the chairmanship of F.E.P. Sandilands (commonly known as the Sandilands Committee). The committee was composed of twelve members possessing diverse backgrounds. Interestingly enough only three of them were chartered accountants. The other nine included four company chairmen, two economists, a tax lawyer, a financial executive, and a retired union leader. From among the three accountants, only one was in public accounting. The other two included a university professor and a financial executive. This concept of wide representation and domination by non-accountants was criticized by some, including Professor Stamp of the University of Lancaster. He labelled the committee as "amateur."[3] Others interpreted the committee's varied composition as an attempt to prevent its deliberations from being overwhelmed by any single institutional bias.[4]

A natural question arises: what prompted the British Government to take this, what many consider rather drastic, action? The inflation problem in the UK had become extremely serious around that time. Moreover, the trends indicated that the country was moving toward the worst period of inflation in its history, causing resultant economic hardships on consumers as well as business entities.

In 1974 a cash shortage of crisis proportions developed and forced many companies to liquidate or reduce their operations drastically. Uncertainties about future profitability also resulted in sharp curtailment of investment by the business sector. In the later part of 1974 the stock market collapsed and stock prices fell to a record low level for many years. This caused drying-up of funds from equity capital sources. Uncertainties and very high short-term interest rates also adversely affected the ability of the corporate sector to borrow on both long and short-term bases, thus compounding the problem.

Though the Sandilands Committee was set up in early 1974, the rate of inflation in the UK was already in double digits and the situation was noticeably deteriorating. When the committee submitted its report in June 1975 the inflation rate had jumped well over 20 percent. Thus the current economic situation, the direction of economic trends, and the dissatisfaction of the government with inflation accounting proposals contained in ED 8 were the reasons for formation of the Sandilands Committee.[5]

In May 1974, while the Sandilands Committee was considering inflation accounting, the Accounting Standards Committee and Councils of the Accountancy Bodies approved a provisional standard, "Provisional Statement of Standard Accounting Practice No. 7" (PSSAP7) pursuant to ED 8, and with the same title.[6] This statement recommended only that companies listed on the London Stock Exchange prepare supplementary current purchasing power statements which restate the conventional statements by use of the retail price index.

In general, PSSAP7 gained considerable support in the business community. Even though compliance to the standard was not mandatory, many companies listed on the London Stock Exchange provided the supplementary current purchasing power statements. In its final report, the Sandilands Committee acknowledged that evidence submitted to the committee revealed more support for PSSAP7 approach (current purchasing power) than for any other method of inflation accounting. The method was regarded useful and acceptable by

---

[3] *The Accountant's Magazine* (December 1975), p. 411.

[4] R. D. Wollstadt, "The Challenge of the Sandilands Report," *Management Accounting* (July 1976), p. 19.

[5] Inflation Accounting Committee, F.E.P. Sandilands, Chairman, *Inflation Accounting* (London: Her Majesty's Stationary Office, September 1975), pp. 1-2.

[6] The Institute of Chartered Accountants in England and Wales, *Professional Statement of Standard Accounting Practice No. 7: Accounting for Changes in Purchasing Power of Money* (London: May 1974).

a large number of companies and other interested parties.[7]

The Sandilands Committee submitted its report to the Chancellor of the Exchequer and Secretary of State for Trade in June 1975. In September 1975 the report was presented to the UK Parliament and also published. Normally the British Government accepts or rejects such reports within a few months, although the legislation to implement an accepted report may take much longer.[8] The government approved the report in November 1975.

The principal recommendation of the Sandilands Committee involved adoption of a system described as "current cost accounting" for basic financial statements. It called for a radical departure from traditional historical cost basis. The committee also rejected the current purchasing power approach which was recommended in PSSAP7.[9] The reason cited by the committee was that the usefulness of such supplementary statements will always be "constrained by the deficiencies of the basic historic cost accounts to which they are attached."[10] Thus the Sandilands Committee viewed the real contrast as being between historical cost accounting and current value accounting and not between price level accounting and current value accounting.[11]

The initial reception given to the Sandilands Report was generally enthusiastic and positive. Immediately after its release two of the most prestigious financial periodicals in the UK, the *Financial Times* and *The Economist* expressed their support. The Consultative Committee of Accounting Bodies effectively withdrew the current purchasing power proposals of PSSAP7 in favor of the basic recommendations of the Sandilands Report.[12] The CCAB expressed qualified approval of the report in its statement of "initial reactions."[13] Although welcoming it as a valuable contribution to accounting thought, the CCAB pointed out that current cost accounting does not take into account all aspects of inflation such as:[14]

1. *The decrease in value of monetary assets*
2. *The decrease in value of obligations represented by monetary liabilities*
3. *The effect of inflation on the value of the proprietor's interest in the company*
4. *The problem of making valid comparisons over a period of time when the unit of measurement is unstable*

The CCAB recommended publication of supplementary additional information on the basis of current purchasing power. In essence, the CCAB was suggesting an inflation accounting approach for financial reporting which would

---

[7] Inflation Accounting Committee, F.E.P. Sandilands, Chairman, *op. cit.*, pp. 120-121.

[8] Andrew M. McCosh, "Implications of Sandilands for non-U.K. Accountants," *Journal of Accountancy* (March 1976), p. 43.

[9] Inflation Accounting Committee, F.E.P. Sandilands, Chairman, *op. cit.*, pp. 135-136.

[10] *Ibid.*, p. 136.

[11] James Don Edwards and John B. Barrack, "Objectives of Financial Statements and Inflation Accounting: A Comparison of Recent British and American Proposals," *The International Journal of Accounting Education and Research* (University of Illinois, Spring 1976), p. 15.

[12] In January 1976 the Accounting Standards Committee issued "Inflation Accounting—The Interim Period." This statement recommended to the companies that until a Statement of Standard Accounting Practice on current cost accounting is issued, historical cost statements be supplemented with a statement based on current cost accounting as described in the Sandilands report (preferably by also taking into account initial reaction of the CCAB), or general purchasing power adjustments as explained in PSSAP7. These guidelines appeared in, "Inflation Accounting—The Interim Period," *Accountancy* (February 1976), p. 92.

[13] The Consultative Committee of Accountancy Bodies, *Initial Reactions to the Report of the Inflation Accounting Committee* (October 30, 1975).

[14] Summarized by, Edward Stamp and Alister K. Mason, "Current Cost Accounting: British Panacea or Quagmire," *The Journal of Accountancy* (April 1977), pp. 67-68.

combine current cost valuation and current purchasing power basis.

The Sandilands Report had recommended setting-up of a "Steering Group" to prepare proposals for implementation of current cost accounting.[15] In accordance with the recommendation, the British Government established Inflation Accounting Steering Group (IASG) under the chairmanship of a Touche Ross partner Douglas Morpeth. Mr. Morpeth was also a former president of the Institute of Chartered Accountants in England and Wales. The IASG, more commonly known as the Morpeth Committee, had eleven other members appointed by the CCAB in consultation with the ASC. Unlike the Sandilands Committee all Morpeth Committee members were accounting and financial professionals, the former being in comfortable majority of eight.

The exact status of the IASG is difficult to define because of the nature of its objectives and methods of its operation. Brennan, a former secretary of the International Accounting Standards Committee, has commented on this aspect:[16]

> *The committee was clearly created to act upon a government report. In the absence of a Sandilands Report, there would not have been a Morpeth Committee. The committee was created with explicit financial support coming, more or less equally, from three sources: accountancy bodies, the government, and private subscriptions from industrial enterprises. Its membership comprised individuals from the same three sources as well....*
>
> *Legally, it was a subcommittee of the ASC. Its ability to issue exposure drafts and ultimate pronouncements was tied to the ASC. Proposals by the Morpeth Group were to be vetted by the ASC, which was to be the formal issuer. Nevertheless, the Morpeth group itself issued the Guidance Manual on Current Cost Accounting. The exposure draft known as ED 18 was issued by ASC without apparently having been subjected to the same degree of deliberation as the first seventeen exposure drafts had been.*

Formation of the Morpeth Committee was announced early January 1976. Its main assignment was to prepare a proposal for an exposure draft based on The Sandilands Report. The Committee was instructed to take into account the comments made by the CCAB and others on the recommendations of the Sandilands Committee. The Morpeth Committee submitted its report to the ASC in early September 1976. After modifications, the revised draft was published as ED 18 on November 30, 1976;[17] concurrently the Morpeth Committee released three related publications.[18] The exposure period on ED 18 was to last six months. It was also decided that the target date for issuance of a Statement of Standard Accounting Practice, based on ED 18, would be January 31, 1978.

ED 18 generally followed the Sandilands guidelines. The Exposure Draft called for adoption of current cost accounting without any adjustment for changes in general price level. However, in response to the CCAB suggestion, it was proposed that gains or losses on monetary items, and the effect of the change in the value of the monetary unit on shareholders'

---

[15] Inflation Accounting Committee, F.E.P. Sandilands, Chairman, *op. cit.*, pp. 3-4.

[16] W. John Brennan, "The Impact of the Inflation Accounting Debate on Accounting Standard Setting Bodies," *The Impact of Inflation on Accounting: A Global View* (University of Illinois Center for International Education and Research in Accounting, 1979), p. 210.

[17] Accounting Standards Committee, Proposed Statement of Standard Accounting Practice ED 18, *Current Cost Accounting* (London: Institute of Chartered Accountants in England and Wales, November 30, 1976).

[18] The Inflation Accounting Steering Group, *Guidance Manual on Current Cost Accounting* (London: Tolley Publishing Company Ltd., November 30, 1976). The other two publications entitled, *Brief Guide* and *Background Papers* have the same source reference as the *Guidance Manual on Current Cost Accounting.*

equity be disclosed in footnotes. Another innovation recommended by the Morpeth Committee was a new statement entitled "Appropriation Account." This statement would bring together the current cost profit, the revaluation surpluses, the amount which the directors consider should be retained within the business to fulfill its needs, and dividends.

Initial response to ED 18 was positive. Adulatory comments poured in, commending the Morpeth Committee on the impressive speed with which it accomplished its mission. Only nine months had elapsed since the inception of the committee when the draft appeared for public comment. However, shortly afterwards the support for the proposal seemed to evaporate, and instead replaced by a swarm of critical and hostile comments. These reactions were often described in vivid superlatives in accounting journals, an uncommon practice for publications of a profession often considered devoid of strong outward expression of collective feelings.

Declarations of dissatisfaction covered the whole spectrum: from broad generalizations to microscopical dissection; from theoretical overview to implemental measures.[19] The most commonly voiced criticisms revolved around the complexities of the requirements, and their inherent subjectivity.[20]

Ultimately the upheaval culminated in the celebrated revolt of July 6, 1977. On that day, a special meeting of The Institute of Chartered Accountants in England and Wales convened to consider the motion: "That the members of The Institute of Chartered Accountants in England and Wales do not wish any system of current cost accounting to be made compulsory." The vote was 55 to 45 percent against implementation.

Theoretically the motion did not carry any formal decision authority. The English Institute is only one of the six accounting bodies in the United Kingdom; moreover, only the council of the Institute is empowered to take a position on matters involving acceptance or rejection of proposed standards. Nonetheless, for all practical purposes the resolution meant demise of ED 18. Though the English Institute is only one of the many professional bodies in Great Britain, it dominates the profession. And as Brennan observed, "the grass roots had spoken";[21] their resolution, though not binding on the council of the Institute, got the message across. Many sources believe that "the leadership of the UK accounting profession has been shell-shocked since."[22]

A special task force of the Accounting Standards Committee was appointed under the chairmanship of William Hyde to develop interim guidelines on inflation accounting. Its proposals, known commonly as the "Hyde guidelines" were published by the ASC in November 1977.[23] These guidelines called for voluntary disclosure of supplementary data by the companies listed on the London Stock Exchange. Senior partners of the ten largest public accounting firms in the UK publicly supported the Hyde recommendations and appealed for voluntary compliance.[24] The chairman of the London Stock Exchange also endorsed the guidelines in the form of a request to the chairmen of all listed companies urging compliance by their companies.[25]

---

[19] For a thorough discussion of the issues see, Edward Stamp, "ED 18 and Current Cost Accounting: A Review Article," *Accounting and Business Research* (Spring 1977), pp. 83-94; and, Stamp and Mason, *op. cit.*, pp. 66-73.

[20] Stewart A. Leech and Denis J. Pratt, "Current Cost Accounting in Australia, New Zealand, and the United Kingdom: A Comparative Study," *The International Journal of Accounting Education and Research* (Spring 1978), p. 111.

[21] Brennan, *op. cit.*, p. 210.

[22] Michael Lafferty, "Move to Get CCA Show Back on the Road," *World Accounting Report* (March 1979), p. 5.

[23] Accounting Standards Committee, *Inflation Accounting—An Interim Recommendation by the Accounting Standards Committee* (London: Institute of Chartered Accountants in England and Wales, November 4, 1977).

[24] Brennan, *op. cit.*, p. 211.

[25] Australian Society of Accountants and The Institute of Chartered Accountants in Australia, *The CCA Working Guide—A Summary* (Melbourne: July 1978). The pages of this brochure are not numbered; this statement appears on the last page.

The Hyde guidelines recommended that the financial statements of listed companies should include a separate statement showing three adjustments to the traditional historical cost income statement. The three adjustments were a depreciation adjustment, a cost of sales adjustment, and a "gearing" adjustment. The "gearing" adjustment was to show how the method of financing the business affected the impact of inflation. Since the Hyde guidelines did not clarify the underlying capital maintenance concept, not everyone understood the reason for the gearing adjustment.[26] It is noteworthy that the Hyde guidelines dealt exclusively with the income statement.

During all this period the Morpeth Committee continued its work on development of a current cost accounting system, as requested by the British Government. Its new proposals were exposed for comment as ED 24 by the ASC on April 30, 1979. This Exposure Draft replaces ED 18, which is now formally withdrawn.[27] Interestingly, ED 24 acknowledges that it had become obvious that the Sandilands' recommendations, and ED 18 which stemmed from them, were not acceptable. It also states that the new proposals have evolved from the Hyde guidelines, with due consideration given to the comments received on both ED 18 and the Hyde guidelines.[28] However, according to one knowledgeable source, ED 24 is a simplified version of ED 18; it is being presented as a development of the Hyde guidelines only for public relations reasons.[29] There is some validity in this assertion. While the Hyde guidelines called for supplementary current cost adjustments in the income statement only, ED 24 proposals, like those of ED 18, require a current cost income statement and a current cost balance sheet. However there is an important difference; while ED 18 required replacement of historical cost statements by current cost statements, ED 24 requires current cost information on a supplementary basis only.

It appears that the general response to ED 24 from the public as well as the government has been overwhelmingly positive.[30]

Four proposals from the UK are examined:

1. *Sandilands Report*
2. *Exposure Draft No. 18*
3. *Hyde guidelines*
4. *Exposure Draft No. 24*

**Sandilands Report.** The principal recommendation of the Sandilands Committee involved adoption of current cost accounting system for basic financial statements. Important historical cost data which are not used in the current cost statements should be disclosed in footnotes.

Financial statements should be based on monetary units. The Sandilands Committee specifically rejected the use of constant purchasing power concept.

Assets in the balance sheet should be based on "value to the business." This concept equates value of the asset with the amount of loss which would be suffered by the company if deprived of its use. Value to the business is usually current replacement cost. If replacement cost is higher than both the economic and net realizable values, then the appropriate valuation is the higher of the latter two amounts. In this context net realizable value is the current disposal value of the asset, and economic value is the present value of expected future net cash inflows from the asset.

The report recommended independent appraisals for land and buildings. For other noncurrent assets, such as plant and machinery, the government's specific price indices should be used. Inventories should be shown at current replacement cost or net realizable value at year-end, whichever is lower. Monetary assets would generally be shown at their nominal monetary value. Marketable securities are to be presented at their market value at the end of the fiscal year.

---

[26] Jenny Cox, "ED 24—The New Proposals Explained," *Accountancy* (June 1979), p. 56.

[27] "Exposure Draft 24, Current Cost Accounting," *Accountancy* (May 1979), p. 37.

[28] *Ibid.*, p. 38.

[29] "Morpeth Tries to Fill the CCA Gap," *World Accounting Report* (May 1979), p. 13.

[30] "UK Inflation Accounting," *World Accounting Report* (December 1979), pp. 4-5.

The value to the business of liabilities is their historical amount and, therefore, no adjustments are necessary.

Gains and losses arising from the revaluation of fixed assets, and charges for backlog depreciation are entered directly in the revaluation reserves in the stockholders' equity, and do not affect net income figure.

Cost of sales should reflect the current cost of goods at the time of sale. This should be accomplished either by using the current purchase price of items when sold or alternatively through a "cost of sales adjustment" based on an averaging technique. The amount of "cost of sales adjustment" is then added to the conventional cost of sales to charge the income for the total amount which approximates the value to the business of inventory sold. The cost of sales adjustment amount appears in the stockholders' equity section of the balance sheet as an inventory adjustment reserve.

Besides the cost of sales adjustment for the inventory sold, an adjustment basing depreciation on year-end valuation of fixed assets was recommended in order to reflect the value of assets consumed in the production of revenue for the period. Thus profits are recognized only after revenues exceed value of assets consumed to earn those revenues.

The Sandilands Report classifies gains as holding, operating, and extraordinary. "Operating gain" is the difference between the amounts realized from a company's earnings from goods or services provided and the value to the business of the assets consumed by the company in generating these amounts. "Extraordinary gain" is the difference between the amounts realized from items which do not fall into a company's normal output and their value to the business at the time of disposal. Both of these gains are reported only when realized. "Holding gain" is the difference between the value to the company of an asset at any point of time and the original purchasing cost of the asset (less depreciation if applicable). Holding gains may be either realized or unrealized. These various types of gains may be viewed as described below.

*Operating gain:* current cost profit after tax;

*Extraordinary gain:* arising from transactions not considered as part of normal operations;

*Holding gain:* movement in reserves.

These three classes of gains are summarized in Exhibit 1.

**EXHIBIT 1  UK'S SANDILANDS REPORT
FORMAT OF SUMMARY STATEMENT OF TOTAL GAINS OR LOSSES
FOR THE YEAR**

|  |  | Monetary Units |
|---|---|---|
| Current cost profit after tax (as shown in current cost profit statement) |  | XXX |
| Extraordinary items less tax |  | XXX |
| Net profit after tax and extraordinary items |  | XXX |
| Movements in reserves net of tax: |  |  |
|    Inventory adjustment reserve | XXX |  |
|    Revaluation reserves: |  |  |
|       Gain/loss due to changes in the basis of valuation of assets | XXX |  |
|       Other gains/losses | XXX | XXX |
| Total gain (loss) for the year after tax |  | XXX |

Source: Adapted from Inflation Accounting Committee, F.E.P. Sandilands, Chairman, *Inflation Accounting* (London: Her Majesty's Stationary Office, September 1975), p. 190.

Another important proposal of the Sandilands Committee was that a funds statement be provided as one of the basic financial statements. Although a funds statement is not a feature exclusively characteristic of current cost accounting, the recommendation was made to provide information on the availability of liquid assets for distribution.

*Exposure Draft No. 18.* This Exposure Draft was prepared to present proposals for implementation of current cost accounting. The Exposure Draft generally follows the guidelines of the Sandilands Committee. Two main innovations include the disclosures regarding effects of change in the value of money, and the introduction of a new statement titled "Appropriation Account."

ED 18 requires that the financial statements should disclose, in a note, the effect of the change in the value of monetary unit on shareholders' net equity interest. In addition, a separate disclosure should present an analysis of the gain or loss on holding monetary items during the period.

The Exposure Draft requires the presentation of a financial statement described as "Appropriation Account." This statement is to show the information regarding current cost profit; the net surplus for the period arising from the revaluation of assets; the amount necessary to be retained in the business, as determined by the directors, to meet its needs; and dividends. An illustration of the Appropriation Account is provided in Exhibit 2.

ED 18 proposals prefer asset-based indices for determining the "value to the business" of plant and equipment, rather than industry-based indices favored by the Sandilands Committee.

*Hyde guidelines.* Recommendations of the Hyde Report deal exclusively with the income statement. The guidelines recommend inclusion of a supplementary income statement adjusted for depreciation, cost of sales, and "gearing" adjustment. Compliance with the guidelines is on a voluntary basis. These adjustments are explained next.

1. Additional depreciation is charged, based on the current replacement cost of fixed assets.
2. A charge is made for the excess of the current cost of inventories over the historical cost as of the date of sale.
3. The gearing adjustment relates to the effect of inflation on monetary items. A charge or credit is made to the income statement depending on the monetary position of the business. In order to derive the formulas, the following notations will be used.

**EXHIBIT 2 UK'S EXPOSURE DRAFT 18
FORMAT OF APPROPRIATION ACCOUNT**

|  |  | *Monetary Units* |
|---|---|---|
| Current cost profit/(loss) for the year |  | X |
| Net surplus for year on revaluation of assets | X |  |
| Appropriated to revaluation reserve* | (X) | X |
| Available for distribution and general reserve |  | X |
| Dividends |  | (X) |
| Added to/(deducted from) general reserve |  | X |

*This transfer is the amount of the net surplus that the directors consider should be retained having regard to the needs of the business: It may exceed or be less than the net surplus. The directors should explain the basis and the reasons for amounts transferred.

Source: Adapted from Accounting Standards Committee, Proposed Statement of Standard Accounting Practice ED 18, *Current Cost Accounting* (London: Institute of Chartered Accountants in England and Wales, November 30, 1976), p. 75.

Total liabilities and preferred stock = ℓ
Total monetary assets = a
Common stockholders' equity
 including reserves = e
Cost of sales adjustment = c
Depreciation adjustment = d

When $\ell > a$, the stockholders are in a favorable position during inflationary economic conditions. Expressed another way the "loss" of an entity's creditors, due to eroding purchasing power of monetary unit, is "gain" to its stockholders. Therefore a gearing credit is made to the income statement for an amount which equals:

Gearing adjustment (credit) = $\dfrac{(\ell - a)}{(\ell - a) + e} \times (c + d)$

If $a > \ell$, on the basis of rationale explained above, a gearing charge is made to the income statement for an amount which equals:

Gearing adjustment (charge) = $(a - \ell) \times$ Percent change in the retail price index during the year

*Exposure Draft No. 24.* The latest proposal in the UK, if finalized as an SSAP, would require an abbreviated (at the minimum) current cost balance sheet, a current cost income statement, and explanatory notes, all on a supplementary basis. The proposed standard would apply, with certain specified exceptions, to all listed companies and other entities with annual gross revenues of at least five million pounds sterling.

The current cost income statement would present two distinct income figures. The "current cost operating profit" is derived by making three adjustments to historical cost income before interest and taxes. The adjustments are for depreciation, cost of sales, and a "monetary working capital adjustment." Then "current cost profit attributable to shareholders" is computed by making a gearing adjustment, and also deducting interest and taxes.

The adjustments for depreciation and cost of sales are the same as in the Hyde guidelines discussed earlier. The monetary working capital adjustment (MWCA) is an innovation included in this Exposure Draft. The MWCA is essentially a short-term adjustment for working capital which enters the calculation of current cost operating profit. A charge is made against income for the increased working capital (excluding inventories) which a business needs to provide in times of inflation. Calculations to compute the MWCA in a simple situation by using the averaging method are illustrated in Exhibit 3. The MWCA recognizes that monetary working capital is an integral part of the net operating assets of the business. In most situations monetary working capital will be the aggregate of the following items arising from normal operating activities of the enterprise:

*1. Accounts receivable, prepayments and trade bills receivable, plus*

*2. Inventories that are not subject to a cost of sales adjustment, less*

*3. Accounts payable, accrued liabilities, and trade bills payable.*

As indicated in (2) above, only those inventories are included in the monetary working capital adjustment which are not subject to a cost of sales adjustment. This is to avoid including the same amount for inventories twice, once in the cost of sale adjustment and again in the monetary working capital adjustment. Obviously it would be erroneous to do so since both of these adjustments have the same objective, i.e., to take into account the effect of changing prices on the working capital needed to continue operations.

As explained earlier, the Hyde guidelines proposed two types of gearing adjustment, appropriateness of each being dependent upon the overall net monetary position of the company. ED 24 requires a gearing adjustment to be made only when the business is financed by "net borrowing."

Net borrowing is defined as the amount by which liabilities in (1) exceed assets in (2), as listed below.

*1. The aggregate of all liabilities and provisions (including convertible debentures*

**EXHIBIT 3   UK'S EXPOSURE DRAFT 24**
**CALCULATION OF THE MONETARY WORKING CAPITAL ADJUSTMENT**

|  | Year-End 19X2 | Year-End 19X1 |
|---|---:|---:|
| Amounts in the historical cost balance sheets: |  |  |
| Accounts receivable—trade customers | $108,500 | $78,000 |
| Accounts payable—raw materials suppliers | 75,000 | 64,800 |

|  | Finished Goods | Raw Materials |
|---|---:|---:|
| Appropriate index numbers: |  |  |
| At year-end 19X1 | 130 | 135 |
| Average for year 19X2 | 145 | 140 |
| At year-end 19X2 | 155 | 150 |

Calculation of the MWCA:

I.  $108,500 - 78,000$ — $30,500$

   Less: $(108,500 \times \frac{145}{155}) - (78,000 \times \frac{145}{130})$ — $14,500$

   $\$16,000$ (A)

II. $75,000 - 64,800$ — $10,200$

   Less: $(75,000 \times \frac{140}{150}) - (64,800 \times \frac{140}{135})$ — $2,800$

   $\$ 7,400$ (B)

III. Monetary working capital adjustment:
    (A − B) — $\$ 8,600$

---

and deferred tax but excluding proposed dividends) other than those included within monetary working capital.

2. The aggregate of all current assets other than those subject to a cost of sales adjustment and those included within monetary working capital.

With reference to the above listing, if the assets in (2) exceed the liabilities in (1), no gearing adjustment would be required by ED 24.

The formula for calculating the gearing adjustment with explanation of the notations used in the formula are presented next.

| Average net borrowing | $(\ell - a)$ |
| Average shareholders' equity | $e$ |
| Cost of sales adjustment | $c$ |
| Depreciation adjustment | $d$ |
| Monetary working capital adjustment | $m$ |

Gearing adjustment (credit)

$$\frac{(\ell - a)}{(\ell - a) + e} \times (c + d + m)$$

The companies making supplemental disclosures in accordance with ED 24 guidelines may present either a complete or a summarized version of current cost balance sheet. ED 24 allows the use of a general price index rather than an asset-based specific index, whenever the former is more appropriate. In general, all fixed assets and inventories would be shown at their value to the business, which is generally current replacement cost. The Exposure Draft contains the proposal that an annual professional appraisal of land and buildings should be made to determine their valuation. The liabilities would be shown at the same amounts in current cost balance sheet as in basic historical cost statements.

ED 24 requires separate summaries of the movements both of fixed assets and the capital maintenance reserve. The capital maintenance reserve reflects the four adjustments required to be made in order to derive current cost profit attributable to shareholders, i.e., cost of sales, depreciation, monetary working capital, and gearing. In addition, the capital maintenance reserve reflects the revaluation surpluses and deficits arising from the differences between historical and current cost of fixed assets and inventories.

# ACCOUNTANTS AND ACCOUNTANCY: IS IT ONLY ACCOUNTANTS WHO CANNOT RECOGNIZE THE EFFECT THAT INFLATION HAS HAD ON ACCOUNTANCY?

by R.F.J. Dewhurst, MA, FCA, MEA

So long as man has traded, so long has he tried to assess what gain he has made. The one subsumes the other, since to fix the terms of a bargain he must first find out what advantage it will be to him.

Early on he began to make a note of these transactions. Setting aside bartering, he must have recorded these dealings in money terms at the date of the transaction. Understandably, with these figures available to him, all his calculations of his gain were based on these historic figures. For centuries since, accountants, in drawing up their estimates of profit, have followed this principle.

**INVIOLATE PRINCIPLE**

With this long background of calculations based on input values it is understandable that, when inflation became severe in the early seventies and some adjustment seemed inevitable, the historic principle was kept inviolate.

For reasons which even now remain a little obscure, the Government set up the Sandilands Committee to look into the matter of inflation in accounts. Some inkling of the answer which the Committee might have been expected to arrive at, could perhaps have been obtained by a close study of the make up of its members. Some of these were experienced in other accounting methods. One of these was replacement costing, developed in the Netherlands in the early 20s, and since used in that country by several large companies, including Phillips.

The solution recommended by the Sandilands Committee was indeed a form of replacement accounting. The Committee called it "current cost accounting" (CCA), though it differed very little from any other type of accounting based on the replacement concept.

To accountants brought up for many years on the principle that input cost was the single firmly-established fact relating to any asset, and that all calculations relating to profit should be related to this, it is understandable that the whole idea should be regarded as near heresy. At one sweep it would have made redundant much of their knowledge and expertise acquired over years of labour.

Perhaps, therefore, it should not have been much of a surprise when last year members of the Institute of Chartered Accountants in England and Wales passed their resolution saying that they did not wish any system of current cost accounting to be made compulsory [*The Accountant*, July 7th, 1977] — even though this was against the advice of the leaders of their profession, who had come, though with reservations, to accept Sandilands.

---

Reproduced by consent from *The Accountant* (UK) of October 12, 1978.

## INABILITY TO AGREE

The consequences of this 'revolt' were enormous. Historic cost, current purchasing power and CCA had been considered and apparently set aside. Apparently no-one, certainly not members of the accounting profession, could agree as to the right basis for accounting.

In the wake of this resolution it was evident that it was necessary to arrive at some agreed solution as a matter of urgency. Equally clearly—considering the great divergence of opinion—the likelihood was that this would be a compromise.

## THE HYDE GUIDELINES

The Hyde proposals [*The Accountant*, November 10th, 1977] were the 'compromise' and, initially, at any rate, they received a great deal of support. Most people seemed glad to settle for any agreed and equitable solution.

But were the Hyde proposals truly equitable, or were they an artificial compromise arrived at just for the sake of convenience? Two of the three adjustments—those for cost of sales and depreciation—are attempts to allow for the effect of inflation on the replacement values of current and fixed assets in the profit and loss account. Indeed, the Hyde working party openly admitted that historic profit needed adjusting and used the standard argument in favour of replacement accounting to justify this.

Since this replacement point is so crucial, at the risk of boring the reader the question is put once again by way of this simple example:

> *At the start of a year a business has one unit in stock, which cost £60. At the end of the year this unit is sold for £70 and on the same day an identical unit is purchased for £70. No other trading or operating takes place. What is the profit?*

Historical cost argues for £10. Common sense says it surely must be nil, and replacement accounting concurs. Hyde, too, says historical is wrong; indeed, this was the point of the 'Hyde' adjustment.

So here is the strange thing. The Hyde Committee, convinced by its own arguments, recommended incorporating these replacement adjustments—but *solely* by way of notes to accounts which will still be in historic terms. It is these historic accounts which will be adjusted, and it is these accounts which will still show the profit figure.

But is this historic profit figure right? Common sense says no. Even Hyde in his convincing statement said it should be adjusted. If this is so, if his argument for an adjustment is so good, why not put it in as the correct profit in the first place? If these adjustments are right, if the replacement cost principle is truly the right one, then why are they not implemented?

Can it be that many professional accountants, with their long training in historical input accounting, are too prejudiced to admit openly that the basis for all their work is wrong? Can they only admit the truth as a temporary adjustment, necessitated by the present strange rates of inflation?

## ACCOUNTANTS AND NON-ACCOUNTANTS

The evidence that years of training 'blinkers' accountants in trying to assess the situation is strong. We have already seen one example of this. The leaders of the accounting profession—presumably people of above-average knowledge and ability—were, in general, prepared to accept Sandilands. But the backwoodsmen were not.

Let us go to the other end of the scale and take a very parochial example. The University of Warwick runs several masters' degree courses in business studies. 'Finance' is a fairly popular option on these degree courses, and each year a number of students who are also qualified accountants take this option.

Earlier this year, as part of this work, the arguments in favour of historical cost, CPP, CCA and Hyde were once again presented. At the end a lengthy argument developed. To try and round the matter off, students were asked to say where they stood. The results are given below:

| In favour of: | Everyone | | Professional accountants | |
|---|---|---|---|---|
| Historical | 5 | | 3 | |
| CPP | 3 | 8 | 2 | 5 |
| CCA | 10 | | 0 | |
| Hyde | 5 | 15 | 0 | 0 |

Whereas the majority of all students were in favour of CCA or at least of the Hyde proposals (which incorporate replacement accounting), no students with professional accountancy qualifications held these views. Solidly they voted for historical or its associated CPP approach.

This difference in the attitude, as between those with a professional accountancy background and other professional men with less formal training in accountancy, can be seen, equally clearly, at other levels. The accounting profession, as such, in the United States has not shown much interest in any form of replacement accounting. Yet since March 1976 the Securities and Exchange Commission—a widely-respected body with powers far exceeding those of our own Stock Exchange—has required companies with over $100 million in fixed assets and stock to supply replacement cost data (and also to show this data by way of notes to their accounts) in respect of cost of sales, stock and depreciation charges. The accounting profession rejects replacement accounting; the SEC and most investment analysts in the States accept the need for it.

Even in the UK this schism is clearly evident. The main body of ICAEW members has voted against any mandatory departure from historical accounting concepts, yet many industrial accountants of large businesses—Ford and ICI are good examples of this—show that they favour replacement cost accounting.

## THE ALTERNATIVES

Throughout the world we can see two opposing forces at work: on the one hand, the feeling that historical accounting has served the accounting profession well and truly for hundreds of years, and that this should not be thrown aside lightly. On the other hand, there is a growing acceptance that inflation has cast doubts on the validity of accounts prepared on the old basis.

Many countries mirror the uncertainty which exists in this country or show their ambivalent feelings in one way or another. The United States is a good example of this. Some countries, such as South Africa, are waiting to see what the rest of the world decides.

A few countries have come down fairly positively on the side of replacement accounting. As might be expected, these are either 'new' countries with a fresh approach to accounting, or those with a reputation for a sophisticated and intellectual attitude. Australia, New Zealand and Canada are good examples of the former. In Europe the outstanding example of the latter is Holland, a small nation but one whose accountants have long been highly respected.

Indeed, it all started in Holland when Professor Limperg, an economist, first worked out in practical detail the consequences of applying replacement cost theory. He did not hold that what has been done for hundreds of years is necessarily right. Mankind has always been able to produce people of like initiative. Perhaps this is as well—otherwise we should surely still be cave-dwellers!

# ACCOUNTANTS AND ACCOUNTANCY: SOME FURTHER COMMENTS ON "INFLATION ACCOUNTING"

by John M.J. Boersema

The ambivalence and uncertainty about the subject of inflation accounting, which Mr. Dewhurst criticizes, are perfectly understandable, since the problem to be addressed is much more difficult than he implies. The choice to be made is not a simple choice between, on the one hand, historical accounting and, on the other hand, acceptance that 'inflation has cast doubts on the validity of accounts prepared on the old basis'.

Rather, the acceptance of this latter fact is only the beginning of the search for an alternative. Choices must be made as to definitions of capital and details of the precise methods to be adopted. This article summarizes some of the issues not addressed by Mr. Dewhurst and presents the existing state of the world in an alternative and, as I believe, a somewhat more realistic light.

## CAPITAL MAINTENANCE

Mr. Dewhurst, in his discussion, advocates a strict physical capital maintenance point of view as typified in his example:

> At the start of a year a business has one unit in stock, which cost £60. At the end of the year this unit is sold for £70, and on the same day an identical unit is purchased for £70. No other trading or operating takes place. What is the profit?
> 
> Historical cost argues for £10. Common sense says it surely must be nil, and replacement accounting concurs.

Justification of the use of replacement cost solely by an appeal to common sense fails to recognize opposing viewpoints expressed throughout the relevant literature. There is another view, held by many, that advocates the maintenance of general purchasing power of financial capital. That is, if, in this example, the general price-level (the only measure of inflation) had increased by 10 per cent, the cost of the unit of stock adjusted for changes in the value of the pound would be £66 and profit would, under a general purchasing power capital maintenance definition, be £4.

The reasons for advocating purchasing power of financial capital can be briefly expressed as follows:

1. All amounts in the financial statements can be stated in a constant measuring unit;
2. Comparability among enterprises is, therefore, achieved since the same yardstick of performance, general purchasing power, is used for all;
3. When combined with a current value alternative, all real changes in wealth are reported in the income statement;
4. Shareholders' wealth–general purchasing power–is maintained so that funds are, over time, available to deploy in other areas than those presently invested in;
5. Purchasing power capital maintenance does not mandate 'excessive' price increases. Normal profits will be reported as long as selling prices are adjusted to reflect general price-level changes;
6. It will report the result of good buying activities in the income statement;
7. It will report the favourable impact of inflation on debt; it does not report exclusively the negative impact of price changes;
8. It is readily definable;
9. It provides better management guidance, in that it best encourages managers to be innovative in new areas;

---

Reproduced by consent from *The Accountant* (UK) of January 11, 1979.

10. It is questionable whether 'productive capacity' is relevant for wasting assets such as oil and gas reserves;
11. Purchasing power capital maintenance uses the traditional concept of financial capital;
12. It is congruent with an inflation-adjusted investment appraisal approach. This seeks to ensure that the purchasing power of the capital to be invested in a project is recovered in addition to a real return on that capital; and
13. It is consistent with the recent tentative decision by the US Financial Accounting Standards Board in favour of a financial capital concept.

Surely, the support for this view is great enough at least to acknowledge its existence!

## REPLACEMENT COSTS

Moreover, the accounting alternatives which can be loosely grouped as 'replacement cost'—Sandilands, ED18, Hyde, the SEC requirements, the Dutch proposals, etc.—are still subject to some very significant problems:

1. These alternatives do not necessarily account for inflation, i.e., changes in the general price-level;
2. A balance sheet valued on this basis does not reflect wealth, financial position or command over goods and services;
3. Valuation at replacement cost erroneously assumes or implies the replacement of assets;
4. These alternatives generally imply some type of physical capital maintenance, but exactly what is to be maintained is often unclear;
5. These alternatives match future costs with past revenues;
6. They account both for assets owned and those not owned by the company;
7. The definition of 'replacement' cost is far from settled;
8. Whether or not technological change must be taken into account is not yet agreed and, if it is, the methodology to be used is complex, subjective and not yet standardized;
9. Replacement cost alternatives are not relevant in the context of stewardship;
10. Replacement cost may be 'counter-intuitive' to general shareholders;
11. Numerous unsettled issues remain; e.g., backlog depreciation, deferred taxes, depreciation, intangible assets and special trading gains;
12. Replacement cost alternatives may be very subjective and largely dependent on management intent. The results are unlikely to be comparable between companies;
13. Replacement cost accounting does not appear applicable for a number of industries or parts thereof; e.g., oil, gas and mineral reserves, property companies, commodity traders and banking;
14. The available experience has been experimental, has not been adequately analysed, and provides little indication that a uniform, standardized version can or should be adopted at this time.

It is no wonder, therefore, that accountants have refused to jump enthusiastically into implementing such alternatives.

## NET REALIZABLE VALUES

Furthermore, the issue is complicated by the existence of another valuation alternative, net realizable value. Although it has received little discussion in professional (as opposed to academic) literature, it does have significant merit:

1. Net realizable values represent wealth, the money's worth at a company's command, command over goods and services;
2. Net income measures changes in wealth;
3. Net realizable values are consistent with maintaining the purchasing power of financial capital;

4. Net realizable values best satisfy the requirements of stewardship;
5. Financial statements based on market resale prices are most comparable among companies, and from period to period for the same company;
6. These statements provide a meaningful calculation of the rate of return;
7. The net realizable value provides the best basis on which to evaluate managerial responsibility;
8. Depreciation and amortization will no longer be arbitrary;
9. Net realizable values are the only values relevant to investment decision that can reasonably be maintained in an accounting system;
10. Comprehensive application of net realizable values provides a balance sheet that is properly additive and provides a meaningful aggregation;
11. An accounting alternative based on net realizable values accounts only for existing assets and events that have actually taken place;
12. Net realizable values may be intuitively understandable to the general shareholder; and
13. While the value obtained may vary somewhat, the estimate of net realizable values is clear on what is being estimated; is concerned with existing assets; is limited by variations in real market prices; does not depend on management's intent; and involves no consideration of possible future cost savings or revenue changes.

While a system of accounting based on net realizable values will no doubt also have implementation problems, these are likely to be no greater than with replacement costs. Certainly, it is incorrect to say at this point that 'current value' is replacement cost. Another contender is available.

**STATE OF THE ART WORLD-WIDE**

Given the complexity of the problem, it is not surprising that differences of opinion exist throughout the world. Concern about replacement cost is, however, not limited to 'backwoodsmen' and accountants with 'blinkers' on. In the United States, the Securities and Exchange Commission is 'presently assessing the disclosures made' and, according to its release 33-5966, 'continues to believe that the disclosure of relevant current economic information, including the current cost of assets as well as the current cost of using assets, is essential to meaningful financial reporting in the existing business environments'.

'The Commission has not, however, determined that these concerns should necessarily lead to the general implementation of a form of current value accounting. The Commission has reservations about the kinds of subjective decisions that would be injected into financial statements by adopting a current value system'.

In general, the response from the companies preparing the SEC data has been negative. Most companies did not include the figure in the annual report to shareholders. The ambiguity of the numbers was particularly stressed as, for example, by US Steel, which noted that its 1976 replacement cost depreciation would be $600 million under one set of assumptions but could be as much as $1,300 million under another approach. On the basis of the published opinion of a sample of companies, one American author concludes that the experiment has been a fiasco and that the SEC should 'go back to square one and do its homework'.

A more recent study conducted for the Financial Executives Research Foundation by Booz-Allen and Hamilton, management consultants, and reported in the *Journal of Accountancy* for September 1978, surveyed 500 corporations representing one-half of all corporations affected by SEC ASR190. It reported that the companies' executives did not believe the data to be 'useful in making investment and credit decisions' and were opposed to the requirement. Also, 'they generally could not derive direct benefit from such disclosure, nor could they find an effective use for it in business management'. They were also 'found to have serious reservations about the conceptual validity of replacement cost disclosure'.

Moreover, it is not true that 'most investment analysts in the US accept the need for it'.

Some analysts have apparently reacted favourably; others have not. For instance, Stewart Specter of Oppenheim & Co is quoted as saying: 'It's a nice set of financial figures that have very little to do with the real business world'.

The Booz, Allen study found that analysts 'generally believe that they have been better off in assessing the impact of inflation through their own individually developed analytical techniques'. Less than 1 per cent of the 200 financial and credit analysts surveyed found that the information 'had significantly altered their investment or credit decisions'. Thus, while a lot of analysis of the SEC experiment can and should still be done, the preliminary results available give little justification for enthusiastic adoption of the concepts elsewhere.

It is also untrue to claim that Canada has come down 'fairly positively on the side of replacement accounting'. After first issuing guidelines for CPP accounting, which have not been withdrawn, the CICA Accounting Research Committee issued in 1976 a discussion paper on current value accounting which admirably sets out the issues involved. 'In order to focus discussion', the committee provided a preliminary position which provided for the use of a 'combination of current entry and current exit prices' and the adoption of a general purchasing power definition of capital. Hardly a positive replacement accounting alternative!

Finally, while it did indeed 'all start in Holland', the position of replacement cost in the Netherlands at this time should not be overrated. A 1977 NIvRA survey of 1975 annual reports concludes that profit calculations were still predominantly shown on the basis of historic costs.

A survey by a Netherlands author, Dr. R. Slot, of the 1976 annual reports of 50 large Dutch companies found only five which show both balance sheets and profit and loss accounts on a full replacement cost basis. He noted various other partial replacement cost practices but his survey combines all forms of price variation accounting, so that the degree of replacement accounting cannot be accurately determined. He did find, however, a great variety of replacement cost practices and criticizes particularly the lack of clarity as to capital maintenance objectives.

Klaassen's 1975 study 'Replacement value: Theory and application in financial reporting' found that about 16 per cent of the Dutch companies listed on the Amsterdam stock exchange value fixed assets and/or stock on the balance sheet, and also calculate profit, on a replacement cost basis. He also found great diversity in the methodology applied. Thus it is clear that replacement cost accounting is not all-pervasive in the Netherlands and that Dutch practice cannot be quoted as an indication that an objective, comparable methodology is available. Rather, as another Dutch author, Jules Muis, has concluded, 'an attempt to impose current value accounting, especially in the case of smaller companies which, unlike the classic Dutch example Phillips, do not have available a sophisticated "accounting think tank", might open a Pandora's box of verifiability problems'.

Moreover, it should not be thought that replacement value theory as developed in the Netherlands has presented clear, unequivocal solutions to all the possible problems. Nor is this theory universally accepted even in the Netherlands.

## CONCLUSION

Overall, then, it is obvious that the solution to the problem caused by inflation is not nearly as simple as Mr. Dewhurst implies.

Controversy surrounds the choice of capital maintenance objective. The replacement cost alternatives entail major problems which must be resolved if a uniform system is to be implemented world-wide. A conceptually more attractive alternative exists in the form of net realizable values. It behooves anyone taking part in the ongoing discussion to show some recognition of these considerations.

# C.C.A.: A COMPARISON OF THE AUSTRALIAN AND U.K. PROPOSALS

*by Russell G. Marriott*

**INTRODUCTION**

This article evaluates how Australia's C.C.A. proposals contained in the Statement of Provisional Accounting Standards "Current Cost Accounting" (DPS 1.1/309.1) and Explanatory Statement "The Basis of Current Cost Accounting (DPS 1.2/309.2), both issued by The Institute of Chartered Accountants in Australia and the Australian Society of Accountants in August 1978, together with the Revised Exposure Draft entitled "The Recognition of Gains and Losses on Holding Monetary Items in the Context of Current Cost Accounting" issued by the Australian Accounting Research Foundation in August 1979, compare with the U.K.'s C.C.A. proposals contained in Exposure Draft 24 "Current Cost Accounting" and accompanying Guidance Notes issued by the U.K. Accounting Standards Committee in April 1979.

This comparison is made in a general way to facilitate understanding of the similarities and differences between the two C.C.A. proposals. There is no attempt in this article to enter into academic debate on technical points, nor to draw any conclusions as to the relative merits of each set of proposals.

**GENERAL COMMENTS**

1. The Australian proposals apply to all listed companies and public corporations, without exception. The U.K. proposals apply only to listed companies and other entities with an annual turnover of £UK5,000,000 or more. The U.K. proposals also exempt insurance, property investment and dealing companies and investment and unit trusts on the grounds that the C.C.A. method does not appear to be wholly appropriate to them.

2. The Australian proposals contain a strong recommendation for publication of supplementary information, relating to current costs of fixed assets and inventories, depreciation charges and cost of goods sold, for accounting periods commencing on and after 1 July 1978.

A suggestion is also made that business enterprises may wish to show other information, including gains or losses on monetary items and the manner in which they have been calculated. The U.K. proposals take a more definite stance, proposing that the standard contained therein should be effective for accounting periods beginning on or after 1 January 1980. However, this date will be kept under review in the light of comments received.

3. The U.K. Exposure Draft (ED 24) and accompanying Guidance Notes cover a complete C.C.A. system. The Australian Provisional Standard (DPS 1.1/309.1), Explanatory Statement (DPS 1.2/309.2) and Revised Monetary Items Exposure Draft (MIED) deal only with fixed assets/depreciation, inventories/cost of goods sold, and monetary items. There are a number of areas for which a C.C.A. treatment has yet to be prescribed in Australia, such as investments, intangible assets, translation of foreign currencies, consolidations, and others.

4. The Australian publications contain much more of the underlying theory and rationale, and are more definite in the C.C.A. treatments prescribed, than the U.K. proposals. ED 24 obviously has been heavily influenced by the adverse comments concerning the length and complexity of ED 18, which was issued in November 1976. As a result ED 24 is much shorter, does not attempt to explain the underlying theory or justify the rationale for the methods selected completely, and suggests experimentation in applying broader guidelines rather than prescribing unique treatments.

---

Reprinted from *The Australian Accountant*, October, 1979. With the permission of *The Australian Accountant* and R. G. Marriott.

5. The same basic concepts underlie both the Australian and U.K. proposals. The capital to be maintained in both cases is determined on the physical productive capacity concept. The current costs of assets in both cases are to be determined on the lower of net current replacement cost or recoverable amount. The U.K. proposals explicitly state that these amounts are to represent the value of the assets to the business. While the Australian proposals do not specifically mention this requirement, the practical implications of the Australian proposals are similar in this respect to the results obtained by applying the U.K. concept.

6. Given the broader nature of the U.K. proposals, C.C.A. results prepared in accordance with the Australian proposals for fixed assets/depreciation and inventories/cost of goods sold would in most cases also be acceptable under the U.K. proposals.

7. The account to which entries for changes in current costs are to be made is termed the current cost adjustment account in the Australian proposals, and the capital maintenance reserve in the U.K. proposals. However, the names should be interchangeable.

8. The only technical differences of any significance between the two proposals relate to:

a. *Calculation of losses/gains on monetary items (in the Australian proposals these include loan capital, which is also involved in the gearing adjustment);*
b. *Calculation of the gearing adjustment,*
c. *The approach to determination of C.C.A. profit, as suggested in illustrative profit and loss statements included in each of the proposals.*

## CALCULATION OF LOSSES/GAINS ON MONETARY ITEMS

1. The Australian proposals calculate a net loss/gain on all monetary assets and liabilities. Loan capital is included, although losses/gains calculated thereon are subsequently transferred out of the profit and loss account to a gearing gains reserve account. This leaves in entity net profit losses and gains on trade debtors and trade creditors and other monetary assets and liabilities.

The U.K. proposals include a monetary working capital adjustment (MWCA). The items subject to adjustment are restricted to:

a. *(i) Trade debtors;*
   *(ii) Stocks not subject to a cost of sales adjustment, e.g., seasonal produce and dealing commodities;*
   *(iii) Trade creditors;*
   *arising from day-to-day operating activities as distinct from transactions of a capital nature.*
b. *Where their exclusion can be shown to be misleading when calculating current cost profit, cash floats and that part of bank balances or overdrafts arising from fluctuations in the volume of stock, trade debtors and trade creditors can also be included.*
c. *For banks and other financial businesses, other current assets and other current liabilities are also included insofar as they also arise from the day-to-day operating activities of the business as distinct from transactions of a capital nature.*

The range of monetary items on which a net loss/gain is calculated under the Australian proposals is thus more extensive than the range of monetary items included in the proposed U.K. MWCA. However, under the U.K. proposals loan capital and, broadly, all monetary assets and liabilities not included in the MWCA are subject to the calculation of a gearing adjustment.

2. Generally speaking, both proposals recommend the use of the most relevant specific indexes to calculate losses/gains on monetary items, other than on loan capital in the Australian proposals.

The Australian proposals specifically suggest that:

a. *For trade debtors and trade creditors, appropriate measures of changes in the* current cost of inputs should be used; inventory price movements would often be suitable.

b. For trade debtors and trade creditors related to financing activities, a general price index should be used. This reflects movements in the average value of money, which is the relevant good in financing activities.

c. In the majority of cases for other monetary assets and other monetary liabilities, a general price index may be used for practical purposes, although efforts should be made to find a more specific relevant index.

d. For loan capital, a general price index should be used.

The U.K. proposals specifically suggest that:

a. For trade debtors and trade creditors, indexes relating to changes in input prices for the current cost of goods or services sold should be used. Indexes of selling prices and the same index as for stock are both mentioned.

b. For monetary working capital of general banking businesses, the general index of retail prices should be used as the best available proxy measure of changes in the prices of the assets of undertakings for which the business provides finance.

3. The mathematical methods suggested for calculation of the losses/gains differ slightly as between the proposals. However, this is only a matter of mechanics and both methods produce substantially the same results.

## CALCULATION OF THE GEARING ADJUSTMENT ON (MAINLY) LOAN CAPITAL

1. This is the only area where there are real conceptual differences between the two proposals. As a very brief summary:

a. The Australian gearing adjustment includes a large component of unrealized holding gains, but none of the adjustment remains in the final net profit, which is determined on an entity basis.

b. The U.K. gearing adjustment is restricted to a portion of the holding gains realized during the period, and the total adjustment remains in the final net profit, which is determined on a proprietorship basis.

2. Under the Australian proposals, the gain or loss on loan capital is calculated simply by applying the movement in a general price index to the average balance of loan capital. Its inclusion in the profit and loss statement in the intermediate result of "profit and gearing gains attributable to shareholders" is intended to satisfy those persons with proprietorship viewpoints. The gain or loss is then transferred to a gearing gains reserve account, before determining entity net profit.

Under the U.K. proposal, the gearing adjustment is calculated by the following recommended method:

a. Ascertain the average net borrowing during the period. This is not confined to loan capital, but broadly includes all monetary liabilities and monetary assets other than those included in the MWCA. Let the average net borrowing be $L$.

b. Ascertain the average shareholders' interest during the period. Let this be $S$.

c. The gearing proportion is the ratio of the average net borrowing to the sum of this and the average shareholders' interest, i.e.,

$$\frac{L}{L+S}$$

d. Ascertain the current cost adjustments made to convert historical cost trading profit to current cost operating profit. These adjustments will comprise additional depreciation, cost of goods sold, loss on fixed asset disposals and the MWCA. Let the sum of these adjustments be $A$.

e. Calculate the gearing adjustment by multiplying the sum of the adjustments by the gearing proportion, so that the adjustment equals

$$\frac{L}{L+S} \times A$$

The U.K. rationale is that shareholders benefit from gearing during a time of rising prices, since the borrowings are normally fixed in monetary amount and the replacement cost of assets exceeds the borrowings that have financed them. In these circumstances the profit attributable to shareholders would be understated if the whole of the current cost adjustments were charged in the profit and loss account; the adjustments must be abated for the effects of gearing. Effectively, this abatement process results in a credit being made to profit for the geared portion of holding gains realized during the period; it does not cause any unrealized holding gains to be credited to profit.

3. It is worth noting that both the Australian and U.K. publications warn against the dangers of distributing gains from gearing as dividends. Relevant quotations are:

Australian MIED:
*As gearing gains on loan capital do not increase entity net profit, distributions made to shareholders from the gearing gains reserve account constitute a reduction in the operating capability of the entity unless replaced by additional equity funds or loan capital.*

U.K. ED 24:
*The current cost profit attributable to shareholders does not necessarily measure the amount that can prudently be distributed since, although it will reflect the impact of price changes on the profits reported under the historical cost system, other factors still need to be considered. Even if the effect of such factors is neutral, a full distribution of the current cost profit attributable to shareholders may make it necessary to arrange additional finance (equal to the gearing adjustment) to avoid an erosion of the operating capability of the business. However, an increase in the value to the business of the assets may provide increased cover for such financing.*

## ILLUSTRATIVE APPROACH TO DETERMINATION OF C.C.A. PROFIT

1. Statements illustrating the approach to determination of C.C.A. profit are included in both the Australian MIED and the U.K. ED 24. Neither are prescriptive, nor are they intended to be used as standard formats.

These statements are set out side-by-side in the following Table. Some very minor changes have been made in this table to the form of presentation included in each of the publications to facilitate a direct comparison, but these changes do not invalidate the principles of the proposals.

2. The major differences as shown by this table are:

a. *Both proposals show a figure for a form of both entity net profit and proprietorship net profit. However, the order in which they appear as between the body of the statement and the bottom line (and therefore the amount available for dividend distribution) is reversed.*

b. *Gearing gains under the Australian proposals are transferred out of the profit and loss account to a gearing gains reserve account. The U.K. gearing adjustment remains in the final net profit figure.*

c. *Interest under the Australian proposals is merely a deduction in arriving at the H.C.A. profit. Under the U.K. proposals interest is offset against the gearing adjustment, to show the net benefit arising to shareholders from borrowing.*

d. *The U.K proposals show a form of current cost operating profit, before gearing adjustment, interest and taxation. There is no such concept in the Australian proposals.*

## CONCLUSION

The major conclusion which can be drawn from the comparison presented in this article is that, apart from some differences relating to adjust-

**TABLE SHOWING INDICATIVE APPROACH TO DETERMINATION OF C.C.A. PROFIT**

| Australian Proposals | | $000 | U.K. Proposals | | £000 |
|---|---|---|---|---|---|
| H.C.A. profit—after interest and tax | | 1970 | H.C.A. profit—before interest and tax | | 2900 |
| Less: C.C.A. adjustments | | | Less: C.C.A. adjustments | | |
| Depreciation | 900 | | Depreciation | 900 | |
| Cost of goods sold | 460 | | Cost of goods sold | 460 | |
| Loss on sale of fixed assets | 50 | | Loss on sale of fixed assets | 50 | |
| Loss/gain on monetary items | | | Monetary working capital adjustment | 100 | 1510 |
| —All other (Gain 30) | | | | | |
| —Loan capital (Gain 200) | (230) | 1180 | | | 1180 |
| Profit and Gearing Gains Attributable to Shareholders | | 790 | Current Cost Operating Profit | | 1390 |
| Less: Transfer of gain on loan capital to gearing gains reserve account | | 200 | Gearing adjustment | 370 | |
| | | | Interest | 200 | 170 |
| | | | Current cost profit before taxation | | 1560 |
| | | | Taxation | | 730 |
| Entity Net Profit | | 590 | Current Cost Profit Attributable to Shareholders | | 830 |

ments for monetary items and gearing and the illustrative approach to determination of C.C.A. profits, the Australian and U.K. proposals are broadly compatible on conceptual and practical grounds.

It will be interesting to watch the progress of the proposals in each country to observe the degree of acceptance which each receives, and also whether there is any move towards an even greater degree of harmonization. This may well be forthcoming in view of the growing movement in many countries towards a form of current cost accounting.

# REPORTING THE IMPACT OF CHANGING PRICES IN NEW ZEALAND

*by M. Zafar Iqbal*

The New Zealand Society of Accountants is the leading professional accounting group in the country. Created by a special statute of Parliament in 1908, it was recognized as the sole legal representative of the profession, one of its stated objectives being to promote interests of the profession. The law also assigned exclusive authority to the society to control and

Excerpted from "SEC Replacement Cost Accounting: Broader Implications" by permission of M. Zafar Iqbal, MBA, Ph.D., CPA, CMA, Professor of Accounting at the California Polytechnic State University, San Luis Obispo. Mr. Iqbal is a member of the American Accounting Association, National Association of Accountants, Beta Alpha Psi, Beta Gamma Sigma, and Sigma Iota Epsilon. He has previously published in numerous professional and business journals.

regulate the accounting profession in New Zealand.[1]

There are no laws in New Zealand which prescribe the use of particular accounting methods. However, the Companies Act 1955 imposes a general standard and specific requirements relating to financial statements of companies. The general standard requires "true and fair" representation in the financial statements. The specific requirements deal with the disclosures.[2]

The New Zealand Society of Accountants has been the only source of official pronouncements related to accounting principles in the country. Until recent years its Statements of Standards of Accounting Practice were recommendations of the society to its members. Now the members are required to adhere to promulgated standards of the society. The role of the society is recognized by the Stock Exchange Association of New Zealand which requires all listed companies to prepare financial statements according to standards prescribed by the society. The Inland Revenue Department, New Zealand's equivalent of the US Internal Revenue Service, has also emphasized in recent years that generally it would recognize for tax assessments the income calculated by following accepted accounting principles.[3]

New Zealand has experienced double digit inflation in most years during the 1970's. This is in sharp contrast to the previous decade when average annual rate of inflation was less than 4 percent.

In March 1975 the New Zealand Society of Accountants published an Exposure Draft, ED 10, which was based on the United Kingdom's provisional standard PSSAP7.[4] The Exposure Draft required all listed companies to present a set of financial statements adjusted for general price level changes. These statements could be in summarized form, and were to be presented as supplementary information. The Society decided in March 1976 to withdraw the Exposure Draft. The reasons given for the decision were that the council of the Society had concluded on the basis of the Sandilands Report and comments from the members of the Society that current purchasing power was neither the most appropriate solution, nor would it receive wide acceptance in New Zealand.[5] Instead the Society decided to shift its focus on current cost accounting approach.

The next inflation accounting proposal by the New Zealand Society of Accountants was ED 14 issued in August 1976.[6] The method recommended in ED 14 was a current cost system similar to the approach adopted by the Sandilands Committee.

The government of New Zealand established a Committee of Inquiry into Inflation Accounting in December 1975. The committee is generally known as the Richardson Committee, after its chairman I.L.M. Richardson. Most members of the committee, including Dr. Richardson, were non-accountants but were supported by a staff which included accountants. Appointment of the Richardson Committee was not necessarily an unwelcome intervention by the New Zealand government in accounting standard-setting process. There are two reasons for this perception.

First, the New Zealand government has traditionally assumed a leadership role in attempts to stabilize the economy. The people

---

[1] R. S. Wasley, "The Status of Accountancy and of Accounting Practices in New Zealand," *The International Journal of Accounting Education and Research* (Spring 1968), pp. 73-77.

[2] Committee of Inquiry into Inflation Accounting, I.L.M. Richardson, Chairman, *Report of the Committee of Inquiry into Inflation Accounting* (Wellington, N.Z.: Government Printer, December 1976), pp. 27-29.

[3] *Ibid.*, pp. 29-30.

[4] New Zealand Society of Accountants, *Accounting for Changes in the Purchasing Power of Money*, Exposure Draft No. 10 of Proposed Statement of Standard Accounting Practice (Wellington, N.Z.: March 1975).

[5] Committee of Inquiry into Inflation Accounting, I.L.M. Richardson, Chairman, *op. cit.*, p. 65.

[6] New Zealand Society of Accountants, *Accounting in Terms of Current Costs and Values*, Exposure Draft No. 14 of Proposed Statement of Standard Accounting Practice (Wellington, N.Z.: August 1976).

of New Zealand suffered greatly in two depressions which occurred in 1890 and 1930. As a result, since the early 1930's it has been the philosophy of the government to be the general guardian of the people and attempt to protect them from all economic ills.[7] Consequently the national government, through its policies, has a definite impact on all facets of the business. Secondly, the government established the Richardson Committee after consultations with representatives of the accounting profession. Because of these reasons the climate in New Zealand was relatively free of friction and suspicion in contrast to the controversy which surrounded the Sandilands Committee in the UK. One can get an idea about the New Zealand situation from the following excerpts of a speech by P.I. Wilkinson, a minister in the cabinet of the New Zealand government:[8]

> *The Government became involved in the question of inflation accounting for two main reasons. First, a major change in the basis of accounting would have very significant implications for the economy. Secondly, a change in the method of accounting would also have implications for taxation and price control policies. The changes which have been proposed extend well beyond the field of accounting and would, if implemented, affect the structure and nature of our economy and the distribution of national income.*
>
> *Your profession was consulted before the setting up of the Committee of Inquiry and discussions were held with the President and Secretary before the Government recently invited further submissions. I am sure that a co-operative approach to this particular problem will be to our mutual advantage.*

The Richardson Committee submitted its report to the government in September 1976, shortly after ED 14 was issued by the New Zealand Society of Accountants. In December 1976 the report was presented to the New Zealand Parliament and also published by the government.[9] The Society effectively withdrew ED 14 in March 1977 when it informed the government it found most of the Richardson Committee recommendations acceptable.[10]

The Richardson Report called for abandonment of historical cost financial statements in favor of statements based on current cost accounting. The report recommended valuation of assets in financial statements at current cost to the enterprise. Profit for a period was to be measured according to operating capability concept of capital maintenance. The committee was the first to adopt the idea of "gearing" adjustment; the general concept was later incorporated in the UK both in the Hyde guidelines and ED 24 proposals. The Richardson Committee drew a distinction between operating profit of the enterprise and the profit attributable to its owners.

The response of the New Zealand government to the report was generally positive but cautious. The government invited comments from all interested parties on two issues. First, whether current cost accounting basis, recommended by the Richardson Committee, should be adopted for financial reporting purposes. If support existed for its introduction, then the second issue involved the specific modifications, if any, required to be made to the proposals contained in the Richardson Report.[11] The New Zealand government encouraged both the business sector and accounting practitioners

---

[7] Wasley, *op. cit.*, pp. 70-71.

[8] P. I. Wilkinson, "Comments by the Hon. P. I. Wilkinson," *Accounting for Inflation: Collection of Papers of the New Zealand Society of Accountants – Wellington and Wairarapa Branch's Summer Convention, 1977* (Wellington, N.Z.: 1977), pp. 1-2. The proceedings are not sequentially numbered; therefore the page numbers refer to the text of individual presentation.

[9] Report of the Committee of Inquiry into Inflation Accounting, I.L.M. Richardson, Chairman, *op. cit.*

[10] "Submissions on the Report of the Committee of Inquiry into Inflation Accounting," *Accountants' Journal* (New Zealand: May 1977), pp. 153-156.

[11] Wilkinson, *op. cit.*, pp. 3-4.

to assess implications of current cost accounting on their own operations, and let their opinions be known before any firm decision was made on introduction of the new method of accounting.

Response from the members of the New Zealand Society of Accountants and the business community indicated that an immediate change to current cost basis would not be acceptable. Instead it was generally felt that for the present time supplementary financial statements in terms of current costs and values will fulfill the need to reflect the impact of changing prices. The New Zealand Society of Accountants issued GU-1 in December 1978 to provide guidelines on preparation and presentation of such supplementary financial statements.[12]

GU-1 guidelines require an abbreviated balance sheet on the current cost basis, and an income statement which incorporates certain adjustments to reflect the impact of changing prices. These adjustments are for depreciation, cost of goods sold, and a gearing adjustment computed according to the method recommended in the Richardson Report.

The Department of Management Studies at the University of Waikato initiated an Inflation Accounting Research Project (IARP) in the later part of 1975.[13] The project is under financial sponsorship of the New Zealand government and the private sector. A working manual has been published under the IARP at the request of the New Zealand Society of Accountants.[14] The manual describes the steps and procedures for implementing the society's guidelines as specified in GU-1.

Implementation of GU-1 is supposedly the first phase of the process leading toward eventual adoption of a comprehensive current cost accounting system in the future. It is hoped that the knowledge gained from experimentation with inflation accounting will facilitate evolution and orderly introduction of the new system to replace the existing one.[15]

Two proposals from New Zealand are analyzed:

*1. The Richardson Report*
*2. Gu-1: CCA Guidelines*

**The Richardson Report.** The report recommended that all companies should adopt the system described as "current cost accounting" for basic financial statements. The essential features of the current cost accounting method are described next.

*1. The assets should be valued at current cost to the enterprise as a continuing entity.*
*2. Operating profit of the enterprise should be derived by recovering current cost of resources consumed to generate the revenue.*
*3. A figure designated as "profit attributable to owners" should be presented which reflects the portion of the movement in the capital maintenance reserve financed from borrowings.*

The Richardson Report recommended that fixed assets should be stated at their deprival value in the financial statement at the year-end. Those assets that are "essential" to the operations should be shown at their current replacement cost. If an asset is not essential for continued operations, it should be valued

---

[12] New Zealand Society of Accountants, *CCA Guidelines GU-1: Supplementary Financial Statements in Terms of Current Costs and Values* (Wellington, N.Z.: December 1978).

[13] One of the publications under this project reports on results of a field-test of three alternative inflation accounting techniques. See, Inflation Accounting Research Project, *Project Report No. 2—The Application of CPP, CCA, CoCoA* (Department of Management Studies, University of Waikato, Hamilton, N.Z.: October 1977). The methods tested under the project include current purchasing power accounting (CPP), current cost accounting (CCA) based on the Sandilands Report, and continuously contemporary accounting (CoCoA) as developed by Professor R.J. Chambers.

[14] Inflation Accounting Research Project, *CCA Working Manual* (Department of Management Studies, University of Waikato, Hamilton, N.Z.: March 1979).

[15] *Ibid.*, p. 1.

at net realizable value. The committee recommended the development of a series of indices by the New Zealand government to provide the basis for current replacement cost.

The proposed current cost accounting method would retain the transaction-based historical cost model, at least for the foreseeable future. Periodic adjustments would be made to historical cost figures to achieve conformity with the proposed system before preparation of current cost financial statements. In order to derive the current cost operating profit of the enterprise, four adjustments would be necessary in most cases.

1. *Depreciation expense would be based on the current cost of related assets at the end of the period.*
2. *Inventory would be valued at current cost to the enterprise at year-end, and a "cost of sales adjustment" is made to charge the revenue for the current cost, at the time of sale, of the items sold.*
3. *An adjustment should be made to reflect the change in the value of "circulating monetary assets." Circulating monetary assets include cash, bank deposits, and trade accounts receivable. These assets are employed in the ordinary course of business and cannot be removed from operations without impairing productive capacity of the enterprise. The Richardson Report recognizes that an entity suffers a loss in the value of such assets to the extent that inflation adversely affects operating capability of those funds. The loss, measured by using an index, is charged to the revenue.*
4. *Interest on borrowed funds should be excluded as a deduction in arriving at the current cost operating profit of the enterprise.*

The last item leads to an important point. One of the distinctive features of the Richardson Report relates to the two profit concept, namely,

1. *The current cost profit to the enterprise, and*
2. *The profit to the owners.*

In order to calculate the profit to the enterprise, the previously discussed adjustments relating to depreciation, cost of sales, and circulating monetary assets are incorporated but interest on borrowed funds is excluded. To move from "profit to the enterprise" to "profit to the owners" interest is deducted and also a gearing adjustment is made. The gearing adjustment essentially increases the owners' profit thus giving recognition to the fact that the corresponding credits to the capital maintenance reserve (arising from charges to the revenue for depreciation, cost of sales, and circulating monetary assets adjustments) were partially financed from borrowings. Thus the gearing adjustment is in the opposite direction of the other three adjustments; it increases the amount of income attributable to owners and reduces the balance in capital maintenance reserve. This statement, of course, presumes that there were upward movements in general and specific price levels during the period.

The amount of the gearing adjustment is computed by this formula:

$$\frac{\text{Average borrowings}}{\text{Average total assets}} \times \text{Net change for the period in the capital maintenance reserve}$$

Since "profit attributable to the owners, before tax" is the taxable income, the gearing adjustment ensures only that part of current cost adjustments which are attributable to shareholders is included as a deduction in the determination of taxable income.

The Richardson Committee termed non-circulating monetary assets as "fixed monetary assets." While the changes in the value of circulating monetary assets is reflected in arriving at the current cost operating profit of the enterprise, the corresponding change in the value of fixed monetary assets is reflected through the capital maintenance reserve. The change in value in the later case does not affect either profit figure.

The current cost statement of profits, prepared in accordance with the Richardson recommendations, is illustrated in Exhibit 1.

*GU-1: CCA Guidelines.* These current cost accounting guidelines became effective in New Zealand for financial statements covering periods beginning on or after April 1, 1979. The require-

**EXHIBIT 1  NEW ZEALAND'S RICHARDSON PROPOSAL
FORMAT OF CURRENT COST STATEMENT OF PROFIT**

| | | |
|---|---|---|
| Gross revenue | | * |
|     Historical cost of sales | * | |
|     Cost of sales adjustment to current cost | * | (*) |
| Current cost trading profit of the enterprise | | * |
|     Deduct— | | |
|         Expenses (excluding interest) | * | |
|         Depreciation on current cost basis | * | |
|     Add (or deduct)— | | |
|         Monetary asset adjustment | * | (*) |
| Current cost operating profit of the enterprise | | * |
|     Add (or deduct)— | | |
|         Capital profits (or losses) | | * |
| Total current cost profit of the enterprise | | * |
|     Deduct— | | |
|         Interest on borrowed funds | | (*) |
|     Add (or deduct)— | | |
|         Movements in capital maintenance reserve financed from borrowed funds | | * |
| Profit attributable to the owners, before tax | | * |
|     Provision for taxation for the period | | (*) |
| Profit attributable to the owners after tax | | * |
|     Provision for dividend (if a company) | | (*) |
| Retained current cost profit for the period | | * |
|     Retained current cost profit brought forward from previous period | | * |
| Retained current cost profit carried forward | | * |

Source: Committee of Inquiry into Inflation Accounting, I.L.M. Richardson, Chairman, *Report of the Committee of Inquiry into Inflation Accounting* (Wellington, N.Z.: Government Printer, December 1976), p. 153.

ments apply to all listed, publicly-held, companies. The affected companies have to provide an abbreviated balance sheet and an income statement, both prepared on the current cost basis as specified in the guidelines. The required current cost information is supplemental to the historical cost financial statements.

GU-1 requires that all non-monetary assets used in the business should be revalued at the end of every period to reflect their value to the business.

The guidelines for such valuation follow the Richardson Committee recommendations. Essential assets are valued at net replacement cost. Those assets which are non-essential to maintain operating capability should be stated at net realizable value. The guidelines suggest various alternatives to determine replacement cost of assets including current market purchase price, estimated current reproduction costs, appraisals, and indices. The backlog depreciation resulting from revaluation should be charged to the capital maintenance reserve account. Intangible assets and inventories should also be shown at their value to the business.

The Capital Maintenance Reserve account is part of the stockholders' equity. It should be adjusted for the following.

1. Unrealized gains or losses on revaluation of non-monetary assets
2. Backlog depreciation
3. Cost of sales adjustment
4. Purchasing power gains or losses on circulating monetary assets
5. Gearing adjustments.

The current cost income statement incorporates three adjustments to the income shown on historical cost basis income statement.

1. Depreciation adjustment
2. Cost of sales adjustment
3. Gearing adjustments.

Guidelines applicable to all three income statement adjustments are essentially the same as in the Richardson Report.

## COMPARISON OF CERTAIN CURRENT COST ACCOUNTING PROPOSALS

|  | *New Zealand CCA Guidelines* | *Australia Amended Provisional Standard* | *United Kingdom and Ireland ED. 24* |
|---|---|---|---|
| *Applicability* | Listed public companies | Listed public companies and public corporations | Listed public companies and other entities with turnover greater than $5 million |
| *Initial Implementation Date* | Years beginning April 1, 1979 (earlier application encouraged) | Years beginning July 1, 1978 | Years beginning January 1, 1980 (earlier application encouraged) |
| *Status of Current Cost Information* | Supplementary profit and loss account and balance sheet | Supplementary profit and loss account and balance sheet | Supplementary profit and loss account and balance sheet |
| *Audited?* | Yes | No | Not specifically mentioned |
| *Size of Publication* | 12 pages and manual | 7 pages, 26 page explanatory statement and manual | 28 pages and 46 page guidance notes |
| *Concept of Capital Maintenance* | Operating capability | Operating capability | Operating capability |

Reprinted from *The Chartered Accountant in Australia*, August 1979.

|  | New Zealand CCA Guidelines | Australia Amended Provisional Standard | United Kingdom and Ireland ED. 24 |
|---|---|---|---|
| General Valuation Rule | "Value to the Business" generally replacement cost | The lower of current cost or "recoverable amount" | "Value to the Business" |
| Cost of Sales | Cost at date of sale via a cost of sales adjustment | Cost at date of sale | Cost at date of sale |
| Depreciation | Based on end of period values | Based on average costs for the period | Based on average values for the period |
| Backlog Depreciation | Capital maintenance reserve account | Current cost adjustment account | Capital maintenance reserve account |
| Revaluation Credits and Debits | Capital maintenance reserve account | Current cost adjustment account | Capital maintenance reserve account |
| Purchasing Power Changes | Adjustment to "operating surplus" for change in circulating monetary assets<br><br>Adjustment to "proprietors profit" for movement in capital maintenance reserve finance from borrowings | Adjustment to current cost profit for holding monetary items in respect of:<br>(a) Monetary working capital<br>(b) Long-term monetary assets | Monetary working capital adjustment to "operating current cost profit" for change in working capital<br><br>"Gearing" adjustment to "current cost profit attributable to shareholders" for movement in capital maintenance reserve financed from borrowings |

# KEEPING UP WITH INFLATION THE CANADIAN WAY

*by Peter Myers*

For the past six years, while Americans have done little more than debate the relative merits of indexation, Canadians have been gaining real-world experience with this controversial system for coping with inflation. The lessons they have learned may be particularly valuable in assessing the probable impact of indexation in the United States.

Although the example usually discussed by economists is that of Brazil, which unquestionably constitutes the classic model for a fully-indexed economy, the type of indexation that has been established in Canada probably is much closer to any system that could be adopted by Americans. Moreover, Canada embraced the concept of indexation in response to economic circumstances that closely parallel those now faced by the United States. Unlike Brazil, which was forced to take its first major steps toward indexation as a means of averting imminent bankruptcy, Canada adopted the concept quite voluntarily—its government simply decided to try an idea advocated in the early Seventies by both American and Canadian economists as a means of reducing the more unpleasant side effects of high inflation.

In its purest form—and Brazil provides the obvious illustration—indexation can be an extremely cumbersome system that forces everyone to become a mathematician, imposes heavy administrative costs, and invites abuse by government officials. And to the extent that an indexation system is successful in eliminating the adverse consequences of inflation, it also reduces the incentive to bring inflation itself under control. A *partial* indexation system such as Canada's, however, can avoid the worst risk while retaining some of indexation's major benefits.

Before discussing how Canada's system actually works, let me review the type of problem any indexation system is supposed to resolve. When inflation is eroding a nation's currency, people no longer have a firm yardstick for measuring the economic value of such items as wages, beef prices, or even taxes. If the rent for your apartment goes up from $400 to $600 a month, then clearly you must cut back on other expenditures. Unless you get a large enough raise, the real value of your income will have been reduced in terms of its buying power. A $25,000 salary today may be worth, in today's terms, only $22,000 in a year's time.

In a largely unindexed economy, such as that of the United States, inflation forces everyone to perform a continual financial balancing act. Inevitably there are winners and losers. Lenders see the value of their money diminishing, for example, while borrowers can repay their loans with "cheaper" money. Unless interest rates exceed the rate at which prices are rising, inflation encourages people to spend their money now rather than save it. When the inflation rate is excessive, it does not take long before major disruptions occur in the relatively delicate mechanism of a free-market economy. These disruptions can lead to social unrest and ultimately to economic chaos, as was demonstrated so disastrously by the impact of hyperinflation on Germany a half century ago.

While many people—particularly the elderly and others with fixed incomes—are badly hurt by the existence of any inflation at all, the general tendency in mature economies is to fight inflation directly with the traditional weapons of fiscal and monetary restraint. Although some individuals make a profit from inflation while others sustain losses, these dislocations usually are considered to be inevitable. Much of the damage can be repaired through such means as a boost in pension levels or welfare payments. Under normal circumstances, when prices are rising slowly enough for each individual to perform his financial balancing act with little difficulty, this makeshift attitude probably makes sense—particularly given the enormous advantages of using a country's currency as a reasonably stable yardstick of value.

---

Reproduced from *Across the Board,* March 1980.

But there has been a more insidious effect of inflation in countries such as the United States and Canada, which levy personal income taxes on the basis of progressive rate structures. The underlying principle of progressive tax rates, of course, is that people with higher incomes should pay relatively larger shares of the cost of government services. Somebody with a taxable income of $50,000 not only pays more tax than somebody with an income of $10,000, he also pays a higher percentage of his taxable income.

While this principle may be socially desirable, it also results in a government's becoming one of the major beneficiaries of inflation. Say the inflation rate from one year to the next is 10 percent and all dollar amounts—including your salary—have risen by precisely that amount. In theory you would have neither lost nor gained. You would need more dollars for every expenditure, but the extra dollar cost would be offset exactly by your extra dollar income. Every financial transaction would involve a larger number of dollars, but those dollars would be worth correspondingly less, leaving the actual value of each transaction at the same level as the previous year. The mere fact of the increase in your dollar income, however, would have pushed you into a higher tax bracket. And given your higher *percentage* tax rate, the government would be demanding a proportionately larger slice of your income. The *real* value of your aftertax income—despite the 10 percent raise—actually would decrease.

Governments can make enormous windfall gains from inflation as a consequence of progressive personal tax rates. The interplay between the tax rates and inflation results in what amounts to automatic annual tax boosts—increases that would not occur if people were taxed on the basis of the real value of their incomes instead of the nominal amounts of shrinking dollars reflected in their paychecks. In the United States, even if one ignores the inflation profits earned by government in the past, the 1980 boost in total taxes will be something on the order of $10 billion, unless inflation soon turns sharply downward. A further boost of similar magnitude is likely to occur next year, lifting the government's windfall gain in 1981 alone to around $20 billion. In just two years the government may make an extra profit of some $30 billion—simply because of the current level of inflation. The net result is a massive hidden transfer of wealth from private hands to the Federal treasury. And the government's windfall gets larger every year.

Governments also may profit from inflation when corporations are compelled to do their accounting—and to determine their taxable incomes—on the basis of current dollars. The equation is far more complex in the area of corporate tax, as inflation has a different impact on the individual income statement items that eventually result in a net income figure. Depreciation charges based on unadjusted historical costs, for example, may be quite unrealistic when they are compared with current replacement costs. The point is that many separate factors are involved in the determination of a company's *real* profit, and the present accounting standards applied to taxation reporting—being based on a depreciating measure of economic value—produce highly misleading profit figures. One indication of the problem is the increasing adoption of inflation accounting within the business communities of both Canada and the United States in order to permit more realistic financial planning. Many executives believe that reported profits are vastly overstated under traditional accounting procedures. If so, this would result in further windfall gains to the government. In other words, corporations may be subject to tax on income that has not really been earned.

Until 1972 Canada and the United States dealt with the tax consequences of inflation in similar fashions. Their governments simply pocketed their windfall tax profits, and tax revenues increased extremely rapidly—even after the occasional tax cut at election time. Few seemed to wonder why the tax collector hauled in more and more cash every year regardless of such cuts. The government's share of the total economic pie just kept on growing. If Federal officials really understood the economic side-effects of inflation, they kept their mouths shut—the extra tax profits permitted them not only to hand out rate reductions from time to time but also to indulge in other politically appealing (and occasionally worthwhile) expansions of basic social services.

This rather cavalier attitude on the part of government has remained the norm in the United States, although the unprecedented level of inflation during 1979—and the sheer size of the government's windfall profits that would result—led many economists to trot out their old proposals for indexation. The last time they had done so was in the early Seventies, when inflation was moving upward on a similar spiral.

The basic principle of indexation is that all economic values—including wages, prices, and assets—should be measured in terms of their true worth rather than in relation to a variable yardstick such as a constantly shrinking dollar. Indexation involves a continuing process of adjusting current values to compensate for changes in the worth of a nation's currency. As this worth usually is measured in terms of buying power for specific items, most economists advocate a nation's consumer price index as the appropriate adjustment factor.

Even in the United States, where the term indexation conveys unfamiliar—and, to many people, revolutionary—connotations, the concept is far from alien. The most obvious example of existing indexation occurs in Social Security payments and the area of wage rates, where cost-of-living adjustments (COLA clauses) provide an automatic mechanism for personal incomes to keep pace with the rising cost of living. In theory, COLA clauses result in periodical wage boosts sufficient to offset increased prices. In practice, however, relatively few existing COLA clauses provide for *full* indexation; the trend has been for them to include only partial compensation for inflation, as is the case when a COLA clause results in a wage boost of six tenths of 1 percent for a full percentage point increase in the Consumer Price Index. Nevertheless, all COLA clauses demonstrate the distinctive feature of indexation—the linkage of economic measures to standard values through a predetermined formula. While ad hoc wage increases may achieve the same result, indexation provides for automatic adjustments.

Wage rates, however, are only one of the forms of economic value that would be subject to automatic adjustment in a fully indexed system. For example, the unpaid principal owed on a mortgage would be adjusted upward on a periodic basis to offset the reduced buying power of the dollars in which it is measured. During the first few years after they take out a mortgage, Brazilians actually find themselves with a larger debt (measured in current cruzeiros) than the amount they originally borrowed. In relation to current buying power, however, the economic value of the debt is unchanged from what it would have been in a zero-inflation environment. As a result, mortgage interest rates reflect *real* investment returns, and future inflation patterns become irrelevant in deciding whether a particular borrowing is worthwhile.

So, controversial as the subject of indexation may be, its economic impact is far from revolutionary—in fact, full indexation simply preserves the status quo. It eliminates the distortions that stem directly from inflation, so that the mere fact of shrinkage in a currency's value no longer creates winners and losers. Needless to say, it is rather horrifying to contemplate the enormous number of adjustment calculations that would be needed every day in an indexation system that extended to mortgages, bank deposits, prices, wages, and every other commodity or transaction that is measured in terms of money. The Brazilian experiment is fascinating from a theoretical point of view, but in practical terms—even though most of the adjustments are effected on a quarterly basis instead of daily—it is appallingly cumbersome.

But many of the most important elements of indexation—including the indexation of a country's tax system to avoid those windfall profits to the government—can be carried out independently. You don't have to buy the entire package. In the case of Canada, indexation has been adopted selectively. As in the United States, the usage of COLA clauses has been spreading gradually without any governmental edicts; the trend has evolved through the regular bargaining process between unions and employers. But a broad range of social welfare payments (including such items as old age pensions and family allowances) have been subject to automatic escalation through indexation formulas for most of the past decade, as have the pensions of government employees. Canada's Federal politicians also were quick to catch on to the benefits of indexation when they realized it could work to their personal advantage: their salaries have been subject to automatic annual escalation since 1974. Now the politicians' incomes are linked to the industrial composite wage index (which just happens to increase at a faster rate than the Consumer Price Index); no longer are there any beefs from the public about elected officials voting themselves hefty raises. They get them automatically, without any need for a vote.

Where Canadian and American practices differ most significantly is in the area of taxation. With a few minor exceptions, Canada's personal tax system has been fully indexed since 1973. The government no longer makes windfall profits from inflation, and taxpayers no longer suffer unfair erosion in their living standards as a result of the interplay between inflation and progressive tax rates. If their incomes merely keep pace with rising prices, the government's percentage slice remains constant. If their incomes fall behind the inflation rate, which would represent a decline in personal buying power, then the government's slice actually shrinks—even though the nominal dollar amount of taxable income may have increased. Canadians move into higher tax brackets only when their incomes rise faster than inflation; they drop into lower brackets when inflation takes the lead.

Given a government's usual vested interest in inflation through its impact on tax revenue, it is worth explaining how tax indexation actually came to be accepted by the Canadian government. The concept initially was put forward by the major opposition party, the Progressive Conservatives, during Canada's 1972 Federal election campaign. The governing party, the Liberals, campaigned strenuously against the proposal. When the votes were counted, the government had been returned to office with a minority—a situation that, in Canada's parliamentary system, carries the risk of a government's being booted out of power (or a new election being called) if the minor parties join forces with the official opposition to defeat the government party on any critical vote (as happened with Joe Clark's government last December, after just six months in office). Under the circumstances, the government had second thoughts about its earlier opposition to the indexation proposal and, before long, it simply "stole" the opposition's idea. The indexation was formally proposed by the government in its first minority budget, and the automatic adjustment procedure became effective in 1974. Political conditions clearly were a major factor in Canada's adoption of tax indexation; if circumstances had been different, the concept may have evoked as little governmental response as it did at the same time in the United States.

The way the system works today is that the basic tax deductions and the individual tax brackets are escalated annually in accordance with increases in Canada's Consumer Price Index. The actual percentage tax rates within each bracket remain constant. The indexation of deductions is needed to maintain the real value of the tax-exempt portion of each individual's income; the indexation of the tax brackets ensures that one's marginal rate remains constant when the taxable portion of one's income increases by the same percentage as average prices. Complicated as this may sound, it is accomplished easily: all that is needed is to revise various figures on the tax forms each year.

On an item-by-item basis the annual changes in each individual figure may not seem enormously important. In 1979, for example, the first $2,650 of each Canadian's income was exempt from taxation because of a basic personal deduction. The deduction amount was determined by applying the 1979 indexation factor of 9 percent to the 1978 deduction level of $2,430. (Most taxpayers are unaware of the details—the 1979 tax forms, for example, simply tell taxpayers to claim a deduction of $2,650.)

The cumulative impact of indexation is far more significant and can be seen by comparing each deduction to the level that applied at the start of the indexation process. In 1972 Canada's basic personal exemption amounted to $1,500. An ad hoc boost of $100 was applied in 1973, bringing the deduction to $1,600. From 1974 onward the $1,600 amount was escalated annually by each year's indexation factor, rising initially to $1,706 in 1974 and then, successively, to $1,878, $2,090 and $2,270 before reaching the 1978 level of $2,430. For 1980 the deduction will be a little under $2,900—or 80 percent higher than the level that would have applied without indexation (or without intervening tax cuts on an ad hoc basis).

As the same ratios apply to the various tax brackets as well as to the deductions, a Canadian who had a taxable income of $25,000 in 1973 could report $45,000 of income in 1980 without any change in the percentage tax rate he paid in 1973. This reflects, of course, the fact that $1.80 in 1980 has the equivalent buying power of $1 in 1973. The Canadian dollar has shrunk by almost 45 percent during this period, when adjusted to reflect changes in the Consumer Price Index.

As far as total government tax revenues are concerned, the cumulative impact of indexation is massive. The Economic Council of Canada estimates that personal taxes in 1978 were $4.8 billion less than they would have been without indexation. Using the 10-to-1 ratio that Canadians use as a means of comparing U.S. and Canadian economic indicators (a ratio that reflects the relative sizes of the two economies), that $4.8 billion figure is the equivalent of around $50 billion in the United States. Given the similarity of the two countries' personal tax systems, the implication is that Americans have suffered hidden annual tax increases that, in the period from 1973 to 1978, had reached an annual level of $50 billion. To reach that level the tax boosts would have been close to $10 billion a year—compounded annually on top of the previous year's boost. So the second year's total boost under indexation would be something in the order of $20 billion, rising to $30 billion in the third year, and so on. Over a five-year period the cumulative government windfall profits from inflation could have reached $150 billion or so.

(By scaling up Canadian figures to measure the probable impact of tax indexation in the United States, the author has obtained results virtually identical to those calculated by Edgar R. Fiedler, Vice President of Economic Research at The Conference Board, Inc., and published in the May 1979 "Commentary" in *across the board*. Those estimates, in turn, were confirmed by Francis H. Schott, vice president and chief economist of Equitable Life Assurance Society, in a letter published in the September 1979 issue of *across the board*. Mr. Schott's fears about the budgetary impact of tax indexation gain some support from recent Canadian experience, as described later in this article.)

Although Canada's system provides for nominal tax cuts each year, while the U.S. rate schedule remains constant, it is important to recognize that taxable income figures in both countries are reported as the actual dollars earned by each individual. In terms of their true worth—or their buying power—those dollars shrink in value each year as inflation pushes up prices. The Canadian system takes this factor into account; the American system does not. Canadian incomes are measured for tax purposes in terms of their real value instead of their nominal value. The result is that the Canadian structure remains "neutral" during inflation, while the American system automatically imposes hidden annual rate boosts. Canada's estimated tax "cut" of $4.8 billion in 1978 was not a tax reduction when one takes into account the *real* value of Canadians' 1978 incomes—instead, it represents the effect of eliminating a confiscatory additional tax that would have resulted from the mere existence of inflation and its consequent distortion of the country's progressive tax rate structure. The status quo in fact had been maintained; without indexation, taxes would have been boosted by $4.8 billion in 1978.

To reemphasize, the impact of indexation is that it maintains the status quo in an inflationary environment. Logical as the system may be, one problem is that governments themselves show little inclination to accept the status quo when it comes to their own programs. Up to 1974, when Canada's indexation formula started operating, the role of the Canadian government had been expanding at an unprecedented rate. Much of the growth had been financed by the government's windfall inflation gains. The politicians got used to spending money at a lavish rate, and they locked the system into programs that could only be financed by continued rapid revenue growth. When indexation was applied to the tax system, revenues kept growing, but they did so at a much slower rate. The government's costs, however, kept rising at their previous rapid rate. The net result is that the Canadian government has experienced growing budgetary deficits. In the current fiscal year (ending March 31) the deficit is expected to be well over $11 billion, equivalent to a U.S. government deficit of more than $110 billion. While many factors have combined to lift Canada's budgetary deficits to such disturbing levels, one of the major causes unquestionably was the impact of careless spending habits developed by the government prior to indexation, when tax revenues were bloated artificially. After a spending binge it is as hard for a government to work its way back into the black as it is for any individual.

Given Canada's swollen deficits, it probably is not surprising that rumors are spreading about the possible abandonment of indexation. Many public figures now argue that Canada cannot afford automatic annual "cuts" in personal tax rates. The underlying principle of indexation is difficult for even some sophisticated individuals to comprehend, so it may be understandable that many people feel they are advocating the elimination of a future tax cut when in fact they are advocating tax increases. To many politicians there is obvious appeal in the idea of ending the indexation of income taxes, as revenue increases could be achieved automatically without the government itself seeming greedy. A decision to drop the indexing formula may seem far more saleable politically than a decision to raise taxes directly. Even when a government does not face a financial crunch, politicians prefer to be able to hand out occasional tax cuts, and indexation eliminates the windfall profits that enable them to do so. Needless to say, nobody really expects the politicians to go so far as eliminating the indexation of their own salaries.

Political considerations such as these are likely to be the ultimate determinant of whether the United States will adopt the indexation approach—and also of whether Canada will retain its present system. At the same time, many voices, including that of Canada's Economic Council, are advocating an expansion of indexation into the area of corporate taxation. Late in 1979 the Council recommended that "corporate tax legislation be reexamined by governments with a view to ensuring that taxes are based on real rather than nominal profits."

The problem with most of the economists' arguments is that they have not managed to get their basic message across to the general public; the message that indexation does not involve tax cuts but merely the maintenance of the status quo. Even in Canada, where people have lived with indexation since 1973, the concept has yet to be fully grasped.

# CURRENT VALUE ACCOUNTING PREFERENCES: THE CASE FOR CANADA

*by Haim Falk*

## INTRODUCTION

There is some published evidence that current value accounting (CVA) measures have been considered by accountants for many years. For example, Djorup suggested some fifty years ago the use of current replacement cost in the calculation of reported value for fixed assets in foreign countries.[1] However, empirical researchers have become interested in this topic only in the last twenty years.[2] Most of the empirical research published to date suggests that some interest in CVA on the part of both users and perparers of financial accounting information is evident.[3] Further, in some countries such as the United Kingdom, the United States, and Australia, some methods of CVA are already, or are becoming, a practice reality through legal or professional requirements.

In Canada, the CICA Accounting Research Committee (ARC) recently issued a discussion paper in which several CVA methods are thoroughly discussed. In its "Preliminary Position" statement,[4] the ARC suggested the introduction of a combination of CVA methods to be utilized in supplementary reports to the historical cost-based financial statements. It is unclear, however, whether the information generated under the suggested CVA combination would indeed be preferred by all segments of investors, and useful in their investment decision-making process. Further, there is some evidence that CVA preferences may vary according to specific investment interest.[5] The research reported here is intended to obtain some insight with this respect.

If CVA is adopted in Canada, sooner or later chartered accountants (CAs) may be expected to extend their audit and express their opinion on CVA-based reports. Therefore, a consensus between the CAs and users of financial statements with respect to CVA information would be desirable. Thus, another objective of this paper is to assess the extent to which such a consensus is evident. More specifically, the present paper reports on CVA

---

*The International Journal of Accounting Education and Research*, Vol. 14, No. 2, Spring 1979 (Urbana, Ill.: Center for International Education and Research in Accounting, 1979).

[1] Christian Djorup, *Foreign Exchange Accounting* (New York: Prentice-Hall, 1926), p. 376.

[2] For an excellent review on empirical research related to CVA, see Thomas R. Dyckman, Michael Gillins, and Robert J. Swieringa, "Experimental and Survey Research in Financial Accounting: A Review and Evaluation," in A. Rashad Abdel-khalik and Thomas F. Keller, eds., *The Impact of Accounting Research on Practice and Disclosure* (Durham, N.C.: Duke University Press, 1978).

[3] For example, American Institute of Certified Public Accountants' Technical Service Division, "Opinion Survey on Price-Level Adjustment of Depreciation," *Journal of Accountancy* (April 1958): 36-42; Ralph W. Estes, "An Assessment of the Usefulness of Current Cost and Price-Level Information by Financial Statement Users," *Journal of Accountancy Research* (Autumn 1968): 200-207; Dan E. Garner, "The Need for Price-Level and Replacement Value Data," *Journal of Accountancy* (September 1972): 94-98; and John R. Hana, *Accounting Income Models: An Application and Evaluation*, Special Study No. 8 (Ontario: The Society of Industrial Accountants, 1974).

[4] See Canadian Institute of Chartered Accountants, Accounting Research Committee, *Discussion Paper: Current Value Accounting* (Toronto: CICA, 1976), pp. 65-70.

[5] See George J. Benston and Melvin A. Krasney "DAAM: The Demand for Alternative Accounting Measurements," *Accounting for Changes in General and Specific Prices: Empirical Research and Public Policy Issues, Journal of Accounting Research* (1978 supplement).

preferences of Canadian financial analysts (FAs), branch managers in chartered banks (Bankers), and CAs who were associated with CA firms in Canada.

## THE QUESTIONS

The questions utilized in this survey were finalized after three separate pilot tests conducted on the target populations. In additon, discussions were held with selected FAs, Bankers, and CAs. As a result, the questions concentrated on four major CVA methods for which some evidence was generated indicating that they are more widely considered than others. These methods are (1) Net Realizable Value (NRV); (2) Current Replacement Cost (CRC); (3) Current Replacement Cost New (CRCN); and (4) discounted Present Value of future expected cash flows (PV).[6]

To increase the reliability of the responses, the respondents were provided with the following definitions for the four methods.[7]

> *NRV*–*The current disposal value of assets net of disposal expense.*

> *CRC*–*The current purchase price of equivalent existing assets on a second-hand market.*

> *CRCN*–*The current purchasing price of new assets (embodying new technological developments) to replace current productive capacity less appropriate depreciation.*

> *PV*–*The discounted Present Value of future expected cash flows. Usually the maximum amount that the corporation is willing to pay for an asset or to settle a liability.*

The results for two questions will be discussed.[8] These questions presented a matrix of ten financial information items by the four CVA methods. The respondents were requested to indicate the importance (question 1) and the monetary value (question 2) of ten information items under each of the four CVA methods. The ten items, listed in exhibit 1, have been selected based on the following criteria:

1. *The item is usually included in the financial statements or the notes accompanying them.*
2. *The item is available to investors through data bases of financial reporting and survey services (e.g., COMPUSTAT). This criterion increases the probability that the items are indeed considered in investment decisions.*
3. *There is an a priori reasonable probability that the item may be affected by the four CVA methods. That is, that the reported value of the item under any or most of the CVA methods may be different from the value under currently accepted accounting principles (GAAP).*
4. *There was some indication by interviewed people (FAs, Bankers, and CAs)*

---

[6] These four CVA methods also serve as the major components of the CVA combination recommended by the ARC. For very marginal cases the ARC also suggested the use of historical costs adjusted for changes in General Purchasing Power. However, in light of the FASB conclusion "that General Purchasing Power information is not now sufficiently well understood by preparers and users and the need for it is not now sufficiently well demonstrated to justify imposing the cost of implementation upon all preparers of financial statements at this time," (FASB, Status Report, 4 June 1966), it was decided to omit this method from the final questionnaire. Further, most of the ones interviewed indicated extremely low interest in this method.

[7] In light of the findings of Rosen which suggest that some potential Canadian users and preparers of CVA information may not understand the differences between the methods, it was viewed desirable to provide the respondents with uniform definitions for the four methods. See Lawrence S. Rosen, *Current Value Accounting and Price-Level Restatements* (Toronto: CICA, 1972).

[8] The research work undertaken covered several issues of CVA. Only part of this work is reported here. Financial support was obtained from Canadian businesses through the School of Business, University of Western Ontario; the Faculty of Management, McGill University; and Zitter, Siblin, Stein, Levine and Co., a Montreal and Toronto based CA firm.

EXHIBIT 1  IMPORTANCE OF INFORMATION ITEMS UNDER CVA METHODS

Means

| Information items | Shares | | | | Loans | | | | CAs | | | |
|---|---|---|---|---|---|---|---|---|---|---|---|---|
| | NRV | CRC | CRCN | PV | NRV | CRC | CRCN | PV | NRV | CRC | CRCN | PV |
| 1. Inventory | 7.25+<br>( 2.4) | 5.86<br>(10.3) | 6.15<br>( 8.4) | 4.44<br>(16.2) | 8.10+<br>( 2.8) | 6.02<br>( 3.0) | 5.78<br>( 3.4) | 5.21<br>(12.5) | 7.49+<br>(13.3) | 5.77<br>(10.0) | 5.98<br>(11.2) | 4.47<br>(22.0) |
| 2. Property, plant & related depreciation | 6.02<br>(10.7) | 6.36*<br>( 8.0) | 7.10+<br>( 4.8) | 5.52<br>(14.6) | 7.67+<br>( 1.4) | 6.54<br>( 3.0) | 6.59<br>( 6.6) | 5.36<br>( 8.9) | 5.90<br>(10.1) | 6.45+<br>( 4.3) | 6.40*<br>( 6.3) | 5.43<br>(16.9) |
| 3. Investments in other companies | 6.89+<br>( 3.6) | 5.26<br>( 8.0) | 5.11<br>(10.8) | 6.20<br>( 9.8) | 7.27+<br>(12.9) | 5.09<br>( 9.1) | 4.56<br>( 3.3) | 5.48<br>(10.3) | 6.95+<br>( 6.3) | 4.89<br>(15.8) | 5.01<br>(18.9) | 6.15<br>(10.8) |
| 4. Cost of goods & services sold | 5.21+<br>(15.7) | 5.13*<br>(14.0) | 5.15*<br>(15.9) | 4.40<br>(20.0) | 6.13+<br>( 8.7) | 5.08<br>(12.5) | 4.80<br>( 1.7) | 4.43<br>(13.2) | 5.02*<br>(11.5) | 5.01*<br>(13.7) | 5.26+<br>(15.3) | 3.96<br>(29.1) |
| 5. Other operating expenses | 4.31*<br>(22.0) | 4.60*<br>(16.3) | 4.80*<br>(18.3) | 4.44*<br>(21.2) | 5.44+<br>(11.4) | 4.55<br>(18.5) | 4.67<br>( 3.3) | 4.75*<br>(14.5) | 4.03<br>(22.1) | 4.44*<br>(17.0) | 4.62+<br>(19.4) | 3.87<br>(30.2) |
| 6. Research & development expenses | 4.06+<br>(22.0) | 3.95*<br>(22.1) | 4.17*<br>(23.2) | 4.34+<br>(26.2) | 5.04*<br>( 7.2) | 4.35<br>(12.3) | 4.56*<br>( 1.5) | 5.22+<br>( 6.9) | 4.65<br>(17.8) | 4.47<br>(17.7) | 4.80<br>(17.5) | 5.38+<br>(17.2) |
| 7. Depreciation & amortization expenses | 5.31<br>(14.5) | 6.06*<br>( 7.1) | 6.46+<br>( 7.4) | 5.25<br>(15.0) | 5.76+<br>( 4.3) | 5.34<br>( 4.6) | 5.10*<br>( 8.3) | 5.15*<br>(10.9) | 5.06<br>(17.7) | 5.87*<br>( 7.5) | 6.01+<br>( 8.3) | 4.78<br>(22.5) |
| 8. Operating income | 5.32*<br>(14.6) | 5.38*<br>(12.6) | 5.65+<br>(11.1) | 5.53*<br>(13.9) | 6.20+<br>( 8.6) | 5.03<br>(10.8) | 5.13<br>( 6.7) | 5.84+<br>( 7.3) | 4.84*<br>(19.2) | 4.85*<br>(16.5) | 4.94*<br>(16.9) | 4.51<br>(25.4) |
| 9. Temporarily idle production capacity | 5.94+<br>( 7.2) | 5.54*<br>( 6.9) | 5.53*<br>(12.0) | 6.44+<br>( 1.5) | | 5.46<br>( 3.1) | 5.30<br>( 5.1) | | 6.03+<br>( 8.9) | 4.74<br>(16.4) | 4.73<br>(14.7) | |
| 10. Excess production capacity | 6.07+<br>( 9.6) | 5.02*<br>(16.1) | 5.11*<br>(15.5) | | 6.39+<br>( 6.0) | 5.20<br>( 7.7) | 5.13<br>( 5.0) | | 6.76+<br>( 8.3) | 4.57<br>(18.4) | 4.59<br>(16.9) | |

+The highest group mean for the information item.
*The mean is not significantly different from the highest group mean for the information item.

Notes: (1) Figures in parentheses = percentage of respondents who attributed negative values (rating points, 1, 2 or 3) to the item. (2) The importance was assessed on a 10 point rating scale (1-3—degree of hindrance; 4—notimportant; 5-10—degrees of importance).

*that the item is considered in investment decisions.*[9]

The two questions attempted to assess the demand for CVA information on an item-by-item basis, and thereby to empirically assess the acceptability of the ARC-suggested CVA combination. Under the first question, the respondents were asked to assume that, in addition to receiving each of the ten items of information under GAAP, they can also obtain for free the current values for each of the items under the four CVA methods.[10] They were then instructed to rate the degree of importance that they would attach to receiving supplementary current values for each item under each of the four CVA methods. The rating procedure was accomplished by utilizing a ten-point rating scale, as presented in exhibit 1. Three rating points represent negative degrees of importance (hindrance), one is neutral (no importance), and the six remaining rating points represent positive degrees of importance. The three negative degrees were introduced to check for the assumption that the supplementary CV information may cause confusion to investors. This assumption was formulated based on arguments expressed in the literature and views voiced by some who were interviewed during the pilot testing period of the questionnaires.

The major purpose of the second question was to assess the intensity of demand for CVA information. Unfortunately, it is very difficult to measure intensity of demand directly. However, a good approximation for intensity may be obtained by learning the degree of monetary value which one attaches to the desired CVA information. Therefore, the degree of financial sacrifice which one would consider incurring in obtaining the CVA information was used here in lieu of the intensity of demand.

The second question was identical to the first question except that the respondents were instructed to rate the ten information items under each of the four CVA methods, based on the degree of financial sacrifice that they would feel is proper to be incurred for obtaining the CV information. That is, in reality information can rarely be obtained free. Thus, if a corporation is required to report additional information, the cost of generating this information may reduce its cash flow available for reinvestment and distribution to owners (dividends) and lenders (payments on interest and principal). The pilot tests, as well as discussions in individual interviews, provide some evidence that this indirect monetary effect of the additional costs is not well perceived by the respondents. Therefore, a direct question to this effect was desirable.

Another purpose of this question was to enable a partial check of the reliability and validity of the answers on question 1. For example, if an information item is evaluated as relatively more important than others, it was expected that its monetary value also be evaluated higher than other items. Should this expectation prove to be fulfilled by the respondents, a dimension of reliability may be added to the results of this survey. Obviously the assignment of a negative monetary value must be interpreted that a respondent expects to be paid for receiving the CVA information. This would be an unreal situation. Consequently, a seven-point rating scale, of which one rating point is neutral (no financial sacrifice) and six

---

[9] Liabilities certainly meet criteria (1) through (3), and therefore were included in the first pre-tested questionnaire. Further, the ARC explicitly considered a CVA treatment for liabilities. However, most of the ones interviewed and some respondents to the pre-tested questionnaire indicated that CV of liabilities is rarely considered in their investment decisions. Thus, liabilities are not included among the ten information items investigated.

[10] While the production cost of generating the CVA information is borne by the reporting company, it may reduce the reported earnings and thereby affect the return on equity investment. Thus, the CVA information is apparently not obtained entirely for free. However, based on the pre-tests and interviews conducted prior to finalizing the questionnaires, it was assessed that investors are not aware of this possible reduction in return. Therefore, the respondents were instructed to assume that the CVA information could be obtained for free. The monetary value of this information was the subject of the second question which will be discussed in later paragraphs.

EXHIBIT 2    WILLINGNESS TO INCUR A FINANCIAL SACRIFICE FOR INFORMATION UNDER CVA METHODS

Means

| Information items | Shares | | | Loans | | | | CAs | | |
|---|---|---|---|---|---|---|---|---|---|---|
| | NRV | CRC | CRCN | PV | NRV | CRC | CRCN | PV | NRV | CRC | CRCN | PV |
| 1. Inventory | 2.54+ | 1.72 | 1.88 | .99 | 3.36+ | 1.96 | 1.75 | 1.46 | 2.94+ | 1.85 | 1.95 | 1.09 |
| 2. Property, plant & related depreciation | 2.21* | 2.26* | 2.69+ | 1.82 | 2.99+ | 2.29* | 2.18 | 1.61 | 2.17 | 2.34* | 2.40+ | 1.93 |
| 3. Investments in other companies | 2.37+ | 1.50 | 1.51 | 2.10* | 2.36+ | 1.23 | 1.16 | 1.43* | 2.56+ | 1.33 | 1.39 | 2.26* |
| 4. Cost of goods & services sold | 1.42* | 1.29 | 1.37 | 1.61+ | 2.11+ | 1.22 | 1.20 | 1.11 | 1.35* | 1.35* | 1.64+ | .91 |
| 5. Other operating expenses | 1.04* | 1.07* | 1.33+ | 1.06* | 1.86+ | 1.17 | 1.10 | 1.24* | .85 | .93* | 1.22+ | .85 |
| 6. Research & development expenses | .94* | .83* | 1.02* | 1.05+ | 1.68+ | 1.15* | 1.18* | 1.55* | 1.08 | 1.00 | 1.22 | 1.62+ |
| 7. Depreciation & amortization expenses | 1.64+ | 1.99* | 2.16+ | 1.62* | 1.86+ | 1.63* | 1.25 | 1.38* | 1.34 | 1.73* | 1.81+ | 1.36 |
| 8. Operating income | 1.59+ | 1.44* | 1.70+ | 1.59* | 2.07+ | 1.35 | 1.27 | 1.71* | 1.42+ | 1.34* | 1.42+ | 1.26* |
| 9. Temporarily idle production capacity | 1.78+ | 1.44+ | 1.40+ | | 2.36+ | 1.62 | 1.23 | | 1.98+ | 1.33 | 1.17 | |
| 10. Excess production capacity | 1.88+ | 1.17 | 1.29 | | 2.35+ | 1.56 | 1.34 | | 2.39+ | 1.12 | 1.06 | |

+The highest group mean for the information item.
*The mean is not significantly different from the highest group mean for the information item.
Note: The degree of financial sacrifice was assessed on a 7-point rating scale (0—none, 1—very little, 2—little, 3—somewhat less than moderate, 4—moderate, 5—somewhat more than moderate, and 6—substantial).

representing degrees of positive monetary values, was employed for the purposes of this question. This scale is also presented in exhibit 2.

The findings related to the two questions are discussed in the fourth section. The section which follows deals with the survey samples and procedures. Some important demographic characteristics are also discussed in the immediately subsequent section.

## THE SURVEY SAMPLES

Questionnaires were mailed to 1000 practicing FAs and Bankers, and to 1000 CAs who were randomly selected from three publicly available sources. The FAs were selected from the 1977 Membership Directory of the Financial Analysts Federation. The Bankers were selected from the latest available telephone directories for eleven principal Canadian cities,[11] and the CAs' sample was drawn from the January 31, 1975, Directory of Canadian Chartered Accountants. The questionnaires directed to the FAs and CAs were mailed to the selected respondents personally. No personal approach was feasible as far as the Bankers were concerned. To ensure the maximum possible response rate, complete anonymity was assured where desired by the respondents.

The first mailing was mailed in July 1977, and a second approximately one month later. After completion of the two mailings, an intensive follow-up procedure for a subsample of the remaining nonrespondents was employed. Randomly selected nonrespondents were contacted by telephone in order to personally explain the importance and relevancy of the survey and its possible contribution to a sound decision with respect to CVA reporting in Canada. Participants who did not return the questionnaire within ten days were contacted a second time and encouraged to take part in the survey. This intensive follow-up procedure had a dual purpose: (1) to increase the actual response rate, and (2) to produce an adequate data base which was later used in assessing a possible nonresponse bias in the survey findings. The described mailing procedure, along with the intensive follow up, resulted in a 51.9 overall rate of response of usable questionnaires. That is, 51.6 and 52.3 percent for the FAs and Bankers, and CAs respectively.

Perceptions of respondents not familiar with CVA information would be of little value in the context of this research. Therefore, the respondents were asked to indicate their degree of familiarity with each of the four CVA methods. Some respondents indicated that they were not familiar with one or more of the CVA methods. These respondents were instructed to ignore the part or parts in questions 1 and 2 which related to the method(s) they were not familiar with. Consequently, depending on the CVA method, the results for questions 1 and 28 reflect the perceptions of 72.2 to 80.4 percent and 62.5 to 77.4 percent of the FA and Banker, and CA respondents respectively.

In recognition of the possibility that the type of investment interest may impact CVA preferences, each of the FA and Banker respondents was asked to indicate the primary type of investment decision with which he or she was involved, for example, investment in shares, bonds, or long- or short-term loans to publicly or closely held businesses. The respondents were also requested to indicate the primary type of firms to which their decision is related (firms in manufacturing, retail stores, public utilities, or extractive industries, etc.). The CA respondents were asked to indicate the primary type of business they were serving. The respondents were then requested to use their selection in these demographic questions as their frame of reference for answering the two questions which deal with the importance and value of the ten CVA information items. These two questions were described in the immediately preceding section.

The analysis of the responses for the above investment interest questions resulted in 27 and 15 categories for the FAs and Bankers, and CAs respectively. An analysis of the findings for each category and a comparison of results among the groups would produce an overwhelming amount of data for presentation and

---

[11] Several efforts to obtain lists of branch managers and investment officers employed by Canadian Chartered Banks turned out to be unsuccessful.

discussion, and would practically be impossible in the context of this paper. Therefore, the following analysis procedure was employed to combine the categories into as few homogeneous clusters as possible. First, the analysis for the FA and Banker respondents will be described.

To assess the degree to which CVA preferences were associated with investment categories, the Kruskal-Wallis one-way analysis of variance by ranks (KW) test was applied to the responses under each information item under questions 1 and 2. A total of 76 tests were performed. Each of the 27 investment categories was considered as a separate respondents' group for the purpose of these tests. However, some of the investment categories accounted for a very small number of respondents. Such small groups are of little significance for a statistical analysis. Therefore, only investment categories with ten or more members who answered questions 1 and 2 were considered. Thus, eight categories which accounted for approximately 80 percent of the FA and Banker respondents entered the KW analysis. The results of these tests indicated that for 14 items (18.4 percent), at least one of the eight investment categories exhibited respondent ratings which were significantly different ($\alpha = .05$) from those of the other categories. These results tend to indicate that the respondents' CVA preferences are significantly associated with the type of investment interest.

Is it the type of investment (for example, shares, loans) or the type of firm (manufacturing, retail stores) which contributes the most to the observed association? To answer this question, the KW test was repeated for questions 1 and 2 based on two independent classifications. The first test was based on categorizing the respondents by type of firm, and the second on categorizing the respondents by type of investment.

The FA and Banker respondents clustered into four firm categories of ten members or more: the (1) manufacturing, (2) retail stores, (3) public utilities, and (4) extractive industries. The KW test for this analysis produced three significant differences (3.9 percent). Therefore, it was decided to eliminate the type of firm as a basis for the investment categories.

Five investment-type groups of ten respondents or more were formed by the FAs and Bankers. They are investment in (1) shares, (2) bonds, short-term loans to (3) publicly and (4) closely held corporations, and (5) long-term loans to publicly held corporations. The KW tests performed on these categories resulted in 17 significant differences. Thus it was concluded that it is the type of investment which mainly impacted the respondents' perceptions regarding CVA information.

In attempting to further reduce the number of investment categories, it was recognized that a number of possible combinations could be supported on an a priori basis. One such breakdown was (1) investment in shares, and (2) granting of loans, including bonds. So, the KW test was repeated on the lending categories, that is, the respondents who were involved in equity (shares) investment were excluded. The results showed that only two of the 76 individual KW tests were statistically significant.

Based on the preceding analysis, the following two user respondents' categories were selected as the basis for subsequent analysis: (1) respondents who were engaged in equity investment, hereafter referred to as Shares, and (2) respondents concerned with lending decisions, hereafter referred to as Loans.

The CA respondents formed nine primary business interest categories of ten members or more. The nine groups were scattered among firms in four industries, categorized into publicly and closely held businesses. The KW test performed on the nine business interest categories resulted in four significant differences (5.3 percent). It was decided, therefore, not to subcategorize the CA respondents for further analysis.

As a consequence of the preceding analysis, the results in the subsequent section will be separately presented for each of the three categories. A comparison among the Shares', Loans', and CAs' perceptions will also be provided.

## THE RESULTS

### Importance of CVA Information

The first question deals with the importance of CVA information to investors. Under this question, the respondents were instructed to rate the degree of importance that they would attach to receiving supplementary current values for ten items under four CVA methods. A 10-point rating scale was provided for this purpose. A "1" represented the qualitative designation "Leads to a great deal of confusing results (hindrance)," a "4" denotes "No importance," and "10" equated to "Invaluable (essential)." The mean response scores for this question are presented in exhibit 1.

To obtain an overall assessment of the importance of CVA information, the highest score for each item under each of the three categories was identified. These scores are denoted by a "+" on the upper right side of the related score. First, the procedure was applied to the Shares and then repeated for the Loans. Thus, for example, the highest score for the first item (inventory) under Shares is 7.25; for the second (property and plant), it is 7.10. By repeating this procedure for all ten items, it was found that five items were evaluated as having at least "some importance" (rated as 6 or higher), three items were evaluated as having between "very little" and "some importance" (rating points 5 and 6), and two items were rated between "no importance" (rating point 4) and "very little importance" (rating point 5).

In general, the Loan respondents rated the CVA information higher than did the Share respondents. Thus, one item (inventory) was rated between "very important" (rating point 8) and "extremely important" (rating point 9), two items between "moderate" and "very important" (rating points 7-8), four items between "some importance" (6) and "moderate importance" (7), and three items were rated as being between "very little" and "some importance" (5-6). While the Loans evaluated seven items as having at least some importance, the Shares found only five items to be at this level of importance.

On the average, the CAs attached a lower degree of importance to the CVA information than the two user groups did. Only one item (inventory under NRV) was rated as having a higher than "moderate importance" (rating point 7). Five items were evaluated as having between "some" (6) and "moderate importance" (7), two items were assessed as having between "very little" (5) and "some importance" (6), and two items were rated between "no" (4) and "very little importance" (5).

The findings in exhibit 1 may lead to the conclusion that there is some support for the contention that some interest in CVA information is evident. On the other hand, at least some of the respondents considered the CVA information as a hindrance. Depending on the information item and the CVA method, between 2.4 and 26.2, 1.4 and 14.5, and 4.3 and 30.2 percent of the Shares, Loans and CAs, respectively, rated the information as leading to confusing results (rating points 1, 2, or 3). The proportions of respondents who viewed the CVA information as a hindrance are higher for the CAs when compared to both Shares and Loans. Another indication for the differences in perceptions between CAs and users of financial accounting information may be obtained by comparing the highest mean score under each item among the three groups. The CAs assigned the highest score to the NRV method for four items. The CRCN came next with four items, and the CRC and PV methods received the highest mean for one item each. This pattern is somewhat similar to the one reported for Shares who assigned the highest mean score to 5, 4, and 1 items under NRV, CRCN, and PV, respectively. It differs materially, however, from the Loans' perceptions, which privileged the NRV method with nine of the ten highest scores.

Is the information under the CVA method with the highest mean score perceived as significantly more important than the information generated under the remaining methods? By answering this question, some assessments could be made as to whether the CVA preferences reported in exhibit 1 are statistically meaningful. Thus, the highest mean score for each item was compared, by utilizing the Student's t test, with each of the remaining mean scores. For example, the highest mean score for item 2 under Shares was found to be related to CRCN (7.10). This mean score was then compared with each of the three mean scores for item 2 under NPV, CRC and PV. The mean score under CRC was found not to be significantly different from the highest mean score and was denoted with an asterisk in exhibit 1. This procedure was followed for each item under each of the three respondent categories.

The analyses just described revealed that for two, eight, and five items under Shares, Loans, and CAs, respectively, the highest mean score was significantly higher than all the remaining scores for the respective item. The results may suggest the three groups exhibited some differential perceptions of importance of information under the alternative CVA methods. However, on the average, a higher degree of significance may be attached to the CVA preferences demonstrated by the Loans and CAs when compared with those expressed by the Shares. It is interesting to note that for items 1 and 3, all three categories rated NRV as significantly higher than the other three methods.

**Monetary Value of CVA Information**

The purposes of the second question were (1) to obtain some insight regarding the perceived monetary value of the CVA information, and (2) to provide some possible validity of the answers on the first question. Thus, the respondents were instructed to indicate the degree of financial sacrifice that they would be willing to incur for obtaining the CVA information for each of the ten information items under each of the four CVA methods. A seven-point rating scale which varies from zero (no financial sacrifice) to six (substantial) was provided for this purpose. The mean response scores for the two subcategories are displayed in exhibit 2.

With one exception, none of the mean scores presented in exhibit 2 is higher than "somewhat less than moderate" (rating point 3). The one exception is the mean score for inventory under the NRV method as assessed by the Loan group, which happened to be 3.36 (between "moderate" [4] and "somewhat less than moderate"). More than 84, 76, and 81 percent of the mean scores under the Shares, Loan, and CA categories respectively are below 2.00 ("little"). Thus, it appears that the respondents perceive the monetary value of the CVA information as being generally low.

To check for reliability and validity of the responses on the first question, the mean scores pattern for question 2 was compared to the pattern obtained for the previous question. The analysis procedure applied to the mean scores under question 1 was also repeated for the mean scores in exhibit 2.

First, the highest mean scores for each information item under each respondents' category in exhibit 2 was paired with the corresponding mean score in exhibit 1. For 9, 9, and 8 pairs under the Shares, Loans, and CAs category respectively, the two paired scores were related to the same CVA method. These results suggest a high degree of consistency among the intragroup preferences exhibited in exhibits 1 and 2.

Next, the highest mean score for each item under each respondents' group in exhibit 2 was compared with each of the remaining three mean scores. For two, eight, and five items under Shares, Loans, and CAs, respectively, the highest mean was significantly higher than all the remaining scores for the respective item. These findings also parallel the corresponding pattern observed for question 1.

The results of the foregoing analyses clearly suggest that while overall the monetary value of CVA information is perceived as being very low, the responses to this question elicited essentially the same set of preferences as for the importance of the CVA information. The results for both questions parallel to a great extent, and therefore an additional dimension of reliability and validity of the results obtained in the first question is added.

**Demand for CVA**

In the preceding sections, the importance and the monetary value attached by each of the three respondent groups was assessed on an item-by-item basis. The perceived monetary value was used here in lieu of intensity of demand for CVA information. This intensity should not be ignored when the demand for CVA information is examined. Therefore, to obtain more insight regarding the groups' CVA preferences, each mean score reported in exhibit 1 was multiplied by its related mean score for financial sacrifice in exhibit 2. The product of this calculation was then standardized to obtain a relative weight for the information generated under each CVA method for each information item. These weights may reflect the relative demand by each of the three respondent groups for the information generated under each CVA method for each information item. The CVA method with the highest demand was then identified and also listed in exhibit 3. By observing the list of the most demanded methods, one may infer the most desired CVA combination preferred by each of the respondent groups. However, such a preference list should be regarded only as indicative, rather than a reflection of a precise preference scale. That is, in analyzing perceptions of respondents in an empirical research, such as the one presented here, minor differences in weights may be ignored. Therefore, CVA methods which received a weight of at least 90 percent of the highest scored method were also listed in exhibit 3.

An illustration of this analysis may be in order. Consider the scores for information item no. 6 under Shares. The mean scores in exhibits 1 and 2 are repeated in columns 2 and 3, exhibit 4. The products of the multiplications of the scores in column 2 by the scores in column 3 are listed in column 4. Each raw weight was then standardized and is presented in column 5, exhibit 4. The PV method received the highest weight. This method is listed in column 2, exhibit 3. The CRCN produced a weight which is higher than 90 percent of the PV score, and is therefore listed in column 3, exhibit 3. This procedure was followed for each item under each of the respondent groups.

As can be seen from exhibit 3, the NRV method was by far the Loan's first preference for all ten items. The Share preferences differ from those of the Loans with respect to five items. Thus, no consensus between the two user groups is evident.

The CA preferences parallel the preferences demonstrated by the Shares. The CA perceptions differ only slightly from those of the Shares with respect to one information item (item 4). It seems that the CAs perceive the information needs of the Shares as more important than the needs expressed by the Loans. One explanation for this observation might be related to auditors' legal responsibility. That is, the fact that auditors address their opinion on the financial statements to the company's shareholders might have an impact on their perceptions regarding the purpose of financial accounting information.

While the equity investors are the owners of the corporation, the information needs of the lenders should not be ignored when the introduction of CVA reporting in Canada is considered. Thus, it might be desirable for corporations with material borrowing activities to consider the adoption of a dual CVA reporting system which may satisfy both equity investors and lenders.

**Comparison with the ARC Proposal**
The ARC proposed the introduction of a CVA combination for supplementary financial accounting reporting by all businesses in Canada. Some of the items, such as liabilities, considered by the ARC were not examined here. On the other hand, only 7 of the 10 items listed in exhibit 3 were explicitly considered by the ARC. Therefore, only a partial comparison between the three respondent groups' preferences and the ARC proposal is feasible here.

The relevant CVA methods proposed by the ARC are listed in column 8, exhibit 3. The comparison of the ARC proposal with the methods listed in the remaining columns in exhibit 3 reveals that by adopting the ARC proposal, none of the user groups may be satisfied. For only two items (items 2 and 7), the ARC proposed a method which was also preferred by the Shares and the CAs who participated in this survey. The use of the NRV method which was preferred by the Loans for all items and by the Shares for 3 out of the 7 comparable items was not proposed by the ARC for even one single item. In the light of these findings, it would be advisable for the ARC to reconsider its proposal.

## EXHIBIT 3  CVA METHODS WITH HIGHEST AND CLOSE TO HIGHEST WEIGHTS

| Information item | Shares | | Loans | | CAs | | ARC |
| --- | --- | --- | --- | --- | --- | --- | --- |
| | Highest Weight | Close to Highest | Highest Weight | Close to Highest | Highest Weight | Close to Highest | Proposal |
| (1) | (2) | (3) | (4) | (5) | (6) | (7) | (8) |
| 1. Inventory | NRV 41.43 | | NRV 47.96 | | NRV 44.74 | | CRC |
| 2. Property, plant & related depreciation | CRCN 33.61 | | NRV 37.65 | | CRCN 28.59 | CRC 28.08 | CRCN |
| 3. Investments in other companies | NRV 36.32 | | NRV 46.95 | | NRV 39.40 | | CRC |
| 4. Cost of goods & services sold | NRV 26.28 | PV 25.14, CRCN 25.07 | NRV 43.37 | | CRCN 33.49 | | CRC |
| 5. Other operating expenses | CRCN 31.14 | | NRV 38.23 | | CRCN 34.20 | | CRC & PV |
| 6. Research & development expenses | PV 28.66 | CRCN 26.71 | NRV 31.44 | PV 30.03 | PV 36.22 | | CRC & GP |
| 7. Depreciation & amortization expense | CRCN 32.26 | | NRV 32.55 | | CRCN 31.70 | CRC 29.60 | CRCN |
| 8. Operating income | CRCN 27.77 | PV 25.40 | NRV 35.51 | | CRCN 26.90 | NRV 26.36, CRC 24.94 | |
| 9. Temporarily idle production capacity | NRV 40.21 | | NRV 49.72 | | NRV 50.24 | | |
| 10. Excess production capacity | NRV 47.80 | | NRV 50.07 | | NRV 61.80 | | |

## EXHIBIT 4  ILLUSTRATION FOR WEIGHT CALCULATION FOR INFORMATION ITEM NO. 6, UNDER SHARES

| CVA Method | Mean Scores | | Raw Weight | Standardized Weight |
| --- | --- | --- | --- | --- |
| | Table 1 | Table 2 | | |
| (1) | (2) | (3) | (4) = (2) × (3) | (5) = [(4)/15.81] 100 |
| NRV | 4.06 | .94 | 3.82 | 24.01 |
| CRC | 3.95 | .83 | 3.28 | 20.62 |
| CRCN | 4.17 | 1.02 | 4.25 | 26.71 |
| PV | 2.34 | 1.05 | 4.56 | 28.66 |
| Total | | | 15.91 | 100.0 |

### Consideration of Nonresponse Bias

The high nonresponse rates of 48.4 and 47.7 percent for FAs and Bankers, and CAs respectively, might suggest that the reported results would not be representative of the perceptions of the entire populations. Therefore, an attempt was made to test for nonresponse bias. It has been suggested that late respondents are roughly similar to nonrespondents.[12] Consequently, the questionnaires returned by the participants who were approached by telephone were separated from those which resulted from the two mailings. This procedure resulted in two sets of questionnaires for each of the three respondents' categories. The two sets of questionnaires for each respondents' group were viewed as two independent samples, and the Mann-Whitney U test was employed to test for significant differences in the distribution of responses for each of the 38 combinations under questions 1 and 2. A total of 76 tests was performed for each of the three respondent groups.

For the Shares, Loans, and CAs, the results of 5, 2, and 4 tests, respectively, indicated significant differences between the late and the prompt responses. While these results may not provide conclusive evidence of a lack of nonresponse bias, they do suggest that such a possible bias is not material.

### CONCLUSION

The results reported here provide some evidence that perceptions (and needs) of prospective users of CVA information are affected by the type of investment decision in which they are engaged. Although some demand for CVA information was demonstrated by the two user groups, the Shares expressed different priorities than the ones demonstrated by the Loans. Both the Shares and the CAs demonstrated a desire for a combination of CVA methods to be utilized, if at all, in generating CVA information. With this respect, the ARC proposal gained some support. The Loan respondents, however, preferred a uniform method, NRV, for all ten information items under consideration. While the CAs' preferences parallel the choices made by the Shares, lenders' needs should not be ignored. It has been suggested that a dual CVA reporting system which may satisfy both equity investors and lenders may be considered.

The foregoing results must be interpreted with caution. First, the conclusions are based on the examination of only ten items of information. Some items considered by the ARC, for example, were not included here. Second, the value attached to the CVA information by all three respondent groups was generally low. Therefore, it might well be that it is too early to consider the introduction of CVA in Canada. Third, all of the index figures for assessing the demand for CVA information, as presented in exhibit 3, are considerably low. That is, none of the items under the Shares category received a weight higher than 47.8 and only one and two items under the Loans and CA categories, respectively, received weights higher than 50 percent. Therefore, it seems that by adopting the CVA compositions presented in exhibit 3, many users may remain unhappy. Finally, under the two questions discussed in this paper, the respondents' preferences were assessed on an item-by-item basis. The question of whether one uniform method of current value accounting as opposed to a combination of methods would be preferred for supplementary financial statements was not discussed here. Preference orders different from those reported here might have resulted under such a question.

The CVA preferences of the respondents in this survey were compared with the ARC proposal. Enough evidence was generated by this comparison to lead to the conclusion that it would be advisable for the ARC to reconsider its proposal before reaching firm conclusions regarding the introduction of CVA reporting in Canada. More research regarding users' preferences would also be desirable before deciding on the CVA issue.

---

[12] Robert Ferber, "The Problem of Bias in Mail Returns: A Solution," *Public Opinion Quarterly* (Winter 1948): 669-79; A. N. Oppenheim, *Questionnaire Design and Attitude Measurement* (New York: Basic Books, 1966).

# Appendixes

# APPENDIX A: FASB-33
# FINANCIAL REPORTING AND CHANGING PRICES, SEPTEMBER 1979

**Definitions**

22. For purposes of this Statement, certain terms are defined as follows:

a. *Constant dollar accounting. A method of reporting financial statement elements in dollars each of which has the same (i.e., constant) general purchasing power. This method of accounting is often described as accounting in units of general purchasing power or as accounting in units of current purchasing power.*

b. *Current cost accounting. A method of measuring and reporting assets and expenses associated with the use or sale of assets, at their current cost or lower recoverable amount at the balance sheet date or at the date of use or sale.*

c. *Current cost/constant dollar accounting. A method of accounting based on measures of current cost or lower recoverable amount in terms of dollars, each of which has the same general purchasing power.*

d. *Current cost/nominal dollar accounting. A method of accounting based on measures of current cost or lower recoverable amount without restatement into units, each of which has the same general purchasing power.*

e. *Historical cost/constant dollar accounting. A method of accounting based on measures of historical prices in dollars, each of which has the same general purchasing power.*

f. *Historical cost/nominal dollar accounting. The generally accepted method of accounting, used in the primary financial statements, based on measures of historical prices in dollars without restatement into units, each of which has the same general purchasing power.*

g. *Income from continuing operations. Income after applicable income taxes but excluding the results of discontinued operations, extraordinary items, and the cumulative effect of accounting changes.*

h. *Public enterprise. A business enterprise (a) whose debt or equity securities are traded in a public market on a domestic stock exchange or in the domestic over-the-counter market (including securities quoted only locally or regionally) or (b) that is required to file financial statements with the Securities and Exchange Commission. An enterprise is considered to be a public enterprise as soon as its financial statements are issued in preparation for the sale of any class of securities in a domestic market.*

**Applicability and Scope**

23. The requirements of this Statement apply to public enterprises that prepare their primary financial statements in U.S. dollars and in accordance with U.S. generally accepted accounting principles and that have, at the beginning of the fiscal year for which financial statements are being presented either:

a. *Inventories and property, plant, and equipment*[1] *(before deducting accumulated depreciation, depletion, and amorti-*

---

Copyright by Financial Accounting Standards Board, High Ridge Park, Stamford, Connecticut 06905 U.S.A. Reprinted with permission. Copies of the complete document are available from the FASB.

[1] For the purposes of this Statement, except where otherwise provided, inventory and property, plant, and equipment shall include land and other natural resources and capitalized leasehold interests but *not* goodwill or other intangible assets.

zation) amounting in aggregate to more than $125 million; or

b. Total assets amounting to more than $1 billion (after deducting accumulated depreciation).

Both amounts shall be measured in accordance with generally accepted accounting principles as reported in the primary financial statements (consolidated if applicable) of the enterprise.

24. The requirements of this Statement do not apply, during the year of a business combination accounted for as a pooling of interests, to an enterprise created by the pooling of two or more enterprises, none of which individually satisfies the size test described in paragraph 23.

25. The Board encourages nonpublic enterprises and enterprises that do not meet the size test in paragraph 23 to present the information called for by this Statement.

26. This Statement does not change the standards of financial accounting and reporting used for the preparation of the primary financial statements of the enterprise.

27. The information required by this Statement shall be presented as supplementary information in any published annual report that contains the primary financial statements of the enterprise except that the information need not be presented in an interim financial report. The information required by this Statement need not be presented for segments of a business enterprise although such presentations are encouraged.

28. An enterprise that presents consolidated financial statements shall present the information required by this Statement on the same consolidated basis. The information required by this Statement need not be presented separately for a parent company, an investee company, or other enterprise in any financial report that includes the results for that enterprise in consolidated financial statements.

**Requirement for Supplementary Information**
29. An enterprise is required to disclose:

a. *Information on income from continuing operations for the current fiscal year on a historical cost/constant dollar basis (paragraphs 39-46)*

b. *The purchasing power gain or loss on net monetary items for the current fiscal year (paragraphs 47-50).*

The purchasing power gain or loss on net monetary items shall *not* be included in income from continuing operations.

30. An enterprise is required to disclose:

a. *Information on income from continuing operations for the current fiscal year on a current cost basis (paragraphs 51-64)*

b. *The current cost amounts of inventory and property, plant, and equipment at the end of the current fiscal year (paragraph 51)*

c. *Increases or decreases for the current fiscal year in the current cost amounts of inventory and property, plant, and equipment, net inflation (paragraphs 55 and 56).*

The increases or decreases in current cost amounts shall *not* be included in income from continuing operations.

31. In some circumstances, there may be no material difference between the amount of income from continuing operations on a historical cost/constant dollar basis and the amount of income from continuing operations on a current cost basis. In those circumstances, the current cost information listed in paragraph 30 need not be disclosed for the fiscal year concerned, but the enterprise is required to state, in a note to the supplementary disclosures, the reason for the omission of the information.

32. Information on income from continuing operations (on a historical cost/constant dollar basis or on a current cost basis) may be presented either in a "statement format" (disclosing revenues, expenses, gains, and losses) or in a "reconciliation format" (disclosing adjustments to the income from continuing operations that is shown in the primary income statement). Whichever format is used, such information should disclose, unless they are immaterial, the amounts of or adjustments to cost of goods sold, depreciation, depletion, and amortization expense and (in the case of historical cost/con-

stant dollar income from continuing operations) reductions of the historical cost amounts of inventory, property, plant, and equipment to lower recoverable amounts as required by paragraph 44. . . .

33. If depreciation expense has been allocated among various expense categories in the supplementary computations of income from continuing operations (for example, among cost of goods sold and other functional expenses), the aggregate amount of depreciation expense, on both a historical cost/constant dollar basis and a current cost basis, shall be disclosed in a note to the supplementary information.

34. An enterprise shall disclose, in notes to the supplementary information:

a. *The principal types of information used to calculate the current cost of inventory, property, plant, and equipment, cost of goods sold, and depreciation, depletion, and amortization expense (paragraph 60)*
b. *Any differences between (1) the depreciation methods, estimates of useful lives, and salvage values of assets used for calculations of historical cost/constant dollar depreciation and current cost depreciation and (2) the methods and estimates used for calculations of depreciation in the primary financial statements (paragraph 61)*
c. *The exclusion from the computations of supplementary information of any adjustments to or allocations of the amount of income tax expense in the primary financial statements (paragraph 54).*

35. An enterprise is required to disclose the following information for each of its five most recent fiscal years (paragraphs 65 and 66):

a. *Net Sales and Other Operating Revenues*
b. *Historical Cost/Constant Dollar Information*

   *(1) Income from continuing operations*
   *(2) Income per common share from continuing operations*
   *(3) Net assets at fiscal year-end*

c. *Current Cost Information (except for individual years in which the information was excluded from the current year disclosures in accordance with paragraph 31)*

   *(1) Income from continuing operations*
   *(2) Income per common share from continuing operations*
   *(3) Net assets at fiscal year-end*
   *(4) Increases or decreases in the current cost amounts of inventory and property, plant, and equipment, net of inflation*

d. *Other Information*

   *(1) Purchasing power gain or loss on net monetary items*
   *(2) Cash dividends declared per common share*
   *(3) Market price per common share at fiscal year-end.*

All enterprises shall report, in a note to the five-year summary, the average level or the end-of-year level (whichever is used for the measurement of income from continuing operations) of the Consumer Price Index for each year included in the summary (paragraphs 40 and 41).

36. If an enterprise chooses to state net assets, in the five-year summary, at amounts computed from comprehensive financial statements prepared on a historical cost/constant dollar basis or on a current cost/constant dollar basis, that fact shall be disclosed in a note to the five-year summary (paragraph 66).

37. Enterprises shall provide, in their financial reports, explanations of the information disclosed in accordance with this Statement and discussions of its significance in the circumstances of the enterprise.

38. The disclosures summarized in paragraphs 29-37 are required by this Statement. Enterprises are encouraged to provide additional information to help users of financial reports understand the effects of changing prices on the activities of the enterprise.

**Historical Cost/Constant Dollar Measurements**

39. The index used to compute information on a constant dollar basis shall be the Consumer Price Index for All Urban Consumers, published

by the Bureau of Labor Statistics of the U.S. Department of Labor.[2]

40. An enterprise that presents the minimum historical cost/constant dollar information required by this Statement shall restate inventory, property, plant, and equipment, cost of goods sold, depreciation, depletion, and amortization expense and any reductions of the historical cost amounts of inventory, property, plant, and equipment to lower recoverable amounts (paragraph 44) in constant dollars represented by the average level over the fiscal year of the Consumer Price Index for All Urban Consumers. Other financial statement elements need not be restated. An enterprise that chooses to present comprehensive financial statements on a historical cost/constant dollar basis may measure the components of those statements either in average-for-the-year constant dollars or in end-of-year constant dollars.

41. If the level of the Consumer Price Index at the end of the year and the data required to compute the average level of the index over the year have not been published in time for preparation of the annual report, they may be estimated by referring to published forecasts based on economic statistics or by extrapolation based on recently reported changes in the index.

42. Inventory and property, plant, and equipment (for computation of the amount of net assets at the end of the current fiscal year for inclusion in the five-year summary of selected financial data paragraph 35(b)(3)), cost of goods sold and depreciation, depletion, and amortization expense shall be measured at their historical cost/constant dollar amounts or lower recoverable amounts. Inventories may need to be reclassified as monetary assets at the date of the use on or commitment to a contract. . . .

43. Measurements of historical cost/constant dollar amounts shall be computed by multiplying the components of the historical cost/nominal dollar measurements by the average level of the Consumer Price Index for the current fiscal year (or the level of the index at the end of the year if comprehensive financial statements are presented) and dividing by the level of the index at the date on which the measurement of the associated asset was established (i.e., the date of acquisition or the date of any measurement not based on historical cost). Those measurements may be restated in base-year dollars for inclusion in the five-year summary (paragraph 65).

44. If it is necessary to reduce the measurements of inventory and property, plant, and equipment, during the current fiscal year from historical cost/constant dollar amounts to lower recoverable amounts, the reduction shall be deducted in the computation of income from continuing operations.

45. Except as provided in paragraphs 42-44 and paragraph 61, the accounting principles used in computing historical cost/constant dollar income shall be the same as those used in computing historical cost/nominal dollar income. Only the measuring unit is changed.

46. Inventory, property, plant, and equipment, and related cost of goods sold and the depreciation, depletion, and amortization expense that are originally measured in units of a foreign currency shall first be translated into U.S. dollars in accordance with generally accepted accounting principles and then restated in constant dollars in accordance with the provisions of paragraph 43.

**Purchasing Power Gain or Loss on Net Monetary Items**

47. A monetary asset is money or a claim to receive a sum of money the amount of which is fixed or determinable without reference to future prices of specific goods or services. A monetary liability is an obligation to pay a sum of money the amount of which is fixed or determinable without reference to future prices of specific goods or services. The economic significance of monetary assets and liabilities (monetary items) depends heavily on the general purchasing power of money, although other factors, such as the credit worthiness of debtors, may affect their significance.

48. All assets and liabilities that are not monetary are nonmonetary. The economic significance of nonmonetary items depends

---

[2] The index is published in *Monthly Labor Review*. Those desiring prompt and direct information may subscribe to the Consumer Price Index (CPI) press release mailing list of the Department of Labor.

heavily on the value of specific goods and services. Nonmonetary assets include (a) goods held primarily for resale or assets held primarily for direct use in providing services for the business of the enterprise, (b) claims to cash in amounts dependent on future prices of specific goods or services, and (c) residual rights such as goodwill or equity interests. Nonmonetary liabilities include (a) obligations to furnish goods or services in quantities that are fixed or determinable without reference to changes in prices or (b) obligations to pay cash in amounts dependent on future prices of specific goods or services.

49. Guidance on the classification of balance sheet items as monetary or nonmonetary is set forth in Appendix D to this Statement.

50. The purchasing power gain or loss on net monetary items shall be equal to the net gain or loss found by restating in constant dollars the opening and closing balances of, and transactions in, monetary assets and liabilities. An enterprise that presents comprehensive supplementary financial statements on a historical cost/constant dollar basis may measure the purchasing power gain or loss in average-for-the-year constant dollars or in end-of-year constant dollars; other enterprises shall measure the purchasing power gain or loss in average-for-the-year dollars. . . .

**Current Cost Measurements**
51. The current cost amounts of inventory and property, plant, and equipment shall be measured as follows:

   a. *Inventories at current cost or lower recoverable amount (paragraphs 57-64) at the measurement date. (This provision is qualified by paragraph 53 in respect of any depletion expense included in the measurement of inventories.)*
   b. *Property, plant, and equipment (excluding income-producing real estate properties and unprocessed natural resources) at the current cost or lower recoverable amount (paragraphs 57-64) of the assets' remaining service potential at the measurement date.*
   c. *Resources used on partly completed contracts shall be measured at current cost or lower recoverable amount at the date of use on or commitment to the contracts.*

52. An enterprise that presents the minimum information required by this Statement on current cost income from continuing operations shall measure the amounts of cost of goods sold and depreciation and amortization expense as follows:

   a. *Cost of goods sold shall be measured at current cost or lower recoverable amount (paragraphs 57-64) at the date of sale or at the date on which resources are used on or committed to a specific contract. (This provision is qualified by paragraph 53 in respect of any depletion expense included in cost of goods sold.)*
   b. *Depreciation and amortization expense of property, plant, and equipment (excluding income-producing real estate properties and unprocessed natural resources) shall be measured on the basis of the average current cost or lower recoverable amount (paragraphs 57-64) of the assets' service potential during the period of use.*

Other revenues, expenses, gains, and losses may be measured by such an enterprise at the amounts included in the primary income statement. An enterprise that chooses to present comprehensive financial statements on a current cost/constant dollar basis may measure the components of those statements either in average-for-the-year constant dollars or in end-of-year constant dollars. (This paragraph is qualified by paragraph 64 for enterprises that are subject to rate regulation or other form of price control.)

53. This Statement does not contain provisions for the measurement, on a current cost basis, of income-producing real estate properties, unprocessed natural resources, and related depreciation, depletion, and amortization expense (paragraph 19). If an enterprise presents information on a current cost basis in an annual report for a fiscal year ended before December 25, 1980, it may measure the assets

and the related expenses, described in this paragraph, at their historical cost/constant dollar amounts or by reference to an appropriate index of specific price changes.

54. The amount of income tax expense in computations of current cost income from continuing operations shall be the same as the amount of income tax expense charged against income from continuing operations in the primary financial statements. No adjustments shall be made to income tax expense for any timing differences that might be deemed to arise as a result of the use of current cost accounting methods. Income tax expense shall not be allocated between income from continuing operations and the increases or decreases in current cost amounts of inventory and property, plant, and equipment.

**Increases or Decreases in
The Current Cost Amounts of Inventory
and Property, Plant, and Equipment**

55. The increases or decreases in the current cost amounts of inventory and property, plant, and equipment represent the differences between the measures of the assets at their "entry dates" for the year and the measures of the assets at their "exit dates" for the year. "Entry dates" means the beginning of the year or the dates of acquisition, whichever is applicable; "exit dates" means the end of the year or the dates of use, sale, or commitment to a specific contract whichever is applicable. For the purposes of this paragraph, assets are measured in accordance with the provisions of paragraph 51.

56. The increases or decreases in current cost amounts of inventory and property, plant, and equipment shall be reported both before and after eliminating the effects of general inflation. An enterprise that represents comprehensive supplementary statements on a current cost/constant dollar basis may measure increases or decreases in current cost amounts in average-for-the-year constant dollars or in end-of-year constant dollars; other enterprises shall measure those increases or decreases in average-for-the-year constant dollars. . . .

**Information About Current Costs**

57. The current cost of inventory owned by an enterprise is the current cost of purchasing the goods concerned or the current cost of the resources required to produce the goods concerned (including an allowance for the current overhead costs according to the allocation bases used under generally accepted accounting principles), whichever would be applicable in the circumstances of the enterprise.

58. The current cost of property, plant, and equipment owned by an enterprise is the current cost of acquiring the same service potential (indicated by operating costs and physical output capacity) as embodied by the asset owned; the sources of information used to measure current cost should reflect whatever method of acquisition would currently be appropriate in the circumstances of the enterprise. The current cost of a used asset may be measured:

*a. By measuring the current cost of a new asset that has the same service potential as the used asset had when it was new (the current cost of the asset as if it were new) and deducting an allowance for depreciation;*

*b. By measuring the current cost of a used asset of the same age and in the same condition as the asset owned;*

*c. By measuring the current cost of a new asset with a different service potential and adjusting that cost for the value of the differences in service potential due to differences in life, output capacity, nature of service, and operating costs.*

Current cost may be measured by direct reference to current prices of comparable assets or methods such as functional pricing or unit pricing under which the current cost of a unit of service embodied in the asset owned is measured and the current cost per unit is multiplied by the appropriate number of service units.

59. If current cost is measured in a foreign currency, the amount shall be translated into dollars at the current exchange rate, that is, the rate at the date of use, sale, or commitment to a specific contract (in the cases of depreciation expense and cost of goods sold) or the rate at the balance sheet date (in the cases of inventory and property, plant, and equipment).

60. Enterprises may use various types of information to determine the cost of inventory, property, plant, and equipment, cost of goods sold, and depreciation, depletion, and amortization expense.[3] The information may be gathered and applied internally or externally and may be applied to single items or broad categories, as appropriate in the circumstances. The following types of information are listed as examples of the information that may be used, but they are *not* listed in any order of preferability. Enterprises are expected to select types of information appropriate to their particular circumstances, giving due consideration to their availability, reliability, and cost:

 a. *Indexation*

   *(1) Externally generated price indexes for the class of goods or services being measured*

   *(2) Internally generated price indexes for the class of goods or services being measured*

 b. *Direct pricing*

   *(1) Current invoice prices*

   *(2) Vendors' price lists or other quotations or estimates*

   *(3) Standard manufacturing costs that reflect current costs.*

## Depreciation Expense

61. There is a presumption that depreciation methods, estimates of useful lives, and salvage values of assets should be the same for purposes of current cost, historical cost/constant dollar, and historical cost/nominal dollar depreciation calculations. However, if the methods and estimates used for calculations in the primary financial statements have been chosen partly to allow for expected price changes, different methods and estimates may be used for purposes of current cost and historical cost/constant dollar calculations.

---

[3] Cost of goods sold measured on a LIFO basis may provide an acceptable approximation of cost of goods sold, measured at current cost, provided that the effect of any decreases in inventory layers is excluded.

## Recoverable Amounts

62. The term "recoverable amount" means the current worth of the net amount of cash expected to be recoverable from the use or sale of an asset. If the recoverable amount for a group of assets is judged to be materially and permanently lower than historical cost in constant dollars or current cost, the recoverable amount shall be used as a measure of the assets and of the expense associated with the use or sale of the assets. Decisions on the measurement of assets at their recoverable amounts need not be made by considering assets individually unless they are used independently of other assets.

63. Recoverable amounts may be measured by considering the net realizable values or the values in use of the assets concerned:

 a. *Net realizable value is the amount of cash, or its equivalent, expected to be derived from sale of an asset net of costs required to be incurred as a result of the sale. It shall be considered as a measurement of an asset only when the asset concerned is about to be sold.*

 b. *Value in use is the net present value of future cash flows (including the ultimate proceeds of disposal) expected to be derived from the use of an asset by the enterprise. It shall be considered as a measurement of an asset only when immediate sale of the asset concerned is not intended. Value in use shall be estimated by discounting expected future cash flows at an appropriate discount rate that allows for the risk of the activities concerned.*

64. An enterprise that is subject to rate regulation or other form of price control may be limited to a maximum recovery through its selling prices, based on the nominal dollar amount of the historical cost of its assets. In that situation, nominal dollar/historical costs may represent an appropriate basis for the measurement of the recoverable amounts associated with the assets at the end of the fiscal year. Recoverable amounts may also be lower than historical costs. However, cost of goods sold and depreciation, depletion, and amortization

expense shall be measured at historical cost/constant dollar amounts (in measurements of historical cost/constant dollar income from continuing operations) or at current cost (in measurements of current cost income from continuing operations) provided that replacement of the service potential provided by the related assets would be undertaken, if necessary, in current economic conditions; if replacement would not be undertaken, expenses shall be measured at recoverable amounts.

**Five-Year Summary of Selected Financial Data**
65. The information presented in the five-year summary shall be stated either:

a. *In average-for-the-year constant dollars or end-of-year constant dollars (whichever is used for the measurement of income from continuing operations) as measured by the Consumer Price Index for All Urban Consumers for the current fiscal year; or*

b. *In dollars having a purchasing power equal to that of dollars of the base period used by the Bureau of Labor Statistics in calculating the Consumer Price Index (currently 1967).*

66. If an enterprise presents the minimum information required by this Statement, it shall measure net assets (i.e., shareholders' equity) for the purposes of the five-year summary:

a. *On a historical cost/constant dollar basis at the amount reported on its primary financial statements adjusted for the difference between the historical cost/nominal dollar amounts and the historical cost/constant dollar amounts or lower recoverable amounts of inventory and property, plant, and equipment*

b. *On a current cost basis at the amount reported in its primary financial statements, adjusted for the difference between the historical cost/nominal dollar amounts and the current cost or lower recoverable amounts of inventory and property, plant, and equipment and restated in constant dollars in accordance with paragraph 65.*

If an enterprise elects to present comprehensive supplementary financial statements on a current cost/constant dollar basis, or on a historical cost/constant dollar basis, it may report the amount of net assets in the five-year summary in accordance with the comprehensive statements.

**Effective Date and Transition**
67. The provisions of this Statement shall be effective for fiscal years ended on or after December 25, 1979. However, information on a current cost basis for fiscal years ended before December 25, 1980 may be presented in the first annual report for a fiscal year ended on or after December 25, 1980.

68. An enterprise is required to state, in the five-year summary of selected financial data, only the following amounts for fiscal years ended before December 25, 1979: net sales and other operating revenues, cash dividends declared per common share, and market price per common share at fiscal year-end (paragraph 35(a), (d)(2), and (d)(3)). Disclosure of the other items listed in paragraph 35, for fiscal years ended before December 25, 1979 is encouraged. Disclosure of current cost information in the five-year summary (paragraph 35(c)) for fiscal years ending before December 25, 1980 may be postponed to the first annual report for a fiscal year ending on or after December 25, 1980.

69. An enterprise that first applies the requirements of this Statement for a fiscal year ended on or after December 25, 1980 is required to state for earlier years, in its five-year summary, only the following items listed in paragraph 35: net sales and other operating revenues (item (a)), cash dividends declared per common share (item (d)(2)), and market price per common share at fiscal year-end (item (d)(3)). Disclosure of the other items listed in paragraph 35 for earlier years is encouraged.

*This Statement was adopted by the affirmative votes of five members of the*

*Financial Accounting Standards Board. Messrs. Mosso and Walters dissented.*

Mr. Mosso dissents because he believes that the Statement does not bring the basic problem it addresses—measuring the effect of inflation on business operations—into focus. Because of that he doubts that it will effectively communicate the erosive impact of inflation on profits and capital and the significance of that erosion on all who have an investment stake in business enterprises. The Statement seems to him to fail the cost-benefit test because potential benefits are diminished by diffusion and some costs are unnecessary regardless of benefits.

The lack of focus stems from the dual reporting requirements imposed by this Statement, reporting on both historical cost/constant dollar and current cost bases, and is compounded by the ambivalence of the income concepts in both approaches. The Statement offers at least four income numbers—historical cost/constant dollar or current cost, each with or without adjustments for purchasing power gains or losses on monetary items. Other income combinations are invited in the current cost approach because of the juxtaposition of the increase or decrease in current cost amounts of assets. This array of income numbers is a good reflection of the range of views existing among the Board's respondents; but a good mirror does not make a good standard.

Mr. Mosso does not share the widely-held view that the historical cost/constant dollar and current cost models have different objectives. The objective is the same: To measure the effect of inflation on a business enterprise. But there are two types of inflation effect. The Board's historical cost/constant dollar model captures one type, the effect of inflation on the purchasing power of money invested in a particular business. The Board's current cost model captures both types. It incorporates some features of the constant dollar model and also the effect on the prices of goods and services that a particular business deals in. Inflation affects different specific prices in different ways. Consequently, information about changes in an index of general inflation does not provide sufficient information about the effect of inflation on a specific business enterprise. The current cost model is a more comprehensive inflation measurement approach and it makes a free standing historical cost/constant dollar model superfluous.

The constant dollar approach has two uses that he would support: One, as a method of computing simple one-line adjustments of net income and owners' equity in the primary historical cost financial statements, in conjunction with current cost supplemental statements (a proposal that deserves more support than it has received so far); or two, as an integral part of a supplemental current cost model, essentially as in the current cost approach required by this Statement. As a complete model, however, the historical cost/constant dollar approach has little to recommend it except seniority.

A major criterion that the Board has established for choosing among alternative disclosures is usefulness of the information for predicting earnings and cash flows. The evidence presented to the Board on usefulness in this sense was sketchy, but virtually all of it favored the current cost approach. In fact, usefulness for predicting earnings and cash flows was rarely associated with the historical cost/constant dollar approach, even by its supporters.

Beyond the investor-oriented usefulness criterion, the current cost model bears directly on an urgent national economic policy issue, that of capital formation and its corollary, productivity. The current cost model is built around the notion of maintaining operating capacity, and the distributable income concept that goes with it is designed to trigger attention at the point where reduction of capacity sets in. The whole system pivots on the point where capital investment begins to rise or fall. In the historical cost/constant dollar model, reduction of operating capacity can occur without showing up in the financial statements. This is not to suggest that it is a function of the Board to design accounting standards to promote economic policy objectives. But it is a function of the Board to design standards that measure business income and investment and to be aware, in doing so, of the broader economic consequences of standards. The current cost model has the potential for measuring and communicating many effects of inflation in ways that will be useful both to investors, to policy makers, and to the business community.

Much of the resistance to current cost accounting derives from two interrelated misconceptions: First that it is a major step toward current value accounting and second that its measurements are subjective and open to income manipulation. These are valid concerns. They should not be dismissed or lulled. But neither is an inherent concomitant of current cost accounting.

The essence of current value accounting is revenue recognition on some prerealization basis. The increases in current cost amounts of assets (so-called "holding gains") arising in a current cost model can be viewed as income equivalents, but that view is not necessary. The model can classify those items as capital maintenance adjustments—necessary to keep the business on a level output trendline.

Subjectivity of measurement is also associated with the current cost model because in theory it breaks the link to historical transaction prices. In practice, this need not be a problem. Indexing can maintain a linkage to historical prices and preserve objectivity and reliability. Many other current costing techniques compare favorably, in terms of objectivity, with historical cost allocation techniques.

In Mr. Mosso's view, conventional accounting measurements fail to capture the erosion of business profits and invested capital caused by inflation. The urgent need is to focus attention on that basic problem. To do that effectively, it is essential to settle on a single inflation-adjusted bottom line within a framework that captures the price experience of individual firms. The door should be closed quickly and firmly on the dual approach with multiple income numbers.

Mr. Walters dissents because he believes that the dual approach in this Statement unfortunately attempts to deal with two very important but fundamentally different issues in combination. The result is most confusing.

The first issue is the need to measure and report the impact on the enterprise of the change in the exchange value of money. This need is urgent. Paton said: "A summation of unlike monetary units, even of the same name, is a misrepresentation." The integrity of the historical cost/nominal dollar system relies on a stable monetary system. We have experienced several decades of continuing debasement of the currency. It is essential to the credibility of financial reporting to recognize that the recovery of the real cost of investment is not earnings—that there can be no earnings unless and until the purchasing power of capital is maintained. The constant dollar information required by this Statement, provided one takes the monetary adjustment into consideration, will generally accomplish this within a reasonable order of magnitude. It is not experimental. It is ready to go.

The second issue is the need to introduce current costs or values into the financial reporting model. The record built in the Board's due process indicates that the Securities and Exchange Commission, some educators, and some financial analysts perceive such a need. Issuers of financial statements and auditors, in the main, either do not perceive a need at this time, or believe the proposed model needs further development and testing or that the costs exceed the benefits.

The current cost information introduced in this Statement has significant limitations. It is neither a comprehensive current cost nor a value system. It identifies as income from continuing operations an amount that is sometimes referred to as "distributable income." This amount may have use in funds flow analysis, but is neither distributable nor income. In most cases, it is a result of subtracting the estimated cost of the next purchase from the revenue from that last sale. It is neither transaction-based income nor real economic income. It has no "bottom line." It is at best an intermediate step, easily misinterpreted.

To reduce complexity, the Board elected to defer action or deal inconclusively with such significant matters as backlog depreciation, holding gains, tax allocation, gearing adjustments, and liability measurement. The sacrifice of completeness for understandability leaves us with a model that falls short of the mark on both counts.

This Statement reflects diverse views on the best way to report the effects of changing prices. The resulting product has something for everybody, but by requiring a number of supplemental income amounts which can be used in various combinations, it does not focus on a concept of real income. It offers a smorgasbord of data that fail to meet the tests of simplicity, understandability, and therefore cost-effectiveness.

The weight of evidence suggests that the Board is promulgating a current cost model that is not ready, for a constituency that is not ready for it. Experimentation with current cost and value information is sorely needed to establish their feasibility, reliability, cost, and usefulness. Mr. Walters believes that this experimentation should be conducted with volunteer companies working through professional organizations of business executives, accountants, and financial analysts. Regulators mandate experiments in financial reports; standard setters should not.

*Members of the Financial Accounting Standards Board:*
    Donald J. Kirk, *Chairman*
    Frank E. Block
    John W. March
    Robert A. Morgan
    David Mosso
    Robert T. Sprouse
    Ralph E. Walters

# APPENDIX B: SAMPLE FINANCIAL STATEMENTS

The following pages illustrate a few examples of financial statements based on the inflation accounting principles outlined in this book. The formats presented herein are not intended to be exhaustive.

### IOWA BEEF PROCESSORS, INC.—1979 ANNUAL REPORT

**Replacement Cost Data:**

In inflationary periods similar to those of the recent past, the cost of replacing certain assets, such as inventories and plant and equipment, with comparable products and productive capacity is generally higher than the cost incurred when these assets were initially acquired. Estimates of replacement cost information for certain assets and the effect of the assumed replacement on certain costs and expenses are reflected in the Company's Annual Report, Form 10-K, filed with the Securities and Exchange Commission.

The Company is presenting, in addition to financial information reported on the conventional basis of historical costs, supplementary current-value financial statements for the years (53 Weeks) ended November 3, 1979 and (52 Weeks) ended October 28, 1978. The current-value financial statements, which are presented on pages 32 through 36 of the 1979 Annual Report to Stockholders, go beyond the requirements of Accounting Series Release No. 190.

Iowa Beef Processors, Inc. and Subsidiaries   SUPPLEMENTARY FINANCIAL INFORMATION
# Current-Value Consolidated Balance Sheets

Amounts in thousands

|  | November 3, 1979 | October 28, 1978 |
|---|---:|---:|
| **Assets** | | |
| CURRENT ASSETS: | | |
| Cash | $ 27,138 | $ 18,189 |
| Accounts receivable, less allowance for doubtful accounts | 155,107 | 141,467 |
| Inventories | 94,022 | 55,261 |
| Prepaid expenses | 1,135 | 1,538 |
| Total Current Assets | 277,402 | 216,455 |
| PROPERTY, PLANT AND EQUIPMENT: | | |
| Land and land improvements | 28,687 | 24,545 |
| Buildings and stockyards | 100,689 | 87,472 |
| Equipment | 248,093 | 193,443 |
| Construction in progress | 7,593 | 4,264 |
|  | 385,062 | 309,724 |
| Less — accumulated depreciation | 144,913 | 106,953 |
| — imputed income tax | 64,028 | 48,153 |
|  | 176,121 | 154,618 |
| OTHER ASSETS | 304 | 1,100 |
|  | $453,827 | $372,173 |
| **Liabilities and Stockholders' Equity** | | |
| CURRENT LIABILITIES: | | |
| Notes payable | $ 20,000 | $ 20,000 |
| Accounts payable and accrued liabilities | 56,625 | 41,313 |
| Federal and state income taxes | 10,559 | 4,137 |
| Current maturities on long-term obligations | 2,948 | 2,546 |
| Total Current Liabilities | 90,132 | 67,996 |
| LONG-TERM OBLIGATIONS | 63,634 | 70,580 |
| STOCKHOLDERS' EQUITY | 300,061 | 233,597 |
|  | $453,827 | $372,173 |

See notes to current-value consolidated financial statements.

Iowa Beef Processors, Inc. and Subsidiaries    SUPPLEMENTARY FINANCIAL INFORMATION

# Current-Value Consolidated Statements of Net Results of Operations and Changes in Value

Years Ended November 3, 1979 (53 Weeks) and October 28, 1978 (52 Weeks)
Amounts in thousands

|  | 1979 | 1978 |
|---|---|---|
| RESULTS OF OPERATIONS: |  |  |
| Net sales | $4,216,370 | $2,968,099 |
| Cost of products sold | 4,114,122 | 2,879,150 |
|  | 102,248 | 88,949 |
| Expenses: |  |  |
| Selling, general and administrative | 34,846 | 32,463 |
| Interest expense | 2,261 | 3,309 |
| Income taxes | 30,433 | 27,224 |
|  | 67,540 | 62,996 |
| Net results of operations | 34,708 | 25,953 |
| CHANGES IN VALUE: |  |  |
| Change in current costs of depreciable assets during the year | 20,891 | 11,714 |
| Change in inventory value during the year | 7,934 | 5,924 |
| Change in current value of debt and interest | 2,080 | 874 |
| Change in other imputed taxes | 831 | 1,148 |
| Amount required to recognize impact on stockholders' equity of increase in the general price level during the year | (20,089) | (13,505) |
| TOTAL OF NET RESULTS OF OPERATIONS AND CHANGES IN VALUE | $ 46,355 | $ 32,108 |

# Current-Value Consolidated Statements of Stockholders' Equity

Years Ended November 3, 1979 (53 Weeks) and October 28, 1978 (52 Weeks)
Amounts in thousands

|  | 1979 | 1978 |
|---|---|---|
| Balance at beginning of year | $233,597 | $188,090 |
| Amount required to recognize impact on stockholders' equity of increase in general price level during the year | 20,089 | 13,505 |
| Restated balance at beginning of year | 253,686 | 201,595 |
| Common stock options exercised | 3,724 | 1,516 |
| Income tax benefits attributable to stock options | 1,334 | 524 |
| Treasury shares issued | — | 215 |
| Cash dividends paid | (5,038) | (2,361) |
| Net results of operations and changes in value during the year | 46,355 | 32,108 |
| Balance at end of the year | $300,061 | $233,597 |

See notes to current-value consolidated financial statements.

Iowa Beef Processors, Inc. and Subsidiaries    SUPPLEMENTARY FINANCIAL INFORMATION

# Notes to Current-Value Consolidated Financial Statements

Years Ended November 3, 1979 (53 Weeks) and October 28, 1978 (52 Weeks)

1. **General:**

    In the inflationary environment of the past several years, financial information reported on the conventional basis of historical costs fails to fully reflect economic reality of the financial condition and results of operations of business enterprises. As a result, the Company is presenting financial statements reflecting the current values of its assets, liabilities, operating results and changes in value by estimating:

    a. The current replacement cost for assets and resources expected to be retained and net realizable value for assets expected to be disposed of.

    b. The present value of estimated future cash outflows for liabilities.

    c. The imputed income taxes relative to the difference in current-value and income tax bases of assets and liabilities.

    d. The effects of changes in general purchasing power on the net resources of the Company.

2. **Current Assets and Liabilities:**

    Current assets and liabilities are stated on the same basis as the historical cost basis financial statements except for inventories (Note 3) and imputed taxes. Imputed taxes have been deducted from accounts payable and accrued liabilities.

3. **Inventories and Cost of Products Sold:**

    Inventories reported at the year ends are stated at amounts that approximate current replacement cost less imputed income taxes. The inventory component of cost of sales is determined using the LIFO method of inventory valuation which approximates replacement cost at date of sale. The inventory value change reported in the Consolidated Statements of Net Results of Operations and Changes in Value represents the net change in the values of inventories held throughout the year net of imputed income taxes.

4. **Property, Plant and Equipment:**

    Property, plant and equipment, including assets under capital leases, are stated at current replacement cost less accumulated depreciation and imputed income taxes. Current replacement cost was developed principally by using engineering estimates for the cost of replacing existing productive capacity after giving recognition to technological changes and methods by which replacement would be expected to be made. The costs so determined have not been adjusted for anticipated reductions in operating expenses as such reductions are not estimated to be significant. Accumulated depreciation has been restated to reflect depreciation which would have been incurred in 1979 and 1978 and prior years based on the current replacements costs. Current-value depreciation expense for 1979 and 1978 was $9,109,000 and $7,538,000 greater than the respective historical cost amounts. Such depreciation was calculated on average replacement costs using the straight-line method and the historical rates for existing facilities.

    Cost of products sold and selling, general and administrative expenses have been charged for the increased current-value depreciation during the years. The increase in replacement cost (net of imputed income taxes) of property, plant and equipment during the years is reported as a value change in the Consolidated Statements of Net Results of Operations and Changes in Value.

5. **Long-term Obligations:**

    Long-term obligations include long term debt and capital lease obligations. These obligations are stated at the present value of future cash flows (net of imputed income taxes) based on the current applicable interest rates at the statement dates. The rates include an element for estimated financing costs. Current-value interest expense is calculated at average current rates for the years.

6. **Income Taxes:**

   Income taxes at rates approximating 50% have been imputed on the difference between current-value and income tax bases of assets and liabilities. The amounts of imputed taxes that have been deducted (added in the case of long-term obligations for 1979) from the related assets and liabilities in the current-value balance sheets are shown below:

   |  | **November 3, 1979** | October 28, 1978 |
   |---|---|---|
   | Inventories | **$12,740,000** | $ 5,933,000 |
   | Property, plant and equipment | **64,028,000** | 48,153,000 |
   | Accounts payable and accrued liabilities | **3,557,000** | 2,726,000 |
   | Long-term obligations | **1,384,000** | 505,000 |

   All changes in imputed taxes are reported as changes in value in the Consolidated Statements of Net Results of Operations and Changes in Value. Income tax expense shown in the current-value results of operations is the amount currently payable.

7. **Stockholders' Equity:**

   The amounts of aggregate earnings required during the years to maintain the general purchasing power of stockholders' equity are shown as decreases in changes in value. Such amounts are measured by the GNP Implicit Price Deflator and are comprised of the following:

   |  | **November 3, 1979** | October 28, 1978 |
   |---|---|---|
   | Net non-monetary assets | **$19,287,000** | $12,944,000 |
   | Net monetary assets-liabilities | **2,294,000** | 1,493,000 |
   | Operations | **(1,492,000)** | (932,000) |
   |  | **$20,089,000** | $13,505,000 |

   Stockholders' equity at the beginning of the years and the amounts shown for sales and purchases of stock and dividends paid during the years have been restated as appropriate to give effect to the increase in general price level during the years.

8. **Restatement of Prior Years Current-Value Statements:**

   The Company adopted the LIFO method of inventory valuation for primary financial reporting during 1978. The current-value financial statements for 1978 have been restated to report inventories on a replacement cost basis. During 1979 the Internal Revenue Service revised their LIFO conformity rules which previously required a company using LIFO to use that method for all financial statements. The effect of the restatement was to increase inventories at October 28, 1978 by $11,857,000 less imputed income taxes of $5,933,000, increase stockholders' equity by $5,924,000 and to increase the Net Results of Operations and Changes in Value by $5,924,000 for the year then ended.

9. **Notes to Historical Cost Basis Financial Statements:**

   The current-value financial statements should be read in conjunction with the notes to the historical cost basis financial statements.

**Current-Value Accountants' Report**

Board of Directors and Stockholders
Iowa Beef Processors, Inc.
Dakota City, Nebraska

The accompanying supplementary consolidated current-value balance sheets of Iowa Beef Processors, Inc. and subsidiaries as of November 3, 1979 and October 28, 1978 and the related current-value statements of net results of operations and changes in value and statements of stockholders' equity for the years then ended have been prepared on a comprehensive current-value basis of accounting as more fully discussed in Note 1. The current-value basis differs significantly from, and is not in accordance with, generally accepted accounting principles applied to the primary financial statements. Further, the current-value financial statements are not intended to measure the net realizable value or market value of the Company taken as a whole.

Because current-value accounting is presently in an experimental stage, uniform criteria for the preparation and presentation of comprehensive current-value financial statements have not yet been established and acceptable alternatives exist as to the nature and content; accordingly, as experimentation proceeds, the principles followed in the accompanying current-value financial statements may be modified.

Our examination of the current-value financial statements was made in accordance with generally accepted auditing standards and, accordingly, included a review of selected data used to obtain current values and such other auditing procedures we considered necessary in the circumstances. In our opinion, the current-value financial statements referred to above are a reasonable and appropriate presentation of the information set forth therein on the basis indicated in Note 1, which basis has been applied in a consistent manner after the restatement for the change, with which we concur, described in Note 8.

**Touche Ross & Co.**  December 20, 1979
Certified Public Accountants
Omaha, Nebraska

# Ford Motor Company and Consolidated Subsidiaries
## Supplementary Inflation Data

### Schedule of Income Adjusted for Changing Prices
For the Year Ended December 31, 1979 (in millions)

| | As Reported in the Financial Statements (Historical Costs) | Adjusted for General Inflation (Average 1979 Constant Dollars) | Adjusted for Changes in Specific Prices (1979 Current Costs) |
|---|---|---|---|
| **Sales** | $43,513.7 | $43,513.7 | $43,513.7 |
| **Costs and Expenses** | | | |
| Cost of goods sold (Note A) | 38,448.3 | 38,907.8 | 38,931.6 |
| Depreciation and amortization of special tools (Note B) | 1,604.4 | 1,939.0 | 2,077.0 |
| Other—net | 1,951.6 | 1,951.6 | 1,951.6 |
| Total costs and expenses | 42,004.3 | 42,798.4 | 42,960.2 |
| **Income Before Income Taxes** | 1,509.4 | 715.3 | 553.5 |
| Provision for income taxes | 330.1 | 330.1 | 330.1 |
| **Net Income** (After minority interest in net income of consolidated subsidiaries) | $1,169.3 | $375.2 | $213.4 |
| **Net Income a Share** | $9.75 | $3.13 | $1.78 |
| **Effective Income Tax Rate*** | 37.9% | 90.7% | 126.7% |
| Net assets at year-end | $10,420.7 | $13,200.5 | $15,100.8 |
| Unrealized gain from decline in purchasing power of net amounts owed | | $451.8 | $451.8 |
| Increase in general price level of inventories and property over increase in specific prices | | | $112.2 |

*Excludes the effect of a $186-million nonrecurring tax credit in Britain.

### Comparison of Selected Supplementary Data Adjusted for Changing Prices

Historical Cost Data Adjusted for General Inflation to Average 1979 Constant Dollars
(in millions except a share amounts)

| | 1979 | 1978 | 1977 | 1976 | 1975 |
|---|---|---|---|---|---|
| Sales—as reported | $43,513.7 | $42,784.1 | $37,841.5 | $28,839.6 | $24,009.1 |
| —in constant dollars | 43,513.7 | 47,601.2 | 45,326.5 | 36,772.5 | 32,379.6 |
| Cash dividends a share—as reported | $3.90 | $3.50 | $3.04 | $2.24 | $2.08 |
| —in constant dollars | 3.90 | 3.89 | 3.64 | 2.86 | 2.81 |
| Market price a common share at year-end | $32 | $46¾ | $54¾ | $62¾ | $47½ |
| Average Consumer Price Index | 217.4 | 195.4 | 181.5 | 170.5 | 161.2 |

The accompanying notes are part of the supplementary schedules.

## Supplementary Inflation Data

Since 1973, inflation in the United States has been at high levels the Consumer Price Index has increased 73% during the period. Present methods of accounting measure costs in terms of the prices actually paid, not the cost of replacing these items after they are used. Consequently, present accounting methods, except for inventories, are not designed to measure the effects of inflation. The distinction between traditional accounting and accounting that measures the effects of inflation is particularly important during periods of high inflation, especially for fixed assets. Because Ford adopted the Last-In, First-Out (LIFO) method of accounting for most U.S. inventories in 1976, the Company's reporting reflects, to some extent, the effects of inflation.

The high rates of inflation in recent years have substantially increased costs required to replace inventories and fixed assets. Because inflation lowers the real value of earnings, it widens the difference between historical accounting and inflation accounting.

Because of concern about the inability of traditional financial reporting to communicate the effects of inflation, the Financial Accounting Standards Board (FASB) issued Statement No. 33, Financial Reporting and Changing Prices. This Statement requires that the Company's Annual Report include supplementary information presenting the effects of general inflation (constant dollars) and changes in specific prices (current costs) on reported financial data. The supplementary inflation data reported on the Schedule of Income Adjusted for Changing Prices and on the Comparison of Selected Supplementary Data Adjusted for Changing Prices have been prepared in accordance with this Statement.

The constant-dollar method is a technique for measuring and reporting the effects of the general rate of inflation on a company's earnings. This method employs the Consumer Price Index for All Urban Consumers to adjust certain costs that are based on historical or noncurrent dollars in the primary financial statements. These costs are material costs included in cost of goods sold, depreciation, and amortization of special tools.

The current-cost method is a technique for measuring and reporting the effects of inflation specifically being experienced by Ford. The current-cost technique used to restate depreciation and tool amortization costs also reflects the effect on fixed assets of foreign currency exchange rate changes and inflation rates overseas.

Both the constant-dollar method and the current-cost method result in lower net income than reported in the primary financial statements. Because these adjustments are not deductible for income tax purposes, the taxation of earnings under present tax law reduces the amount of earnings that are available to support future business growth. The effects of the higher taxation of earnings are demonstrated in the effective tax rates shown on the supplementary schedule.

In the opinion of the FASB, further experimentation is required in order to determine the usefulness of the data presented. The FASB also believes that the information required by the Statement will promote a better understanding of the problems caused by inflation. The Company agrees with the general approach, but it is important to note that implicit in the technique is the assumption that the Company would replace all of the affected assets at 1979 prices. Further, although the reporting requirements are new, management long has recognized the substantial impact of inflation on business operations. The business-planning policies followed by Ford incorporate the effects of inflation as a factor in management decisions.

Inflation during 1979 exceeded 13% – the highest level since 1946. Ford's ability to meet the demands of the 1980s will depend importantly on how the U.S. government shapes the environment in which our customers live and we do business. The high level of inflation is one of our country's most serious domestic problems. Effective and consistent government policies are required that will control inflation, stabilize energy supply, and increase incentives for capital formation – which would improve productivity, lower inflation, and help make U.S. industry more competitive.

## Notes to Supplementary Inflation Data

### Note A. Cost of Goods Sold and Inventory

Cost of goods sold on a constant-dollar basis was determined by applying the average (for the year) Consumer Price Index for All Urban Consumers (CPI-U) to the historical cost of beginning and ending inventory balances. The Company uses the LIFO accounting method for most inventories in the United States, so no adjustment was required to reported cost of goods sold related to U.S. inventories. Cost of goods sold related to inventories maintained on a FIFO basis was restated to a current-cost basis using the specific level of prices at the time the goods were sold.

The current cost of inventory at December 31, 1979 was $6,730 million. This cost was based on the most recent purchase prices, which approximated year-end 1979 prices.

## Notes to Supplementary Inflation Data (continued)

### Note B. Depreciation and Amortization

Property includes land, buildings, machinery, equipment, unamortized special tools, and construction in progress. Current-cost and constant-dollar depreciation and amortization expense were determined using the same depreciation and amortization methods and productive lives as are used in preparing the Company's financial statements.

The constant-dollar value of property and of related accumulated depreciation was determined by adjusting the historical cost of each category of asset by the change in the CPI-U since the original acquisition dates.

The current cost of land was valued using commonly available indices applicable to the country in which the land is located. Current cost for buildings and site improvements in the United States was determined by applying new-facility construction costs-per-square-foot to the square footage of existing buildings. The estimated current cost for machinery and equipment in the United States was calculated by applying specific indices published by the U.S. government to the historical cost of homogeneous categories of machinery and equipment. The current cost of fixed assets for operations outside the United States generally was calculated by applying local indices to historical costs. The current costs in local currency were translated to U.S. dollars by applying the exchange rate in effect on December 31, 1979. Current cost of special tools was calculated on the basis of indices developed from cost changes experienced by the Company. At December 31, 1979, the current cost of property, net of accumulated depreciation, was $12,474 million.

## Supplemental Information on Inflation Accounting

Inflation during 1979 continued at a high rate in the United States, further eroding the purchasing power of the dollar. This trend continues to distort the conventional measures of financial performance. Historical dollar accounting (as reflected in the financial statements) during times of significant and continued inflation does not reflect the cumulative effects of increasing costs and changes in the purchasing power of the dollar.

Investments in plant and equipment, for example, made over an extended period of time are treated as though the dollars from these periods were stated in common units of measurement. Since the purchasing power of the dollar has declined significantly from the time these investments were made (the 1979 dollar, for example, is worth $.53 compared with the 1970 dollar), this decline should be considered for a proper assessment of economic results.

Inflation also affects monetary assets, such as cash and receivables, which lose a part of their purchasing power during periods of inflation since they will purchase fewer goods or services in the future. Conversely, holders of liabilities benefit during periods of inflation because less purchasing power will be required to satisfy these obligations in the future. This benefit is illustrated when a 1970 debt of one dollar can be satisfied with a payment of a 1979 dollar which has the equivalent purchasing power of $.53.

The following information is presented in an experimental fashion to help overcome these shortcomings of historical accounting. The adjustments made to the historical dollar results are made in accordance with the principles of inflation accounting as enumerated in Financial Accounting Standards Board Statement No. 33—Financial Reporting and Changing Prices, which forms the basis for these supplemental statements.

The first approach is to adjust the historical dollars to dollars of the same general purchasing power. For example, if the inflation rate is 5 percent from one year to the next year, then 5 percent more dollars are needed in the second year just to maintain the same general purchasing power. This adjustment to common units of measurement—constant dollars—is accomplished by using an index which measures inflation. Statement No. 33 prescribes the use of the Consumer Price Index for All Urban Consumers (CPI). Therefore, the constant dollar method starts with historical dollars as recorded using generally accepted accounting principles and adjusts these dollars to reflect changes in purchasing power (inflation) using the CPI.

A second approach is also used in the accompanying statements to adjust for the current costs of inventory and plant and equipment, which for Exxon have generally increased over time at a rate higher than that of the CPI. Current replacement costs have been used for these items. That is, specific prices that would have to be paid currently have been used as replacement costs for inventory of crude oil and products and property, plant and equipment. Prices for these items have increased at a different but generally much higher rate than general inflation as a result of, for example, the increased cost of crude oil and the escalation in the costs to build and equip petroleum refineries.

For the most part, the replacement data represent replacement in-place and in-kind. No consideration has been given to the replacement of assets with a different type, to improved operating cost efficiencies of replacement assets, and similar situations. The replacement costs used, while believed reasonable, are necessarily subjective. They do not necessarily represent amounts for which the assets could be sold or costs which will be incurred, or the manner in which actual replacement of assets will occur. Land has been valued based on appraisal or on estimated current market prices. Development costs of oil and gas producing facilities have been updated by use of appropriate indices.

In the first table, the first column shows the results of operations as shown in the Consolidated Statement of Income on page 25. The middle column reflects restatements for the effects of general inflation. Since in 1979, the cost of goods sold was already stated in 1979 dollars only one adjustment is necessary. The adjustment of $1,243 million to depreciation is to restate this cost in terms of 1979 dollars based upon the restatement of property, plant and equipment as shown in the second table. In the third column, the further adjustment of depreciation to reflect the increases of the specific costs of the facilities over the effect of general inflation adds $662 million to the current charge for this item. The two depreciation adjustments maintain the same methods, useful lives and salvage values as used in computing historical depreciation.

After these adjustments, the income from continuing operations of $4,295 million has been lowered to $3,052 million in terms of constant purchasing power (general inflation) and to $2,390 million on the basis of specific prices. Dividends paid in 1979 represent 40 percent, 56 percent and 72 percent, respectively, of these income amounts.

Statement No. 33 requires that income taxes paid not be modified for the effects of either constant dollar or specific price adjustments. Therefore, the 68 percent effective tax rate for historical earnings becomes an effective 75 percent for constant dollar results and 79 percent for specific price earnings.

## Supplemental Information on Inflation Accounting (continued)

This table also shows other changes in shareholders' equity, which occurred during the year as a result of inflation. The first is the gain, applicable to both methods, resulting from the decline in purchasing power of the dollar in the net monetary amounts owed by the company. Most of the company's current assets, except inventories, and the current liabilities and long-term debt are considered to be monetary items. Since the monetary liabilities at year-end 1979 were larger than the monetary assets, a gain is shown. This gain represents the change in the amount of purchasing power required at the end of 1979 to pay these net liabilities versus the higher amount of purchasing power that would have been required to pay them at the end of 1978. With inflation at 10 percent, for example, a gain of $100 thousand would occur for each million dollars of net liabilities held throughout the year.

The second adjustment is applicable only to the specific price method and represents the added increase in costs during the year due to increases in the specific costs for inventory and property, plant and equipment over that which is attributed to the increase due to the effects of general inflation as measured by the CPI. This increase is written off by means of the increased depreciation charge previously mentioned.

These changes in shareholders' equity when added to income from continuing operations resulted in adjusted net income of $4,050 million using the general inflation or constant dollar method and in net changes in shareholders' equity of $6,087 million using the specific cost method. This compares with the $4,295 million of historical net income.

The second table presents the balance sheet at year-end 1979. The first column is a summary of the historical dollar balance sheet shown on page 24. The middle column restates the inventory and property, plant and equipment for the effects of general inflation. The categories "All other assets" and "Total liabilities" are merely restated in average 1979 dollars using the CPI. Both the LIFO inventory and property, plant and equipment have been built up over the years as inventory quantities have increased and as plant capacities have been added or replaced. The adjustments shown on the table restate these prior year additions in terms of average 1979 dollars. That is, an inventory or plant addition made in 1970 is increased in amount to reflect the increased number of 1979 dollars required to equal the general purchasing power originally invested. For example, it takes almost twice as many 1979 dollars to equal the same purchasing power as that used for an investment in 1970.

The last column shows the adjustments for specific prices paid by Exxon which have increased faster than the CPI. The inventory has been restated based upon the cost of replacing the entire inventory at current costs. Since the purchase prices of crude oil and petroleum products have increased faster than general inflation, particularly in 1979, and since the inventory has been carried on the LIFO basis, the inventory using specific prices is about $3,973 million greater than the results after adjustment for general inflation. The adjustment to property, plant and equipment made in a similar fashion results in a $10 billion adjustment indicating the magnitude of the higher costs being incurred by Exxon over and above the level of general inflation. The specific replacement cost data were mainly based on internally developed plant construction and equipment purchase indices.

The sum of all of these adjustments results in the restatement of shareholders' equity—the investment base. The adjustment for general inflation increases the historical shareholders' equity, as shown on the second table, of about $23 billion to a constant dollar basis of $35 billion. In other words, it would take $35 billion of 1979 dollars to provide the same purchasing power as the $23 billion represented in the financial statements. Additional adjustments for specific prices raise the shareholders' equity to $48 billion. This means that an additional $13 billion investment of 1979 dollars would be required to provide for the replacement costs of specific inventories and plant, over the adjustment for the effects of general inflation.

The third table is a five-year summary of results. The historical cost information for the years 1975 through 1978 have been adjusted for the effects of general inflation and for specific prices (from 1976) in the same manner as has been discussed for the year 1979. Income from continuing operations is composed of the same factors as shown on the first table. As shown on this table and in the discussion in the Financial Highlights section (page 4), the return on average shareholders' equity is considerably lower when both the results and the investment base are adjusted for the effects of general inflation. The return is also lower when adjusted to a specific price basis. These decreases reflect the erosion taking place in the capital base of the company from the continuing high levels of inflation now being faced by the general public, the oil and gas industry, and Exxon.

## Income from continuing operations and other changes in shareholders' equity adjusted for changing prices
For the year ended December 31, 1979 (millions of dollars) (millions of average 1979 dollars)

|  | As reported on page 25 | Adjusted for General inflation | Adjusted for Specific costs |
|---|---|---|---|
| **Income from continuing operations** | | | |
| Total revenue | $84,809 | $84,809 | $84,809 |
| Costs and other deductions | | | |
| Crude oil and product purchases | 40,831 | 40,831 | 40,831 |
| Depreciation and depletion | 2,027 | 3,270 | 3,932 |
| Other | 14,070 | 14,070 | 14,070 |
| Interest expense | 494 | 494 | 494 |
| Income, excise and other taxes | 23,092 | 23,092 | 23,092 |
| Total costs and other deductions | $80,514 | $81,757 | $82,419 |
| Income from continuing operations | $ 4,295 | $ 3,052 | $ 2,390 |
| Gain from decline in the purchasing power of net amounts owed | | 998 | 998 |
| Increase in current cost of inventories and property, plant and equipment during 1979 | | | 9,333 |
| Less effect of increase in general price level during 1979 | | | 6,634 |
| Excess of increase in specific prices over increase in the general price level | | | 2,699 |
| **Net income** | $ 4,295 | | |
| **Adjusted net income** | | $ 4,050 | |
| **Net change in shareholders' equity from above** | $ 4,295 | $ 4,050 | $ 6,087 |

## Summarized balance sheet adjusted for changing prices
at December 31, 1979 (millions of dollars) (millions of average 1979 dollars)

|  | As reported on page 24 | Adjusted for General inflation | Adjusted for Specific costs |
|---|---|---|---|
| **Assets** | | | |
| Inventories | $ 5,481 | $ 7,585 | $11,558 |
| Property, plant and equipment | 26,293 | 35,796 | 45,418 |
| All other assets | 17,716 | 16,892 | 16,892 |
| **Total assets** | 49,490 | 60,273 | 73,868 |
| **Total liabilities** | 26,938 | 25,599 | 25,599 |
| **Shareholders' equity** | $22,552 | $34,674 | $48,269 |

## Supplementary financial data
(millions of dollars except per share amounts)

|  | Years ended December 31 | | | | |
|---|---|---|---|---|---|
|  | 1975 | 1976 | 1977 | 1978 | 1979 |
| **Unadjusted for inflation** | | | | | |
| Income from continuing operations | $ 2,456 | $ 2,615 | $ 2,443 | $ 2,763 | $ 4,295 |
| Per share | 5.49 | 5.84 | 5.45 | 6.20 | 9.74 |
| Return of income from continuing operations on average shareholders' equity, percent | 15.4 | 15.1 | 13.1 | 14.0 | 20.1 |
| **Historical cost information adjusted for general inflation** (average 1979 dollars) | | | | | |
| Income from continuing operations | 1,961 | 2,355 | 1,983 | 2,052 | 3,052 |
| Per share | 4.38 | 5.26 | 4.43 | 4.60 | 6.92 |
| Gain from decline in purchasing power of net amounts owed | 337 | 277 | 441 | 617 | 998 |
| Adjusted net income | 2,298 | 2,632 | 2,424 | 2,669 | 4,050 |
| Per share | 5.14 | 5.88 | 5.41 | 5.99 | 9.19 |
| Total revenue | 65,765 | 67,059 | 70,023 | 72,191 | 84,809 |
| Dividends, per share | 3.37 | 3.47 | 3.59 | 3.67 | 3.90 |
| Market price at year-end, per share | 58 | 69 3/8 | 56 1/4 | 52 5/8 | 52 1/8 |
| Net assets at year-end | 30,114 | 31,146 | 31,847 | 32,599 | 34,674 |
| **Return of adjusted net income on average shareholders' equity, percent** | 7.7 | 8.6 | 7.7 | 8.3 | 12.0 |
| **Historical cost information adjusted for specific costs** (average 1979 dollars) | | | | | |
| Income from continuing operations | | 1,944 | 1,336 | 1,245 | 2,390 |
| Per share | | 4.34 | 2.98 | 2.79 | 5.42 |
| Gain from decline in purchasing power of net amounts owed | | 277 | 441 | 617 | 998 |
| Excess of increase in specific prices over increase due to general inflation | | 2,999 | 1,807 | (377) | 2,699 |
| Net change in shareholders' equity | | 5,220 | 3,584 | 1,485 | 6,087 |
| Per share | | 11.66 | 8.00 | 3.33 | 13.81 |
| Net assets at year-end | | 42,781 | 44,642 | 44,211 | 48,269 |
| **Return of net change in shareholders' equity on average shareholders' equity, percent** | | 12.8 | 8.2 | 3.3 | 13.2 |
| Average consumer price index | 161.2 | 170.5 | 181.5 | 195.4 | 217.4 |

# Financial issues: the impact of inflation

Inflation is commonly defined as a loss in value of money due to an increase in the volume of money and credit relative to available goods and services, resulting in a rise in the level of prices. Inflation in the U.S. is generally recognized to be caused by a combination of factors, including government deficits, sharp increases in energy costs, and low productivity gains including the effect of proliferating government regulations.

Although loss of purchasing power of the dollar impacts all areas of the economy, it is particularly onerous in its effect on savings — of both individuals in forms such as savings accounts, securities and pensions, and of corporations in the form of retained earnings.

**For the individual,** with inflation of 6% a year, the dollar saved by a person at age 50 will have lost three-fifths of its value by the time the person is age 65. With a 10% inflation rate, almost four-fifths of the dollar's value is lost in 15 years. This problem affects almost everyone, including those presently working and especially those who are on fixed incomes.

The situation is rendered even more difficult by the progressive income tax system. A Congressional staff study reports that a family of four with an income of $8,132 in 1964 would need a 1979 income of $18,918 to have kept pace with the increase in the Consumer Price Index over the years. However, the 1979 income of $18,918 puts the family into a higher tax bracket which, when coupled with increased Social Security taxes, reduces real after-tax income $1,068 below the equivalent 1964 level.

**Your Company and all U.S. businesses** face a similar problem. Business savings are in the form of retained earnings — the earnings a company keeps after paying employees, suppliers and vendors, and after payment of taxes to government and dividends to share owners. If a company is to continue in business, much less grow, it must be able to save or retain sufficient earnings, after providing a return to its share owners, to fund the cost of replacing — at today's inflated prices — the productive assets used up. Retention of capital in these inflationary times under existing tax laws is a challenge facing all businesses.

U.S. tax regulations permit recognition of the impact of inflation on a company's inventory costs by use of the LIFO (last-in, first-out) inventory method. In general, under the LIFO method, a company charges off to operations the current cost of inventories consumed during the year. With inflation averaging over 11% last year, the negative impact on operations of using current costs with respect to a supply of goods is substantial. Financial results are portrayed more accurately when the LIFO method is used in periods of high inflation, and GE has used LIFO for most of its U.S. manufacturing inventories for a quarter-century. The Statement of Earnings on page 32 is on that basis. As supplementary information to that Statement of Earnings: use of the LIFO method increased 1979 and 1978 operating costs by $430.8 million and $224.1 million (to $20,330.7 million and $17,695.9 million), respectively, with a corresponding reduction of reported pre-tax profits.

Unfortunately, U.S. tax regulations fail to provide an equivalent to LIFO for the impact of inflation on a company's costs of property, plant and equipment. Instead, deductions for wear and tear on these assets are based on original purchase costs rather than today's replacement costs. In general, the resulting shortfall must be funded from after-tax earnings.

**The supplementary information** shown in Table 1 restates operating results to eliminate the major effects of inflation discussed above. Table 1 compares GE operating results as reported on page 32 with results adjusted in two ways. First, results are restated to show the effects of general inflation — the loss of the dollar's purchasing power — on inventories and fixed assets. The second restatement shows results restated for changes in specific prices — the current costs of replacing those assets. Your management feels that the last column in Table 1 is the more meaningful and has therefore shown, in Table 2 on page 30, five years of results on that basis, also adjusted to equivalent 1979 dollars to make the years comparable. While the techniques used are not precise, they do produce reasonable approximations.

In these earnings statements, specific adjustments are made to (1) *cost of goods sold* for the current cost of replacing inventories and (2) *depreciation* for the current costs of plant and equipment. The restatements for inventories are relatively small because GE's extensive use of LIFO accounting already largely reflects current costs in the traditional statements. However, a substantial restatement is made for the impact of inflation on fixed assets, which have relatively long lives. The $624 million of depreciation as traditionally reported, when restated for general inflation, increases to a total of $880 million. But the restatement necessary to reflect replacement of these assets at current costs grows to $980 million. The net effect of these restatements lowers reported income of $6.20 a share to $4.68 on a general inflation-adjusted basis and $4.34 on a specific current cost basis.

*It is significant to note that for the five years 1975-1979, even after adjustment for inflation, your Company has shown real growth in earnings and a steady increase in share owners' equity over the entire period. After adjusting earnings for current costs and restating all years to equivalent 1979 dollars, your Company's average annual growth rate in real earnings was 21% since 1975 and 8% since 1976. This means that the growth in GE's earnings has been real, not just the product of inflation.*

**An important insight** from these data is depicted in the pie charts at right. These show that, over the five years 1975-1979, because of inflation 10% more of GE's earnings were taxed away than appeared to have been the case using traditional financial statements. While the traditional earnings statements indicated an effective tax rate of 41% over this period, the "real" tax rate averaged 51% of profits before taxes. Consequently, earnings

## Table 1: supplementary information – effect of changing prices (a)

(In millions, except per-share amounts)   The notes on page 30 are an integral part of this statement.

| For the year ended December 31, 1979 | As reported in the traditional statements | Adjusted for general inflation | Adjusted for changes in specific prices (current costs) (b) |
|---|---|---|---|
| Sales of products and services to customers | $22,461 | $22,461 | $22,461 |
| Cost of goods sold | 15,991 | 16,093 | 16,074 |
| Selling, general and administrative expense | 3,716 | 3,716 | 3,716 |
| Depreciation, depletion and amortization | 624 | 880 | 980 |
| Interest and other financial charges | 258 | 258 | 258 |
| Other income | (519) | (519) | (519) |
| Earnings before income taxes and minority interest | 2,391 | 2,033 | 1,952 |
| Provision for income taxes | 953 | 953 | 953 |
| Minority interest in earnings of consolidated affiliates | 29 | 16 | 13 |
| Net earnings applicable to common stock | $ 1,409 | $ 1,064 | $ 986 |
| | | | |
| Earnings per common share | $ 6.20 | $ 4.68 | $ 4.34 |
| Share owners' equity at year end (net assets) (c) | $ 7,362 | $10,436 | $11,153 |

**Use of each dollar of earnings**
Based on total earnings before taxes 1975-1979

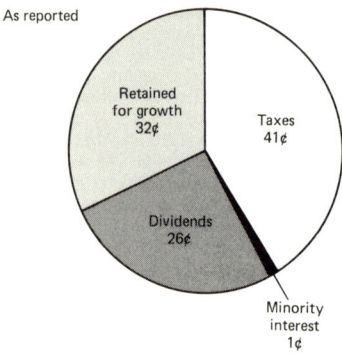

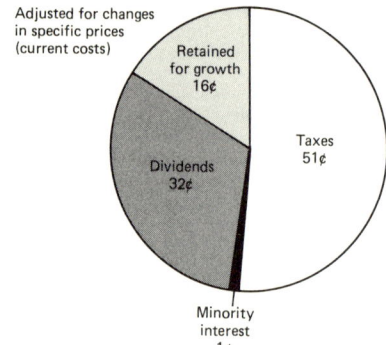

retained for growth were cut in half to 16% of income before tax, not 32% as reflected in the traditional financial statements. Over the period, share owners received a measure of protection against inflation's impact as about two-thirds of after-tax earnings were distributed — equivalent to an average annual growth rate of about 8% in *real* dividends.

**An area receiving special attention** by management is experimentation with the use of inflation-adjusted measurements at the individual business and project level for capital budgeting. Since 1973, your Company has been experimenting with various techniques to measure the impact of inflation, to incorporate the perspectives provided by such measurements into decision-making, and to stimulate awareness by all levels of management of the need to develop constructive business strategies to deal with inflation. The objective is to ensure that investments needed for new business growth, productivity improvements and capacity expansions earn appropriate *real rates of return* commensurate with the risks involved. Such supplemental measurements can assist in the entire resource allocation process, starting with initial project approval, implementation and subsequent review.

**Improving productivity** to offset inflationary forces is a primary goal established by top management that is being stressed throughout General Electric. As discussed on the back cover of this Annual Report, the Company has committed significant levels of resources to research and development activities to accelerate innovation and increase productivity. In addition, General Electric's production base continues to be expanded and modernized through increasing investments in plant and equipment. For example, $1,262 million and $1,055 million were spent on strengthening General Electric's production base in 1979 and 1978, respectively. Imaginative and diligent coupling of production techniques and equipment is critical to the maintenance and improvement of your Company's profitability.

## Table 2: supplementary information – effect of changing prices (a)

(In millions, except per-share amounts)

### Current cost information in dollars of 1979 purchasing power (b)

| (All amounts expressed in average 1979 dollars) | 1979 | 1978 | 1977 | 1976 | 1975 |
|---|---|---|---|---|---|
| Sales of products and services to customers | $22,461 | $21,867 | $20,984 | $20,015 | $19,022 |
| Cost of goods sold | 16,074 | 15,548 | 14,793 | 14,145 | 13,914 |
| Selling, general and administrative expense | 3,716 | 3,566 | 3,606 | 3,360 | 3,018 |
| Depreciation, depletion and amortization | 980 | 1,000 | 986 | 979 | 1,006 |
| Interest and other financial charges | 258 | 249 | 238 | 222 | 251 |
| Other income | (519) | (466) | (467) | (350) | (235) |
| Earnings before income taxes and minority interest | 1,952 | 1,970 | 1,828 | 1,659 | 1,068 |
| Provision for income taxes | 953 | 995 | 926 | 853 | 620 |
| Minority interest in earnings of consolidated affiliates | 13 | 13 | 20 | 26 | 26 |
| Net earnings applicable to common stock | $ 986 | $ 962 | $ 882 | $ 780 | $ 422 |
| Earnings per common share | $ 4.34 | $ 4.22 | $ 3.88 | $ 3.45 | $ 1.88 |
| Share owners' equity at year end (net assets) (c) | $11,153 | $11,020 | $10,656 | $10,526 | $10,056 |

### Other inflation information

| | 1979 | 1978 | 1977 | 1976 | 1975 |
|---|---|---|---|---|---|
| Average Consumer Price Index (1967 = 100) | 217.4 | 195.4 | 181.5 | 170.5 | 161.2 |
| (Loss)/gain in general purchasing power of net monetary items | $(209) | $(128) | $ (61) | $ (20) | $ 19 |
| Dividends declared per common share | 2.75 | 2.78 | 2.52 | 2.17 | 2.16 |
| Market price per common share at year end | 47⅞ | 50½ | 58¼ | 69⅜ | 60¼ |

### Notes to supplementary information — Tables 1 and 2

(a) This information has been prepared in accordance with requirements of the Financial Accounting Standards Board (FASB). Proper use of this information requires an understanding of certain basic concepts and definitions.

The heading "As reported in the traditional statements" refers to information drawn directly from the financial statements presented on pages 32 to 44. This information is prepared using the set of generally accepted accounting principles which renders an accounting based on the number of actual dollars involved in transactions, with no recognition given to the fact that the value of the dollar changes over time.

The heading "Adjusted for general inflation" refers to information prepared using a different approach to transactions involving inventory and property, plant and equipment assets. Under this procedure, the number of dollars involved in transactions at different dates are all restated to equivalent amounts in terms of the general purchasing power of the dollar as it is measured by the Consumer Price Index for all Urban Consumers (CPI-U). For example, $1,000 invested in a building asset in 1967 would be restated to its 1979 dollar purchasing power equivalent of $2,174 to value the asset and calculate depreciation charges. Similarly, 1978 purchases of non-LIFO inventory sold in 1979 would be accounted for at their equivalent in terms of 1979 dollars, rather than in terms of the actual number of dollars spent.

The heading "Adjusted for changes in specific prices (current costs)" refers to information prepared using yet another approach to transactions involving inventory and property, plant and equipment assets. In this case, rather than restating to dollars of the same general purchasing power, estimates of current costs of the assets are used.

In presenting results of either of the supplementary accounting methods for more than one year, "real" trends are more evident when results for all years are expressed in terms of the general purchasing power of the dollar for a designated period. Results of such restatements are generally called "constant dollar" presentations. In the five-year presentations shown above, dollar results for earlier periods have been restated to their equivalent number of constant dollars of 1979 general purchasing power (CPI-U basis).

Since none of these restatements is allowable for tax purposes under existing regulations, income tax amounts are the same as in the traditional statements (but expressed in constant dollars in the five-year summary).

There are a number of other terms and concepts which may be of interest in assessing the significance of the supplementary information shown in Tables 1 and 2. However, it is management's opinion that the basic concepts discussed above are the most significant for the reader to have in mind while reviewing this information.

(b) Principal types of information used to adjust for changes in specific prices (current costs) are (1) for inventory costs, GE-generated indices of price changes for specific goods and services, and (2) for property, plant and equipment, externally generated indices of price changes for major classes of assets.

(c) At December 31, 1979, the current cost of inventory was $5,251 million, and of property, plant and equipment was $7,004 million. Estimated current costs applicable to the sum of such amounts held during all or part of 1979 increased by approximately $1,111 million, which was $329 million less than the $1,440-million increase which could be expected because of general inflation.